Child Psychotherapy and the Games Children Play

I0131066

In this thought-provoking book, Celine Maroudas presents an intriguing psychoanalytic reappraisal of middle childhood. She re-examines both developmental theory and psychodynamic approaches to psychotherapy with this age group, exploring in particular the therapeutic power of games and play therapy in a psychoanalytic setting.

This book offers a comprehensive review of classic and contemporary views of development in middle childhood, from a historical, philosophical, and psychoanalytic perspective, calling into question the classical psychoanalytic concept of the latency period. Throughout, Maroudas highlights the emotional turbulence, psychic complexity, and momentous cognitive and psychosocial development of this critical stage of child development. She argues for a shift in psychodynamic thinking on middle childhood from an emphasis on rigidity, structure, and psychosocial dormancy to a focus on flux, change, and psychic fragility. Maroudas goes on to consider why school-aged children intuitively prefer playing games with rules and boundaries, and looks at how these games might be used as a safe, developmentally appropriate analytic technique for expressing and exploring violent and visceral anxieties, impulses, and passions. Through moving clinical examples and incisive clinical thinking, she shows how these games can serve as a developmentally appropriate framing structure for expressing and exploring the child's inner world, alongside the vicissitudes of the transference–countertransference matrix.

Offering a recalibration of the technique and language of child analytic treatment to better fit the unique challenges and needs of middle childhood, *Child Psychotherapy and the Games Children Play* provides psychoanalysts, psychotherapists, clinical psychologists, and educators with vital new insights into this critical stage of child development.

Celine Maroudas, PhD, is a senior consulting child and adult psychoanalytic psychotherapist and clinical psychologist, and has worked for many years with children, their parents, and adult patients, in the public sector and in private practice. She is a clinical supervisor and teacher in a variety of advanced diploma programmes in psychoanalytic psychotherapy.

Child Psychotherapy and the Games Children Play

A Psychoanalytic Toolkit for Middle Childhood

Celine Maroudas

Routledge
Taylor & Francis Group

LONDON AND NEW YORK

Designed cover image: Getty Images © Ekaterina Andreeva

First published 2026
by Routledge
4 Park Square, Milton Park, Abingdon, Oxon OX14 4RN

and by Routledge
605 Third Avenue, New York, NY 10158

Routledge is an imprint of the Taylor & Francis Group, an informa business

© 2026 Celine Maroudas

The right of Celine Maroudas to be identified as author of this
work has been asserted in accordance with sections 77 and 78 of
the Copyright, Designs and Patents Act 1988.

All rights reserved. No part of this book may be reprinted
or reproduced or utilised in any form or by any electronic,
mechanical, or other means, now known or hereafter invented,
including photocopying and recording, or in any information
storage or retrieval system, without permission in writing from the
publishers.

For Product Safety Concerns and Information please contact our
EU representative GPSR@taylorandfrancis.com. Taylor & Francis
Verlag GmbH, Kaufingerstraße 24, 80331 München, Germany.

Trademark notice: Product or corporate names may be trademarks
or registered trademarks, and are used only for identification and
explanation without intent to infringe.

British Library Cataloguing-in-Publication Data
A catalogue record for this book is available from the British Library

ISBN: 978-1-032-54507-3 (hbk)
ISBN: 978-1-032-54506-6 (pbk)
ISBN: 978-1-003-42522-9 (ebk)

DOI: 10.4324/9781003425229

Typeset in Times New Roman
by codeMantra

To all those children who have had their childhood
years of play and games cruelly snatched from them,
be it through loss, deprivation, and abuse, through war
and dislocation, or through mere bad fortune and twist
of fate.

Contents

Figures

Acknowledgements

"It takes an entire village to raise a child" – so too, it has taken an entire village to bring this book to fruition. Without the dedication and generosity, insight and wisdom, and love and support of those who have accompanied me through these last few challenging years of research and writing, I would never have dared embark on this journey, let alone managed to complete it.

This volume is based on my doctoral research, which I carried out in the Department of Counselling and Human Development at the University of Haifa. First and foremost, I would like to express my deepest thanks and appreciation to Prof Hadas Wiseman, for so generously offering to take me on as her doctoral student, despite my hardheaded insistence on a conceptual theoretical approach to the research, with all the associated methodological complications and pitfalls that this would inevitably entail. In addition to her broad knowledge and extensive experience in the field of psychotherapy research, which underpinned this supervision, Hadas guided me and challenged me through this difficult journey with a quiet, profound wisdom, empathy, and sensitivity, combined with her incisive critical thinking and insight. Equally, I am profoundly grateful to Prof Judith Harel, for agreeing to co-supervise this doctorate, for her generosity and unwavering encouragement and belief in me and in this project. Her deep wisdom and innate common sense combined with her thinking on children's play and the wealth of knowledge of child psychoanalytic theory and clinical practice she brought to bear on my research were invaluable. I could not have wished for a more supportive but challenging, wise, generous, and intuitively complementary joint supervision!

I am also very grateful to Prof Maria Rhode and Prof Yolanda Gampel for so generously agreeing to read and appraise my doctoral proposal, for their time and their thoughtful critiques, which were so very helpful in carving the path that the research took. In addition, I would like here to express my gratitude to Prof Maria Rhode also for providing me (and the other participants) with the English text of her online lecture *On a knife-edge: Looking for the right distance in work with children on the autism spectrum*, which took place on June 25th, 2023, hosted by the Frances Tustin Memorial Trust. I am also indebted to her for generously granting me permission to quote from the text in Chapter 7.

I would also like to express my profound appreciation and thanks to Prof Nick Midgley for the most generous effort and time put into reading and judging my final PhD thesis, despite its considerable length! I am also indebted to Prof Midgley for the many very helpful and insightful comments, and moreover for his belief in my research and insistent encouragement to publish my work, both this book and the papers published based on my PhD.

Heartfelt thanks also to Prof Dana Amir for inviting me to join her unique seminar for doctoral and post-doctoral students in the interdisciplinary doctoral programme in psychoanalysis at Haifa University (headed by Prof Amir), despite my "extraterritorial" academic background. Prof Amir, together with Prof Michal Ben Naftali, guided this group on an extraordinarily enriching, inspiring, challenging, and yet thoroughly enjoyable journey of intellectual and personal discovery and creativity. Thank you both for your sensitive and generous sharing of a boundless wealth of knowledge and creative thinking! I am deeply grateful to my fellow travellers, Dr Rakefet Efrat-Levkovich, Dr Einat Feldhay, Dr Nehama HaCohen, Dr Guy Perel, Dr Shani Samai-Moskovich, and Dr Anat Tzur Mahalel, for their friendship, acceptance, encouragement, and support, for enriching my mind and my world and for the many laughs and tears shared along the way.

Special thanks also to Michal Rieck and Dr Meir Steinbock, of the Israel Winnicott Centre, who encouraged me to delve deep into psychoanalytic thought and dare to find and develop my own psychoanalytic voice.

An alternative version of the same proverb quoted above translates from the Lunyoro (a language spoken in Western Uganda) "Omwana takulila nju emoi" roughly as "a child does not grow up only in a single home".[1] Psychoanalytic psychotherapy and psychoanalysis can often provide the distressed, deprived, or traumatised child or adult, with a home in which their psyche can finally grow and begin to heal. Without the encouragement, patient guidance, teaching, and reverie of those who raised me in the peculiar village that is the world of child psychotherapy and psychoanalytic thought and practice, the seeds of curiosity and enquiry into the psyche of the developing child that led to this research would never have been sown. My deep thanks to Dr Dorit Maoz and Nitsa Riklin, past and present directors of the Haifa Child, Adolescent and Family Mental Health "Ehad Ha'Am" Clinic, who provided me and so many colleagues through many years, with a professional home and secure base in which to grow and develop as a child psychotherapist and later as supervisor and teacher.

I would like to express my deepest gratitude to my dear late colleague and friend, Anna Iofan, child and adult psychoanalytic psychotherapist, and clinical social worker, for sharing with me her work with Kim (described in the clinical example in Chapter 7.3) and for generously granting me permission to use this example in my research and academic writing.

And no less, I am deeply indebted to the many children in the Haifa Clinic and in my private practice, who have been my patients and therefore also my teachers. These children have never failed to make me think, rethink, listen, adapt, create, and recreate, and thereby challenge me to always do my best to meet their inner worlds and their emotional and developmental needs.

Other children outside my clinical work have also been my playful and creative teachers – my nephews, my children's friends, my friends' children, and many others. A special thanks here to two highly thoughtful and expressive children, H and G, from London, for sharing with me their wonderful insights on collecting and trading cards and on making and discovering the joys of slime, and to their very special mum, Karen, for generously and dutifully typing up their every word!

I feel very fortunate and so deeply grateful to have been accompanied and guided on this journey by two wise and wonderful clinical supervisors, Dorit Lavon and Dr Marit Goren, who have supported, mentored, encouraged, and challenged me unfailingly along the way to become the "good-enough" psychotherapist and supervisor I endeavour to be.

My especially profound gratitude to my psychotherapist and analyst over many years, Dr Kareen Ben-Ari Smira, for being there through thick and thin, always with deep clinical wisdom, patience, warmth, and a rare simple common sense. This was a journey of slow and often painful thawing of frozen and long-hidden parts of my psyche; of witnessing through with-nessing; of battling with demons and angels of many shapes and forms; and eventually of rediscovering my ability to play, to think, to create, and to recreate. A journey that enabled me to become the person I am today, made possible only through Kareen's patient sensitive humanity and keen clinical insight. Personal analysis, it is often said, is the best form of clinical supervision and teaching. So too, the developmental and clinical thinking that run through this book are the direct product of experiencing – personally, viscerally – psychoanalytic concepts and ideas, living and surviving them together, in the secure safe reliable framework of psychoanalysis. Holding and containing; projective identification and splitting; trauma and disassociation; survival of the object; standing in the spaces; submission and surrender; alive creation and recreation, all these were part and parcel of the life-changing psychoanalytic voyage through which Kareen steered me over many years, and without which this volume would not have been written.

This book would never have been dreamed of, conceived, let alone seen the light of day, without the loving support, joyful companionship, and down-to-earth common sense of the close friends I have been extraordinarily lucky to have from childhood, through university days and up to the present, and to whom I owe so much. My special deep gratitude to Tami Shaked Lewkowitz and Dr Jenny McCleery for their generosity in sharing their playful and creative thinking and their willingness to read, reread, and tactfully but honestly critique my writing. Alongside their abiding encouragement and immeasurable support over many years.

Needless to say, the process of writing has brought me often to think of my own childhood and the influence my childhood had and still has on my clinical work and thinking. I have my brothers Fred and Alec to thank for teaching me the thrills and skills, the traps, and the pitfalls of the childhood games that today are my invaluable tools of the trade. I am deeply appreciative of my parents for instilling in me the joys of learning, exploration, and creative writing, which gave me the impetus and the confidence to pursue my doctoral research and to write this book.

And, from the depths of my heart, words do not seem enough to express my love and gratitude to my family. To my partner, Rafael, for believing in me and for being by my side through all these years of learning to become a child psychoanalytic psychotherapist and researching and developing the thoughts and ideas in this book. And for your invaluable help, enormous effort, and generosity during the editing and proofreading process. I could not have managed without you! To our children, Yonit, Naama, and Tal, for being just the way you are! Thank you, all three of you, so very much for your patience, tolerance, and even encouragement, to follow my path as a psychotherapist, even when this meant I was at work, playing with, giving attention to, and helping other children and their parents find their souls and begin to heal. Each one of you has given me the privilege of giving you what I can, and of accompanying you as you grow and discover the world and who you are in the world. You have all, together with your wonderful partners, Metar and Yishay, always challenged me each in your own way, to listen, to stop and think, to play with joy and curiosity, and to create and recreate on a daily basis what it means to be a parent, and lately, a grandparent too!

*****

I am deeply indebted to Routledge/Taylor & Francis for giving me the opportunity to publish this volume, and especially to my editors Zöe Meyer and Deepika Batra, for their time, patience, help, and support, and keen editorial eye throughout this long process. My special thanks to Zöe Meyer for initially showing interest in this book, for believing in the ideas presented here, for encouraging me to go ahead and submit my proposal, and also for her invaluable creative input in the search for a suitable title for this book. My appreciation and thanks to Sophie Dixon-Dash, the Production Editor at T&F books, for your sensitivity and generous support during the final editing and production process. My thanks also to Lakshmi Priya Megavannan for her work and dedication as project manager during the production process at Codemantra.

I am very grateful to Taylor & Francis for granting me permission to reuse material from the three papers published by them based on my PhD thesis: Maroudas, C., Wiseman, H., & Harel, J. (2023). The "wave-particle" child: Reconnecting the disconnect in the concept of latency. *Journal of Child Psychotherapy*, *49*(3), 412–431; Maroudas, C. (2024). Petrification, chaos, primitive triangulation and the therapeutic power of game-play. *Journal of Infant, Child, and Adolescent Psychotherapy*, *23*(3), 213–223; and Maroudas, C. (2024). But it's against the rules!! Structured competitive games as a neglected resource in child psychodynamic psychotherapy. *The International Journal of Psychoanalysis*, 1–21. My thanks to both Prof Hadas Wiseman and Prof Judith Harel, co-authors of the first of these three papers, for permission to reuse material from that paper in this volume. Likewise, I am grateful to the editors of this book for permission to reuse material from these three papers in this volume.

Equally, I am indebted to the following publishing companies: American Psychological Association, Cambridge University Press, Elsevier, John Wiley and Sons, Oxford University Press, Sage Publications, Springer Nature, and Taylor and Francis, for kind permission to quote from the many different papers cited in this book and to the myriad of authors whose work and writing I have quoted, without whose wisdom and experience I could not have developed the thinking in this volume.

My profound gratitude to the artist Francis Alÿs and the Alÿs Studio for their generous permission to reuse the poignant images of children's games from his video artwork: *Children's Games #18, #19, #21, #26, #27, and #46* in the preface.

I wish to thank the publishers HarperCollins Publishers Ltd, Penguin Random House LLC (US), and Curtis Brown Group Ltd. on behalf of The Pooh Properties Trust, for permission to reproduce material from The House at Pooh Corner by A.A. Milne, quoted in Chapter 3.

Likewise, I wish to thank the following museums for their kind permission to use the images of their artwork, reproduced in the Preface and in Chapter 2 of this volume: the Yad Vashem Holocaust Memorial Museum; the National Gallery, London; the Museo del Prado; the New York Metropolitan Museum; the National Galleries of Scotland; the Kunsthistorisches Museum, Vienna; the Petit Palais Museum, Paris; and the Musee Marmottan Monet of Paris.

Note

1 https://www.bookbrowse.com/expressions/detail/index.cfm/expression_number/443/it-takes-a-village-to-raise-a-child

Preface

It is nearly ten years since I first embarked on this project, with a wish to commit to paper ideas that had only begun to form in my mind about school-aged children, about the nature of their oft-misunderstood psyche, their peculiar language of play, and the special needs of this age group in child psychotherapy.

This project took me on a journey back to my own childhood, to the often-turbulent games of Monopoly played on the sitting room floor with my elder brothers or the hours spent with them in the garden playing *Three-and-in* games of football and *Six-and-out* games of cricket (in both I was "out" most of the time!). I have fonder memories of the tamer and more benign games of *Scrabble, Rummy, Pairs,* and *Frustration/Trouble*, played with my late mother on cold, wet, winter afternoons. Nevertheless, ours was not a playful home. Vast swathes of my parents' psyches were blocked to simple, spontaneous Winnicottian and Milnerian play. My mother had lost her childhood to the ravages of the Holocaust, and my father had spent most of his childhood ensconced for hours in the local library as an escape from a home life of deprivation and abuse. And yet, both my parents played and created, each in their own way. My mother, at work in her lab with her test tubes and slide rule, or at home within the clear and safe confines of board games and card games, and my father played all his life with words, reading, writing, and reciting ditties from Lewis Carroll or Hilaire Belloc, or Shakespeare soliloquies. He also taught us to play tennis, ride a bicycle, swim, and dive. It is thus perhaps no coincidence that, in my endeavour to understand the years of middle childhood, I found myself both researching academic papers and also reading A.A. Milne, Enid Blyton, and Lewis Carroll, playing not only with footballs and Monopoly money but also with the written word, as my ideas took shape.

I suppose I was drawn to psychotherapeutic work with children in the first place to try and unravel the dark, distorted, and damaged places in my parents' souls and so to uncover, explore, and heal the inescapable transgenerational trauma passed down to me and my brothers. But no less, I can see now that I was searching for answers to the seemingly prosaic question that had burned unconsciously inside me all these years: What does "normal" childhood really look like? I sensed that my own childhood and that of my parents had left me with very little clue. In this book, the phrases "6–12-year-olds" and "between the ages of 6 and 12" come up again and again. But it was only towards the end of my doctorate that it finally dawned on me that these were the very years of middle childhood, precisely between the ages of 6 and 12, that my mother had spent as a young Jewish child in Poland in the Second World War, first under Soviet rule and then surviving Nazi persecution. Intuitively, as I progressed through my research, I realised that in order to help my child patients (the child in me?) imagine the child they could be(come) and to reclaim their psychic aliveness and creativity, it was imperative for me to understand more fully what the benign, untraumatised psyche of middle childhood looks like.

Freud deemed these years of middle childhood a period of psychic stagnation and dormancy (Freud, 1940). Indeed, the average 8- or 9-year-old can often seem boring, their conversation repetitive and rambling, they are obsessed with rules and regulations, and are not nearly as cute and beguiling as their younger siblings. But during my nearly 40 years working with children aged 6–12 (and older) in the public and private sectors, I have also often found myself captivated by the inquisitiveness, depth, and creativity of school-aged children. I have come to recognise and learn to interpret the rich psychic vocabulary and grammar hidden behind the smoke screen of talk of football, Minecraft, classroom gossip, and quirky childhood crazes such as slime, Minions, or the Yu-Gi-Oh cards of yester-year. Countless games of Monopoly, ping pong, TAKI/UNO, football, and Speed/Spit taught me to my surprise (and admittedly at first to my frustration) that it is often only in these rule-bound, seemingly superficial, games that the psyche of the school-aged child comes alive, and their true self emerges. It is this often mis-understood and underestimated world of middle childhood and the games these children play that I have set out to describe and explore in the first few chapters of this book.

As I was nearing the end of my doctorate, my dear cousin Bronia Engel from Australia, whose parents had also been Holocaust survivors, mentioned to me that in the Sydney Jewish Museum there is a replica of a hand-drawn Monopoly board made in Theresienstadt. The therapeutic value of the drama, art, and music groups run by the adult prisoners for the children in the ghetto/concentration camp has been chronicled extensively, but I had never heard discussion and never asked myself about the role the traditional, more structured childhood games might have played in children's psychic survival in the Holocaust? What did the makers of that game of Monopoly in the ghetto understand about the psychic needs of older school-aged children that child psychoanalytic thinkers have yet to formulate?

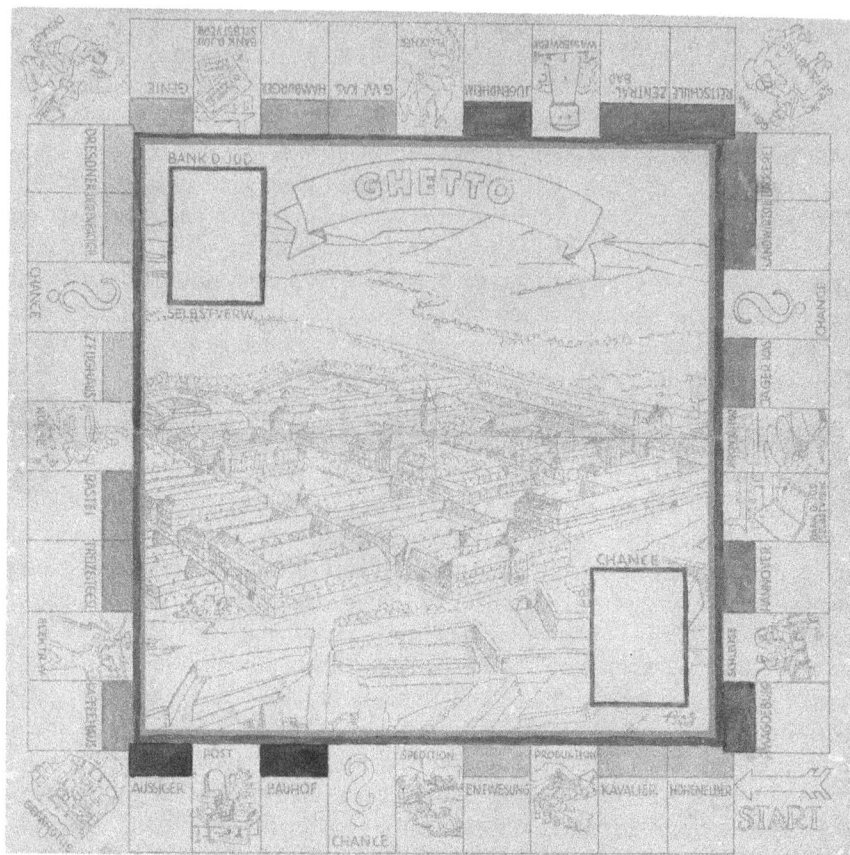

Figure 0.1 Monopoly game received by the brothers Pavel and Thomas Glass in Theresienstadt.

The game board, created in the Theresienstadt graphics workshop by Oswald Poeck, depicts the fortress city of Theresienstadt, and the game stations reflect the life of the Jews in the ghetto. The two children were deported to the ghetto with their mother Francesca from the city of Brno and remained there until liberation.

Credit: Yad Vashem Artifacts Collection. Gift of Micah Glass, Ramat Gan, and Dan Glass, Jerusalem

According to an article in the Haaretz newspaper from 2014,[1] based on an interview with Yehudit Inbar, then Director of Yad Vashem's museums, the world Holocaust memorial centre based in Jerusalem, the centre has three original sets of Monopoly: one based on the streets of Budapest and containing cards such as "pay a hunger tax" or "pay a sick tax"; one regular set played by children in the Shanghai Ghetto; and the one pictured above from Theresienstadt, designed by the artist Oswald Poeck and made secretly in the Theresienstadt Ghetto graphics workshop in 1943. The game featured key locations in the ghetto, such as the main kitchen, the bakery, the prison, and the train station, as well as "chance" cards based on the written and unwritten rules of the ghetto. The ultimate prize of the game was a day of rest, and the severest penalty card instructed you to leave the game on account of your name being on the transport lists (to Auschwitz or Treblinka) for the next day. Play and survival were inexorably, shockingly intertwined.

This discovery led me once again to think about my mother's lost childhood and the games she nevertheless played with us as children: ball games, *Rummy* and *War*; *hopscotch*, and *Jacks*. These were games she could not have learnt before the war; she had been too young. Were these the games she had played with the local children when living under false papers in the small then Polish village of Tlumacz as a 9-, 10-, and 11-year-old? Did these games save parts of her soul too, like the Theresienstadt game of Monopoly, enabling her to be momentarily free and play, even give expression to anxieties and the need to control frustration, jealousy, and even anger and aggression, all under cover of the safety of games with clear rules and boundaries? What other games did she play in those years? I never asked her; it always seemed too frivolous a question, and now it is sadly too late.

In the dark days in which I write this Preface, living in a region of the world wracked by terrible armed conflict, my thoughts wander from the war-torn Lwow of my mother's childhood, to the Lviv of today, to the Ukrainian children experiencing once again the constant threat of ground invasion, aerial bombardments, death, and destruction. And closer to home, what of children caught up in the horrors of the war in Gaza, and here in Israel, their psyches, as well as their bodies, scarred forever? What games are all these children playing? What games can they play? What games do they need to play to keep their psyches alive? I think back to an interview with the grandfather of two young children whose parents were murdered in front of their eyes on one of the kibbutzim in Israel attacked on October 7, 2023. The interviewer asked the grandfather about the conversations he was having with his grandchildren. "There are no words," the grandfather answered, "Their eyes say it all... And in any case, they definitely don't want to talk, they just need me to be there, to go outside and play football with them, whenever they want, as much as they want".[2] Like the maker of the Theresienstadt Monopoly game, Oswalk Poeck, this grandfather knew intuitively that children often do not use words to process what is unimaginable and unbearable, but they speak through their eyes and their bodies, through the language of the games they play. Rather, it is on the Monopoly board, in a game of cards, on the makeshift football pitch in a rubble-strewn street that children intuitively seek to find psychic aliveness and healing.

Children the world over continue to play *Jenga* and football, *Minecraft*, and *Five Stones*, anywhere and everywhere, be it in backstreet alleys or abandoned inner city lots, the school playground, or in the back garden or living room of the family home. Sadly, children continue to be the victims of deprivation and abuse, armed conflict, and political strife. Recently, my attention was drawn to the work of the Belgian-born Mexico-based artist, Francis Alÿs, and his long-running film series *Children's Games*, recently featured in a specially dedicated exhibition *Ricochets* in the Barbican Centre, London.[3] These films present us with poignant and yet strikingly vibrant studies of the games children play across continents and cultures, from the DRC to Nepal, from London to Ukraine, and from the refugee camps of the Middle East to the quiet suburbs of Paris: games like football, marbles, *knucklebones* (*Jacks/Five Stones*), skipping, *hopscotch*, and paper-rock-scissors, that span across nations, socio-economic status, race, creed, and language; and others, like conkers, *Elsakat*, and *Chapitas*, that are peculiar to the local country or culture but so often share common features with games children are playing thousands of miles away, in different surrounds, with different props, in different languages. The games are filled with vitality and energy, unbounded creativity, humour and playfulness, aggression and rivalry, all combined with a seriousness, intense concentration, skill, and a clear determination and sense of purpose, all qualities so typical of middle childhood. The players Alÿs filmed are all children or young adolescents, often surrounded by a crowd of enthusiastic similarly aged onlookers – adults are significant only in their absence.

Figure 0.2 Francis Alÿs, Children's Games (1999 – present).

Clockwise from top left corner: *Children's Game #18: Knucklebones*, Kathmandu, Nepal, 2017; *Children's Game #19: Haram Football*, Mosul, Iraq, 2017; *Children's Game #26: Kisolo*, Tabacongo, DR Congo, 2021; *Children's Game #46: Conkers*, London, United Kingdom, 2024; *Children's Game #27: Rubi*, Tabacongo, DR Congo, 2021; *Children's Game #21: Hand Stack*, Nerkzlia, Iraq, 2019.

Stills captured from original video publications and reproduced with kind permission from the artist Francis Alÿs (https://francisalys.com/category/childrens-games/)

During the Covid-19 pandemic, children were isolated from their peers for months on end, often holed up in their homes, even going out to play in the street or local park with their peers was illegal. Looking on in dismay as a child psychotherapist, it seemed to me that a whole generation of elementary school children seemed to have been forgotten by governments across the globe. It turns out those children who could, turned to game-play at home and online to keep in touch and keep sane. The sales of board games and membership of online board game sites soared, children (and adults of all ages) were not just playing Minecraft and Fortnite but also rediscovering the playfulness, creativity, and the hidden power of interpersonal connection in games like Monopoly, Chess, and even simple card games.

I have been playing board games, ball games, and card games with my child patients in psychotherapy for many years. I have to confess that, at first, the choice was definitely not mine: I had been trained as a student in what is called today the "Jerusalem Hills Therapeutic Centers", a psychoanalytically oriented therapeutic children's home founded some 80 years ago. The therapy rooms were kitted out with toy animals and cars, dollhouses, a sandbox, a couch, a table, a couple of balls, crayons, paints, and paper. No packs of cards, no board games to be seen. I had been taught Melanie Klein and Winnicott, had read *Dibs in Search of Self* (Axline, 1975), and this is what I had expected to find in a psychoanalytic playroom. But then, 30 years ago, I moved north and began work as a clinical psychology/child psychotherapy trainee in the "Ehad Ha'Am Child, Adolescent and Family Mental Health Clinic" in Haifa and found myself faced with a toy cupboard full of board games and ball games: *Monopoly, Cops and Robbers, Guess Who, Battleships, Mastermind/Code:Breaker, Chess*, Basketball, Ping Pong, and *TAKI/UNO*. Some familiar, others less familiar, but almost all instilled in me a sense of dread – I had no wish to revisit those feelings of inadequacy, helplessness, anger, rivalry, and hurt I had experienced so often as a child, playing these games with my older, cleverer, and physically much stronger brothers. So, in my first weeks in the clinic, I kept the cupboard doors tightly shut and hoped for the best. But my child patients, most of whom were behaviourally disruptive boys aged 9–11, had other ideas. They almost all refused point blank to engage in painting, digging tunnels in the sandbox, or pretend play with dolls or toy soldiers (except to use these play materials as weapons of mass destruction when the impulse struck them). They insisted on playing football (thank goodness I had grown up in Britain), basketball (which I had never played in my life), *TAKI* (over and over again), *War* (which I found tedious), and *Monopoly* (which I loathed with a vengeance). Initially, I presumed that by choosing to play games with rules, boxes, and inbuilt symbols, these children were playing safe, keeping their psychic pain at an arms distance. But I soon found myself struggling to contain therapeutic equanimity in the face of the emotional maelstrom that these games stirred up in these children and in me too, despite my best efforts. Instinctively, I understood that playing according to the rules was way beyond these children's emotional capacities. These were children who more often than not had grown up without control over their daily lives and had experienced deprivation and abuse and long-term instability in their home life. So, I let them lock me in jail and refuse to pay their debts in Monopoly, cheat and move their ships in Battleships whilst repeatedly sneaking a peek at my board, steal my best cards in WAR, and discount all my well-deserved goals in our makeshift games of football.

My supervisors gently and wisely helped me open up and dare to explore the minefield of the intense transference–countertransference interactions I experienced in these sessions. They taught me key theoretical conceptualisations to help me withstand and make sense of what was taking place in these tumultuous games with the school-aged children I was treating: survival of the object, living the experience together, projective identification, narcissistic rage, nameless dread, countertransference as key to understanding the patient's psyche, containment (malignant and benign), beta elements, and alpha elements. All these I experienced viscerally, powerfully, in the emotional storm of these supposedly tedious, repetitive, emotionally restrictive, "non-therapeutic" games. Through the years, these clinical-theoretical concepts became my friends and allies in maintaining psychic space and the ability to think in the face of the "emotional violence" my child patients intuitively channelled through *Monopoly*, football, *War*, and *Cheat*.

Like many, in times of trouble, I turn to books to find solace and meaning. In my clinical work, it is to the psychoanalytic literature that I turn to regain my psychic equilibrium and create sense out of the chaos and confusion that is part and parcel of psychoanalytic psychotherapy. But as a trainee, and later as a clinical supervisor myself, I found that my clinical experience with school-aged children was not reflected in the psychoanalytic literature. I struggled to find papers with clinical examples from the world of game-play in middle childhood that could provide clinical-theoretical conceptualisations for the intra-psychic and inter-psychic processes taking place when we play these traditional structured competitive games in the child psychotherapy room. What do so-called latency-aged children need psychologically and developmentally that is different from preschoolers and adolescents? Why is their language of play and inter-psychic communication so different from the pretend play of early childhood, and what therapeutic power do these games hold? The literature, I discovered, lacked in-depth answers to these and other basic clinical-developmental questions about latency, a period I prefer to refer to as middle childhood (for reasons that will become apparent in the pages that follow). As a supervisor seeking to help my supervisees deepen their clinical-developmental thinking in the child psychotherapy room, I came to the rather shocking realisation that neither I nor my students and trainees had ever been offered, let alone attended, a course on the developmental stage of middle childhood.

This was a developmental and clinical-theoretical lacuna I had not even noticed during my own child psychotherapy training. This book, based on my PhD thesis, is an attempt to begin to fill that very lacuna, to shine the spotlight on children aged 6–12, who, according to age-old wisdom, should be "seen and not heard" and "left well alone". Children who are so often overshadowed, both at home and in the literature, by their more vociferous and behaviourally challenging older and younger siblings. Children whose mental health, according to recent WHO statistics,[4] is increasingly under threat in the aftermath of the Covid-19 pandemic, in a world still wracked by terrible armed conflicts and large-scale wars, 80 years after Oswald Poeck created the Theresienstadt Ghetto Monopoly set.

Notes

1 https://www.haaretz.com/jewish/2014-10-02/ty-article/.premium/toys-tell-story-of-shoahs-kid-victims/0000017f-e4d0-d568-ad7f-f7fb8add0000
2 For the sake of preserving privacy and anonymity, the grandfather's answer as written here is not an exact translation nor an exact transcript of his actual words, but I have tried to be as faithful as possible to the message he conveyed.
3 I am very grateful to Ms Xiaowei Yan, a trainee child psychotherapist at the Anna Freud Centre, London, who brought this Francis Alÿs exhibition to my notice.
4 Kessler, R.C., McLaughlin, K.A., Green, J.G., Gruber, M.J., Sampson, N.A., Zaslavsky, A.M., Aguilar-Gaxiola, S., Alhamzawi, A.O., Alonso, J., Angermeyer, M. and Benjet, C., 2010. Childhood adversities and adult psychopathology in the WHO World Mental Health Surveys. *The British Journal of Psychiatry*, 197(5), 378–385.

Chapter 1

Introduction

Until the turn of the 20th century, most child development texts sketched out the stage of middle childhood only cursorily, painting these years of development in monochrome tones, compared to the florid vibrant colours used to describe the psyches of their younger and older vociferous and proverbially unruly siblings. Except perhaps for Jean Piaget's pioneering research in cognitive development, the period of middle childhood has often been overlooked: detailed studies and descriptions of the neurological and physiological changes of this age group are relatively sparse, and the psychosocial and cognitive achievements, challenges, and needs of this stage have been insufficiently investigated (Cincotta, 2008; Cooper et al., 2005). In a seminal interdisciplinary review of research on middle childhood carried out in the early 1980s in the US (Collins, 1984, 2005), the editor cites a general "lack of concern among scholars about the significance of changes in middle childhood". Similarly, he noted that whilst children ages 6–12 were "arguably the most frequently studied participants in research on children, largely because they are [conveniently] congregated in schools" (Collins, 2005, p. ix) [and comparatively compliant experimental subjects CM] "surprisingly, few theoretical formulations have included extensive treatments of this age group, in contrast to the amount of theoretical attention given to infancy, early childhood, and adolescence" (Collins, 1984, pp. 3–4). In society at large, this age group has historically attracted less attention: with whole generations of school children seen, but neither properly heard nor properly held in the collective mind of practitioners and educationalists.

Likewise, in the field of psychoanalysis, perhaps more than in any other area of developmental research, the view of middle childhood as an unremarkable stage of child development holding little scientific interest has held sway for decades. Freud unashamedly wrote of post-oedipal children as "losing their charm" and as "stupider" (Freud, 1926, p. 215) than their younger siblings. He understood the years of middle childhood as a period of psychosexual dormancy and even stagnancy and, following Breuer's suggestion, coined the term "the latency period" to reflect this view. The founding mothers and father of child psychoanalysis saw the latency years in similar light: Anna Freud emphasised the defences and the obsessional tendencies of school-aged children; Klein bemoaned the restricted imagination and reserved attitudes of the latency-aged child; Winnicott asserted that children of this

DOI: 10.4324/9781003425229-1

age should be left well alone, unless "very ill indeed". All three used words such as dull, boring, limited, repressed, and obsessional to describe this critical stage of child development.

It is only in the last three decades that it has been more widely understood that the years of middle childhood are not only a period of psychosexual, physical, and cognitive consolidation, but are also a period of momentous cognitive, physical, and psychosocial advances, a time of flux and change, of ongoing psychological development and transformation (Canham, 2018; Diem-Wille, 2018; Etchegoyen, 1993). Equally, there is an increasing awareness that for many children, these years between early childhood and adolescence are far from tranquil and can often be fraught with considerable psychological challenges and problems. Recent surveys of school children carried out on national and international levels reveal similar patterns of mental health problems in children across the globe: it seems that over half of lifetime mental health problems appear by the age of 14, and around 12% of children in primary school suffer from some form of emotional or behaviour problem, two-thirds of these boys (Costello et al., 2005; Green et al., 2005; Kessler et al., 2007; Merikangas et al., 2010; Ormel et al., 2015; Polanczyk et al., 2015; Smith et al., 2018; WHO; World Health Organization, 2020). Furthermore, the age of onset for the majority of phobias and separation anxieties and over 90% of behaviour and conduct disorders and attention-deficit disorders lies between the ages of 6 and 12 (Kessler et al., 2007; Ormel et al., 2015, see Figure 1.1). Multiple studies have found that mental health issues early in life are directly correlated with

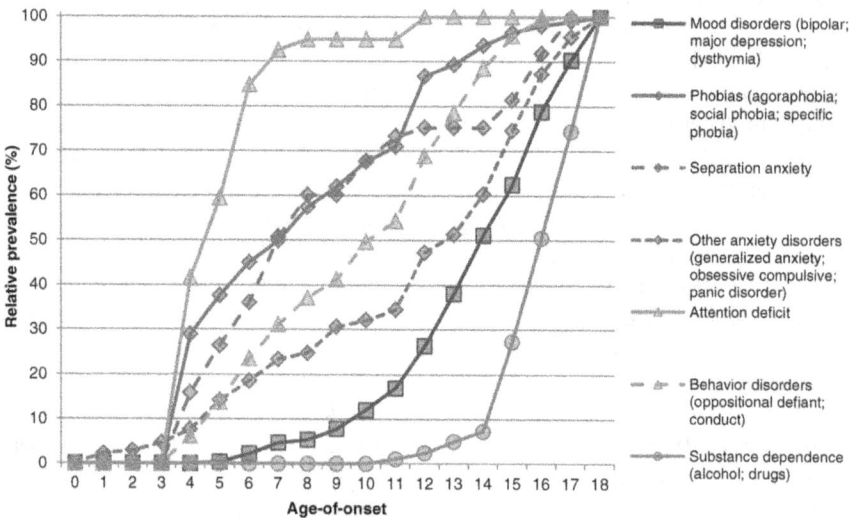

Figure 1.1 Standardised cumulative prevalence curves for *Diagnostic and Statistical Manual of Mental Disorders, 4th edition (DSM-IV)* disorders (reproduced from Ormel et al., 2015, p. 350), with permission © Cambridge University Press.

mental health problems in the long term (Kessler et al., 2010). Psychotherapy for this age group is therefore of the utmost importance in promoting psychological well-being not just in childhood but also into adolescence and beyond.

In tandem with an increased awareness of mental health issues in children and adults alike, the last three decades have also seen a dramatic rise in referral rates of school-aged children to mental health clinics in many countries around the world, even more so in the wake of the Covid-19 pandemic (Collishaw, 2015; Costello et al., 2005; Crenna-Jennings & Hutchinson, 2018; Green et al., 2005; Kessler et al., 2007; Mental Health of Children and Young People in England 2022, NHS Digital, 2022; Samji et al., 2022; Singh et al., 2020). It appears from these and other studies that roughly 40% of these referrals are of children in the age range 6–12 years, and yet, even today, clinical training institutions rarely include courses devoted exclusively to middle childhood. Moreover, the clinical literature focusing on psychodynamic treatment of this age group remains scant, and theoretical and clinical models for adapting psychoanalytic play technique to meet the particular needs of this age group are sorely lacking (Bellinson, 2013; Etchegoyen, 1993; Jemerin, 2004; Oren, 2008).

A closer look at the data reveals that these mental health referrals are not distributed evenly between the genders. Boys in middle childhood are referred to at least twice as frequently as girls of the same age, probably because of the tendency of boys to express emotional distress through externalising disruptive behaviour, which catches the attention of parents, teachers, and school counsellors. (In adolescence this trend is largely reversed, seemingly due to an increase in depressive symptomatology in teenage girls.) With respect to psychodynamic child psychotherapy, outcome research has shown lower rates of drop-out and greater effectiveness for younger children and for girls in general, and higher rates of drop-out (of up to 50%) for older boys in general and for boys with conduct disorders in particular (Deakin et al., 2012, 2009; Kazdin, 1991; Kazdin & Mazurick, 1994; Midgley & Kennedy, 2011). Taking all these findings together, the implication is that traditional child psychotherapy approaches may well not be suited to many school-aged children and that a reappraisal of psychodynamic theory and practice vis-à-vis middle childhood is critical to success in tackling the mental health problems of this age group across the globe.

1.1   The children seen and not heard: "latency" re-examined

Sometimes called the "golden years of childhood", the stage of middle childhood is heralded by the sharp transition from dependent, clumsy, tempestuous toddler to self-contained, physically and cognitively adept, and knowledge hungry schoolchild. Ptolemy aptly named this stage of development (between the ages of 4 and 14 according to Ptolemy) "Mercury", after the youthful, winged messenger of the Greek and Roman gods, famed for his intelligence, athletic prowess, and mischief making. Writers through the centuries, from Homer to Erich Kästner to Michel

Paver, have vividly captured and chronicled the often-confounding combination of physical energy and astounding cognitive achievements with the rigid conformity and morality that are also characteristic of this period of childhood.

Between the ages of 6 and 12, children rapidly acquire multiple and sophisticated physical, cognitive, and social skills, moving from a position of great physical and emotional dependence on the parents to relative independence, competence and self-sufficiency (Cincotta, 2008). It is at this age that children are traditionally assigned or assume increasingly important familial and societal responsibilities (Lancy & Grove, 2011). Thanks to their newly acquired abilities and competencies, and in contrast to the tantrum-prone clingy toddler, children in middle childhood increasingly seek out and enjoy autonomy, peer-group relationships and activities outside of the familiar home environment. And unlike the typical stroppy, hormonal adolescent, battling parental authority, the pre-pubertal school-aged child tends still to be relatively easy-going, cooperative, productive, and organised – Erikson's (1950) proverbial "industrious good citizen". The following picture, painted by Hamish Canham (2018), albeit with a typically British slant, captures the essence of this age group:

> I think of them as wearing school uniforms, being relatively polite and respectful, going out to play, and doing things like football for boys, French skipping for girls, ball games against the wall, clapping games, clubs and secret societies, crazes like yo-yos, conkers, and hopscotch, and lots of collecting and swapping of stamps, marbles, etc. They go to "cubs" or "brownies" [elementary school scouts] and take great pride in getting badges...
>
> [A]n up-to-date list might not be so very different. There would still be football and probably some of the traditional playground games such as skipping and chase. Collections might be of Pokémon cards, Harry Potter badges, or football stickers, but these would be traded and swapped in much the same way as before.
>
> (Canham, 2018, p. 37)

But this perceived equanimity and self-sufficiency of middle childhood comes at a price. Often "seen and not heard", these children tend to spend their time sitting quietly in the corner somewhere, diligently colouring in, reading, or simply playing on their smartphone. Or they might be off somewhere with friends and neighbours investigating the latest interactive internet game together or playing football in the park. "Out of sight and out of mind", the average 6–12-year-old can easily slip under the radar, their[1] needs, and indeed their charms, unheeded and unnoticed. Repeatedly neglected by researchers, practitioners, theoreticians, and policymakers alike, these years of middle childhood are all too easily overshadowed by the momentous physical, emotional, and psychosexual growth and development that are the challenge and hallmark of infancy and toddlerhood on the one hand and puberty on the other (Cooper et al., 2005; Diem-Wille, 2018; Knight, 2014).

Freud's psychoanalytic theory of personality development was revolutionary in its time both because of his detailed investigation into unconscious processes and because of his then highly controversial focus on infantile sexuality. But it was precisely this insight of Freud's into infantile sexuality and his profound belief in the primacy of early psychosexual development and object relations that led, by corollary, to the long-term neglect of the period of middle childhood in psychoanalytic theory. Borrowing from Fleiss, Freud first coined the term *"latency"* in 1905 (Freud, 1905) to describe the post-oedipal years until puberty (roughly 6–12), a developmental period which he viewed as one of psychosexual dormancy and of little significance psychoanalytically, paling in comparison to the seething primeval world of the libidinal and aggressive urges and fantasies of infancy and of the oedipal years of early childhood:

> [T]he most remarkable thing about the sexual life of children seems to me that *it passes through the whole of its very far-reaching development in the first five years of life*. From then onwards until puberty there stretches what is known as the period of latency. During it, sexuality normally advances no further; on the contrary, the sexual urges diminish in strength and many things are given up and forgotten which the child did and knew.
>
> (S. Freud, 1926, p. 210)

Freud held on to this view of the post-oedipal years to the end of his life. In the *Outline of Psychoanalysis* (S.Freud, 1940), he wrote of the latency period thus:

> It is further found that these phenomena which emerge in early childhood form part of a regular process of development, that they undergo a steady increase and reach a climax towards the end of the fifth year, after which there follows a lull. *During this lull, progress is at a standstill and much is unlearnt and undone*. After the end of this so-called period of latency, sexual life is resumed with puberty, or, as we might say, it bursts once more into flower. Here we come upon the fact that sexual life has a dichronous onset...
>
> (S. Freud, 1926, p. 134, emphases added)

The term "latency period" has remained stubbornly embedded in the psychoanalytic discourse ever since Freud (as shall be seen in Chapter 3). The word latency is defined in the Cambridge English dictionary,[2] as "the fact of being present but needing particular conditions to become active, obvious, or completely developed", implying a state of quiescence before an event occurs, but also a state of potential. Freud's particular use of the word latency in psychoanalysis, and the theory behind it, has confounded thinking about emotional development in middle childhood throughout most of the 20th century. As shall be seen in the following chapters, during middle childhood sexuality is indeed partially subverted. It seems that Freud's psychoanalytic ear was tuned especially to psychosexual development in its more florid forms. It may be that the diffidence and the rather ambivalent quality of sexuality and sexual exploration in middle childhood led his thinking on development in the post-oedipal, pre-pubertal years somewhat astray – a pattern in psychoanalytic developmental theory that continues to this day.

In psychoanalytic parlance, the term latency has thus come to be synonymous with calmness and even stagnation, and hence of lesser interest psychoanalytically than the preceding oedipal phase or subsequent pubertal phase, "a time of relative order and composure, in many ways unexceptional and quick to pass over" (Wilson, 1989, p. 59):

> Latency is essentially a time of growth and learning – altogether exhilarating, but essentially held and protected within a sense of structure, both internally and externally. A "good" latency, in effect, refers to a few years of peace and quiet, freed from the turmoil of infantile or adolescent passions and anxieties in which there is access to learning and to new experiences beyond the family, without disruption from within or intrusion from without. What is of essence in this notion of latency is a kind of psychic truce.
>
> (Wilson, 1989, p. 63)

Typical of this view of middle childhood as relatively trouble-free and productive is the following excerpt from Gilmore and Meersand's (2014) important psychodynamic developmental textbook *The Little Book of Child and Adolescent Development*:

> Amplified societal demands – expectations for learning, compliance, social control – interface with the child's newfound abilities and mounting desire for independence and friendship creating *a developmental period that is synonymous with cooperation, diligence, and productivity,* and in which peer norms begin to exert a powerful influence.
>
> (Gilmore & Meersand, 2014, p. 102, emphases added)

Articles and books specifically on this phase of childhood are few and far between (Diem-Wille, 2018; Etchegoyen, 1993; Jacobs, 2004; Knight, 2014). In the eyes of many contemporary writers in the field, this stage of childhood has been treated until recently as "the neglected stepchild in psychoanalytic research" (Knight, 2014). However, with the increase in scientific interest in development in middle childhood across the fields of neurobiology, physiology, cognition, and psychology (see Chapter 3) has come a concomitant rethinking of psychoanalytic theory on the so-called latency period. In sharp contrast to the concept of developmental stagnation and even "unlearning" posited in Freud's psychosexual developmental theory, more recent psychoanalytic writers have begun to turn their attention to the manifest and significant changes that occur throughout this period. The focus of psychoanalytic developmental research has ventured beyond the psychosexual, building on formulations both from within and from outside of mainstream psychoanalysis, to encompass and explore the broader intra-psychic and psychosocial developmental achievements and challenges of the years of middle childhood. In such contemporary psychoanalytic articles, these years of middle childhood are described today not only as a period of relative quiescence, obsessive, and defensive tendencies, but also as "a period of emotional growth and maturation" (Etchegoyen, 1993); years which see a "quantum shift in the child's mental organization, relationships and behaviour" (Gilmore & Meersand, 2013, p. 141):

> Despite the child's outwardly dutiful and compliant attitude, modern psychodynamic theorists recognize latency as a vibrant period of cognitive growth, inner conflict, and elaborate fantasizing... The confluence of brain maturation, sweeping changes in cognition and emotional self-regulation, diminishment of oedipal pressures, and increasing societal demands generates this critical period of childhood.
>
> (Gilmore & Meersand, 2013, p. 141)

Indeed, it can be seen that the very concept of latency is coming under question. Phrases such as "the latency period does not exist" (Janus & Bess, 1976) or "there is nothing latent about latency" (Ohrenstein, 1986) appear repeatedly in the literature. Likewise, even the very division into developmental phases and stages is being re-examined (Jacobs, 2004; Janus & Bess, 1976; Knight, 2014).

It can be seen from this discussion that many in the field today concur that latent means latent: not stagnant, not inert; but hidden and concealed (as implied by the etymological origin of the word), energy stored in potential, available to be released at any time given certain conditions. Psychosexual development is no longer universally viewed as coming to a halt at the age of six, but is recognised by many as continuing to evolve throughout the childhood years, just in a less overtly tumultuous and bodily manner than in toddlerhood or in adolescence. Many practitioners and theoreticians understand today that even in the most well-balanced "post-oedipal" school-aged child, intra-psychic conflicts and anxieties remain alive and kicking throughout the childhood years, albeit often out of sight and out of mind.

Despite this contemporary psychodynamic re-conceptualisation of middle childhood, the majority of clinical papers and case studies are surprisingly still mostly stuck in the paradigm of classical child psychoanalytic approaches to "latency" aged children. In middle childhood, a momentous shift occurs in children's play away from fantasy and imaginary narrative play towards rule-bound, competitive games: card games and board games, computer console games, competitive physical games, such as tag, hopscotch, football, and basketball, become the mainstay of children's play at home and outside. Although this shift is widely documented in the psychoanalytic literature (Diem-Wille, 2018; Freud, 1963; Gilmore, 2011; Gilmore & Meersand, 2013; Piaget, 1962), little has changed in the field to integrate these forms of play and communication into clinical theory and practice. It is to this issue that I shall now turn, an issue that I judge to be central to the success of psychotherapeutic treatment of school-aged children, and central to the tenets of this book.

1.2   The games not played – a brief historical overview

Historically, psychodynamically oriented child psychotherapy was founded on two main paradigms: "fantasy play", as pioneered by Melanie Klein (1927, 1955), a technique that facilitates the projection, interpretation, and working through of archaic conflicts, suitable mainly for younger children; and the "talking cure" (S.

Freud, 1910), as adapted by Anna Freud (1926, 1946) for children, aimed at the exposition and solution of inner "neurotic" conflicts through the interpretation of the child's dreams, stories, and drawings. Later, in the post-War years, Winnicott (1971) expanded the theory and technique of child psychotherapy in a radical new third direction, and in so doing expanded the theory of playing, of mental health and of psychotherapeutic space itself. Rather than focusing on the exposition and resolution of unconscious conflicts, he emphasised the significance of the patient-analyst interaction in the transitional space and the critical role of spontaneous creativity and of play per se in psychotherapy in particular, and in emotional development in general. However, in his work with children, Winnicott's psychotherapeutic tools remained largely the same as Klein's and Anna Freud's: unstructured dramatic play with dolls and small toys, drawing, and working with dreams and stories his child patients related. These traditional child psychotherapy techniques based on expressive play or verbal techniques are, almost by definition, potentially problematic for older latency-aged children and younger adolescents. Developmentally, children of these ages tend to have outgrown communication through dramatic pretend play or drawing and painting but have yet to develop adult verbal communication skills, insight, and openness (Gilmore & Meersand, 2013; Levy, 2008; Oren, 2008). These are children whom Bellinson (2000) aptly describes as being in the "shrugging, 'fine', 'nothing' stage of communication". And they also instinctively spurn dolls, puppets, paper, and paints in their play, preferring bats and balls, cards and dice, or today, any available interactive electronic gadget. It is these structured competitive games with clear rules and boundaries, winners and losers, that constitute the natural mode of social interaction and interpersonal communication in middle childhood.

The importance of playing such competitive rule-bound games for older children is widely recognised today across the fields of education and child development (Gilmore & Meersand, 2013; Lanyado & Horne, 2007; Peller, 1954; Plaut, 1979). And yet, paradoxically, as shall be seen in Chapter 4, playing these very games in the child psychotherapy room, even with older children, has traditionally been frowned upon and the theoretical discussion of their therapeutic use foreclosed (Bellinson, 2002; Caruth, 1988; Oren, 2008). Both Klein and Anna Freud regarded playing board games and card games as defensive and detrimental to the therapeutic process. Even Winnicott similarly overlooked the potential therapeutic power inherent in the interactive and familiar nature of these everyday board games and card games, despite his emphasis on the transitional space of patient–analyst interaction (Winnicott, 1971). The resistance to playing competitive structured games in the psychotherapy room common to Klein, Freud, Winnicott, and their followers is especially perplexing given the intuitive empathic understanding all three of these founding "parents" of child psychoanalysis had for the need for the child of any age to feel as at ease as possible in the therapeutic setting.

So much for theory. De facto in the child psychoanalytic psychotherapy room, the attitude towards interactive play (and the use of structured rule-bound games themselves) seems to have been less black and white than the statements in the literature would lead us to believe. Klein, for example, argues vehemently against participating in the "latency" child's play and emphasises the dormancy and defensiveness of the latency period, and yet throughout her writings, she gives numerous examples of interactive imaginary play with her young patients. Moreover, towards the end of her life, she tended to emphasise the ongoing oscillatory nature of development during the latency years rather than stagnation and stultification (see Chapters 2 and 4). Anna Freud, for her part, famously argued that the value of the toy had been overstated, and she dismissed board games as defensive and unproductive therapeutically (Sandler et al., 1980). However, she had a special interest in the workings of the ego in this age group and her writings on the latency-aged child repeatedly describe the developmental shift in play from pretend play towards competitive rule-bound games typical of this age group (Peller, 1954). Similarly, Winnicott elevated free imaginary play to an almost hallowed position, but at one and the same time, he invented his own structured game to engage more defensive older children – *the squiggle game* – a game of contained and guided "spontaneous" drawing with clear rules and instructions where patient and therapist take turns to draw squiggles and to elaborate on the squiggles drawn by the other (see Chapter 4).

1.3 Structured games enter the child psychoanalytic therapy room

By the 1970s, playing structured games in child psychotherapy was more accepted, more "above board", so to speak, especially amongst ego psychologists in the US, albeit here too paradoxes and contradictions abound in the literature. Paulina Kernberg (2000, 2008, 2012), for instance, perhaps one of the most prominent US child psychoanalysts of her time, does not engage in any direct discussion of the therapeutic use of board games and card games in her earlier copious writings on child psychotherapy in general and on play in child psychotherapy in particular. However, she repeatedly emphasises the need for adjusting technique to the child's level of psychic functioning and providing age and gender-appropriate toys and games to suit different child patients. Moreover, reading between the lines in her writings, it is clear that playing structured games such as bowls, checkers, and pick-up sticks was part and parcel of child therapeutic work for Kernberg and her colleagues for many years (Kernberg, 2000; Kernberg et al., 2008, 2012).

Reviewing the literature on child psychoanalytic psychotherapy published in the US during this period, one can find a handful of authors who go a few steps further than Kernberg did, and positively endorse the therapeutic benefits of board games (Beiser, 1979b,a; Coriat, 1941; Fried, 1992; Green, 1978; Levinson, 1972; Loomis, 1976; Meeks, 1970). Although the majority of these papers refer only to specific therapeutic applications of board games or carry firm caveats regarding their use, nonetheless they bear witness to the presence and growing use of board games in various child psychotherapy clinics across the US during the last quarter of the 20th century. Notable amongst these child psychoanalytic therapists writing on the subject in the 1970s and 1980s is Helen Beiser, who strongly and proactively advocated the use of board games in diagnosis and treatment, from an ego psychology, object relationship perspective (Beiser, 1979a):

> I have found that children from 6 to 12 often select formal games from an array of toys in preference to the more usual fantasy-stimulating toys. If games are not offered, they may bring their own, or make them up. If the goal of psychotherapy is to help the child reach an appropriate developmental level, then it is to the latency child's advantage to diagnose his game playing difficulties, and, in the treatment process, help him to enjoy this normal activity. Latency children who cheat, cry if they don't win, or give up too easily are not accepted by peers. Of course, games may be used as resistance in therapy, but so may talk, doll play, or even dreams. The essence of psychotherapy is in the relationship, and I would like to see more therapists add formal games to their other modes of interaction.
> (Beiser, 1979a, p. 481)

Since the turn of the last century, the tide has begun to turn regarding the use of formal games in child psychoanalytic psychotherapy and papers on the subject have mushroomed. In tandem with the changing psychoanalytic views of latency, the field has seen a more widespread recognition amongst child psychotherapists of the developmental need of children of this age to play structured games both inside and outside the psychotherapy playroom (Bellinson, 2002; Gilmore & Meersand, 2013; Krimendahl, 2000; Oren, 2008; סער et al., 2017). As Bellinson (2002) writes, children aged 9–12 do not tend to engage naturally in make-believe play, but "they do play board games…And we want them to. A 10- or 11-year old who continued to play exclusively in the doll house or with action figures would strike us as infantile, regressed" (Bellinson, 2002, p. 3). These authors maintain that older children seek out and need toys and games in psychotherapy that are more age appropriate and more acceptable to their own self-image, games that are more familiar and at a "safe" psychic distance from their inner private selves. They suggest that the language of the board game – like the fantasy play of the pre-schooler or the dreams and verbal material of an adult patient – is a psychodynamic language like any other, to be intuited, interpreted, and worked through with the child.

The shift seen recently in many schools of psychoanalytic thought away from content interpretation and towards process, and from a one-person to a two-person psychology, has it seems led indirectly to an increasing number of articles and conference papers that describe playing board games, internet games, and discussing social media content with children and adolescents in psychoanalytically oriented psychotherapy (Brady, 2012; Chung & Colarusso, 2013; Molinari, 2017). Notable amongst these are the post-Bionian, post-Winnicottian "field theory" child psychoanalysts such as Ferro (2003, 2017), Moilnari and Brady (see Chapter 12) who view playing as a "mental function" and view psychoanalysis primarily as a process of expansion of the intra-psychic and inter-psychic space through the inter-psychic experience lived together in the context of the psychotherapy. From this perspective, the specific games played or not played are of minor relevance compared to the form of inter-psychic and intra-psychic interaction taking place in the child psychotherapy room.

1.4   Middle childhood: rethinking developmental theory and clinical practice

Drawing on the foregoing discussion, it can thus be seen that middle childhood is seen by many developmentalists and practitioners today not only as a period of momentous cognitive, physical, and psychosocial advances, but also as a time of vulnerability and emotional fragility – a far cry indeed from the period of quiescence, "latency", or even developmental stagnation that Freud described. The familiar structured games of middle childhood – card games, ball games, board games, and today's console games – reflect this complex and paradoxical developmental picture. These games are bounded in time and place by rules and predetermined contents, but the course of play is unpredictable; the games are often challenging cognitively and physically, and highly emotionally charged. It is for these reasons that several contemporary authors in the field have suggested that game-play can offer the school-aged child a safe and developmentally appropriate medium through which they can express and explore their intra-psychic and inter-psychic world in a psychotherapeutic setting (Bellinson, 2000; Maroudas et al., 2023; Meeks, 1970, 2000). Despite the recent contributions of these and other authors, the field of child psychotherapy still lacks a broad, deep, and detailed psychodynamic formulation of game-play in the analytic playroom.

1.5   Towards a reformulation of developmental theory and clinical practice in middle childhood – methodological approach

1.5.1   Methodological Approach

Given the multiple lacunae with respect to middle childhood that can be seen to exist in the field, the goals I set in this book are threefold. The first is to present a reappraisal of the literature and integrate the extant psychodynamic theories about middle childhood into a reformulation of developmental theory on middle childhood that can contribute towards psychodynamic theory and clinical practice for this age group. The second is to re-examine the psychodynamic approaches to treatment of "latency-aged" children as reflected in the literature of the last hundred years, with special focus on revising and refining conceptions and preconceptions of the nature and role of play and playing in the context of "game-play" (the term I use throughout this book to denote playing the traditional competitive structured games of middle childhood) in the child psychotherapy room. The third and central aim is to build on these two critiques and revised conceptualisations, and to develop a clinical psychodynamic formulation of the psychotherapeutic use of game-play as the primary language of intra-psychic and inter-psychic communication in children of this age.

In theory building, it is the critical re-examination of the existing literature that highlights the conceptual gaps, contradictions, and oversights in thinking in the field and this in turn directs the researcher in the specific areas of contemporary theory that need to be integrated into the new conceptual formulations (Leuzinger-Bohleber et al., 2003; Stein, 2005). In line with this approach, Part I presents a critical re-examination of the psychoanalytic body of literature in order to uncover the gaps, contradictions, and myths in the psychodynamic developmental theory of middle childhood and present a new developmental formulation of middle childhood based on this critique. In Part II, I present a similar critique regarding play, playing and game-play in psychoanalytic psychotherapy with this age group. In Part III, the results of these theoretical and hermeneutic critiques are used as a basis on which to construct a new psychodynamic formulation of game-play in child psychotherapy as the natural mode of intra-psychic and inter-psychic communication for older children inside and outside of the psychoanalytic playroom (Chapters 6–8).

Joseph Sandler referred to the process of clinical conceptual research as a "progressive spiral" (Sandler, 1962, p. 288) from observation to conceptualisation, to more carefully attuned clinical observation and description in the light of the clinical-theoretical conceptualisation, and back to more refined clinical observation. The starting point for clinical conceptual research in psychoanalysis has traditionally been the individual case study (Hinshelwood, 2018) or the examination of clinical vignettes from multiple cases. As in other behavioural and medical sciences, inquiry into individual cases in psychotherapy research constitutes a vital tool for theory building and for in-depth understanding of processes over time and across situations (Bromley, 1986; Fishman & Westerman, 2011; Hoshmand, 1991; Mackay & Poser, 2004; Messer, 2011; Midgley, 2006). Stiles (2007), who has written much on the subject of case studies in psychotherapy research, has stressed the importance of incorporating clinical observations into explicit theory in order to improve and expand understanding. In his view, psychotherapy practitioners have unique access to multiple repeated observations of the workings of the human psyche and are therefore in a position to use these daily careful observations to test and modify theories of psychic development and psychotherapy. He suggests that these observations are critical to theory building and naturally permeate theory such that "new words", explanations, and "mini-theories" are woven into existing theory to "accommodate to the new observations" (Stiles, 2007). The case studies presented in the psychoanalytically oriented journals today tend to be significantly shorter than they once were and are mostly used to *illustrate* points of theory and clinical technique, rather than to prove new theoretical conceptualisations or as a basis for generalisation beyond the particular case in question. Widlöcher (1994) notes a similar trend towards the use of abbreviated focused clinical vignettes as illustration and for teaching purposes, which he conjectures is the result of both an increasing awareness of the need to protect patient confidentiality and constraints of space in academic journals.

Therefore, in this book, I use clinical material to illustrate, augment, and bring to life the theoretical clinical concepts developed in the body of the conceptual discussion, rather than using systematic case studies as a basis for complete theory building. This choice was also determined by the necessity to limit the bulk of the clinical material presented, given the number of clinical examples required to illustrate the multiple aspects of clinical theory explored conceptually in this book. Moreover, since the focus here is on *child* psychotherapy, issues of confidentiality (addressed in detail below) were even more pressing, given that it is the parents and not the child patients themselves who have the final say over matters of consent to publish case material. Reducing the case material to brief clinical descriptions had the additional benefit of rendering the need to obtain consent for publication of clinical material optional rather than obligatory, thus avoiding the risk of exposing children and their parents needlessly to issues of informed consent before the children were old enough to understand the matter in depth.

1.5.2 Clinical material and patient confidentiality

The clinical material in this book (from about 15 different cases) is therefore confined to brief vignettes and partial, focused case descriptions. All the vignettes are taken from psychoanalytically oriented psychotherapies with children ranging in ages from 7 to 14 years. All except one of these vignettes, which was generously contributed by a late colleague of mine, were based on case notes from psychotherapies, completed in my capacity as clinical psychologist and child and adult psychotherapist over the last two decades, and conducted in the framework of a public child mental health clinic in Israel and in private practice.

Ethical considerations of patient confidentiality concerning clinical case studies and vignettes

Over recent decades, the complexity of issues of patient confidentiality in case presentations and clinical illustrations has been widely addressed in the literature, in discussions in training institutes, and in international professional associations. Guidelines in international and national, medical, psychological, and psychotherapy journals vary from the more "old-school" positions of leaving the decision of disguise versus informed consent up to the practitioner (*Journal of Clinical Psychoanalysis*), to blanket across-the-board requirement for informed consent (International Committee of Medical Journal Editors) (Aron, 2016; Tuckett, 2000). The APA (American Psychological Association) adopts a middle-of-the-road position, which has been widely adopted by contemporary psychotherapy and psychoanalytic journals:

> Principle 4.07 of the APA Ethics Code, Use of Confidential Information for Didactic or Other Purposes: "Psychologists should not disclose in their writings, lectures, or other public media confidential, personally identifiable information

concerning their clients/patients, students, research participants, organizational clients, or other recipients of their services that they obtained during the course of their work unless 1) they take reasonable steps to disguise the person or organization, 2) the person or organization has consented in writing, or 3) there is legal authorization for doing so".

(https://www.apa.org/ethics/code)

Professional opinions on matters of patient confidentiality in published case studies similarly vary across the spectrum:

from the most conservative or reactionary—we own our stories and we are the experts who have an obligation to publish with appropriate disguise—to the most radical—the patient owns his or her story, patients should read what the therapist is saying or publishing and give explicit written permission [informed consent] before the therapist proceeds, and no facts should be changed because that would constitute scientific fraud.

(Aron, 2016, p. 286)

Whilst the option of informed consent may appear superficially to be the best route to follow, even with adult patients, the issues are complex. Transference, the intricacy and length of the therapeutic relationship and the ongoing nature of the relationship, even after treatment has ended, all combine to make the issues of informed consent highly problematic and multifaceted. Many articles on the subject of publication of case material from psychotherapies or psychoanalyses note that, because of the confusing and conflictual feelings that may be aroused in the patient, informed consent may not always be in the patient's best interest and may damage the therapeutic alliance and interfere with the treatment process (Aron, 2000; Gabbard, 2000; Kantrowitz, 2010; Sieck, 2012; Tuckett, 2000; Williams & Gabbard, 2007). A variety of alternative approaches to protect patient confidentiality and reduce the need for informed consent have been recommended by these and most other authors writing on the subject. These include heavy disguise (changing or omitting as many biographical and descriptive details as possible, such as age, gender, profession, religion, number of siblings, all without compromising the clinical material); concentrating on internal states of mind rather than external details of the patient; on treatment process rather than content; the use of vignettes (focused extract or briefcase descriptions, omitting details of personal history and background) for illustration of specific aspects of theory or of clinical technique, rather than detailed case studies; and careful assessment of the pros and cons of obtaining informed consent (see especially Kantrowitz, 2010, and Sieck, 2012, for detailed discussions and recommendations on these issues.)

Where children are concerned, these issues become even more complicated. As with adults, disguise is paramount also in paediatric clinical psychology research, but with children, it is consent from the parent or guardian that is usually recommended (Ernst et al., 2013). This having been said, in contemporary psychological research with child participants, there is a growing trend towards obtaining consent also from children: the guiding rule in many studies today is to explain to children in age-appropriate language the details and meaning of the research, so that informed consent by children is truly informed (Einarsdóttir, 2007). However, given children's limited understanding of ethics, of the world of research, and even of their own rights versus those of adults in authority, I would seriously question whether informed consent can ever truly be *informed* in the case of children. Retrospective consent, exposing young adults to clinical material from their childhood, is even more problematic. Many adults are indeed curious about the psychotherapy process they went through as children and may even seek information from their former therapist, sometimes approaching them many years later to explore their treatment together, through adult eyes and psychic knowledge. However, this is very different from situations when it is the practitioner who, for purposes of publication or research, initiates contact with adults who were former child patients, but who are now in a very different stage in life and often have little memory of the process and are not necessarily interested in thinking about it. It is likely that for adults who were in psychotherapy as children, confronting the details of their own childhood psychotherapeutic encounter at the uninitiated behest of their ex-therapist may be at best a surprise, and a disconcerting "bolt from the dark", and at worst, may well be detrimental to their emotional stability.

Taking all these issues into account, I concluded that the safest and most appropriate solution to the question of preserving child patient anonymity in the clinical case illustrations presented in this book was a three-pronged approach: to present only brief descriptions of clinical material; to focus only on aspects of the case relevant to the particular clinical concept under discussion; and to omit or heavily disguise all identifiable biographical and personal details, as recommended by the APA and the papers cited above.

Given that only vignettes and partial case descriptions were used, and considering the complexities discussed above regarding consent for publication of case material in child psychotherapy, consent for publication was therefore not sought from either the child or the parents. Except for gender and approximate age, which were often changed rather than omitted, identifying details, such as marital status, family background and profession of parents, town of residence of the child, birth order, and number of siblings were almost all entirely omitted and much thought and consideration were given to disguising and obscuring those biographical details. In a few of the clinical examples, the cases described are a composite of clinical interactions with several different children, since the clinical phenomena described in this volume tend to appear in multiple cases. This approach has been used increasingly in the last couple of decades as another method of protecting patient confidentiality, whilst preserving the essence of the clinical encounter (Acheson & Papadima, 2023).

Notes

1 Throughout this book, the singular pronoun they (and its derivatives – their and them) will be used instead of he, she, him, her, his, and hers, when the gender of the child or adult is not known or not specified. This is in line with the APA guidelines on non-sexist and gender-inclusive language in academic writing:

The singular "they" is a generic third-person singular pronoun in English. Use of the singular "they" is endorsed as part of APA Style because it is inclusive of all people and helps writers avoid making assumptions about gender. Although usage of the singular "they" was once discouraged in academic writing, many advocacy groups and publishers have accepted and endorsed it. https://apastyle.apa.org/style-grammar-guidelines/grammar/singular-they.

2 https://dictionary.cambridge.org/dictionary/english/latency

Bibliography

Acheson, R., & Papadima, M. (2023). The search for identity: Working therapeutically with adolescents in crisis. *Journal of Child Psychotherapy*, *49*(1), 95–119. https://doi.org/10.1080/0075417X.2022.2160478

Aron, L. (2000). Ethical considerations in the writing of psychoanalytic case histories. *Psychoanalytic Dialogues*, *10*(2), 231–245.

Aron, L. (2016). Ethical considerations in psychoanalytic writing revisited. *Psychoanalytic Perspectives*, *13*(3), 267–290.

Beiser, H. R. (1979a). Formal games in diagnosis and therapy. *Journal of the American Academy of Child Psychiatry*, *18*(3), 480–491.

Beiser, H. R. (1979b). The problem of infantile omnipotence. *Annual of Psychoanalysis*, *7*, 113–132.

Bellinson, J. (2000). Shut up and move: The uses of board games in child psychotherapy. *Journal of Infant, Child, and Adolescent Psychotherapy*, *1*(2), 23–41.

Bellinson, J. (2002). *Children's Use of Board Games in Psychotherapy*. Jason Aronson.

Bellinson, J. (2013). Games children play: Board games in psychodynamic psychotherapy. *Child and Adolescent Psychiatric Clinics of North America*, *22*(2), 283–293.

Brady, M. T. (2012). To know or not to know: An application of Bion's K and –K to child treatment1. *J. Child Psychother*, *38*(3), 302–317.

Bromley, D. B. (1986). *The Case-Study Method in Psychology and Related Disciplines*. Wiley.

Canham, H. (2018). Latency. In B. Youell & H. Canham, *The Learning Relationship* (pp. 47–58). Routledge.

Caruth, E. G. (1988). How you play the game: On game as play and play as game in the psychoanalytic process. *Psychoanalytic Psychology*, *5*(2), 179–192.

Chung, S. J., & Colarusso, C. (2013). The use of the computer and the internet in child psychoanalysis. *The Psychoanalytic Study of the Child*, *66*(1), 197–223.

Cincotta, N. F. (2008). The journey of middle childhood. In S. G. Austrian (Ed.), *Developmental Theories Through the Life Cycle* (pp. 79–132). Columbia University Press.

Collins, W. A. (Ed.). (1984). *Development During Middle Childhood: The Years from Six to Twelve*. National Academy Press.

Collins, W. A. (2005). Contextualizing middle childhood: Beyond 1984. In W. A. Collins (Ed.), *Developmental Pathways Through Middle Childhood: Rethinking Contexts and Diversity as Resources*. National Academy Press.

Collishaw, S. (2015). Annual research review: Secular trends in child and adolescent mental health. *Journal of Child Psychology and Psychiatry*, *56*(3), 370–393.

Cooper, C. R., Coll, C. T., Bartko, W., Davis, H. E., & Chatman, C. E. (2005). *Developmental Pathways Through Middle Childhood: Rethinking Contexts and Diversity as Resources*. Lawrence Erlbaum Associates.

Coriat, I. (1941). The unconscious motives of interest in chess. *The Psychoanalytic Review (1913–1957)*, *28*, 30.

Costello, E., Egger, H., & Angold, A. (2005). 10-year research update review: The epidemiology of child and adolescent psychiatric disorders: i. methods and public health burden. *Journal of the American Academy of Child and Adolescent Psychiatry*, *44*, 972–986.

Crenna-Jennings, W., & Hutchinson, J. (2018). *Access to Children and Young People's Mental Health Services: 2018*. Education Policy Institute.

Deakin, E. K., Gastaud, M., & Nunes, M. L. T. (2012). Child psychotherapy dropout: An empirical research review. *Journal of Child Psychotherapy*, *38*(2), 199–209.

Deakin, E. K., & Tiellet Nunes, M. L. (2009). Effectiveness of child psychoanalytic psychotherapy in a clinical outpatient setting. *Journal of Child Psychotherapy*, *35*(3), 290–301.

Diem-Wille, G. (2018). *Latency: The Golden Age of Childhood*. Routledge.

Einarsdóttir, J. (2007). Research with children: Methodological and ethical challenges. *European Early Childhood Education Research Journal*, *15*(2), 197–211.

Erikson, E. H. (1950). *Childhood and Society* (2nd ed.). Norton (1963).

Ernst, M. M., Barhight, L. R., Bierenbaum, M. L., Piazza-Waggoner, C., & Carter, B. D. (2013). Case studies in clinical practice in pediatric psychology: The "why" and "how to". *Clinical Practice in Pediatric Psychology*, *1*(2), 108.

Etchegoyen, A. (1993). Latency—A Reappraisal. *International Journal of Psycho-Analysis*, *74*, 347–357.

Ferro, A. (2003). *The Bi-Personal Field: Experiences in Child Analysis*. Routledge.

Ferro, A. (Ed.). (2017). *Contemporary Bionian Theory and Technique in Psychoanalysis* (1 edition). Routledge.

Fishman, D. B., & Westerman, M. A. (2011). A key role for case studies: Theory building. *Pragmatic Case Studies in Psychotherapy*, *7*(4), 434–439.

Freud, A. (1926). Introduction to the technique of the analysis of children. In A. Freud (Ed.), *The Psychoanalytical Treatment of Children* (pp. 3–62). Imago (1946).

Freud, A. (1946). *The Psychoanalytical Treatment of Children*. Imago.

Freud, A. (1963). The concept of developmental lines. *Psychoanal. St. Child*, *18*, 245–265.

Freud, S. (1905). Three essays on the theory of sexuality. In J. Strachey, Ed. & Trans., *The Standard Edition of the Complete Psychological Works of Sigmund Freud, Volume VII (1901–1905): A Case of Hysteria, Three Essays on Sexuality and Other Works* (pp. 123–246). Hogarth Press, 1953.

Freud, S. (1910). Five Lectures on Psycho-analysis. In J. Strachey, Ed. & Trans., *The Standard Edition of the Complete Psychological Works of Sigmund Freud Volume XI (1910): Five Lectures on Psycho-Analysis, Leonardo da Vinci and Other Works,*.

Freud, S. (1926). The Question of Lay Analysis. In S. Freud (Ed.), *The Standard Edition of the Complete Psychological Works of Sigmund Freud Volume XX (1925–1926): An Autobiographical Study, Inhibitions, Symptoms and Anxiety, The Question of Lay Analysis and Other Works*. Hogarth Press, 1959.

Freud, S. (1940). An outline of psycho-analysis. In J. Strachey, Ed. & Trans., *The Standard Edition of the Complete Psychological Works of Sigmund Freud, Volume XXIII (1937–1939): Moses and Monotheism, An Outline of Psycho-Analysis and Other Works* (pp. 139–208).

Fried, S. (1992). Chess: A psychoanalytic tool in the treatment of children. *International Journal of Play Therapy*, *1*(1), 43.

Gabbard, G. O. (2000). Disguise or consent: Problems and recommendations concerning the publication and presentation of clinical material. *International Journal of Psycho-Analysis*, *81*(6), 1071–1086.

Gilmore, K. (2011). Pretend play and development in early childhood (with implications for the oedipal phase). *Journal of American Psychoanalytic Association*, *59*(6), 1157–1181.

Gilmore, K., & Meersand, P. (2013). *Normal Child and Adolescent Development: A Psychodynamic Primer*. American Psychiatric Pub.

Gilmore, K., & Meersand, P. (2014). *The Little Book of Child and Adolescent Development*. Oxford University Press.

Green, A. H. (1978). Psychiatric treatment of abused children. *Journal of the American Academy of Child & Adolescent Psychiatry*, *17*(2), 356–371.

Green, H., McGinnity, A., Meltzer, H., Ford, T., & Goodman, R. (2005). *Mental Health of Children and Young People in Great Britain, 2004: (557702010-001)* [Dataset]. American Psychological Association. https://doi.org/10.1037/e557702010-001

Hinshelwood, R. D. (2018). Psychoanalytic research: Personal reflections. *British Journal of Psychotherapy*, *34*(4), 539–548.

Hoshmand, L. T. (1991). Clinical inquiry as scientific training. *The Counseling Psychologist*, *19*(3), 431–453.

Jacobs, M. (2004). The perils of latency. *Psychodynamic Practice*, *10*(4), 500–514.

Janus, S. S., & Bess, B. E. (1976). Latency: Fact or fiction? *The American Journal of Psychoanalysis*, *36*(4), 339–346.

Jemerin, J. M. (2004). Latency and the capacity to reflect on mental states. *Psychoanalytic Study of the Child*, *59*, 211–239.

Kantrowitz, J. L. (2010). Using disguised clinical case material. *Part of a Special Section: Writing About Clients: Ethical and Professional Issues in Clinical Case Reports*, *54*(2), 117–134.

Kazdin, A. E. (1991). Effectiveness of psychotherapy with children and adolescents. *Journal of Consulting and Clinical Psychology*, *59*(6), 785.

Kazdin, A. E., & Mazurick, J. L. (1994). Dropping out of child psychotherapy: Distinguishing early and late dropouts over the course of treatment. *Journal of Consulting and Clinical Psychology*, *62*(5), 1069.

Kernberg, P. F. (2000). The forms of play. In K. von Klitzing, P. Tyson, & D. Burgin (Eds.), *Psychoanalysis in Childhood and Adolescence* (pp. 25–41). Karger Publishers.

Kernberg, P. F., Ritvo, R., Keable, H., & of Child, T. A. A. (2012). Practice parameter for psychodynamic psychotherapy with children. *Journal of the American Academy of Child & Adolescent Psychiatry*, *51*(5), 541–557.

Kernberg, P. F., Weiner, A. S., & Bardenstein, K. K. (2008). *Personality Disorders in Children and Adolescents*. Basic Books.

Kessler, R. C., Matthias, A., Anthony, J. C., De Graaf, R. O. N., Demyttenaere, K., Gasquet, I., De Girolamo, G., Gluzman, S., Gureje, O. Y. E., Haro, J. M., & others. (2007). Lifetime prevalence and age-of-onset distributions of mental disorders in the World Health Organization's World Mental Health Survey Initiative. *World Psychiatry*, *6*(3), 168–176.

Kessler, R. C., McLaughlin, K. A., Green, J. G., Gruber, M. J., Sampson, N. A., Zaslavsky, A. M., Aguilar-Gaxiola, S., Alhamzawi, A. O., Alonso, J., Angermeyer, M., Benjet, C., Bromet, E., Chatterji, S., Girolamo, G. de, Demyttenaere, K., Fayyad, J., Florescu, S., Gal, G., Gureje, O., ... & Williams, D. R. (2010). Childhood adversities and adult psychopathology in the WHO World Mental Health Surveys. *The British Journal of Psychiatry*, *197*(5), 378–385.

Klein, M. (1927). The psychological principles of infant analysis. *The International Journal of Psycho-Analysis*, *8*, 25.

Klein, M. (1955). The psychoanalytic play technique. *American Journal of Orthopsychiatry*, *25*(2), 223–237.

Knight, R. (2014). A hundred years of latency: From Freudian psychosexual theory to dynamic systems nonlinear development in middle childhood. *Journal of American Psychoanalytic Association, 62*(2), 203–235.

Krimendahl, E. (2000). "Did you see that?": A relational perspective on children who cheat in analysis. *Journal of Infant, Child, and Adolescent Psychotherapy, 1*(2), 43–58.

Lancy, D. F., & Grove, M. A. (2011). Getting noticed. Middle childhood in cross-cultural perspective. *Human Nature (Hawthorne, N.Y.), 22*(3), 281–302.

Lanyado, M., & Horne, A. (2007). *A Question of Technique: Independent Psychoanalytic Approaches with Children and Adolescents*. Routledge.

Leuzinger-Bohleber, M., Dreher, A. U., & Canestri, J. (2003). *Pluralism and Unity? Methods of Research in Psychoanalysis*. International Psychoanalytical Association.

Levinson, B. M. (1972). Use of checkers in therapy. *Psychological Reports, 30*(3), 846–846.

Levy, A. J. (2008). The therapeutic action of play in the psychodynamic treatment of children: A critical analysis. *Clinical Social Work Journal, 36*(3), 281–291.

Loomis, E. A. (1976). Use of checkers in handling resistance. In C. E. Schaefer (Ed.), *The Therapeutic Use of Child's Play* (p. 385). Jason Aronson.

Mackay, N., & Poser, S. (2004). The case study in psychoanalytic education. *Modern Psychoanalysis, 29*(2), 171–183.

Maroudas, C., Wiseman, H., & Harel, J. (2023). The 'wave-particle' child: Reconnecting the disconnect in the concept of latency. *Journal of Child Psychotherapy, 49*(3), 412–431.

Meeks, J. E. (1970). Children who cheat at games. *Journal of the American Academy of Child Psychiatry, 9*(1), 157–170.

Meeks, J. E. (2000). Reflections on children who cheat at games: A commentary. *Journal of Infant, Child, and Adolescent Psychotherapy, 1*(2), 71–75.

Mental Health of Children and Young People in England 2022, NHS digital. (2022). NDRS. https://digital.nhs.uk/data-and-information/publications/statistical/mental-health-of-children-and-young-people-in-england/2022-follow-up-to-the-2017-survey

Merikangas, K., He, J.-P., Burstein, M., Swanson, S., Avenevoli, S., Cui, L., Benjet, C., Georgiades, K., & Swendsen, J. (2010). Lifetime prevalence of mental disorders in U.S. adolescents: Results from the national comorbidity survey replication–adolescent supplement (NCS-A). *Journal of the American Academy of Child and Adolescent Psychiatry, 49*, 980–989.

Messer, S. B. (2011). Theory development via single cases: A case study of the therapeutic relationship in psychodynamic therapy. *Pragmatic Case Studies in Psychotherapy, 7*(4), 440–448.

Midgley, N. (2006). The 'inseparable bond between cure and research': Clinical case study as a method of psychoanalytic inquiry. *Journal of Child Psychotherapy, 32*(2), 122–147.

Midgley, N., & Kennedy, E. (2011). Psychodynamic psychotherapy for children and adolescents: A critical review of the evidence base. *Journal of Child Psychotherapy, 37*(3), 232–260.

Molinari, E. (2017). Variations on a theme: Child and adolescent analysis. In Ferro, A. (Ed), *Contemporary Bionian Theory and Technique in Psychoanalysis* (pp. 176–216). Routledge.

Ohrenstein, L. (1986). There is nothing latent about latency: Its impact on parents. *Child and Adolescent Social Work Journal, 3*(3), 143–150.

Oren, A. (2008). The use of board games in child psychotherapy. *Journal of Child Psychotherapy, 34*(3), 364–383.

Ormel, J., Raven, D., van Oort, F., Hartman, C. A., Reijneveld, S. A., Veenstra, R., Vollebergh, W. A. M., Buitelaar, J., Verhulst, F. C., & Oldehinkel, A. J. (2015). Mental health in Dutch adolescents: A TRAILS report on prevalence, severity, age of onset, continuity and co-morbidity of DSM disorders. *Psychological Medicine, 45*(2), 345–360.

Peller, L. E. (1954). Libidinal phases, ego development, and play. *The Psychoanalytic Study of the Child, 9,* 178–198.

Piaget, J. (1962). *Play, Dreams and Imitation.* Norton.

Plaut, E. A. (1979). Definition of play. *Psychoanalytic Study of the Child, 34,* 217–232.

Polanczyk, G. V., Salum, G. A., Sugaya, L. S., Caye, A., & Rohde, L. A. (2015). Annual research review: A meta-analysis of the worldwide prevalence of mental disorders in children and adolescents. *Journal of Child Psychology and Psychiatry, 56*(3), 345–365.

Saar, N., Bar, M., & Gothelf, D. (2017). Understanding Cheating in Board Games Play Therapy with Children. *Sihot/Dialogue: Israel Journal of Psychotherapy, 31*(3), 211–217.

Samji, H., Wu, J., Ladak, A., Vossen, C., Stewart, E., Dove, N., Long, D., & Snell, G. (2022). Review: Mental health impacts of the COVID-19 pandemic on children and youth – a systematic review. *Child and Adolescent Mental Health, 27*(2), 173–189.

Sandler, J. (1962). Research in psycho-analysis—The Hampstead index as an instrument of psycho-analytic research. *International Journal of Psycho-Analysis, 43,* 287–291.

Sandler, J., Kennedy, H., & Tyson, R. L. (1980). *The technique of child psychoanalysis: Discussions with Anna Freud.* Harvard University Press.

Sieck, B. C. (2012). Obtaining clinical writing informed consent versus using client disguise and recommendations for practice. *Psychotherapy, 49*(1), 3.

Singh, S., Roy, D., Sinha, K., Parveen, S., Sharma, G., & Joshi, G. (2020). Impact of COVID-19 and lockdown on mental health of children and adolescents: A narrative review with recommendations. *Psychiatry Research, 293,* 113429.

Smith, J., Kyle, R. G., Daniel, B., & Hubbard, G. (2018). Patterns of referral and waiting times for specialist Child and Adolescent Mental Health Services. *Child and Adolescent Mental Health, 23*(1), 41–49.

Stein, Y. (2005). *The Psychoanalysis of Science: The Role of Metaphor, Paraplax, Lacunae, and Myth.* Sussex Academic Press.

Stiles, W. B. (2007). Theory-building case studies of counselling and psychotherapy. *Counselling and Psychotherapy Research, 7*(2), 122–127.

Tuckett, D. (2000). Reporting clinical events in the journal: Towards the construction of a special case. *International Journal of Psycho-Analysis, 81*(6), 1065–1069.

WHO; World Health Organization | *Child and adolescent mental health.* (2020). Mental Health ATLAS 2020 https://www.who.int/publications/i/item/9789240036703

Widlöcher, D. (1994). A case is not a fact. *International Journal of Psycho-Analysis, 75,* 1233–1244.

Williams, P., & Gabbard, G. O. (2007). *Key Papers in Literature and Psychoanalysis.* Karnac Books.

Wilson, P. (1989). Latency and certainty. *Journal of Child Psychotherapy, 15*(2), 59–69.

Winnicott, D. W. (1971). The use of an object and relating through identifications. In Winnicott, D.W., *Playing and Reality* (pp. 101–111). Penguin Books.

Part I

Towards a developmental reformulation of middle childhood

Chapter 2

Latency

A misnomer? Reconnecting the disconnect in the concept of latency

All the world's a stage,
And all the men and women merely players;
They have their exits and their entrances;
And one man in his time plays many parts,
His acts being seven ages. At first the infant,
Mewling and puking in the nurse's arms;
And then the whining school-boy, with his satchel
And shining morning face, creeping like snail
Unwillingly to school. And then the lover,
Sighing like furnace, with a woeful ballad
Made to his mistress' eyebrow. Then a soldier,
Full of strange oaths, and bearded like the pard,
Jealous in honour, sudden and quick in quarrel,
Seeking the bubble reputation
Even in the cannon's mouth. And then the justice,
In fair round belly with good capon lin'd,
With eyes severe and beard of formal cut,
Full of wise saws and modern instances;
And so he plays his part…
As You Like It Act 2, scene 7, 139–143 (Emphases added)
William Shakespeare

The idea that man and woman pass through a progression of stages in life, from the helpless "mewling" and innocence of infancy, through the trials and tribulations of the adolescent, "jealous in honour, sudden and quick in quarrel", to the "wise saws" of adulthood, dates back to ancient times. Evidence of an awareness of life cycle stages is to be found in ancient biblical texts, in the writings of the Chinese sage Confucius, and in an abundance of artefacts and written records from ancient Egypt, Greece, and Rome. Specific references to the "Seven Ages of Man", as immortalised by Shakespeare, seem to originate, at least formally, in the writings of Ptolemy, one of the first known scholars to define and describe seven life cycle stages, which he named for the sun, the moon, and five planets. Life cycle stages such as these

DOI: 10.4324/9781003425229-3

seven have been variously delineated and defined through the ages and across societies. However, most ethnographic and anthropological studies identify and describe
four major distinct phases that appear to transcend cross-cultural and historical differences and are almost universally recognised. These four life cycle stages can be
loosely defined as a stage of dependency and rapid growth and change in infancy and
toddlerhood (in Roman and medieval times known as *infantia*: roughly ages 0 to 5);
a stage of increasing autonomy and self-sufficiency, in the older child, marked by
slowed physical growth, on the one hand, and rapid acquisition of sophisticated cognitive, physical, and social skills, on the other (*pueritia*: middle childhood, roughly
ages 6 to 11/12); puberty and adolescence marked by dramatic hormonal changes and
bodily changes (*adolescentia*, ages 13–20); and adulthood, when growth more or less
comes to a halt and full societal and parental responsibilities are usually assumed.

Historically, in European societies through the centuries, the age "7+/–1" held particular significance (Shapiro & Perry, 1976): this was the age at which formal education traditionally commenced and children were deemed to be morally, and in some
societies also legally, responsible for their actions. As shall be discussed in more detail
in Chapter 3, the period of childhood from 6 to 12 was regarded as critical for appren-
ticeship, education, and for induction into the ways of society and training for future
roles in adulthood. And this meant that children over the age of five or six were often
regarded as miniature, desexualised, but morally imperfect adults, to be seen and not
heard and to be trained to become steadfast, sensible, upright citizens of society. And
yet as we shall see in the following sections, multiple portraits of middle childhood
can also be found in art and literature through the ages that testify to the remarkable
cognitive plasticity and boundless physical energy that is characteristic of school-aged
children, and their tendency to mischief and appetite for discovery and adventure.

2.1   A painting is worth a thousand words

Pictorial art from the 15th to the 19th centuries bears witness to these two almost
contradictory stereotypes of middle childhood – miniature desexualised adult and
"impish rascal". These works of art can serve as a visual introduction to the conflicting views of childhood prevalent in Western society that shaped psychoanalytic
thinking throughout most of the 20th century. On the one hand, paintings commissioned to serve the Church and the ruling aristocracy depicted children in a manner that reflected the power, wealth, and institutionalised holiness of those who
commissioned these works. The paintings of children of nobility portray them as
dressed almost exclusively in adult clothing and engaged in adult pastimes: their
apparel ranges from elaborate, stiff, and formal evening wear, to overly majes-
tic, pompous ballgowns and suits, to entire suits of armour and full royal regalia.
Likewise, they were usually depicted in adult roles well beyond their years: strong
brave princes on their sturdy steeds; beautiful young princesses standing regally
near the royal throne; solemn young boys earnestly hard at work at their lessons;
and prim and proper sweet-tempered young girls seated studiously at the piano or
serenely reading or sewing in a chair (see Figures 2.1–2.4). Even when the children

Figure 2.1 Leonardo da Vinci (1452–1519).

The Virgin and Child with Saint Anne and the Infant Saint John the Baptist ("The Burlington House Cartoon"), about 1506–1508, charcoal with white chalk on paper, mounted on canvas, 141.5 × 104.6 cm.

Purchased with a special grant and contributions from the Art Fund, The Pilgrim Trust, and through a public appeal organised by the *Art Fund, 1962*.

Permission ©The National Gallery, London. All rights reserved.

Figure 2.2 Diego Rodríguez de Silva y Velázquez (1599–1660).

Las Meninas, 1656, Oil on canvas, Height: 320 cm; Width: 279 cm, Madrid, Museo Nacional del Prado. Inventory number P001174.

Permission ©Photographic Archive, Museo Nacional del Prado.

are depicted as strong and powerful, they lack agency of their own and their true whimsical child selves remain hidden from the viewer's eye. The child subjects in religious works, on the other hand, are depicted as infants or young innocent toddlers: either as rosy-cheeked saintly cherubs or as the precociously wise but pure and holy "baby" Jesus.

During the Early Modern period and beyond, art that depicted children as subjects with their own unique world of play and discovery, and of suffering,

Figure 2.3 Robert Peake the Elder (British, ca. 1551–1619 London).

Henry Frederick (1594–1612), Prince of Wales, with Sir John Harington (1592–1614), in the Hunting Field, 1603, Oil on canvas, Dimensions: 201.9 × 147.3 cm.

The Metropolitan Museum of Art, New York, Purchase, *Joseph Pulitzer Bequest, 1944,* Object number: 44.27. www.metmuseum.org

Figure 2.4 Edwin Henry Landseer (1802–1873).

Study of Rachel Russell (1826–1898), daughter of Georgina, the second wife of John, sixth Duke of Bedord. 1835.

Oil on panel 35.5 × 25.4 cm signed.

Private collection, Open access image.

poverty, and exploitation, became more common. Much of this art originated initially from the Dutch school of the 16th and 17th centuries, painted by artists who aimed to portray the children in their true reality, in all their ebullience and mischief and also in their misery and poverty. Jan Steen's (in)famous picture, *A School for Boys and Girls* (Figure 2.5), is a fitting counterpart to Shakespeare's literary description of the "whining schoolboy with his shining morning face", whilst Bruegel's *Children's Games* (Figure 2.6) provides a rare, but rich and detailed, picture of children's street games of the 16th century, many of which are familiar still today.

Many 18th- and 19th-century European artists continued to focus both on the hardships of child labour and on children's play and natural pastimes. And yet, romanticism and overemphasis of the innocence and freedom of childhood nevertheless often crept into many of these later paintings, especially those of the Impressionists of the late 19th century, contemporary with Freud (Figures 2.7–2.10).

Of these two conflicting depictions of childhood typical of the Early Modern period and beyond, it was the puritanical and the romantic that won out over the truer-to-life portrayals of misery, hardship, mischief, and vitality of middle childhood throughout history. Especially for the educated and moneyed classes of 19th- and early 20th-century Europe, to which Sigmund Freud belonged, the perception of childhood was coloured, or rather discoloured, by this rather strait-laced, monochrome, and lacklustre stereotypical portrayal of school-aged children.

Figure 2.5 Jan Steen (1625/6–1679).

A School for Boys and Girls, About 1670.

Oil on canvas, 81.7 × 108.6 cm.

National Galleries of Scotland collection. Accepted by HM Government in Lieu of Inheritance Tax and allocated to the National Galleries of Scotland, 2008 / Purchased by Private Treaty with the aid of the National Heritage Memorial Fund 1984.

Image and permission: National Galleries of Scotland.

Figure 2.6 Pieter Bruegel the elder (c. 1525–1530–1569).

Children's Games, 1560.

Oil on panel 118 × 161 cm.

Kunsthistorisches Museum Wien, Gemäldegalerie, 1017, 1594 acquired by Archduke Ernst in Brussels.

Permission and Image rights: Kunsthistorisches Museum Wien, Gemäldegalerie.

Figure 2.7 Fernand Pelez (1843–1913).

The Violet Seller, 1885.

Oil on canvas.

Measurements: 89.5 × 104 cm.

Petit Palais, musée des Beaux-arts de la Ville de Paris.

Open access image: Paris museums, Petit Palais Creative Commons 0 (CCO).

Figure 2.8 David Allan (1744–1796).

Lead Processing at Leadhills, Pounding the Ore, probably 1780s.

Oil on canvas.

Measurements: 38.3 × 58.0 cm.

National Galleries of Scotland collection. Accepted by HM Government in lieu of Inheritance Tax and allocated to the National Galleries of Scotland, 2008 / Purchased by Private Treaty with the aid of the National Heritage Memorial Fund 1984.

Image and permission: National Galleries of Scotland.

Figure 2.9 Jean-Siméon Chardin (1699–1779).

The House of Cards (Portrait of Jean-Alexandre Le Noir), about 1740–1741.

Oil on canvas, 60.3 × 71.8 cm.

Bequeathed by Mrs Edith Cragg, as part of the John Webb Bequest, 1925.

Image and permission © The National Gallery, London.

Figure 2.10 Berthe Morisot (1841–1895).
Children at the Basin, 1886.
Oil on canvas, 73 × 92 cm.
Copyright© Musée Marmottan Monet, Paris.

2.2   Historical overview

2.2.1   *Sigmund Freud and the "latency period"*

The post-oedipal pre-pubertal years are indeed a period in childhood where emotional turmoil and physical and hormonal changes are less pronounced than in the volatile periods of adolescence and of early childhood. In Freud's day, this picture of the schoolchild as quiet, well-behaved, rational, and industrious citizen was even more accentuated. Freud was keenly aware of the clearly discernible sharp developmental transition that occurs in children at around six years of age from the libidinal and aggression filled turmoil of infancy and early childhood to the relative quiescence of middle childhood. Observations of the children around him, and his retrospective reconstructions through his own self-analysis and other adult psychoanalyses, led Freud to suggest that this phase transition is due both to the solution of the oedipal complex and also to biological/physiological changes. He posited these years of middle childhood as years of stagnation or "latency" in psychosexual development, when infantile sexual urges and desires go underground (Freud, 1905). In contrast to the almost extravagant lack of sexual inhibition characteristic of the pre-oedipal and oedipal phase, Freud maintained that libidinal sexual drives are experienced unconsciously by the latency child as forbidden and dangerous, to be kept strictly under lock and key. According to Freud, these impulses are psychically a source of "unpleasure", to be "dammed" and redirected via defence mechanisms to socially acceptable ends: children in this phase of development transfer their attention and energies to the acquirement of bodily and physical skills, towards outer reality, cognitive prowess, and to friendships and socialisation within the peer group. He emphasised that sexual energy is not "stopped" during the latency phase, but rather it is repressed and remains hidden/"latent", subordinated to other vital developmental goals via such defence mechanisms as reaction formation and sublimation.

Notwithstanding these significant insights into the psyche of the post-oedipal child, Freud speaks only of a *period* of latency, rather than a *stage*, a reflection of his view that during the latency years, "there is strictly speaking no new organization of sexuality" (quoted in Alvarez, 1989, p. 72). Similarly, he was not able to free himself of his narrow Victorian view of latency as a period of stagnation, even of unlearning and mental inhibition, a view which clouded psychoanalytic thinking on middle childhood for decades to come:

> It is hardly to be believed what goes on in a child of four or five years old. Children are very active minded at that age; their early sexual period is also a period of intellectual flowering. I have an impression that with the onset of the latency period they become mentally inhibited as well, stupider. From that time on, too, many children lose their physical charm.
>
> (S. Freud, 1926)

2.2.2   Anna Freud: drives and ego defences in latency

Freud's emphasis on defence mechanisms and their workings in the latency period was elaborated and expanded on greatly by his daughter, Anna Freud, and later, by leading ego psychologists such as Hartmann (1958), Kris (1951), and Loewenstein (1954), in Europe and especially in the US. In adherence to her father's teachings, throughout her life Anna Freud stalwartly maintained a dual focus on both the unconscious conflicts between the id, ego, and superego and the more observable conscious ego functioning. Her writings abound with rich examples of ego defence mechanisms, and of the role of daydreaming and fantasy in the developing child's struggle with their instinctual life.

Coming to the field of psychoanalysis as she did, not only as Freud's daughter and protégé, but also as a trained and devoted schoolteacher, Anna Freud dedicated her life's work to children in general and to this age group in particular:

> Looking back into my analytic past [she said in 1979, when she was eighty-three], I realize now why, with regard to children, I have always been more attracted to the latency period than the pre-Oedipal phases. In the latter, the id reveals itself quite un-ashamedly. But the latency period presents the observer with all the efforts of the ego to deal with the id. This is of course what makes child analysis

in the latency period so very difficult, since the patient strenuously opposes the analyst's wish to undo the defenses which he has built up in good faith, and with so much trouble.

(Anna Freud, quoted in Young-Bruehl, 1988, p. 457)

Given Anna Freud's profound interest in latency-aged children and their welfare, I suspect she might not have agreed wholeheartedly with her father's perception of school-aged children as stupider and less interesting psychoanalytically than their pre-oedipal siblings. As she herself puts it in her *magnum opus, The Ego and the Mechanism of Defence* (A. Freud, 1946):

...[w]e must not forget that these mental performances ... [of the oedipal child and in puberty], brilliant and remarkable as they are, remain to a great extent unfruitful...*The intellectual work performed by the ego during the latency period and in adult life is incomparably more solid, more reliable,* and, above all, much more closely connected with action.

(A. Freud, 1946, p. 164-165, emphases added)

Nevertheless, she remained resolutely Freudian throughout her life and regarded middle childhood as a period of instinctual dormancy, dominated by a strict adherence to the reality principle and strong and rigid ego defence mechanisms at the expense of creativity and imagination. Her clinical and theoretical discussions focus on the child's more conscious oedipal strivings and forbidden masturbatory urges, often to the exclusion of more complex and deeply hidden unconscious fantasies and anxieties. The proverbial "wood" that is the child's rich fantasy life and inner world is often all too easily lost in Anna Freud's lengthy detailing of the five main ego defences of repression, regression, projection, reaction formation, and sublimation, typical of the Freudian latency period. And yet, Anna Freud's influence on psychoanalytic thinking on middle childhood remains strong to this day. Even in papers and textbooks that purport to re-examine the latency period, from Bornstein's seminal paper *"On latency"* (Bornstein, 1951) to more recently published reformulations such as that of Jemerin (2004), (quoted below) and Diem-Weil's (2018) recent book entitled *Latency* (sic) (quoted in section 3.7), these childhood years are still described and understood largely in terms of drives, impulses, and the defences against them:

Beginning with Freud, psychoanalytic theorists have detailed the growth and reorganization of the ego that occurs on entry into the state of latency... Chief among these are the formation of the superego and the ego ideal via identification with the values, standards, and prohibiting function of the parents. ... Mental organization in the state of latency is characterized by a constellation of defenses, including regression from genital to anal-sadistic drive organization, sublimation, reaction formation, and obsessive-compulsive defenses. Preconscious and conscious fantasy are particularly important in maintaining psychological equilibrium during latency.

(Jemerin, 2004, p. 212)

2.2.3 Melanie Klein: the ebb and flow of the depressive position in latency

Unlike Anna Freud, Melanie Klein initially focused on psychoanalytic work with toddlers and pre-schoolers, and consequently, there is less to glean about the period of middle childhood from Melanie Klein's writings. She carried out few analyses with older "post-oedipal" children, since in her view, children of this age had "too strong a tendency to repression" and "too limited an imagination" (Klein, 1932) to allow useful psychoanalytic work to take place:

> Added to this is the general attitude of reserve and distrust so typical of this period of life, an attitude which is in part an outcome of their intense preoccupation with the struggle against masturbation and thus makes them deeply averse to anything that savours of search and interrogation or touches on the impulses they just manage to keep under control.
>
> (Klein, 1932, quoted in Alvarez, 1989, p. 73)

Melanie Klein, in line with both Sigmund Freud and Anna Freud, also conceived of the latency years as a hiatus in psychosexual development. However, her thinking on psychoanalytic developmental theory was radically different from Anna Freud's and the ego psychologists, and Klein indirectly expanded thinking on latency in critical theoretical and clinical directions. Her analysis of defence mechanisms focused on mechanisms of splitting and projection rather than on repression, sublimation, and reaction formation. She suggested that many of the latency child's libidinal and aggressive instincts and internal conflicts were split off rather than repressed and played out in the external world through physical games and activities or held under strict control through obsessional behaviours. Her formulation of the depressive position as accompanying the solution of the oedipal conflict and her subsequent suggestion of the idea of positions rather than stages in psychic development allows for a more fluid, less rigid view of latency. Klein held that there exist both pre-genital and genital forms of the Oedipus conflicts and contrasted the associated pre-genital harsh archaic superego and defences based on splitting and projection with a less puni-tive more flexible superego and more adaptive defences based on "moderate" repression and sublimation of the genital stage. She, and the post-Kleinians after her, postulated that even the healthy mature psyche is always in a state of flux between pre-oedipal schizoid modes of functioning and oedipal and post-oedipal depressive modes. The transition is neither sudden nor clear-cut, but is the result of incremental working through paranoid and depressive anxieties and gradual integration of part objects into whole objects:

> [T]he resolution does not occur as an abrupt discontinuity, as a crisis, with mas-sive repression of infantile sexuality, but as a process of progressive and more complex elaboration throughout latency.
>
> (Etchegoyen, 1993, p. 349)

In her paper *"Some theoretical conclusions regarding the emotional life of the infant"*, originally published in 1952, and later in *Envy and Gratitude* (Klein, 1975), Klein outlines her understanding of the developmental process as a gradual *decline* (rather than *resolution*) of the Oedipus complex that culminates in the onset of latency. Whereas Anna Freud's focus was on ego structures and functions, Klein emphasised superego development, unconscious impulses, and primal anxieties. Klein's use of comparative adjectives and the notion of incremental change they imply, alongside the notions of fluidity and porosity of defences and emotional states, indicate a view of oedipal resolution as the result of a gradual non-linear process spanning the entire period of early childhood:

> Viewed in the light of the vicissitudes of anxiety, the changes characteristic of the onset of the latency period could be summarized as follows: the relation with the parents is more secure; the introjected parents approximate more closely to the picture of the real parents; their standards, their admonitions and prohibitions are accepted and internalized and therefore the repression of the Oedipus desires is more effective. All this represents a climax of the super-ego development which is the result of a process extending over the first years of life.
>
> (Klein, 1952, p. 230)

This understanding that the decline of the oedipal complex is not a precipitous event but a result of a process of gradual emotional development, represents a radical departure from Freud's theory. It is perhaps Klein's most significant contribution to the contemporary view of latency as a period of flux and progressive working through rather than of rigidity and stagnation (Etchegoyen, 1993):

2.2.4   Winnicott: the "sanity" of the latency-aged child and the squiggle game

Donald Winnicott, oft regarded as the "father" of child psychoanalysis alongside the two founding mothers, Anna Freud and Melanie Klein, himself paid little attention in his writings to the latency years per se. This is in and of itself surprising given the then traditional paternal attitude of reserve and reticence towards infants and toddlers and increased investment and interest in the older child. It would seem that in the psychoanalytic world, the latency-aged child was destined to be ignored, even in the eyes of the father. A supervisee and pupil of Klein, Winnicott was drawn instead to the psychoanalytic exploration of the emotional world of the infant and he repeatedly emphasised the importance of searching beyond the realm of the classical oedipal complex to early childhood and infancy. Despite his self-professed extensive professional experience with children of this age group ("thousands" in child psychiatry, "hundreds" in individual psychotherapy, and between "twelve and twenty" in psychoanalysis) (Winnicott, 1958a), Winnicott wrote sparsely about the emotional life and intra-psychic world of the post-oedipal child as such. Uncharacteristically, in his theoretical formulations regarding this age group, he retained a remarkably static, rigid, classically Freudian (Sigmund and Anna) perception of this phase of child development and largely ignored the complex developmental tasks to be negotiated in middle childhood:

> Biologically it would seem necessary to assume that in these few years, 6–10, the *development of instinct ceases*, so that for the time being the child is left with an instinctual life based on what has been built up in the earlier period…Whatever else may be said about the latency period it seems fairly clear that there *are big defences organized and maintained.*
>
> (Winnicott, 1958a, p. 118 emphases added)

> 'Towards independence' describes the strivings of the toddler child and of the child at puberty. In the latency period children are usually contented with whatever dependence that they are lucky to be able to experience.
>
> (Winnicott, 1958b, p. 92)

His numerous clinical examples, by contrast, reflect a deep sensitivity to the emotional needs, trials, and tribulations of the "latency-aged child", their hidden "madness", and desperate need for "sanity":

> I am thinking of an exercise book that I have in my possession. Each page of this book represents very constructive work done by a girl in the latency period… The characteristic of this exercise book as one looks at it is that it is mainly composed of very well-constructed pictures done with coloured chalks. The analysis was extremely boring for me. The girl seemed to blot me out. Of the fifty or so pictures only two or three in the middle lose the characteristic of organized defence… If this child had been three years old it would have been much easier to have got at the child incontinent or disintegrated; but because she was in the latency group I had to be contented with reaching to an illustration of her hidden madness. Whereas a small child is often 'mad' and yet healthy, because naturally controlled by those in care, a latency child who is 'mad' is very seriously ill, and needs nursing.
>
> (Winnicott, 1958a, p. 121)

By "sanity", Winnicott is referring to the post-oedipal transition from primary process to secondary process, a developmentally vital transition, but one which renders older children unwilling to express their dreams and phantasies directly and spontaneously and leads to their characteristic rigidity and supposed limited imagination.

> In a general way, however, it seems to be important that we should realize when we are treating children of this age that they have achieved a sanity and they have left the primary process. Their ego achievement must not be broken into.
>
> (Winnicott, 1958a, p. 356)

Sanity is essential in the latency phase, and the child in this phase who cannot maintain sanity is clinically very ill.

(Winnicott, 1958a, p. 357)

As was his wont, Winnicott here uses a familiar psychiatrically loaded word, "sanity", and applies it in an unfamiliar context, to describe the psychological achievement of the latency stage. And thus, imperceptibly, but radically, he shifts theoretical perspective on the underlying psychodynamics of the older child.

Winnicott's intuitive grasp of the psychological needs and sensitivities of this age group is perhaps nowhere more apparent than in his trademark "squiggle game". Reading between the lines, I would suggest that the game was at least partially a result of both the self-confessed boredom Winnicott experienced with post-oedipal children and his understanding that most 6- to 12-year-olds will not and should not (developmentally speaking) spontaneously play in a "mad" way, but need to be cajoled and tempted into doing so. Thus, *"in order to reach to the child's ease and so to his fantasy and so to his dreams"* (Winnicott, 1971, p. 115), Winnicott invented the playful, but "latency-safe", game of turning random squiggles into meaningful drawings, a game in which there are rules and no rules simultaneously, which provides the older child with a "sane" framework (your turn, my turn, paper and pencil) within which to express their islands of "madness" indirectly and unconsciously.[1] Winnicott's detailed descriptions of squiggle game sequences with a variety of child patients convey a vivid picture of the rich world of fantasy and dreams, anxieties, and impulses that lies waiting to be tapped beneath the older child's veneer of superficiality and orderly calm. And yet, like Klein, the post-Kleinians, and so many child psychoanalysts since, Winnicott remained blinded by the lure of the bright lights of early childhood, and these clinical insights were never integrated into a detailed developmental description of the psyche of the school-age child.

2.3   *Latency* – disconnect between noun and adjective, theory and practice

This classical psychoanalytic view of the post-oedipal pre-pubertal years as a period of "latency", as first described by Freud, has held fast and remained virtually unchanged to this day (Etchegoyen, 1993; Knight, 2014). Take, for example, the following extract, by no means unusual in its conservative approach to middle childhood, from the recently published psychoanalytic textbook, *On Latency* mentioned above (Diem-Wille, 2018):

This *relatively tranquil* period, where libidinal development is put on the back burner, is the time every society appropriates for children to start school [or similar] – the time of scholastic readiness. At this age children's interest is no longer fixed on their bodies or their parents' bodies, but the outer world...They wish to acquire knowledge that will allow them a new kind of independence....

The ship of child development, after the storms of the early years, now navigates through relatively calm waters.

(Diem-Wille, 2018, p. x, emphases added)

Likewise, the profound disjoint highlighted in the writings of Anna Freud, Klein, and Winnicott, between clinical findings and developmental theory is widespread still today. I would hazard a guess that the majority of the child psychoanalytic individual case studies in the literature are of children aged 5–11 (Diem-Wille, 2018; Knight, 2014), but these papers focus almost always on pre-oedipal and oedipal themes and processes arising in the child analysis and are very rarely used as a basis for deepening psychodynamic understanding of the "latency" stage itself.

As mentioned in the introduction, Freud's term latency has its etymological roots in the Latin participle, *latens* or *latentis*, meaning being in a state of being hidden or concealed. Traditionally, the word latent has been used both colloquially and scientifically as a qualifying adjective to describe a phenomenon that is present, but not yet manifest or fully developed; the emphasis is on the potentiality, not on the inactivity or dormancy per se. Noun and adjective are intimately wedded one with another: *latent talent, latent buds, latent energy, or latent disease*. But within the psychoanalytic discourse, the adjective has become noun, a thing in itself, "latency" as a developmental phase itself, as a hiatus, interruption, and stagnation in development, disconnected from the psychosexual energy that is purported to be latent. It is this fateful disconnection between noun and adjective, between latency and the ongoing partially concealed psychological processes and psychic energies, which has been perpetuated by authors in the field throughout the 20th century. There continues to be a confounding disparity in the literature between rich clinical material from numerous analyses and psychotherapies with older children, and a paucity of descriptions and formulations of the psychosocial and psychosexual achievements, complexities and challenges peculiar to middle childhood. It is almost as if the psychodynamics of middle childhood are fated to follow the same preordained path of "latency" itself in the psychoanalytic discourse: to remain repressed and hidden below the surface, barely voiced, out of sight, and often out of the collective psychoanalytic mind. This, despite the fact that the clinical picture in the field tells a strikingly different story of years that are fraught with upsets and difficulties: more than 10% of children aged 6–12 around the world suffer from some form of mental health problem (see Chapter 1) and around 70% of children in psychotherapy are in fact in the middle childhood age range (Diem-Wille, 2018).

2.4 Children's literature as developmental textbook

What was disconnected and split off in the mainstream ruling strata of society through the ages, and then in the field of psychoanalysis as established in early 20th-century Europe of the intelligentsia and the elite, has remained alive and kicking in children's literature. It is indeed true that popular novels of the 19th century such as Charles Dickens' *David Copperfield*, Charlotte Brontë's *Jane Eyre*, or Louise Alcott's *Little Women* were frequently educational in tone, emphasising morals and upright "responsible" behaviour over mischievous play, adventure, and discovery. But just as in the examples of pictorial art presented earlier, where a less romantic, multifaceted portrayal of childhood could be found alongside the prim and proper, so too in children's literature. From Peter Pan, Tom Sawyer, and Pippi Long-Stocking to Harry Potter, Mulan and Roald Dahl's Matilda, the heroes and heroines of many children's stories, rich and poor, educated and uneducated alike, are full of pluck, oblique sexuality and less oblique anger and aggression, childish hubris, ingenuity, imagination, and creativity. These much-loved tales of middle childhood, written about children and for children, have much to teach the field of child psychoanalysis about the inner psyche and interpersonal world of the post-oedipal, pre-pubertal "sandwich" child. These are stories that possess a magical combination of fantasy and the mundane reality of everyday life, adventure, and structure. Typically, these childhood adventures take place far from the eagle eyes of supervising adults, they are characterised by a clear objective, teamwork, forward planning, and pre-agreed upon codes of conduct, alongside creative invention and plenty of plain childish mischief and boundless energy, a modicum of infantile omnipotence, good fun and humour as well as disagreements, jealousies, hurt, and anger. The fantasy narrative frame of children's literature appears often as a product of children's daydreams and imagination, as interpreted and "translated" by the author (as in the Alice books by Lewis Carroll, for example) but, like the children they portray, these stories are always anchored firmly in reality. Interestingly, many of these books such as the *Chronicles* of *Narnia* (C.S. Lewis), *His Dark Materials* (Philip Pulman), *Harry Potter* (J.K. Rowling), or the *Chronicles of Ancient Darkness* (Michel Paver), feature animals endowed with supernatural powers of communication who join the children on their quests to fight against evil and injustice. These brave and faithful animal companions often play a crucial role in sensing and warning of hidden danger and revealing crucial aspects of the fantasy world hitherto concealed from the child heroes and heroines of the story – the ultimate Winnicottian teddy bear morphed into age-appropriate form.

Creativity, adventure, collaboration, ingenuity, spontaneity, and libido and aggression, combined with a smattering of magical thinking and fantasy all within a rule-bound reality, define much of children's literature through the ages. All this interspersed with the fears, tears, and fist fights that are part and parcel of childhood. These are the very aspects of middle childhood that were largely underestimated and even ignored in child psychoanalysis of the same period, but which are now finally being integrated into contemporary psychoanalytic understanding of middle childhood. Unlike the physical and mental torpor stereotypically attributed to adolescents, school-aged children are portrayed in these novels as "Duracell" or "Energizer" bunnies: their minds, as well as their bodies, constantly on the move, questioning, memorising, learning, inquiring, thinking, and working things out. Any visit to a school playground or inner-city street or local park tells the same story.

This remarkable propensity for new mental activity and discoveries in middle childhood goes hand in hand it seems with an "innate" craving for rules and structure, for labelling, sorting, ordering, and categorising on the one hand, and escape to the world of fantasy and magic (Knight, 2014), on the other. The need for structure and structuring or temporary escape to fantasy and imagination can be understood as healthy and necessary coping mechanisms in the face of the burgeoning capacities and novel experiences that threaten to overwhelm the school-aged child's young and still fragile psyche. Until such time as the neurological and psychological processes of selection and consolidation get under way in adolescence, the developing child's mind, it seems, needs some sort of temporary structure and order, containing and scaffolding, to avoid overload and potential meltdown. It is this scaffolding that has been mistaken in the field of psychoanalysis for rigid stone walls of a rather staid and boring house that is the psyche of the "latency-aged" child.

2.5   Integrating developmental perspectives from adjacent fields of research

Interestingly, the marked transition that occurs around the age of six, from dependent young child to productive and active "juvenile" (Sullivan, 1972), has been noted in academic fields outside of child psychoanalysis from education and cognition to comparative anthropology to neurology and appears to be universal across countries and cultures. Furthermore, recent findings suggest that these profound developmental changes are physiologically and neurologically based (Blakemore, 2018; Campbell, 2011a,b; Hagelin, 1980; Shapiro & Perry, 1976). From a phylogenetic perspective, this period is akin to what biologists have defined as the "juvenile phase", seen in animals as diverse as birds and primates, a phase when the animal young have already become proficient hunters or gatherers, and are largely responsible for feeding themselves, but are not yet reproductively capable and are still under the social influence and protection of their parents.

As is apparent from the following quote, contemporary historical and anthropological research reveals a complex picture of middle childhood that chimes well with the rich, vibrant, and multifaceted world of middle childhood, long recognised in children's literature:

> This stage encompasses the years typically thought of and remembered as…a time of carefree activities, with simultaneous overwhelming *cognitive growth*. The naiveté of infants and toddlers gives way to the inquisitive nature of children, who seek beyond the repetitive "why" question, *to learn in detail who, what, where, when, and how.*
>
> (Cincotta, 2008, p. 69, emphases added)

It is to these "extraterritorial" findings that I now turn to help flesh out the contemporary developmental picture of middle childhood being advanced here.

2.5.1   Education and cognition – Locke, Rousseau, and Piaget

It was the 17th-century radical British thinker, John Locke, and the French philosopher and writer, Jean Jacques Rousseau, who perhaps most notably and profoundly influenced modern theorists in the fields of education and child development. John Locke's widely read educational tome *Some Thoughts Concerning Education*, first published in 1693, popularised the idea of children as *tabula rasa*, clean slates, born innocent and ignorant, whose natural inquisitiveness, playfulness, and physical energy feed their thirst for knowledge and desire for rationality. In many ways centuries ahead of his time, Locke emphasised the child's need to assert their independence of thought and action and advocated strongly that both at home and at school, the child's playfulness should be fostered rather than stifled. The art of education was, according to Locke, "to make all that [children] have to do, sport and play too" (Locke, 1712, p. 63).

Jean Jacques Rousseau, writing over half a century later, was greatly influenced by Locke's ideas of encouraging free thinking, curiosity, and learning by experience in children and proposed an even more radical view of child development and education. In *Emile, or On Education* (Rousseau, 1894 [1762]), Rousseau, like Locke, emphasised that the child is a person whose needs, knowledge, and capabilities are different from those of adults and should be understood and addressed accordingly:

> We know nothing of childhood, and with our mistaken notions the further we advance the further we go astray. The wisest writers devote themselves to what a man ought to know without asking what a child is capable of learning. They are always looking for the man in the child without considering what he is before he becomes a man.
>
> (Rousseau, 1894 [1762](Author's preface page 1))

Rousseau stressed the different stages of child development and the educational (in the broad philosophical sense of the word used by early educationalists) approaches appropriate to each stage. On the second stage of life, the stage of the *enfant* (child) between the ages of 5 and 12, Rousseau writes:

> The development of their physical strength makes complaint less necessary to children. When able to help themselves, they have less need of the help of others. Knowledge to direct their strength grows with that strength. At this second stage the life of the individual properly begins; he now becomes conscious of his own being. Memory extends this feeling of personal identity to every moment of his existence; he becomes really one, the same one, and consequently capable of happiness or misery. We must therefore, from this moment, begin to regard him as a moral being.
>
> (Rousseau, 1894, p. 42)

Perhaps not coincidentally, given Rousseau's classical education and European background, this view of the 5- to 12-year-old "child – *enfant*" with an emergent sense of self, a distinct personality and increasing self-reliance, matches up well with the classical and medieval view of the transition from infancy to childhood at aged 5–7.

Rousseau's descriptions of developmental stages served as the philosophical-educational bedrock on which Jean Piaget later based his highly influential theory of cognitive development in children. (Indeed, Piaget spent some years in the 1920s as director of the *Rousseau Institute* in Geneva, an institute founded with the specific aim of turning educational theory into a science.)[2] Piaget's research revealed the same qualitative leap in cognitive abilities in children at around aged 5/6, which he formulated as a shift from egocentric, "preoperational", one could say illogical, irrational, thinking to what he called "concrete operational" thinking, governed by a logical understanding of concepts such as reversibility, cause and effect, conservation of matter, and temporo-spatial relations (Piaget, 1971). Piaget began to frame his theory already in the 1930s, though it became popularised only in the 1960s, and it has constituted *the* central paradigm in cognitive developmental theory ever since.

Piaget's emphasis on the maturational jump seen at aged 5–7 in the child's ability to comprehend the complexity of the physical and interpersonal world around, stands in strong contrast to classical Freudian and post-Freudian views of latency, which posited a phase of emotional stagnation and even "unlearning". According to Piaget, children in this "concrete operational" stage become interested in reasoning things out, in naming things and mastering classes and relationships (Wilson, 1989). Subsequent cognitive developmentalists have described this stage of middle childhood similarly:

> This stage encompasses the years typically thought of and remembered as…a time of carefree activities, with simultaneous overwhelming *cognitive growth*. The naiveté of infants and toddlers gives way to the inquisitive nature of children, who seek beyond the repetitive "why" question, *to learn in detail who, what, where, when, and how.*
>
> (Cincotta, 2008, p. 69, emphases added)

Piaget's theory therefore had and still has far-reaching implications for psychodynamic understanding of the so-called "latency" phase of development, but it took until the 1970s for his theory even to begin to influence and be incorporated into psychoanalytic thinking on middle childhood (Knight, 2014).[3]

2.5.2   Psychosocial developmental theory

In parallel to Piaget's pioneering work in the field of cognitive development, perceptions of psychosocial development also changed radically in the scientific world and in wider society in the second half of the last century, owing in large part to two prominent non-Freudian psychoanalytic thinkers of the 1940s and 1950s, Harry Stack Sullivan and Eric Erikson. Both Freudian trained psychoanalysts, each developed independent theories of psychosocial development across the lifespan that were outside of mainstream psychoanalysis and which, pertinent to this discussion, highlighted the achievements and challenges of middle childhood, rather than its quiescence.

Harry Stack Sullivan, one of the founders of American interpersonal theory, emphasised for his part the relational shift typically seen in middle childhood from *family to peer relations*, relations with schoolteachers, sports coaches, and the like. Sullivan called this period of childhood the "juvenile era" (Sullivan, 1972 [1933]):

> ...a time when children experience social norms and customs that are different from their family culture, when they have to learn to conform to a peer group and experience peer pressure, and when they have to evaluate themselves in contrast to their peers—all necessary skills for future adolescent and adult relationships.
>
> (Knight, 2014, p. 209)

Erikson's (1950) theory was more Freudian at its heart, based on sublimation of the biological urge to procreate, but, unlike Freud, Erikson's focus was not on repressed conflicts and sublimated drives, but rather on the psychological consequences of success, struggle, and failure. Erikson termed this stage the "age of industry versus inferiority", during which the child acquires sophisticated physical, cognitive, and social skills, moving from a position of great physical and emotional dependence on the parents to relative independence and self-sufficiency.

> With the oncoming latency period, the normally advanced child forgets, or rather sublimates, the necessity to "make" people by direct attack or to become papa or mama in a hurry; he now learns to win recognition by producing things. He has mastered the ambulatory field and the organ modes. He has experienced a sense of finality regarding the fact that there is no workable future within the womb of his family and thus becomes ready to apply himself to given skills and tasks, which go far beyond the mere playful expression of his organ modes or the pleasure in the function of his limbs. He develops a sense of industry – i.e. to adjust himself to the inorganic laws of the tool world. He can become an eager and absorbed unit in a productive situation.
>
> (Erikson 1950, pp. 258–259)

This developmental change is accompanied by a growing sense of competence and achievement in relation to the child's own body and intellect and to their immediate social and physical environment. If this process is disrupted for whatever reason, the child's sense of agency and competence is damaged and feelings of inferiority and futility set in, which detrimentally affect later psychosocial development.

Erikson's theory of psychosocial development across the lifespan continues to be highly influential to this day across the fields of education, social psychology, and sociology. I would suggest that the paradigm shift Erikson proposes from the psychosexual to the domain of self-image, self-confidence, and sense of agency is also critical to building a broader psychodynamic understanding of the emotional development in middle childhood.

2.5.3   Contemporary views of middle childhood in the fields of history and anthropology

According to multiple ethnographic studies of subsistence-based societies around the world, a dramatic shift can be seen at around age "6+/–1"[4] in the roles children assume, both in the home and outside, in the majority of such hunter-gatherer and pastoral tribes and chiefdoms across the continents (Lancy, 2018; Lancy & Grove, 2011; Rogoff et al., 1975). This shift typically takes place between the fifth and seventh years, the age at which children in these societies are deemed to have achieved a sufficient level of physical and cognitive competence and capability to begin learning in earnest from their elders and to be assigned specific roles, chores, and duties, in accordance with their age and capabilities. Children of this age are perceived by their elders to have reached the age of "sense", and they are expected to reduce the time spent in play and to behave in an increasingly socially responsible and acceptable manner. Interestingly, these societal attitudes are often also reflected in the language used to describe this transition from younger, dependent, innocent "infant" to older, "sense"-ible, "responsible" child. Two such evocative examples are described and quoted in Lancy (2018, p. 100):

> For Fulani pastoralists [a semi-nomadic, ethnic group living in the central regions of Nigeria]: "It is when children begin to develop haYYillo (social sense) that adults in turn change their expectations and behavior."
>
> (Riesman 1992, p. 130)

> Osh is the Bakkarwal [nomadic tribe based in the Pir Panjal and Himalayan mountains of South Asia] expression for the "sense" that enables a (seven+ year-old) shepherd to tend his flocks well, day and night.
>
> (Rao 1998, p. 59)

And, following this phylogenetically driven perception of child development, formal education begins in earnest almost universally at this very same critical stage of development of 6+/–1.

In ancient Rome, the infant stage (infantia) was defined as ending around the age of five, the age at which children were perceived to have developed rational minds, and as such were expected to assume domestic responsibilities, be inducted into various trades, and were even eligible for betrothal (though critically not yet for marriage, which took place at puberty). The unique cognitive plasticity of children of the 6+/–1 to 12+/–1 age group was widely recognised also in Europe during the Middle Ages and is reflected in various literary texts from the time, such as Chaucer's colourful descriptions of children and childhood (Salisbury, 2017). Apposite here are the eloquent words of St Anselm, the 11th-century theologian and Archbishop of Canterbury, who famously likened the educational malleability of the child to the propensities of sealing wax:

> …[I]f the wax…is too hard or too soft it will not, when stamped with the seal, receive a perfect image. But if it preserves a mean between these extremes of hardness and softness, when it is stamped with the seal it will receive the image clear and whole. So it is with the ages of men…Take a man…altogether set in [his] ways… He is the hardened wax…. Now consider a boy of tender years and little knowledge, unable to distinguish between good and evil, or even to understand you when you talk about such things. Here indeed the wax is soft, almost liquid, and incapable of taking an image of the seal. Between these extremes is the youth and young man…. If you teach him, you can shape him as you wish.
>
> (Eadmer, 1972, pp. 20–21)

In the medieval Church and the guilds, this proclivity for learning and adaptation, characteristic of the "juvenile", "puerita" years, was well appreciated and moreover well exploited: at age seven, boys and girls were often sent off to monasteries and nunneries, or to work away from home as apprentices or servants. Likewise, in the Roman Catholic Church today, children take their first communion at the age of seven, dubbed "the age of discretion" or the "age of reason", when the child is deemed to have matured and developed sufficiently to be capable of distinguishing between right and wrong.

2.5.4   Physiological and neurological markers of middle childhood

Significantly, over the last 50 years, the view of middle childhood as a well-defined and formative stage in human development has been substantiated by evidence collected from research in the fields of developmental biology, neurobiology, and endocrinology. Campbell (2011b, 2011a) cites an abundance of evidence of biological changes observed in children between five and seven years of age that have been found to coincide with the cross-cultural cognitive behavioural and psychosocial transitions described above. Such changes include the loss of milk teeth and the eruption of the first molars; a rebound in adiposity and the development of axillary hair and odour (Campbell, 2011a); and a maturation in neuromuscular development and fine and gross motor coordination (Hagelin, 1980; Jemerin, 2004; Shapiro & Perry, 1976). Hormonal changes are no longer seen as exclusively belonging to the years of adolescence. Campbell has emphasised the onset of adrenarche (increase in the adrenal production of the neurosteroid dehydroepiandrosterone sulfate) and proposes the radical suggestion that this might be the possible driving force behind the physiological changes and even the psychological and behavioural changes that take place in children aged 5–7. In the introduction to a 2011 special edition of *Human Nature* on middle childhood, he writes:

> [M]iddle childhood in humans now appears to be marked by the physiological changes of adrenarche on one end and gonadarche [puberty] on the other, providing not only a reliable marker by which to judge middle childhood across cultures but a substrate for its evolution as well.
>
> (Campbell, 2011b, pp. 247–248)

Middle childhood is also marked by the consolidation of gross brain volume (the brain in the seven-year-old child is 90% of its final adult volume) and the onset of cortical maturation (Campbell, 2011b; Shapiro & Perry, 1976). As early as the 1970s, Shapiro and Perry (1976) highlighted evidence from research for "functional changes in the child's neurobiological, perceptual, and cognitive development that cluster about the 7th year of life" (Shapiro and Perry (1976), p. 80). It is now known that white matter in the brain increases markedly during middle childhood, as millions of new synapses are formed as the child learns and develops, investigates, and discovers. These synapses are later pruned back, honed, and specified during adolescence as thinking becomes more refined, efficient, and abstract and cognitive and emotional understanding of the world deepens (Blakemore, 2018; Mah & Ford-Jones, 2012):

> …During middle childhood, the brain is in a constant state of flux: myelination is occurring within the corpus callosum and subcortical areas, which enables increased conduction speed and synaptic transmission between the right and left hemisphere, while at the same time, the cortical gray matter is actively adapting. As this takes place, brain activity and behavioural responses advance. Across tasks, young children exhibit patterns of diffuse and widespread activation on functional magnetic resonance imaging while older children show more select regional activation. This is because synaptic pruning enables the brain to attenuate activity in certain areas, while maintaining or enhancing activity in other areas. Thus, with age, fewer and more select regions of the brain are activated for specific tasks by responding selectively to the same stimuli.
>
> (Mah & Ford-Jones, 2012, p. 81)

This neurological picture matches with the observational developmental evidence that during the years of middle childhood, the child amasses a multiplicity of new abilities and interests, behaviours, and beliefs from which the teenager and young adult later pick and choose, consolidating their identity and future life path (Diem-Wille, 2018; Etchegoyen, 1993; Gilmore & Meersand, 2013; Knight, 2014; Shapiro & Perry, 1976; Waddell, 1998; Youell & Canham, 2006).

2.6   Reconnecting the disconnect: re-reading the term latency

I wish now to revisit the metaphor of the physico-chemical concept of latent energy of transformation of one state of matter into another. The findings outlined in this chapter lead to a picture of post-oedipal pre-pubertal child's psyche as far less stable and rigid than classical psychoanalytic thought would have us believe. I would suggest that the psyche in middle childhood be viewed metaphorically as a newly formed solid structure, in delicate equilibrium. As any parent knows, even the most balanced, tranquil, and cooperative school-aged child is also bursting with energy and ideas, insecurities and fears, and tantrums or tears are not such a rare occurrence. It is this concealed emotional instability that Bion (1976), who wrote little on the subject of latency, aptly dubbed "emotional turbulence" lurking below the surface in children of this age.

The psyche of the latency child is indeed structured and bounded, and it is this psychic organisation that gives children of this age their distinct qualities and character. But I think it would be more accurate to conceive of the "intra-psychic bonds" of the post-oedipal pre-pubertal child as vibrating at a more intense level than classical psychoanalytic theory implies. The oscillations are perhaps not so intense and violent as to be permanently at breaking point, as is the case in the effervescent, turbulent toddler or the volatile, explosive adolescent. However, the potential for disruption in middle childhood is nevertheless ever-present. Disturb the equilibrium, add a catalyst, heat the surrounds, loosen the outside containing structure, and the internal bonds destabilise. In the heat of the moment, under internal or external stress, forceful primal anxieties and instinctual impulses temporarily break through and break apart the bonds of the child's newly constructed inner psyche. Splitting and primary processes replace rational behaviour. At such moments of emotional meltdown, after an overwhelming birthday party or an especially important football game, the child's psyche loses its well-defined structure, the "psychic substructures" slipping and sliding over one another in random disorganised fashion, and irrationality and unbridled emotion take over. And yet, unlike in the pre-oedipal child or older pubertal adolescent, the child's psyche in middle childhood is naturally and even phylogenetically and neurologically oriented towards coherence and construction (Blakemore, 2018; Campbell, 2011b). When the system cools down and external boundaries are firmly placed – often in the form of a few reassuring words from a trusted adult, a good night's sleep, or a square meal – a cohesive structure forms once again, and rhyme and reason, calm and rationality return to the child.

2.7   The wave/particle school-age child

Certain contemporary psychoanalytic developmental texts do reflect this less rigid, multifaceted, and more fragile view of middle childhood (Knight, 2014; Novick & Novick, 1994; Shapiro & Perry, 1976; Waddell, 1998; Youell & Canham, 2006). All of these authors describe a period of exponential cognitive growth and psychosocial development. Some emphasise consolidation, autonomy and agency, and the relative robustness of the psyche of the older schoolchild, seeing middle childhood as a time for acquiring and stockpiling emotional, intellectual, social, and physical provisions in preparation for the turbulent storms of adolescence to come:

> Latency is also the time when the child moves from the relatively exclusive tie to parents to important relationships with peers and other adults. The power of new object relations is such that even a seemingly stalemated therapy of a latency child can produce change. All the above-mentioned normal transformations, superego formation, changes in drive organization, cognitive growth, and new object relations, allow for profound transformations in the type and use of fantasy, the capacity to tolerate delay and frustration, an increase in resilience, and the capacity to grow rather than disintegrate in the face of adversity.
>
> (Novick & Novick, 1994, pp. 158–159)

Others emphasise the fragility and precariousness of the still immature psyche of the school-aged child:

> By age nine all of the children had consolidated a new phase of separation and autonomy… *[BUT]* their higher-level ego functions were *not yet sufficiently established to protect them from their strong feelings, which were more powerful than their defenses at this point, resulting in a breakdown of defense functioning and feelings of considerable distress.* That such a failure of defenses occurs after consolidation of separation, the development of a more autonomous self, and the emergence of newly developed ego structures is compatible with the idea that *the most recently established functions are the first to show vulnerability during a maturational change that includes a surge of strong feelings….*
>
> (Knight, 2014, p. 221, emphases added)

> The state of latency, however well achieved and consolidated, sits almost by definition in *a precarious position* – not far removed from the memories and experiences of early childhood and in uneasy anticipation of puberty. *Latency is, in effect, laden with anxieties associated with semi-dormant pressures lurking below the surface*, waiting for puberty and the awesome activity of adolescence. In these terms, the phase of latency is under constant siege – and it may be of no surprise that in a study in 1952, of 4587 children of latency age 62% bit their nails between the age of 6 and 8 years.
>
> (Malone and Massler, 1952) (Wilson, 1989, p. 64, emphases added)

Anne Alvarez (1989) also posits a "relatively new [psychic] organisation at latency", one which may superficially appear defensive to the outside observer, but she stresses that this is a defensiveness that in fact facilitates psychological (not just cognitive and physical) growth and development. In her view, it is by dint of these very defences typical of the latency child that psychological growth is enabled, [de]fences that keep the allegorical wolves of unbridled passions at bay:

> Such splitting has an important developmental function, which is by no means purely defensive...If a farmer encloses a field so that his "sheep may safely graze", the hungry wolves outside may see the fence as defensive; the sheep also, may feel – in their anxious moments – that the fence is for their defence. But in their safer moments, they may feel protected by it so that the flock may graze peacefully and flourish.
>
> (Alvarez, 1989, p. 75)

Moreover, Alvarez and some other authors (Etchegoyen, 1993; Waddell, 1998) go one step further and suggest that the classical psychoanalytic descriptions of rigid defensive obsessive "latency" defensive structures do not in fact represent a picture of normal psychodynamic development but rather are a sign of neurotic pathology or "pseudo-latency" (Etchegoyen, 1993).

Further to these reconceptualisations of this stage of development, I suggest that an apt metaphor for this confounding, almost self-contradictory, nature of the psyche of the older post-oedipal pre-pubertal child can be found in the paradoxical world of quantum physics. This is the enigmatic world of Schrodinger's famed cat, governed by the "Heisenberg uncertainty principle[5]" where waves can be particles and particles waves, depending only on the experimental environment and the measurements taken. Einstein is quoted as summarising this perplexing theoretical state of affairs thus:

> It seems as though we must use sometimes the one theory and sometimes the other, while at times we may use either... We have two contradictory pictures of reality; separately neither of them fully explains the phenomena of light, but together they do.
>
> (Quoted in Kisak, 2016, p. 1)

Similarly for the psyche of post-oedipal child: both stable and in flux, both rigid and volatile, no one theory can suffice. Some aspects of the psyche do seem to settle and go underground in the post-oedipal years, conflicts, and impulses to be classified and boxed away for later times, whilst other aspects develop and change at an astounding rate. Observation in any school playground reveals these contradictory "wave-particle"-like states: children's ceaseless physical energy alongside an extraordinary ability to concentrate for hours mastering a new skill, obsessively collecting Pokémon on their smartphone app, or endlessly classifying and reclassifying forms of "Slime"; the passionate quest for knowledge and physical prowess combined with a coquettish shyness and exaggerated disgust at the merest hint of sex and sexuality; the perplexing admixture of fierce adherence to rules and regulations, with creativity, curiosity, and ingenuity and barely sublimated aggression.

Holding all this in mind, it becomes clear that when thinking about middle child-hood, it is critical to understand the psychic organisation of middle childhood as dynamic and fluid, rather than static and rigid. As Gilmore and Meersand (2014) put it, psychosexual development has now been relegated in psychoanalytic devel-opmental theory to an "ensemble role" alongside the "cognitive, semiotic, object relational, self-regulatory, and affective developments" (Gilmore and Meersand 2014, p. 86), all of which are necessary for what I would term "good-enough" transition into middle childhood. Emotions, drives, and impulses may indeed often be latent, but they are nevertheless always simmering away just below the sur-face. Old theory is no longer sufficient: it seems we need a new developmental grammar and vocabulary to understand this not-so-calm, not-so-stable, paradoxical "wave-particle" stage of middle childhood. It is to the construction and detailing of such a new developmental formulation that I now turn.

Notes

1 For details of the Squiggle game, see Chapter 6.
2 Rousseau's ideas similarly influenced the educational approaches of the Austrian-born philosopher and educationalist Rudolf Steiner (1861–1925) and the Italian physician and educator Maria Montessori (1870–1952). Although differing in their approaches, they emphasised the importance of recognising the specific and distinct educational and emotional needs and abilities of the 5/7–12/14-year-old (particularly to explore and learn independently) in the revolutionary education systems they each founded.
3 See Sarnoff (1971) and Sandler (1975).
4 The term "6+/–1" is borrowed from Shapiro and Perry's (1976) reference to the critical age of 7+/–1 in their seminal article *Latency Revisited*.
5 Heisenberg's uncertainty principle states that until a quantum "particle" interacts with another (is observed) its position remains uncertain and can only be predicted approxi-mately by what can be thought of as a statistically described probability cloud. Like-wise, the properties of a quantum particle can never be known fully – the more precisely its position is known, the less can be known about its momentum (and vice versa). The uncertainty principle together with the concept of the wave-particle duality of quan-tum "particles" in their modern form describe the inherent uncertainty or blurriness of the quantum world (and indeed today are thought by some to be equivalent statements mathematically) (Coles et al., 2014).

Bibliography

Alvarez, A. (1989). Development toward the latency period: Splitting and the need to forget in borderline children. *Journal of Child Psychotherapy*, *15*(2), 71–83.
Bion, W. R. (1976). Emotional turbulence. In Bion, F. (Ed.), *Clinical Seminars and Other Works*, pp. 223–333 Karnac.
Blakemore, S.-J. (2018). *Inventing Ourselves: The Secret Life of the Teenage Brain*. Doubleday.
Bornstein, B. (1951). On latency. *The Psychoanalytic Study of the Child*, *6*(1), 279–285.
Campbell, B. C. (2011a). Adrenarche and middle childhood. *Human Nature*, *22*(3), 327.
Campbell, B. C. (2011b). An introduction to the special issue on middle childhood. *Human Nature*, *22*(3), 247–248.

Cincotta, N. F. (2008). The journey of middle childhood. In S. G. Austrian (Ed.), *Developmental Theories Through the Life Cycle* (pp. 79–132). Columbia University Press.

Coles, P. J., Kaniewski, J., & Wehner, S. (2014). Equivalence of wave–particle duality to entropic uncertainty. *Nature Communications, 5*(1), 5814.

Diem-Wille, G. (2018). *Latency: The Golden Age of Childhood.* Routledge.

Eadmer. (1972). *Life Of St Anselm* (R. W. Southern, Ed.; Reprint Edition). Oxford University Press.

Erikson, E. H. (1950). *Childhood and Society* (2nd ed.). Norton (1963).

Etchegoyen, A. (1993). Latency—A Reappraisal. *International Journal of Psycho-Analysis, 74,* 347–357.

Freud, A. (1946). *The Ego and the Mechanisms of Defence.* Univ. Press.

Freud, S. (1905). Three essays on the theory of sexuality. In J. Strachey & A. Freud (Eds.), *The Standard Edition of the Complete Psychological Works of Sigmund Freud, Volume VII (1901–1905): A Case of Hysteria, Three Essays on Sexuality and Other Works* (pp. 123–246). Hogarth Press, 1953.

Freud, S. (1926). Postscript to the question of lay analysis. In J. Strachey (Ed.) *The Standard Edition of the Complete Psychological Works of Sigmund Freud, Vol. XX (1927),* pp. 251–258 Hogarth Press, 1959.

Gilmore, K., & Meersand, P. (2013). *Normal Child and Adolescent Development: A Psychodynamic Primer.* American Psychiatric Pub.

Gilmore, K., & Meersand, P. (2014). *The Little Book of Child and Adolescent Development.* Oxford University Press.

Hagelin, A. (1980). On Latency. *International Review of Psycho-Analysis, 7,* 165–182.

Hartmann, H. (1958). *Ego psychology and the problem of adaptation.* (D. Rapaport, Trans.). International Universities Press, Inc.

Jemerin, J. M. (2004). Latency and the capacity to reflect on mental states. *Psychoanalytic Study of the Child, 59,* 211–239.

Kisak, E. by P. F. (2016). *Wave-Particle Duality* (1st edition). CreateSpace Independent Publishing Platform.

Klein, M. (1932) Technique of analysis in the latency period In: *The Writings of Melanie Klein,* (Vol. 2, pp. 58–79) London: Hogarth Press, [1975]

Klein, M. (1952). Some theoretical conclusions regarding the emotional life of the infant. In Klein, Heimann, Isaacs and Riviere (Eds.), *Developments in Psycho-Analysis* (Vol. 3, pp. 198–236). Hogarth Press.

Klein, M. (1975). *Envy and Gratitude and Other Works 1946–1963: Edited By: M. Masud R. Khan.* Hogarth Press.

Klein, M. (1932). *The Psychoanalysis of Children. (The International Psycho-analytical Library, No. 22.).* Hogarth.

Knight, R. (2014). A hundred years of latency: From Freudian psychosexual theory to dynamic systems nonlinear development in middle childhood. *Journal of American Psychoanalytic Association,* 62 (2): 203–235.

Kris, E. (1951) Ego Psychology and Interpretation in Psychoanalytic Therapy. *Psychoanalytic Quarterly,* 20, 15–30

Lancy, D. F. (2018). Becoming Workers. In Lancy, D.F., *Anthropological Perspectives on Children as Helpers, Workers, Artisans, and Laborers* (pp. 85–129). Palgrave Macmillan.

Lancy, D. F., & Grove, M. A. (2011). Getting noticed. Middle childhood in cross-cultural perspective. *Human Nature (Hawthorne, N.Y.), 22*(3), 281–302.

Locke, J. (1712). Some Thoughts Concerning Education. A. & J. Churchill.

Loewenstein, R. M. (1954). Some remarks on defences, autonomous ego and psycho-analytic technique. The International Journal of Psychoanalysis, 35, 188–193.

Mah, V. K., & Ford-Jones, E. L. (2012). Spotlight on middle childhood: Rejuvenating the 'forgotten years.' Paediatrics & Child Health, 17(2), 81–83.

Malone, A. J., & Massler, M. (1952). Index of nailbiting in children. The Journal of Abnormal and Social Psychology, 47(2), 193.

Novick, K. K., & Novick, J. (1994). Postoedipal transformations: Latency, adolescence, and pathogenesis. Journal of the American Psychoanalytic Association, 42(1), 143–169.

Piaget, J. (1971). The theory of stages in cognitive development. In Green, D. R., Ford, M. P., & Flamer, G. B. (Eds.), Measurement and Piaget (pp. ix, 283–ix, 283). McGraw-Hill.

Rao, A. (1998). Autonomy: Life cycle, gender, and status among Himalayan pastoralists. Berghahn Books.

Riesman, P. (1992). First find your child a good mother: The construction of self in two African communities. Rutgers University Press.

Rogoff, B., Sellers, M. J., Pirrotta, S., Fox, N., & White, S. H. (1975). Age of assignment of roles and responsibilities to children: A cross-cultural survey. Human Development, 18(5), 353–369.

Rousseau, J.-J. (1894). Émile; Or, Concerning Education: Extracts Containing the Principal Elements of Pedagogy Found in the First Three Books. DC Heath & Company.

Salisbury, E. (2017). Chaucer and the Child. Springer.

Sandler, A. (1975). Comments on the significance of Piaget's work for psychoanalysis. International Review of Psycho-Analysis, 2, 365–377.

Sarnoff, C. A. (1971). Ego structure in latency. The Psychoanalytic Quarterly, 40(3), 387–414.

Shapiro, T., & Perry, R. (1976). Latency revisited. The Psychoanalytic Study of the Child, 31(1), 79–105.

Sullivan, H. S. (1972). Personal Psychopathology; Early Formulations. Norton New York.

Waddell, M. (1998). Inside Lives: Psychoanalysis and the Growth of the Personality. Taylor & Francis.

Wilson, P. (1989). Latency and certainty. Journal of Child Psychotherapy, 15(2), 59–69.

Winnicott, D. W. (1958a). Child analysis in the latency period. In D. W. Winnicott, The Maturational Processes and the Facilitating Environment (pp. 115–123). Karnac 1965.

Winnicott, D. W. (1958b). From dependence towards independence in the development of the individual. In D. W. Winnicott, The Maturational Process and the Facilitating Environment (pp. 83–92). Karnac 1965.

Winnicott, D. W. (1971). Therapeutic Consultations in Child Psychiatry. Hogarth Press.

Youell, B., & Canham, H. (2006). The Learning Relationship: Psychoanalytic Thinking in Education. Karnac Books.

Young-Bruehl, E. (1988). Anna Freud: A Biography. Summit Books.

Chapter 3

The intra-psychic and inter-psychic grammar[1] of middle childhood

A contemporary psychodynamic developmental reformulation

Developmental models can be formulated in various and multiple ways according to theoretical framework and proposed future clinical application. My aim here is to present a developmental picture rooted firmly in psychodynamic theory, whilst taking into consideration contemporary findings and developmental descriptions from relevant fields of child psychology and cognition. The developmental descriptions and conceptualisations presented here are not embedded in any one specific psychoanalytic developmental theory, and the discussion focuses neither on theoretical detail, nor the merits of one theory over another with regards to middle childhood. Rather, my aim is to construct an eclectic conceptual framework for thinking about the psyche and its development in middle childhood for application in the clinical situation across the gamut of psychoanalytic psychotherapeutic approaches. The developmental picture presented here is therefore painted with broad conceptual brush strokes. For the sake of simplicity, I begin by describing three separate spheres of development: the body and the physical; the mind, the ego, and the superego; and, borrowing Winnicott's (1987) phrase, *The Child, the Family and the Outside World*. Later in this chapter, I bring these spheres together in a reworking of the developmental picture beyond the triangular into what I have termed the polygonal psychic space.

3.1 The body, the physical and the sexual[2]

The ego, Freud wrote, "is first and foremost a bodily ego" (Freud, 1923), its archaic container being in effect the skin ego. The growing baby and toddler experiments with their bodies and their functions, deriving pleasure, satisfaction, and self-esteem from learning to turn over, crawl, walk, and run, as well as feed themselves and gain control over the sphincter muscles. The toddler and young preschooler is often an exhibitionist, openly taking a healthy narcissistic pride and joy in his body and shamelessly curious about others. But as the child moves developmentally towards middle childhood, they become increasingly self-conscious and self-aware, and the energy and pleasure in bodily motility and functioning are redirected and take on more sophisticated and complex, less overt, more constructive forms (Diem-Wille, 2018; Gilmore & Meersand, 2013a; Waddell, 1998; Youell & Canham, 2006). The

DOI: 10.4324/9781003425229-4

bodily focus in middle childhood is on the acquisition of physical skills: running, climbing, gymnastics, and football, learning to swim and ride a bicycle, or hunting, building, tending to the animals, or handling tools in more traditional societies. Children of this age are in perpetual motion, practising and honing these skills for hours on end, sometimes on their own, more often with their peers. Anne Alvarez (1989) suggests an innovative alternative interpretation of the child's focus on developing and perfecting physical skills, not as sublimation of psychosexual drives, but as a consequence of psychic development towards the depressive position. In her view, when the child repeatedly and seemingly obsessively practices a physical feat such as turning cartwheels or bowling or pitching a cricket ball/ baseball, these activities serve not only to channel the child's aggression and their craving to beat their peers/dethrone the parent, but also are an expression of the child's strivings towards grace, style, and aesthetic beauty, associated with Klein's depressive position.

Psyche and soma are intimately linked in infancy and toddlerhood, but so too in middle childhood. Not only does the psyche develop from the body-ego, but the way the child experiences their body, sits within their skin, depends not only on their natural genetic endowment but also, and probably more significantly, on the reflection of their body in the eyes of the parents, and how the parents relate to their body, physical growth, and achievements. Diem-Wille poignantly describes this inseparable connection between the "body and soul" in the developing child:

> ...[A] lovingly contemplated child will feel well in his own skin – "cathecting" (occupying) his own body positively...and regard his body as do his loving parents, experiencing himself as something vital. When parents are in a difficult situation and cannot devote themselves lovingly to their baby, their child consequently cannot cathect his body in a positive fashion: instead he feels a stranger in his own skin...
>
> One could also say that the body is a mirror of the soul. Psychic blocks, guilt feelings, and fears are manifested through clumsy movements, frequent bruises, and inhibited forms of expression. An emotionally secure child with a good relationship to her parents moves with security and ease. She shows her lust for life by not just walking but jumping, estimating her own capabilities realistically and only climbing up where she can realistically climb down.
>
> (Diem-Wille, 2018, p. 3)

Sexuality in middle childhood

It is well accepted today that both aggressive and sexual drives are never entirely redirected or sublimated and continue to be expressed overtly and directly from infancy through to adolescence and beyond. Parents and teachers know all too well that anger, physical fights, and violent fantasies are part and parcel of middle childhood, albeit less frequent and extreme than the toddler's temper tantrums or the teenager's volcanic tirades. By contrast, our conceptions about sexuality in middle childhood are still heavily influenced by the fiction of childish sexual innocence and by the classical psychoanalytic concept of psychosexual dormancy as discussed in the previous chapter. Over the last 50 years, however, an increasing number of studies of sexuality[3] in the 5–11-year age range have revealed that sexual knowledge, sexual fantasies and curiosity, and sexual behaviour in the form of masturbation and sexual play with peers (most often homosexual in nature) all remain very much in the forefront of development during middle childhood – sexuality is not as latent during this developmental period as classical psychoanalysis would have us believe (Clower, 1976; Janus & Bess, 1976; Knight, 2014; Ohrenstein, 1986; Wurtele & Kenny, 2011). According to Wurtele and Kenny's (2011) extensive review of the literature, curiosity about nudity and their own and others' genitalia continues in children throughout these years, and sexual play is much more common than adults would like to think. Retrospective research amongst college students in the US reveals that more than half of all students recall engaging in sexual games in elementary school, but only around a quarter of these students recalled being discovered by adults (Reynolds et al., 2003). Freud himself noted that sexual drives do not go completely underground during latency. The major difference between the interest in matters sexual in middle childhood and that of preschoolers is not, it seems, the level of sexual curiosity or strength of impulse per se, but the care these older children take to avoid being discovered, and their insistence on privacy and modesty. Unlike adolescents, sexual exploration is oriented towards voyeurism and nudity, anatomical exploration, and same-sex sexual play, rather than towards imitation or actualisation of the adult heterosexual sexual act. Indeed, children of this age tend to express pseudo disgust of all things sexual, such as kissing or open physical intimacy, and their understanding of adult sexuality and the sexual act is often superficial, confused, and "childish". Today, more than a century after Freud's *Three Essays* (Freud, 1905), not only should masturbation and sexual play in children be understood to be natural and even developmentally important, but parents and educators should be encouraged to talk with children more freely and openly about bodies and sexuality. Having said this, it is important to keep in mind that whilst these children eagerly seek knowledge and understanding of gender and sex, they are not yet adolescents and information regarding issues such as menstruation, night emissions, the sexual act, pregnancy, and birth need to be age-appropriate, neither too sparse and inaccurate, nor too overwhelming and detailed (Wurtele & Kenny, 2011).

Pulling these ideas together, and without rejecting the classical developmental view of middle childhood as years of relative psychosexual calm, it can be stated that the school-aged child is indeed both "wave and particle" vis-à-vis sexuality and sexual behaviour. The developmental literature today suggests that aggressive drives, sexuality, and sexual urges are not in fact held in psychic suspended animation during the post-oedipal prepubertal years, but rather, they are better contained and compartmentalised, expressed more privately and indirectly (Diem-Wille, 2018; Gilmore & Meersand, 2013a; Knight, 2014; Youell & Canham, 2006). The healthy-enough older child has gained the ability to hold sexual urges and fantasies at bay, in the words of Anne Alvarez, in order to engage in age-appropriate learning and play and enable *"other activities or perceptions to develop and mature"*. Alvarez concludes:

> I would suggest that it is important to think of the latency period, not only as a period of hiatus and repression, but also as a period of very important development. The notion of hiatus or repression of defences against sexuality, may be useful for understanding the problems of the neurotic latency child, but not for the healthy latency child nor for the borderline psychotic latency child. The healthy child with some degree of depressive position development may have achieved adequate symbol formation for his sexuality, or, in Bion's terms, learned techniques for the modification of frustration and anxiety, rather than techniques leading to evasion of frustration [CM such as excessive repression and rigid defences].
>
> (Alvarez, 1989, pp. 81–82)

3.2 The mind, the ego, and the superego

Psychoanalytic theory has traditionally emphasised the ego defences and structure constructed to ward off and channel the powerful and potentially fragmenting nature of unbridled bodily id drives and oedipal impulses in the post-oedipal child. In this classical view, the ego and ego functions are conceived as developing in the child's psyche in response to parental prohibitions and chastisements, cultural mores, and taboos, these latter gradually internalised and integrated into the developing child's superego (Freud, 1946; Freud, 1905, 1963 [1915]). Sublimation of sexual curiosity and oedipal aggression is seen in classical theory as the driving force behind the post-oedipal prepubertal child's insatiable thirst for knowledge and acquisition of physical and cognitive skills.

Contemporary psychodynamic developmental theory takes a more holistic etiological approach to the development of the mind in the growing child. The following extract from Gilmore and Meersand (2013a, 2014) exemplifies this wider conceptual perspective, echoed by many other contemporary child psychoanalytic authors (Etchegoyen, 1993; Knight, 2014; Novick & Novick, 1994; Sarnoff, 1971; Shapiro & Perry, 1976; Waddell, 1998):

> The mind of the latency child is characterized by an unprecedented capacity for logical reasoning, a consolidation of parental identifications, and a proliferation of defensive resources such as repression, sublimation, intellectualization, and fantasy formation. Together, these advances in ego and superego functioning reinforce reality testing and self-other differentiation, facilitate relations beyond the family, and help transform infantile wishes and daydreams into latency-phase pursuits and daydreams.
>
> …The child's prodigious cognitive advances and the proliferation of symbolic capacities are seen as major contributors to a distinct latency psychic structure, maintained largely by fantasy formation, sublimation and repression.
>
> (Gilmore & Meersand, 2014, pp. 101, 102)

Middle childhood is characterised by a mushrooming of interests, activities, and abilities, the learning "about" and learning "how" modes become more dominant and visible in order to support new abilities necessary to engage with wider and more complex experiences. These are the years in which children learn to read and write, often in more than one language, to add, subtract, multiply, and divide. They become proficient in arts and crafts and electronic wizardry, in music, fishing, hunting, cooking, and animal husbandry, depending on the family and cultural environment. Ideally, these years are marked by the sense of pleasure and growing self-confidence experienced by children as they acquire these new skills and gradually learn to manage their world, guided and encouraged by significant adults at home and outside. However, these developmental achievements do not always come easily. Many children encounter painful battles along the way as they struggle not only with difficult, even traumatic, family situations and life events, but also with intrinsic learning difficulties, issues with concentration and attention, coordination and sensory modulation, physical weakness, and disabilities, which in turn adversely affects self-esteem, sense of agency, and general emotional well-being, sometimes with long-lasting and highly damaging effects (Kessler et al., 2007; Merikangas et al., 2010).

The quantum leaps in cognitive capacities and intellectual activity in middle childhood can be described variously: in terms of Piaget's theory and the transition from the pre-operation to concrete operational mode of thinking (Piaget, 1971); in Freudian terms as the development of the capacity for secondary process thinking, sublimation and fantasy formation (Freud, 1946; Freud, 1905, 1963 [1915]); or equally in terms of the Kleinian symbol formation (Klein, 1975; Segal, 1989), Bionian theory of thinking (Bion, 1962), or Winnicottian transformations in the transitional space (Winnicott, 1971). As stated earlier, it is not my purpose here to discuss the details or merits of one theory over the other, but rather highlight what can be seen as a common thread running through all these developmental approaches: that is, the emphasis all these authors place on the acquisition of cognitive and physical abilities and skills in the school-aged child. "Mental development and thinking", as Anne Alvarez (1989) puts it, should be conceived of "as processes going ahead in their own right, not purely as defensive against more 'fundamental' fantasies" (Anne Alvarez (1989), p. 74). The metaphor of 3-d perspective, of decentring (Gilmore & Meersand, 2014), of "bifocal" (Bion, 1962) emotional and cognitive thinking and of developing the space in which to think and imagine (Milner, 1957), is found across the theoretical spectrum, from Freud's Oedipal triangulation, the Kleinian depressive position, Winnicott's transitional space, to Piaget's transition from egocentric to concrete operational thinking.

But this decentred mode of thinking, new in middle childhood, is still in its fledgling state, and rigidity and one-tracked thinking often constrict and confound these newly developed capacities for reason and logic. Younger children in the 6–8 year age range, especially, have little tolerance for ambiguity: they are notorious for their insistence that there is only one way to do things, usually according to what they have heard from their friends, teachers, or local scout leader or sports coach.

Wilson (1989) stresses the uncertainty and immaturity of newly developed cognitive capacities and the compensatory need for certainty that characterises latency:

> [T]here is a premium in latency on preserving a sense of order: a kind of compensatory process in which certainty is emphasised as an adaptation to and defence against the prevailing and surrounding uncertainty and anxiety...[T]he fundamental dynamic behind the quest for certainty is a fear of its opposite – of being rendered unsure and helpless under the sway of unrepressed emotions: overly aroused, confused and terrified by parents and adult activities.
>
> (Wilson, 1989, p. 68)

Anne Alvarez (1989) and Canham and Youell (2006), after her, suggest that this concentrated and highly focussed, almost one-tracked, form of thinking, typical of this stage, is developmentally critical and remains important throughout our lives:

> Concentration on a thought, a task or a subject requires focussing of attention, but it also requires the capacity to ignore other thoughts, tasks and subjects, the capacity to put aside those others. It also seems to require the willingness of thoughts, tasks, subjects, to remain in the background and wait their turn, so it is also a certain sort of object-relation with one's own thoughts.
>
> (Alvarez, 1989, p. 75)

Superego development has similarly been reformulated in terms of the mechanisms of self-regulation and self-control[4] that are gradually established and reinforced during middle childhood, in tandem with these developmental advances:

> In a sense the mind may be likened to a passport: once a border is crossed, the passport is ineradicably stamped with the port of entry. Once having entered latency, the psychic apparatus is permanently transformed to include elements of intentionality, choice, responsibility, and guilt. Any subsequent mental activity is marked by this transformation, which must always be taken into account.
>
> (Novick & Novick, 1994, p. 151)

Kohlberg famously developed Piaget's theory of cognitive decentring into the realm of moral reasoning and behaviour (Kohlberg & Hersh, 1977). Whilst his model has come in for much criticism for its simplicity and for its cultural and sexist bias, the basic idea of children shifting from a simplistic quid pro quo, tit-for-tat morality and reciprocity guided by what is good for themselves (you scratch my back, I scratch yours) to a view of morality that takes into account social convention and expectations, and conformity to the rules and prohibitions in their immediate peer group, can clearly be seen over the span of middle childhood. This moral code is very different from the preschool egocentric "morality" which still largely lacks a concept of reciprocity, and also distinct from the shift one sees in adolescence into the realm of the abstract and the moral codes of society at large. Contemporary authors have gone beyond Kohlberg's fairly rudimentary theory and described significant transition from egocentric empathy to sympathetic empathy during middle childhood (Hoffman, 2000) and an increased awareness in older children of the emotional complexities in others, and the influence of context on other people's behaviour and feelings (Gibbs, 2003). All of this points to a superego in middle childhood that initially tends towards the classically static and the rigid, but grows in complexity and flexibility in the later years of primary school.

3.3   "The child, the family and the outside world"

Between the ages of 6 and 12, the child becomes their own person with an increasingly clear sense of self as an individual with a personality and unique and separate identity. As Canham (2018) puts it:

> One of the most important discoveries is who you are. Before he can explore all the different aspects of his character, as happens in adolescence, a child needs to feel safely grounded in his identity [and sense of self].
>
> (Canham 2018, p. 40)

Similarly, Waddell (1998) holds that one of the most important tasks of middle childhood is to develop "a sufficiently strong sense of inner identity to enable [the child] to undertake the psycho-social tasks of, for example, going to school in the first place, at five, and contemplating 'big school', at eleven" (Waddell 1998, p. 64).

The child's developing cognitive capacities and physical abilities bring with them a growing sense of self: of self-awareness and self-reliance; a sense of separateness, of agency and intentionality; of existing in a body and mind that are unique and recognisable as theirs and belonging to them (Canham, 2018; Diem-Wille, 2018; Etchegoyen, 1993; Fonagy & Target, 1998; Waddell, 1998). The ability to think and fantasise and to distinguish reality from fantasy fosters in the child the experience of owning a private internal world, their own inner sanctuary, safe from the intrusion of bothersome parents and siblings, teachers, and peers. Children at this stage become concerned with privacy, of mind and body, ensconcing themselves in their bedrooms, or in secret hide-outs and dens: creating their own little worlds with the help of siblings or friends, often carefully furnished and ordered, often inspired by fictional worlds and characters (Canham, 2018; Diem-Wille, 2018; Knight, 2014; Waddell, 1998; Wilson, 1989).

Drawing from fictional examples in children's literature, Waddell (1998) describes these secret retreats with deep sensitivity and perspicuity: as "private places in the [child's] mind/world" as "expressions of interiority", versions of Virginia Woolf's "room of one's own". These spaces where the child can temporarily create the illusion of independence and mastery in their own world, and where "important aspects of growing up take place" (Waddell 1998, p. 76). I would add that these private hide-outs of middle childhood can usefully be viewed as

Winnicottian transitional spaces, spaces between the inner world and outer reality, between the make-believe world of pretend play of the younger child and the rebellious moody lockdowns of the teenage years.

This emerging sense of self and identity in the child is still closely linked to the parents and the home and as such is still unstable and insecure, not yet cohesive. As a result, children of this age tend to hold inflexible concepts of who they are, of their likes and dislikes, abilities and weaknesses, beliefs and interests, as a defensive guard against the danger of fragmentation and merger (Diem-Wille, 2018; Wilson, 1989). These are the very elements that give the illusory impression of rigidity to the psyche of middle childhood and led to the myth of the ego-defensive immutable structure of the psyche in latency (Sarnoff, 1971).

Building on various psychoanalytic theories of the self (Fairbairn, 1952; Kohut, 1977; Winnicott, 1960 amongst others), Fonagy and Target (1998) link the development of the child's sense of self with the perception and representation of the infant, and later the child, in the mind of the parent or carer, as a thinking, feeling, intentional, whole being. This developmental achievement of differentiation between what is internal and what is external reality only begins to take hold around four years of age and crystallises during the years of middle childhood. It develops in tandem with the ability to think in concrete operations and cognitively perceive reality from different perspectives (cf. Piaget, 1971), which can be conceived as the cognitive basis of mentalisation. These developmental achievements underpin the ability to understand metaphorically and symbolically the other's point of view, to understand the connection between action and reaction, which in turn enable psychological mentalisation: the ability to conceive of the self and the other as thinking, feeling, and experiencing separate beings. Disturbance and inhibition of this capacity for mentalisation lead to social deficits, serious behaviour problems, and emotional instability in older children and adolescents.

This relative self-reliance and developing sense of self, capable of interaction with the outside world as a separate entity with agency and autonomy, enables the tectonic change in middle childhood from familial relationships and the home to school and peer relationships, highlighted by Sullivan (1972) and Erikson (1950). These achievements are predicated, not just on a sense of self, but also on relative security in attachment figures, and the ability for self-regulation and the capacity for reflection and mentalisation (Canham, 2018; Diem-Wille, 2018; Gilmore & Meersand, 2013a; Jemerin, 2004; Knight, 2014; Shapiro & Perry, 1976; Waddell, 1998). Middle childhood is a time for socialisation, for venturing out from the (hopefully) protective environment of the family and home to the wider world of peer relationships and external adult "authority" figures such as teachers and mentors. Conformity with the peer group supersedes loyalty to parental mores, and friends and group activities take preference over time spent with parents. As previously noted, Sullivan (1972) in particular viewed social skills, social integration, and the development of close same-sex friendships ("chums" or "buddies") as paramount for healthy psychic development in the adolescent years and into adulthood. Keeping a child on track socially is of the utmost importance at this stage of life. Difficulties in the area of peer relations can have catastrophic consequences: children who suffer from social rejection or fail to develop close friendships with their peers are liable to suffer from loneliness and low self-esteem, which in turn can lead to self-harm, depression, and school dropout in the teenage years (Gilmore & Meersand, 2013a).

3.4   Psychic space in middle childhood: from the oedipal and the triangular to the polygonal

From here, building on this contemporary conceptual developmental picture of a paradoxical, not-so-calm, not-so-stable, wave-particle, middle childhood state of mind, I shall now re-examine the traditional concepts of the Oedipus complex, of triangularity, sexuality, and gender identity. According to classic psychoanalytic theory, the transition to latency is heralded by the solution of the oedipal complex and is contingent upon the successful mediation by the child's developing ego between the erotic and aggressive id drives and impulses on the one hand, and the strictures and prohibitions of the nascent superego on the other. This is a move from the mother–infant dyad towards the mother–father–child triad, where the infantile fantasy of their "majesty" the baby (Freud, 1914) has been replaced by the sobering reality of father-king sitting on his rightful throne, mother-queen loyally by his side, the child excluded from the royal parental couple. This exclusion, though painful and difficult to tolerate, and even harder to internalise, is at the same time emancipating; the child is liberated to explore and discover the outside world, in the knowledge that the parental couple are safe from the child's dangerous incestuous parricidal impulses.

The original Oedipus complex, as conceived by Freud, and the associated phallocentric concepts of castration anxiety, the castration complex, and penis envy, have of course all undergone major revisions in the last hundred years in the light of historical, socio-political, and psychoanalytic critiques (Benjamin, 1988; Buhle, 2009; Chodorow, 1994). These contemporary reformulations tend towards a more humanistic, nuanced, complex view of the Oedipus complex as a universal "watershed in individuation" and emancipation in human development (Loewald, 1979, 1985). Nevertheless, the basic concept of the child moving from dyadic to triadic relations, and from the illusion of omnipotence to symbolic thinking and an objective "binocular" (Bion, 1962) perception of reality, has stood the test of time in the field of psychoanalysis.

Contemporary psychoanalytic literature continues to be dominated by an overarching tendency to concentrate on the infant–mother dyad and its regressive pull, in tension with the role of the father as agent of separation–individuation. The more complex aspects of triangularity encompassing the wider interpersonal and intersubjective field in which the child grows up and develops have been largely neglected. Middle childhood is a period of negotiation through a multiplicity of relations: siblings, aunts, uncles, grandparents and cousins, peers, teachers, scout leaders, and sports coaches. I believe that the term triangularity does not do justice to these intra-psychic and inter-psychic complexities the child increasingly encounters in these "post-oedipal" years, and that psychoanalytic theory needs a new term, wider in scope, to describe psychic space beyond the mother–father–infant "oedipal" triangle. I would like to suggest here coining the term *polygonality* (or even the 3-D term polyhedrality) as a metaphor for this wider interpersonal and intersubjective field. If one imagines the infinite variety of possible regular and irregular polygonal shapes, it becomes immediately apparent that the multiplicity of relational possibilities that can be represented using this polygonal metaphor is far greater and more complex than in the triangular metaphor. As such, I would argue that the term polygonality more truly reflects the intrapsychic and interpsychic space of middle childhood.

As I have said, this polygonal psychic space can be conceived as encompassing the multiplicity of the child's own relations with significant others in their own interpersonal world beyond the mother–father–child triad. Furthermore, I would like to propose that the polygonal is seen as extending also to the parents' social and professional world, from which the child is excluded but whose presence as significant others in the parents' world is strongly felt. This polygonal inter-psychic and intra-psychic complexity, which the child gradually internalises through middle childhood and needs to learn to negotiate both psychically and in the real world, presents a particularly challenging developmental task for the immature and as yet unstable psyche of the school-aged child.

3.4.1   Gender identity and childhood sexuality in the polygonal space: the "enigma of difference" and the "fact of incompleteness"

Attaining a relatively stable degree of identity integration and gender identity is a central developmental task of middle childhood. The child's sense of security and pleasure in their own body, combined with flexible, non-punitive, non-intrusive parental attitudes towards sexual curiosity and childhood sexuality, enable healthy, and initially fluid, gender identification to develop as the child moves through middle childhood. Research shows that most boys and girls entering middle childhood have a clear sense of the anatomical differences between themselves and the opposite sex, and an understanding of the connection between these differences and gender identity on the instinctual, bodily, and cognitive levels (Gilmore & Meersand, 2013b; Knight, 2014). Indeed, gender identification in this age group tends to appear superficially to be rigid and black and white, with girls and boys often obstinately shying away from joint play or activities associated with members of the opposite sex. However, here too the picture is paradoxical: whilst at first glance these divisions seem fixed and firmly held, boys and girls of this age also typically maintain a surprisingly flexible dual gender role identity in fantasy and in play well into middle childhood (Knight, 2014).

Twenty-first century psychoanalysts, many writing from a feminist standpoint, have now begun to breathe sexuality back into psychoanalytic theory of early childhood, allied to these questions of gender identity and the self. These approaches have moved away from the binary concepts of feminine and masculine, maternal and paternal, and have begun to redraw the developmental map in multi-gendered language, without disregarding the importance of sexuality, aggression, the body, and the bodily (Balsam, 2001; Bassin, 1996; Ben-Ari Smira, 2015; Benjamin, 1995; Chodorow, 1994; Fiorini, 2019; Mitchell, 2000; Palgi-Hecker, 2005; Scarfone, 2013). From this standpoint, notions of lack and difference signified in classical psychoanalysis in terms of the phallus, the womb and breasts, penis envy, and castration anxiety have been restated in terms of the fundamental "incompleteness" that is intrinsic to the human condition. "Incompleteness" that goes well beyond the manifest differences between the sexes and the generations to encompass the very "enigma of difference" (Fiorini, 2016, 2019; Fogel, 2006; Mieli, 1993) between the self and the other, an ineffable difference that perhaps can never be fully comprehended, let alone fully accepted (for explanations of these terms and for more detail, see Fiorini, 2016; Laplanche, 1999, 2007; Scarfone, 2019).[5]

Balsam (2001, 2010, 2018), who has written much on these subjects from a 21st-century feminist psychoanalytic perspective, elegantly preserves the "baby" when throwing out the "bathwater" of classical psychoanalytic theory. She emphasises Freud's revolutionary insights into infantile psychosexual development and the intergenerational instinctual drama of early childhood, but her conceptual formulation of this "oedipal" stage of development crucially takes into account "the existence of bodies of two natal sexes" (the biologically male and female bodies) and a multiplicity of combinations of gender identifications and sexual orientation in development. She suggests laying aside the terms oedipal and pre-oedipal, since these terms tend to confound thinking on psychosexual development and proposes instead adopting a "multi-gendered system of operations that deals in spectra of difference and description of differing modes of sexual behaviour, aims, and the choice of objects can coexist". Such multi-gendered systems of operations, Balsam argues, relieve "[t]he pressure to compare male and female so narrowly as in a phallocratic scheme" (Balsam, 2018, p. 12).

Classical psychoanalysis has often confounded the myths of the matronly goddesses associated with nurturing and reproduction, the home, the hearth, and mother earth – Demeter, Hestia and Gaia – with the mythological ideal of female beauty and sexuality associated with Aphrodite, Andromeda, and Helen of Troy. The feminine, the female, is equated in the literature with boundlessness and space; receptivity, emotionality, and intuition; fluidity and softness; beauty and aesthetics; creativity; passivity and being; connection and relations. Likewise, the paternal, the masculine, and the male have been confounded together and traditionally confined to the myth of the strong, heroic, powerful male and the stern, disciplinarian father. Our "infantile theories" (Scarfone, 2019) are skewed towards a two-dimensional masculinity that is defined by outmoded stereotypes: rigidity, boundaries, and rules; aggression and penetration; separation and individuation; cognition and abstraction; production, activity, and doing; competition and potency; work and the outside world. Many contemporary writers argue for preserving the traditional terms masculine and feminine, whilst decoupling these terms from the biological male and female. They paradoxically suggest using these heavily overladen gendered terms to denote a particular cluster of human attributes accrued during development, independent of sex and gender of the particular individual (Bassin, 1996; Fogel, 2006). I would contend that such a decoupling is culturally, linguistically, and psychologically self-contradictory and that maintaining the very terms masculine and feminine, even if decoupled from biological sex, nevertheless preserves the lacunae, distortions, and myth surrounding gender and sexuality.

In contrast to this language couched in terms of the traditional masculine/feminine binary dichotomies, I propose, in line with Balsam (2001), Fiorini (2016, 2019), Scarfone (2019), and others, a counter-stereotypical approach to identity integration and gender identity development in particular. Specifically here, with regards to gender identity development in childhood, this requires the conceptualisation of developmental gender identity conflicts and challenges of the child not in terms of maternal and paternal dichotomous identifications, of the feminine and the masculine, but rather in terms of gender integration and flexibility.

Contemporary research has revealed that the reality of motherhood and fatherhood as experienced by children and as rated by observers, from infancy and into adolescence, is far less polarised than the stereotypes suggest. Fathers today are likely to be involved in handling and holding in infancy, mothers play physical games with their children (albeit on average slightly less than fathers), and are equally responsible for introducing and engaging babies, toddlers, and older children in linguistic and cognitive activities and interactions. In multiple studies, fathers have been found to be as emotionally receptive as mothers, and mothers as responsible for rules and regulations as fathers (Ben-Ari Smira, 2015; Bronstein, 1984; Cath et al., 2013; Davies & Eagle, 2013; Etchegoyen & Trowell, 2005; Lamb, 2010; Russell & Russell, 1987). The list of findings from contemporary gender and child development research that run counter to traditional stereotypes is comprehensive and surprisingly unequivocal. Even in the most stereotypical, traditional homes and environments, children experience the "masculine" and the "feminine", the "maternal" and the "paternal" in both parents of whatever sex, and in other adults inside and outside the home. And this has probably been at least partially true, if only to a limited extent, throughout the ages and across cultures, despite the myths and distortions propagated in the public, educational, and psychoanalytic discourse.

The implications of this multi-gendered view of identity, sexuated subjectivity, and parental identification are far-reaching. The psychological task in middle childhood is for the child to align themselves in multi-gendered and multifaceted ways, and move freely within the polygonal space between identifications with one or other (or several) of the internalised parental objects (in whatever familial situation the child is growing up). This, whilst critically accepting the "enigma of difference" and the fact of "incompleteness" (the latter related to, but not restricted to, the biological anatomical differences between the sexes and the generations). In the home, the school, the playground, and the psychotherapy room alike, this means enabling the child to explore aspects of activity and passivity, competition and rivalry, creativity and cognition, space and boundaries, yielding and aggression, sexuality and gender, fantasies of production and reproduction and parenthood, of home and of work, all irrespective of biological sex and of gender.

3.5 The language of play in middle childhood

Christopher Robin was going away. Nobody knew why he was going; nobody knew where he was going; indeed, nobody even knew why he knew that Christopher Robin was going away. But somehow or other everybody in the Forest felt that it was happening at last. Even Smallest-of-all, a friend-and-relation of Rabbit's who thought he had once seen Christopher Robin's foot, but couldn't be quite sure because perhaps it was something else, even S. of A. told himself that Things were going to be Different.

(Milne & Shepard, 1961, p. 162)

As noted poignantly by A. A. Milne in the final chapter of the House at Pooh Corner, reaching the age of six and going "away" to school (literally or metaphorically), marks both an ending and a beginning in childhood, when children's play changes radically in both form and content. This is a time when children begin to spend less time playing in their "enchanted places…walking along and listening to things you can't hear, and not bothering" (Milne & Shepard, 1961, p. 162) and turn their attention to their peers and the outside world.

Fantasy play continues to be dominant in the early years of middle childhood (6–8-year olds), but such play becomes more complex, symbolic, and deeply layered in the older child, and day-dreaming and creative outlets such as arts and crafts, writing, dance and music, slowly replace the pretend play of the younger child (Gilmore, 2011; Meersand, 2009). As Waddell (1998) writes, children of this age have

an increasing need to develop a world apart, a world of one's own, separate and yet not cut-off from that of the adults. Time for engaging with one's own experience is needed, for experimenting with it, and developing a stronger sense of self as a consequence.

(Waddell 1998, p. 73)

It is play, both individual and group play, which provides children with this very arena of experimentation and psychic growth. Unlike adolescents, whose dominant mode of communication is verbal (though parents and teachers of many a sullen teenager may seriously doubt this), for school-aged children, play still serves as the principal mode of communication and intra-psychic and inter-psychic interaction (Bellinson, 2002; Diem-Wille, 2018; Meersand, 2009; Waddell, 1998).

The preferred modes of play in these years naturally reflect the distinctive developmental picture of middle childhood detailed above. The momentous shifts in all spheres of development propel the school-aged child towards rule-bound, competitive games, and organised group activities (Freud, 1963; Piaget, 1962; Plaut, 1979). Card games and board games, computer console games, competitive physical games, such as tag, hopscotch, football, and basketball, become the mainstay of children's play at home and outside. These are games that have been designed and refined, usually unintentionally, by generations of creative children and adults to engage children's attention and enable them to practice their burgeoning physical, cognitive, and social abilities, whilst simultaneously releasing and working through emotional and physical steam and sexual and aggressive impulses, all within the metaphor and under cover of the game.

Children of this age also tend to collect all sorts of weird and wonderful items, from seashells and conkers (horse chestnuts) to football stickers and Pokémon cards. These collections often serve as an outlet for more infantile issues of hoarding and anality, but they also act as an organising axis of shared common interest in the peer group, with children's emotional investment waxing and waning with the trends of the times (and influenced of course by the commercial market):

> Middle latency is also the time when children amass huge collections of things, and if a group of friends all collect similar things, it binds them together in a tight unit where rivalries over who has collected what can be played out safely. Children can learn to compare, barter, and swap. They can feel rich, either because of their possessions or their accumulated specialist knowledge.
>
> (Canham, 2018, p. 41)

These common trends are shaped by the need for conformity described by Sullivan (1972) and Erikson (1950) and often take the form of fads and crazes that spread through schools and neighbourhoods like wildfire. Waddell (1998) suggests that this world of competitive play, "hierarchy", and "acquisitiveness", has vital developmental significance:

> [This] world of acquisitiveness and commerce, of competitiveness and hierarchy, of collecting for the sake of it (football stickers, match boxes,… beads) is by no means merely a kind of caricature of the adult world. It may, especially for the more secure and enquiring child, involve a way of beginning to discover the meaning of his own world, one which may strongly resemble, and yet be importantly different from, that of his parents and family.
>
> (Waddell 1998, p. 73)

The dominant language of communication of the 6–12-year-old, then, is still play, but the dialect spoken in this land of middle childhood is distinct and specialised. It is a dialect that possesses a grammar instantly recognisable by its rhythm, rhyme, rules, and reason, and a vocabulary, which, though superficially perhaps a little poor and simplistic in some regards, comprises a rich variety of intellectual and physical activities: sports, competitive games, arts and crafts, building, constructing, and collecting.

3.6   Summary and conclusions

The period of middle childhood, ranging roughly from aged 6 to 12 has often been overlooked in society at large (children who "should be seen and not heard"), and in developmental research and literature in particular. School-aged children are often perceived by educators, practitioners, and even grandparents as boring and less engaging than their older and younger counterparts. In the field of psychoanalysis too, this developmental period was traditionally deemed of little consequence, as a period of dormancy and quiescence.

Research over the last 50 years across a range of fields has revealed a very different picture. It appears that the psychological and developmental needs and challenges of this age group are in fact profoundly different from those of toddlers and pre-schoolers on the one hand, or fully fledged adolescents, on the other. Middle childhood today should no longer be conceived as a time of developmental stagnation, but as a period of momentous cognitive, physical, and psychosocial advances, a time of flux and change, of ongoing psychological development and transformation.

Focusing on psychological development, the ideas and research findings presented in this and the previous chapter point not to a stable inert psychic structure, but rather to a dynamic fluid psychic organisation in the "latency-aged" child, thinly concealed behind a veil of superficially structured and defensive thinking and behaviour. It is helpful to think of the psychic structure of the 6–12-year-old child not as a stable neatly compartmentalised solid crystal structure, but more like the elusive and illusory crystalline structure of iodine or the paradoxical duality of the "wave-particle" nature of light.

The world of play in middle childhood is similarly easily mistaken for being obsessively structured and lacking in imagination and creativity, seemingly governed by the rules and strictures of the outside world. Look once at children playing in the backyard or local park, and you will find a superficially strictly organised lattice work structure of play and games. Look again and scratch a little beneath the surface, and you will discover a rich and volatile wave-like world of emotions and sexual and aggressive passions. The natural channels of emotional expression of the 6–12 child take place within the rich and largely interactive domain of structured games and complex rule-bound fantasy worlds, a domain that allows the rapidly developing child a safe arena in which to express these underlying anxieties, urges, and passions, whilst maintaining a veneer of "good" "Eriksonian" citizenship.

As regards psychotherapeutic intervention for this age group, the conventional wisdom in the past was often largely to "leave well alone" and "let time take its course" (see Chapter 2), an attitude that remains prevalent amongst many parents and educators even today. The developmental formulation in this chapter highlights the dangers of this misconception: it can be clearly seen that the years from 6–12 present developmental challenges in all spheres of the child's life and these children are more emotionally vulnerable and fragile than was believed in the past. As Wilson (1989) puts it:

What is implicit is that latency is an achievement that has to be maintained. It is not something ordained or inevitable, despite maturation. Rather it is a state that has to be earned and looked after, given adequate environmental facilitations. Despite its virtue of composure and orderly growth, it nevertheless sits perilously at the mercy of numerous disruptive forces.

(Wilson 1989, p. 63)

Sadly, children in middle childhood experience loss, deprivation, and disruption no less than in early childhood or in adolescence, and their psychological welfare is every bit as critical as in any other stage of development. Just as the very term latency has come under question, so the techniques and theory of child psychoanalytic psychotherapy with this age group need to be reassessed in line with contemporary understanding of the sometimes contradictory and elusive "wave-particle" school-age child. In the Tavistock seminars, Bion pointed out the pliability of the young child's mind (in contrast to the "myelinated" mind of the adult), and its remarkable capacity for growth and:

… people say, "It's no good to psychoanalyse a child of two or three or five." I have even heard fantastic statements about not being able to do anything when "the fibres are not myelinated." The trouble with the myelinated fibres is that the person who has them is often so rigid, so structured, that you can't get another idea through their myelin.

(Bion 2005, p. 15, quoted in Brady, 2012, p. 302)

I would argue that just as for the young child, so for the wave-particle child, their brain is still wonderfully pliable and malleable, and the myelination process is far from complete, which makes psychoanalytic intervention both highly effective and also of the utmost importance in cases where the "myelination" may be taking a damaging and distorting form and direction.

Notes

1 After Alvarez' (1997) paper "Projective identification as a communication: its grammar in borderline psychotic children".
2 In this section, the emphasis is on the bodily and the sexual, and questions of gender and gender identity are tackled below in Section 3.2.1.
3 There is a large body of literature today on the development of self-regulation and its connection to early attachment. See the work of Fonagy and his colleagues in UCL for details of this work, beyond of the scope of the present discussion. (Diamond & Aspinwall, 2003; Fonagy et al., 2018; Fonagy & Target, 2002).
4 Such are the winds of change that the 2019 IPA centenary conference was devoted entirely to the The Feminine, with the aim of "updating and rethinking classical psychoanalytic views on the feminine [and by corollary the masculine also] and their repercussions in psychoanalysis" and addressing such questions as how "the feminine develop[s] in childhood and adolescence, and how … we deconstruct the infantile theories about the feminine at work in our psyches" (IPA 2019 conference handbook: p. 5, p. 7 respectively).

Bibliography

Alvarez, A. (1989). Development toward the latency period: Splitting and the need to forget in borderline children. *Journal of Child Psychotherapy, 15*(2), 71–83.

Alvarez, A. (1997). Projective identification as a communication its grammar in borderline psychotic children. *Psychoanalytic Dialogues, 7*(6), 753–768.

Balsam, R. H. (2001). Integrating male and female elements in a woman's gender identity. *Journal of American Psychoanalytic Association*, 49(4): 1335–1360.

Balsam, R. H. (2010). Where has oedipus gone? A turn of the century contemplation. *Psychoanalytic Inquiry*, 30(6), 511–519.

Balsam, R. H. (2018). "Castration anxiety" revisited: Especially "Female castration anxiety". *Psychoanalytic Inquiry, 38*(1), 11–22.

Bassin, D. (1996). Beyond the he and the she: Toward the reconciliation of masculinity and femininity in the postoedipal female mind. *Journal of American Psychoanalytic Association, 44*S(Supplement), 157–190.

Bellinson, J. (2002). *Children's Use of Board Games in Psychotherapy*. Jason Aronson.

Ben-Ari Smira, K. (2015). *The Hidden Father: Reintroducing the Father into Psychoanalytic Discourse*. Reisling.

Benjamin, J. (1988). *The Bonds of Love: Psychoanalysis, Feminism, and the Problem of Domination*. Pantheon.

Benjamin, J. (1995). *Like Subjects, Love Objects: Essays on Recognition and Sexual Difference*. Yale University Press.

Bion, W. R. (1962). The psycho-analytic study of thinking. *International Journal of Psycho-Analysis, 42*, 4–8.

Brady, M., Tyminski, R. and Carey, K. (2012). To know or not to know: An application of Bion's K and –K to child treatment1. *Journal of Child Psychotherapy*, 38(3), 302–317.

Bronstein, P. (1984). Differences in mothers' and fathers' behaviors toward children: A cross-cultural comparison. *Developmental Psychology, 20*(6), 995.

Buhle, M. J. (2009). *Feminism and Its Discontents: A Century of Struggle with Psychoanalysis*. Harvard University Press.

Canham, H. (2018). Latency. In B. Youell & H. Canham (Eds.), *The Learning Relationship* (pp. 47–58). Routledge.

Cath, S. H., Gurwitt, A. R., & Ross, J. M. (2013). *Father and Child: Developmental and Clinical Perspectives*. Routledge.

Chodorow, N. J. (1994). *Femininities, Masculinities, Sexualities: Freud and Beyond*. University Press of Kentucky.

Clower, L. (1976). Theoretical implications in current views of masturbation in latency girls. *Journal of the American Psychoanalytic Association, 24*, 109–125.

Davies, N., & Eagle, G. (2013). Conceptualizing the paternal function: Maleness, masculinity, or thirdness? *Contemporary Psychoanalysis, 49*(4), 559–585.

Diamond, L. M., & Aspinwall, L. G. (2003). Emotion regulation across the life span: An integrative perspective emphasizing self-regulation, positive affect, and dyadic processes. *Motivation and Emotion, 27*(2), 125–156.

Diem-Wille, G. (2018). *Latency: The Golden Age of Childhood*. Routledge.

Erikson, E. H. (1950). *Childhood and Society* (2nd ed.). Norton (1963).

Etchegoyen, A. (1993). Latency—A Reappraisal. *International Journal of Psycho-Analysis, 74*, 347–357.

Etchegoyen, A., & Trowell, J. (Eds.). (2005). *The Importance of Fathers: A Psychoanalytic Re-Evaluation*. Routledge.

Fairbairn, W. R. (1952). *Psychoanalytic Studies of the Personality*. Basic Books.

Fiorini, L. G. (2016). Intersubjectivity, otherness, and thirdness: A necessary relationship. *International Journal of Psycho-Analysis*, *97*(4), 1095–1104.

Fiorini, L. G. (2019). Deconstructing the feminine: Discourses, logics and power. Theoretico-clinical implications. *The International Journal of Psychoanalysis*, *100*(3), 593–603.

Fogel, G. I. (2006). Riddles of masculinity: Gender, bisexuality, and thirdness. *Journal of American Psychoanalytic Association*, 54(4), 1139–1163.

Fonagy, P., Gergely, G., & Jurist, E. (Eds.). (2018). *Affect Regulation, Mentalization and the Development of the Self*. Routledge.

Fonagy, P., & Target, M. (1998). Mentalization and the changing aims of child psychoanalysis. *Psychoanalytic Dialogues*, *8*(1), 87–114.

Fonagy, P., & Target, M. (2002). Early intervention and the development of self-regulation. *Psychoanalytic Inquiry*, *22*(3), 307–335.

Freud, A. (1946). *The Ego and the Mechanisms of Defence*. Univ. Press.

Freud, A. (1963). The Concept of Developmental Lines. *Psychoanal. St. Child*, *18*, 245–265.

Freud, S. (1905). Three essays on the theory of sexuality. In J. Strachey (Ed. & Trans.) *The Standard Edition of the Complete Psychological Works of Sigmund Freud, Volume VII (1901–1905): A Case of Hysteria, Three Essays on Sexuality and Other Works* (pp. 123–246). Hogarth Press, 1953.

Freud, S. (1914). On narcissism: An introduction. In J. Strachey (Ed. & Trans.) *The Standard Edition of the Complete Psychological Works of Sigmund Freud, Volume XIV (1914-1916)* (pp. 67–102).

Freud, S. (1923). The Ego and the Id. In J. Strachey (Ed. & Trans.) *The Standard Edition of the Complete Psychological Works of Sigmund Freud, Volume XIX (1923–1925): The Ego and the Id and Other Works, 1–6*. Hogarth Press.

Freud, S. (1963). Introductory lectures on psychoanalysis. In J. Strachey (Ed. & Trans.) *The Standard Edition of the Complete Psychological Works of Sigmund Freud, Volume XV (1915–1916): Introductory Lectures on Psycho-Analysis (Parts I and II)* (pp. 1–240).

Gibbs, J. C. (2003). *Moral Development and Reality: Beyond the Theories of Kohlberg and Hoffman* (pp. xvi, 299). Sage Publications Ltd.

Gilmore, K. (2011). Pretend play and development in early childhood (with implications for the oedipal phase). *Journal of American Psychoanalytic Association*, 59(6), 1157–1181.

Gilmore, K., & Meersand, P. (2013a). *Normal Child and Adolescent Development: A Psychodynamic Primer*. American Psychiatric Pub.

Gilmore, K., & Meersand, P. (2013b). *Normal Child and Adolescent Development: A Psychodynamic Primer*. American Psychiatric Pub.

Gilmore, K., & Meersand, P. (2014). *The Little Book of Child and Adolescent Development*. Oxford University Press.

Hoffman, M. L. (2000). *Empathy and Moral Development: Implications for Caring and Justice* (pp. x, 331). Cambridge University Press. https://doi.org/10.1017/CBO9780511 805851

Janus, S. S., & Bess, B. E. (1976). Latency: Fact or fiction? *The American Journal of Psychoanalysis*, *36*(4), 339–346.

Jemerin, J. M. (2004). Latency and the capacity to reflect on mental states. *Psychoanalytic Study of the Child*, *59*, 211–239.

Kessler, R. C., Matthias, A., Anthony, J. C., De Graaf, R. O. N., Demyttenaere, K., Gasquet, I., De Girolamo, G., Gluzman, S., Gureje, O. Y. E., Haro, J. M., & others. (2007). Lifetime prevalence and age-of-onset distributions of mental disorders in the World Health Organization's World Mental Health Survey Initiative. *World Psychiatry*, *6*(3), 168–176.

Klein, M. (1975). *Envy and Gratitude and Other Works 1946–1963: Edited By: M. Masud R. Khan*. Hogarth Press.

Knight, R. (2014). A hundred years of latency: From Freudian psychosexual theory to dynamic systems nonlinear development in middle childhood. *Journal of American Psychoanalytic Association*, *62*(2), 203–235.

Kohlberg, L., & Hersh, R. H. (1977). Moral development: A review of the theory. *Theory Into Practice*, *16*(2), 53–59.

Kohut, H. (1977). *The Restoration of the Self*. International Universities Press.

Lamb, M. E. (2010). *The Role of the Father in Child Development*. John Wiley & Sons.

Laplanche, J. (1999). *Essays on Otherness*. Psychology Press.

Laplanche, J. (2007). Gender, sex, and the sexual. *Studies in Gender and Sexuality*, *8*(2), 201–219.

Loewald, H. W. (1979). The waning of the Oedipus complex. *Journal of the American Psychoanalytic Association*, *27*, 751–775.

Meersand, P. (2009). Play and the older child: Developmental and clinical opportunities. *The Psychoanalytic Study of the Child*, *64*(1), 112–130.

Merikangas, K., He, J.-P., Burstein, M., Swanson, S., Avenevoli, S., Cui, L., Benjet, C., Georgiades, K., & Swendsen, J. (2010). Lifetime prevalence of mental disorders in U.S. adolescents: Results from the national comorbidity survey replication–adolescent supplement (NCS-A). *Journal of the American Academy of Child and Adolescent Psychiatry*, *49*, 980–989.

Mieli, P. (1993). Femininity and the limits of theory. *Psychoanalysis and Contemporary Thought*, 16(3): 411–427.

Milne, A. A., & Shepard, E. H. (1961). *The House at Pooh Corner*. E. P. Dutton & Co.

Milner, M. (1957). The ordering of chaos. In Milner, M. (Ed.), *The suppressed madness of sane men: Forty-four years of exploring psychoanalysis.* (pp. 216–233). Routledge/ Taylor & Francis Group.

Mitchell, J. M. (2000). *Psychoanalysis and Feminism: A Radical Reassessment of Freudian Psychoanalysis*. Basic Books.

Novick, K. K., & Novick, J. (1994). Postoedipal transformations: Latency, adolescence, and pathogenesis. *Journal of the American Psychoanalytic Association*, *42*(1), 143–169.

Ohrenstein, L. (1986). There is nothing latent about latency: Its impact on parents. *Child and Adolescent Social Work Journal*, *3*(3), 143–150.

Palgi-Hecker, A. (2005). *Mother in Psychoanalysis: A Feminist View*. Am Oved.

Piaget, J. (1962). *Play, Dreams and Imitation*. Norton.

Piaget, J. (1971). The theory of stages in cognitive development. In Green, D. R., Ford, M. P., & Flamer, G. B. (Eds.), *Measurement and Piaget* (pp. ix, 283–ix, 283). McGraw-Hill.

Plaut, E. A. (1979). Definition of play. *Psychoanalytic Study of the Child*, *34*, 217–232.

Reynolds, M. A., Herbenick, D. L., & Bancroft, J. (2003). The nature of childhood sexual experiences: Two studies 50 years apart. *Sexual Development in Childhood*, *7*, 134–155.

Russell, G., & Russell, A. (1987). Mother-child and father-child relationships in middle childhood. *Child Development*, *58*(6), 1573–1585.

Sarnoff, C. A. (1971). Ego structure in latency. *The Psychoanalytic Quarterly*, *40*(3), 387–414.

Scarfone, D. (2013). A brief introduction to the work of Jean Laplanche. *International Journal of Psycho-Analysis*, 94(3), 545–566.

Scarfone, D. (2019). The feminine, the analyst and the child theorist. *International Journal of Psycho-Analysis*, 100(3), 567–575.

Segal, H. (1989). *Melanie Klein*. Karnac Books.

Shapiro, T., & Perry, R. (1976). Latency revisited. *The Psychoanalytic Study of the Child*, 31(1), 79–105.

Sullivan, H. S. (1972). *Personal Psychopathology: Early Formulations*. Norton New York.

Waddell, M. (1998). *Inside Lives: Psychoanalysis and the Growth of the Personality*. Taylor & Francis.

Wilson, P. (1989). Latency and certainty. *Journal of Child Psychotherapy*, 15(2), 59–69.

Winnicott, D. W. (1960). Ego distortion in terms of true and false self. In Winnicott, D.W. (1965) *The Maturational Processes and the Facilitating Environment: Studies in the Theory of Emotional Development* (pp. 140–152). Hogarth Press, 1965.

Winnicott, D. W. (1971). The use of an object and relating through identifications. In *Playing and Reality* (pp. 101–111). Penguin Books.

Winnicott, D. W. (1987). *Child, the Family, and the Outside World*. Addison-Wesley Pub. Co.

Wurtele, S. K., & Kenny, M. C. (2011). Normative sexuality development in childhood: Implications for developmental guidance and prevention of childhood sexual abuse. *Counseling and Human Development*, 43(9), 1–24.

Youell, B., & Canham, H. (2006). *The Learning Relationship: Psychoanalytic Thinking in Education*. Karnac Books.

Part II

The place of play, playing, and game-play in child psychoanalytic psychotherapy

Historical background and contemporary questions of clinical technique and practice

Chapter 4

Technique in child psychoanalytic psychotherapy: historical background

The place of play, playing, and game-play

4.1 Early days

Until around 70 years ago, play was often eclipsed from centre stage in psychoanalytic theory and practice. Freud was the first to recognise the importance of play in childhood and, prescient to Winnicott half a century later, he even understood children's play as a precursor of adult creativity and as taking place in the intermediate sphere between fantasy and reality (Freud, 1908). Nevertheless, Freud saw children's play primarily as a means to an end, the endpoint being the renunciation of instinctual satisfactions and adaptation to reality. Children's play, according to Freud, is essentially a defence against unpleasure (Alvarez, 1989) and, unlike work and love, was not seen by him to be of primary importance to adult psychological health. This somewhat undervalued psychoanalytic view of play began to change with the birth of child psychoanalysis, first pioneered by Hug-Hellmuth (1921), and developed in very different directions by Melanie Klein (1927) and Anna Freud (1926) respectively. But it took until after the Second World War for child psychoanalysis and child psychotherapy to become well established and for the significance of play as a psychoanalytic/psychotherapeutic tool to gain widespread recognition in the psychoanalytic world.

Freud himself strongly doubted whether children could undergo psychoanalysis "proper" because of what he saw as the "insuperable" technical difficulties involved, such as the child's immature verbal and cognitive abilities and their natural reluctance to sit or lie still, on a chair, or a couch, in fact, anywhere. When Freud did undertake the first psychoanalytic treatment of a child, in the case of "Little Hans" (Freud, 1909), he did so almost entirely indirectly, via correspondence with the child's father. And this was only by dint of Hans's father's special connection with his son, his profound interest in psychoanalysis, and his unique position as a member of Freud's inner circle of friends and colleagues. In Freud's eyes, "the authority of a father and of a [psychoanalytically informed] physician were united in a single person" (Freud, 1909, p. 5). It is this amalgamation of father and analytical physician that allowed Freud and Hans' father to apply the analytic technique to cure Hans' phobias. It is interesting to note that already in this very first attempt of some form of child analysis, the child's creative and imaginative play figure prominently: Hans' drawings of horses, carts, and their "widdlers", and his pretend play, are presented and analysed in detail.

DOI: 10.4324/9781003425229-6

Hermine Hug-Hellmuth, a teacher by profession, began working psychoanalytically with children as early as 1913. In her treatise published in 1913: *The Mental Life of a Child: A Psychoanalytic Study* (von Hug-Hellmuth, 1921; von Hug-Hellmuth et al., 1919), and later in her lecture *On the Technique of Child Analysis* (von Hug-Hellmuth, 1921) presented at the International Congress at The Hague in 1920 (attended by both Melanie Klein and Anna Freud), Hug-Hellmuth described various modes of play in children and emphasised the role of play in early emotional and cognitive development. Furthermore, she described how play could be used not only to help facilitate a therapeutic bond with the child, but, more significantly, she understood that play had symbolic meaning and could act as a window into the child's unconscious. In essence, she presented a form of child psychoanalysis where play was used as a tool to replace the verbal free associations central to adult psychoanalysis. Hug-Hellmuth's relative professional isolation and premature death meant that she failed to develop these ideas into an organised body of theory: it remains unclear exactly how she used play therapeutically, what toys and games she had in the room, and to what extent she interpreted the child's play.

4.2 Melanie Klein, the Kleinians, and the psychoanalytic play technique

Melanie Klein's paradigm of child psychoanalysis based on fantasy play began in earnest with her experimental analysis of her younger son Erich (Fritz in her papers), as she puts it: "in his own home with his own toys". She intuitively realised that verbal free association would not work and that "the child expressed his anxieties and fantasies mainly in play [and by] consistently interpret[ing] its meaning to him… additional material came up in his play" (Klein, 1980, p. 123). Her proposition, that children project their inner world, fantasies, and object relations onto the arena of fantasy play, directly onto the playroom floor as it were, was revolutionary and opened the way for direct psychotherapeutic work with children. For Klein, "play itself was the technique that made it possible to analyse the child" (Geissman & Geissmann, 1998, p. 122). As Hanna Segal put it:

> Klein's stroke of genius lay in noticing that the child's natural mode of expressing himself was play, and that play could therefore be used as a means of communication with the child. Play for the child is not 'just play'. It is also work. It is not only a way of exploring and mastering the external world but also, through expressing and working through phantasies, a means of exploring and mastering anxieties. In his play the child dramatises his phantasies, and in doing so elaborates and works through his conflicts.
>
> (Segal 1989, quoted in Geissman & Geissmann, 1998, p. 123)

Later, as Klein worked with other people's children in their homes, she came to the conclusion that "psychoanalysis should not be carried out in the child's home".

Klein believed that separation of consulting room from the child's home was vital for the establishment of transference:

> [I] found that the transference situation… can only be established and maintained if the patient is to feel that the consulting room or the play-room, indeed the whole analysis, is something separate from his ordinary home life. For only under such conditions can [s]he overcome his resistance against experiencing and expressing thoughts, feelings and desires, which are incompatible with convention, and in the case of children, felt to be in contrast to much of what they have been taught.
>
> (Klein, 1980, p. 125)

And hence the birth of the Kleinian consulting room and the analytic therapist removed from the home or school environment, a *tabula rasa* with a variety of toys and creative materials such as pencils and paper available for the child to use to express their inner conflicts and "phantasies". Likewise, Klein also regarded drawings and the associations arising from them, particularly in the older child, as an especially useful analytic tool for children.

4.2.1 Play, transference, and unconscious phantasy

It seems that Klein invested much thought in what "props" the young child needs to give expression to their inner world fully and freely:

> Each child's playthings are kept in one particular drawer, and he therefore knows that his toys and his play with them, the equivalent of the adult's associations, are known only to the analyst and to himself… I have found it essential to have small toys because their number and variety enable the child to express a wide range of phantasies and experiences… [The toys] are mainly: little wooden men and women, …wheelbarrows, swings, trains, aeroplanes, animals, trees, bricks, houses, fences, papers, scissors, a knife, pencils, chalks or paints, glue, balls and marbles, plasticine and string….[The room should have] a washable floor, running water, a table, a few chairs, a little sofa, a few cushions and a chest of drawers.
>
> (Klein, 1980, p. 126)

This intuitive choice of small objects was critical for accessing the child's inner world; the very smallness of the toys creates an all but irresistible urge, in younger children especially, to project their phantasy world onto the blank screen of the playroom floor. Winnicott was to call this "the most significant advance" in child analysis (Segal, 1989).

Another revolutionary aspect of Klein's child psychoanalytic technique was her realisation that, as in adult analysis, aspects of the child's unconscious object relations are directed towards the analyst, played out and worked through in the child's play, often enacted in dramatic role play directly involving the analyst. In her paper "Personification in the play of children" (Klein, 1975, pp. 207–208), she gives some beautiful playful examples:

> If a child's phantasy is free enough, he will assign to the analyst, during a play analysis, the most varied and contradictory rôles. ... Thus, the same boy ... repeatedly made me act the part of a boy who crept by night into the cage of a mother-lioness, attacked her, stole her cubs and killed and ate them. Then he himself was the lioness who discovered me and killed me in the cruellest manner. The rôles alternated with the analytic situation and the amount of latent anxiety. At a later period, for instance, the boy himself enacted the part of the miscreant who penetrated into the lion's cage, and he made me be the cruel lioness. But in this case the lions were soon released by a helpful fairy-mamma whose part also I had to play...

***

> From the conclusion that the transference is based on the mechanism of character-representation I have taken a hint as regards technique...As the analyst assumes the hostile rôles required by the play-situation and thus subjects them to analysis, there is a constant progress in the development of the anxiety-inspiring imagos towards the kindlier identifications with their closer approximations to reality.

(Klein, 1975, pp. 207–208)

This led Klein to an equally significant advance in psychoanalytic technique, critical to psychoanalytic work with both children and adults: the concept of transference as a transfer of "total situations" of early experiences, emotions and phantasies into the "here and now" of the analyst-patient relationship and into the "total situation" of the psychoanalytic setting. Klein's understanding of children's play as a vivid enactment of the child's inner phantasies and conflicts in the present led her to the concomitant realisation that the equally intense transference she observed in the psychoanalytic treatments of children, and indeed in adults, should likewise be interpreted not so much as a re-enactment of past relationships, as Freud had proposed, but rather *as an enactment in the "here and now" in the child-therapist relationship of the child's or adult's current unconscious inner phantasy world and object relations.* Taking this one step, or rather one giant leap, further, Klein showed that all free associations arising from the patient, both verbally or through play, can, and should, be referred to the transference.

Analysis of the patient's material in this light thus exposes unconscious elements of the transference not expressed directly towards the analyst. The interpretation of these elements in turn enables access to deeper unconscious aspects of the patient's inner phantasy world, emotions, and past experiences, even of the young child, which can then be gradually worked through with the analytic therapist. *Seen through this prism, the child's play in the psychoanalytic setting can therefore be understood as an expression of the unconscious phantasy world projected simultaneously into the arena of imaginary play and onto the relationship with the analyst. For Klein, play, transference, and unconscious phantasy are all inexorably linked to one another.*

Klein's approach to interpretation in both child and adult psychoanalysis also diverged from classical Freudian theory. Klein saw the power of interpretation as lying not so much in making the unconscious conscious per se, but rather in the direct articulation of these primitive anxieties and phantasies, in the here and now, in order to reduce their potency and facilitate the production of more and deeper unconscious material. Klein noticed that when she interpreted in depth in this way, the child's anxiety reduced almost instantaneously, enabling further unconscious phantasies to be expressed and enacted by the child. These in turn could be explored and interpreted by her, all within the framework of the child's play, often without stepping outside the very play-acting roles assigned to the analyst by the child. From the Kleinian point of view, "the impact on the patient of an interpretation that articulates the depth of anxiety is a process, *a here-and-now process*" (Hinshelwood, 2007, p. 1490, emphases added).

Klein's focus was on in-depth interpretation of unconscious anxieties and phantasies, which led to a deeper understanding of infantile mental states, unconscious phantasies and defence mechanisms, particularly of primitive mechanisms of splitting and projection. Of these, perhaps the most significant for future psychoanalytic theory and technique was Klein's concept of projective identification, the powerful unconscious projective mechanism she posited whereby aspects of the self or an internal object are "split off", attributed to, and "forcibly" projected into an external object. This revolutionary notion of unconscious communication via powerful unconscious projective and introjective mechanisms eventually led to the realisation amongst the Kleinians and post-Kleinians that the analyst's reactions to the patient are in fact more often than not indicative of the patient's primitive unconscious states rather than of the analyst's unanalysed internal conflicts. This realisation, combined with the Kleinian understanding of transference "total situation" in the here and now, led to a clinical theoretical shift in emphasis to the here-and-now transference–countertransference inter*play* between the child and the analyst, and to a focus on the analyst's mind as receptacle for the patient's primitive unconscious emotions and phantasies (Alvarez, 1993; Alvarez & Phillips, 1998; Bion, 1962; Bleiberg et al., 1997; Heimann, 1950, 1977; Joseph, 1985; O'Shaughnessy, 1981). Equally, over the last 30 years, there has been a gradual shift in technique away from lengthy "there and then" verbal interpretations to "bitesize", "here and now", interventions through the language and metaphor of the game at hand, with the aim of communicating back to the child unconscious contents and communications in digested and attuned, "ingestible" form (Alvarez, 2012; Blake, 2011) (see especially Chapter 8).

4.2.2   Melanie Klein, latency games, and Kleinian attitudes to board games

The shifts in Kleinian psychoanalytic theory towards a focus on the infantile intra-psychic world of archaic (part)-object relations and powerful unconscious phantasies did indeed constitute a radical development of, or some would say departure from, Freud's theory. However, in other aspects of theory and technique, Klein strictly and rigidly followed Freud's psychoanalytic method, in particular his emphasis on free association, the analyst as *tabula rasa* and the central role of interpretation of content in analytic therapy. This loyalty to the Freudian ideal of the analyst as blank screen and as translator of the language of the unconscious had deep repercussions with regard to two central aspects of Klein's psychoanalytic play technique relevant to this book: the range and type of toys and games she deemed suitable for use in the consulting room and her adherence to an interpretive and observatory analytic stance. Thus, according to Segal (1989), Klein insisted that play should (as far as possible) not be dictated by the toys available in the consulting room:

> As in the analysis of adults, the [child] analyst must not suggest the theme of the associations, so the toys must not suggest the theme of play. There should be no toys which have their own special meaning, such as toy telephones, or games which impose rules, such as draughts; the human figures [...] are quite unspecific. They should be no uniforms or special dress nor any indication of occupation or role which would suggest a particular kind of play.
>
> (Segal, 1989, p. 41)

In particular, Klein held that especially the older child's play and games tend to be "more adapted to reality and ... [characterised by] more intense repression of their imagination [and] an obsessional over-emphasis of reality" (Klein, 1932, p. 97). For Klein, such games, and by implication board and card games especially, should be discouraged in the psychoanalytic playroom: she judged them to stultify the child's imagination and impede access and interpretation of unconscious sexual experiences and phantasies.

Likewise, in contrast to the lively interactive games Klein described playing with her younger child patients, and the flexibility in transference roles and inter-pretation such play enables, Klein viewed her involvement as a partner in the older child's play as undesirable in psychoanalytic terms and as one of the "unfortunate" adaptations needed in analyses with latency-aged children:

> A great part of this analysis was by means of toys and with the help of draw-ing. I was obliged [sic] to sit beside him [Klein's 9 year old child patient] at the play-table and to play with him to a greater extent than I usually have to with even quite small children.
>
> (Klein, 2011, p. 66)

This apparent contradiction will be taken up and examined in later chapters. Suffice it to say at this stage that these two Kleinian strictures vis-à-vis formal games and interactive play with the older child all but automatically exclude all board and card games from the Kleinian analytic playroom. Indeed, Klein, at least initially, considered latency-aged children unsuited to her play technique, due to their limited imaginative life (in her view) and "strong tendency to repression" typical of their age (Klein, 2011):

[They have] "neither the insight into their illness nor the desire to be cured characteristic of the adult patient, nor are they under the influence of instinctual experiences and fantasies the way a small child is"[...] "who puts things in front of us straight away".

(Klein, 2011, p. 58)

And so, for Klein, the latency-aged child presented a problem for the psychoanalytic play technique. But maybe the reverse is also true? I would suggest that Klein's psychoanalytic play technique, though revolutionary and extraordinarily powerful therapeutically, in fact presents a problem for school-aged children, a problem both of technique and of clinical theory that needs addressing.

The practice of excluding structured games from the child's toy box and avoiding participation in the child's play was maintained by most Kleinian psychoanalysts well after Klein's death. For instance, in her paper "Thinking about a playroom", Betty Joseph (1998) makes a clear case against any playing "games" with the child in psychoanalysis. Using an example of a simple game of throwing and catching a ball, she warns against situations where the child draws the therapist into play, which turns into a game and ceases, in her eyes, to be communication. When this happens, it is upon the therapist to understand the "acting in" and interpret. However, Joseph continues, this does not always achieve the desired effect:

[t]he child may then try defensively to continue the activity, as a 'game', in order not to think about the interpretation and any anxiety it might have touched. This would need to be understood and interpreted and the therapist probably then [should] stop joining in the activity.

(Joseph, 1998, p. 363)

This somewhat remote, non-interactive approach is particularly surprising given the latter-day Kleinian and post-Kleinian emphasis on projective identification and transference–countertransference in the here-and-now. Betty Joseph herself wrote much on the subject, repeatedly underscoring the therapeutic significance of these sometimes subtle enactments which take place between patient and analytic therapist. Paradoxically, she highlights these exact issues in the closing paragraphs of this very same paper:

To my mind, the most important area of growth in child analysis recently has been the increasing awareness of the importance of enactment in the transference — the way in which the patient subtly influences the analyst and nudges or manipulates him into some kind of attitude or behaviour, touching the analyst's unconscious defences or wishes, etc.

(Joseph, 1998, p. 364)

These two views regarding therapist-child interaction in play put forward simultaneously in the same paper seem to be somewhat at odds with one another. Betty Joseph clearly advocates a non-interactive, observational, interpretive analytic stance where the therapist should avoid being drawn into joining in the child's game. And yet in her closing paragraph, she suggests that being "drawn into some kind of acting in" is essential to the therapeutic process and awareness of associated projective identifications and counter transference feelings constitutes "the growing edge in psychoanalytic work with children today" (Joseph, 1998, p. 366). Both these approaches are firmly grounded in Kleinian theory, but confusingly seem to point to radically different, if not opposing, technical approaches: "to be drawn in" or "not to be drawn into" the child's play, that is the question. (This topic is critical to child analytic treatment and will be taken up and examined in depth in Chapter 8.)

Perhaps it is not surprising that this inconsistency comes to the fore so clearly in this particular paper, published as it was in the closing years of the last century by Betty Joseph, who was both a staunch disciple of Klein's, but also influenced strongly by Bion and a pioneer in her own right of psychoanalytic thinking about transference–countertransference "enactments" in work with children. To my mind, this paper is a prime example of the deep-seated opposition to participatory structured or semi-structured games in child analytic treatment harboured by many Kleinians and post-Kleinians up to the present day. Many contemporary texts on child analytic treatment reflect this entrenched position regarding play materials in the Kleinian analytic playroom, exemplified in the following extract from the recently published volume, *Psychodynamic Child and Adolescent Psychotherapy: Theories and Methods* (Grunbaum & Mortensen, 2018):

> Games are not appropriate materials in object relation-based psychotherapy as they hinder rather than further the child's phantasies and usually lead to situations where the child becomes caught up in competing with the therapist, which risks reducing the therapist into a dialogue with the child that is more educational than therapeutic.

Kegerreis (2009) writes in similar vein in her textbook *Psychodynamic Counselling with Children and Young People: An Introduction*:

> What matters in choosing equipment is whether it is likely to enhance or inhibit emotional expression, and whether it is flexible rather than in some way dictating how it can be used. Most board games for example can easily be used defensively and as a barrier rather than an aid to communication.

(Kegerreis 2009, p. 26)

Taking all these statements together, there appears to be a clear consensus amongst many Kleinian and post-Kleinian authors that children tend to use structured games defensively and that the games, being too rule-bound, stultify the child's imagination and inhibit the expression of unconscious phantasies and therefore should be excluded as far as possible from the analytic playroom. It is these statements and others like it arising from other schools of thought of child psychoanalytic treatment, explored in the remainder of this chapter, that I tackle from a theoretical conceptual standpoint in the next chapter and in the context of the clinical setting in the later chapters.

4.3   Winnicott's contribution

Donald Winnicott, former pupil of Klein's turned "independent", developed Klein's thinking on the psychoanalytic theory of play in a new and revolutionary direction. Like Klein, he was spurred to develop new theory and technique by his work with deeply disturbed children and adults, whom he found could not engage and cooperate in the classical Freudian psychoanalytic process. Given Winnicott's Kleinian background, it is to his theory of play and transitional space that I will now turn, before discussing Anna Freud's approach to play and games in child psychoanalysis.

Winnicott's writings on play (Winnicott, 1971b, 1989) constituted a radical theoretical shift in emphasis away from the classical Freudian and Kleinian emphasis on the content of unconscious material exposed through free association. He did not mince his words on the subject: "I seem to see in the psychoanalytic literature the lack of a useful statement on the subject of play….The psychoanalyst has been too busy using play content to look at the playing child, and to write about playing as a thing in itself" (Winnicott, 1971b, p. 40). For Winnicott, it is the process of play and the quality of that process that are of significance developmentally and psychotherapeutically. Play is an act of spontaneous creativity; it is "universal and… belongs to health" (Winnicott, 1971b, p. 48). "[It] is an experience, always a creative experience, and it is an experience in the space-time continuum, a basic form of living" (Winnicott, 1971b, p. 50).

According to Winnicott, play takes place in the transitional space, the undefined space between the subjective and the objective worlds, between "me" and "not me". The origins of play are in the potential space between the parent and the infant, at the stage of separation from a state of absolute dependence of the infant on the parent. As the infant develops, the need for absolute or near absolute adaptation to the infant's primal physical/psychic needs diminishes over the first few weeks of life, and a potential space develops between the infant and parent. It is in this potential transitional space that the infant begins to differentiate between their own omnipotence and inner reality (me) and that which is beyond omnipotent control in outer reality (not me). This is contingent on an initial stage of development with a parental figure, who is adapted and attuned to the needs of the infant – the good-enough parent (Winnicott's "good-enough mother"). It is precisely the primary caring parent's almost total adaptation and merger that paradoxically enables the infant to experience the illusion of omnipotent control of their inner and outer world (according to Winnicott, these two worlds are initially experienced by the infant essentially as one). As the infant develops and becomes stronger physically and psychically, separation begins to occur naturally, epitomised in the trusting and trustworthy phrases so commonplace in parenting: "Just hang on one sec"; "It's OK, Mommy/Daddy is coming to pick you up right now". It is in this "time and place", in the hair's breadth of a gap between parent and infant, that the infant begins to discover the outside world and their creative influence on this outside world.

This is the place and time where baby discovers and creates what was already there, the Winnicottian transitional object. The parent accepts this paradox and the baby's omnipotent illusion within this paradox. This is a stage of discovery and manipulation (think of a baby discovering their fingers and hands, toes and feet, or the squeaky toy in the cot), the result of spontaneous gestures meeting a flexible, responsive, non-impinging environment. The infant infuses the outside objects, discovered in reality, Winnicottian "external phenomena", with the colours and phantasies of their inner world and manipulates these outside objects in accordance with inner reality. Play, according to Winnicott, can thus be seen to take place between the subjective and the objective, at the intersection between imagination and reality. The movement of play and creativity is outwards and inwards simultaneously, thereby creating psychic space.

Winnicott stresses that play is no trivial matter and cannot and should not be taken for granted. By dint of its creative nature, the discovery of the unknown, and the alive destruction involved in the act of creative play, the act of playing in Winnicott's eyes "involves trust [and is] precarious", even psychically dangerous. This makes playing not only the source of aliveness and psychic development, but also, simultaneously, arouses anxiety (Winnicott, 1971b). Like a toddler taking their first steps towards "the other", the outside world, full of excitement, but no less full of trepidation, such is our emotional experience each time we play and create.

Not all children and adults can play in this Winnicottian sense of the word, and no one is always able to play this way. At times of intense stress, anxiety, and trauma, playing is supremely difficult for all. But there are children and adults for whom Winnicottian play in the transitional potential space is beyond their capacity much of the time, whose experience of the primary environment was neither reliable enough nor trustworthy enough to allow spontaneous creativity to emerge. It should be stressed that this is not necessarily because of "not good-enough parenting", but can often be due to intrinsic and extrinsic environmental impingements such as chronic illness, hospitalisations, genetic endowment, or to external trauma such as war and natural disasters. Whatever the origins of inhibitions, perversions, and generalised difficulties in the capacity to play, this is where psychotherapy comes in, not only as a channel for access to the unconscious, but equally as a vehicle for the expansion of the transitional area of play and psychic space *per se*. Relevant here is Winnicott's deceptively simple statement about psychotherapy:

> Psychotherapy takes place in the overlap of two areas of playing, that of the patient and that of the therapist. Psychotherapy has to do with two people playing together. The corollary of this is that where playing is not possible then the work done by the therapist is directed towards bringing the patient from a state of not being able to play into a state of being able to play.
>
> (Winnicott, 1971a, p. 44)

Winnicott sees psychotherapy as a "highly specialised form of playing in the service of communication with oneself and others" (Winnicott, 1971, p. 48). Psychotherapy, according to Winnicott, offers a unique opportunity to introduce new and challenging, even surprising, elements into the area of overlap between the therapist and patient by manipulating the "external phenomena" available (words and play materials alike). It is the element of surprise, of the novel and the unexpected, introduced at a pace attuned to the child's state of mind and capacities, which facilitates the expansion of the transitional space, the area of play. However, playing and creating are also acts of discovery and of alive destruction that inevitably arouse considerable anxiety, even a sense of psychic danger, and as such require the therapeutic couple to take repeated "leaps of faith" (Eigen, 1981) into uncharted and often stormy waters. It is the therapist's responsibility to ensure that this anxiety does not get out of hand, does not overwhelm the patient and block playing:

From Winnicott's perspective, the therapeutic and developmental power of play is twofold. First, play is the child's natural form of communication and expression; second and even more significantly, play takes place in the transitional space, the undefined space between the subjective and the objective worlds, between "me" and "not me". As Levy (2008) puts it in his paper "The therapeutic action of play in the psychodynamic treatment of children", play allows a

> 'plausible deniability' concerning troubling material. i.e. it permits the parties to suspend and if necessary, to disavow its reality. After all it's really only a game. Play therefore frees the participants to express and explore these issues [the troubling material] in ways that would be far more difficult if one was to pursue a more exclusively verbal means of communication.
>
> (Levy, 2008, pp. 284–285)

In his writings on play in psychotherapy, Winnicott stressed that the "external phenomena" we present to the child or adult patient for their and our "manipulation" should feel safe. His case studies describe child-therapist interaction/"play" through drawing, particularly the "squiggle game", and play with soft toys, dolls, string, and other ordinary objects that happened to be in his office, including, famously, his doctor's metal spatula. And yet, Winnicott too, like Klein and the Kleinians of Winnicott's time, strongly eschewed the use of structured games in child psychotherapy:

> It is good to remember always that playing is itself a therapy. To arrange for children to be able to play is itself a psychotherapy that has immediate and universal application, and it includes the establishment of a positive social attitude towards playing. *This attitude must include recognition that playing is always liable to become frightening. Games and their organization must be looked at as part of an attempt to forestall the frightening aspect of playing.* Responsible persons must be available when children play; but this does not mean that the responsible person need enter into the children's playing. When an organizer must be involved in a managerial position then the implication is that the child or the children are unable to play in the creative sense of my meaning in this communication.
>
> (Winnicott, 1971b, p. 50, emphases added)

Winnicott clearly perceived organised games with rules as contradictory to the essential spontaneous creative nature of play. Even more surprisingly, Winnicott discourages entering into the child's play in the case of such competitive childhood games, whereas he freely enters the child's play with toys and dolls and soft animals and is often even proactive in these games. Like Klein before him, Winnicott overlooked the potential therapeutic power inherent in the interactive and familiar nature of everyday board games and card games, this despite the emphasis he placed in general on the patient–analyst interaction in the transitional space.

It was Masud Khan, Winnicott's analysand and protégé turned disowned prodigal son, who promoted the idea of applying Winnicottian ideas on the therapeutic importance of play to the world of board games, ping pong, and card games, albeit with adult patients. Masud Khan, though a prolific and innovative psychoanalytic writer and thinker, became notorious for his destructively wild behaviour outside and inside the consulting room. Unhappily for the fate of board games in child and adolescent psychoanalytic treatment, Khan was eventually thrown out of the British Psychoanalytic Society (see Green, 2005, for a scathing critique of Khan's work on play). It is nevertheless worth quoting here, in the context of this discussion, Khan's innovative clinical work with a severely narcissistic and dysfunctional, but highly intelligent, 24-year-old male patient who brought Khan a gift of a "magnificent backgammon board" and proceeded to challenge him to a series of hard-fought games:

> While Jonathan was setting up the board to play, myriad ideas and apprehensions scampered through my head. Was he intent on asserting his omnipotence and humiliating me? Was he trying to subvert the whole analytic process by this ruse? Then I recalled that only a few weeks earlier, when he was bemoaning his incapacity to converse with people, I had interpreted that he always tried to astonish or dominate with what he spoke, and *did not realize that conversation*

in ordinary social intercourse is playing. Now he had brought me a game. I had the potential space to change his gamesmanship into playing. I took that chance, recalling Prince Hamlet's device: 'The Play is the thing wherein I shall catch the conscience of the King!'

... Of course, he slaughtered me in each game and collected his ten pence per game. In one session I took the opportunity and said: 'You realize, Jonathan, you do not play, you slaughter!' This had a curiously significant effect on him, and he told me how he used to drive his mother, his Nanny and his therapist crazy when he was about eleven years of age. He would build complex structures from Meccano sets, and just as they would begin to get excited, he would complete whatever he was doing and would smash it all up. From this point onwards, it was possible to show him that he had missed the experience of playing in childhood and had instead taken to asserting his will.

... I must describe one of the last games we played. I was winning, and suddenly he introduced a new rule of which I knew nothing and of course he won. Then he rather sheepishly asked: 'Do you think that was dishonest?' I said bluntly, 'No, it was not dishonest,' since he had also given me a book on how to play backgammon, and if I had read it, I would have known the rule; but that he was secretive for sure, and that worried me, because it was out of character with his general behaviour. For the first time, Jonathan began to cry in a session.

(Khan, 2012, pp. 93–94)

This extract probably constitutes one of the earliest detailed and powerful description of the use of a board game for analytic work on the pre-oedipal infantile "subjective-object" level. However, Khan's approach to game-playing in his analytic work became so severely tarnished by his outrageous and even vindictive game-playing in his social life that his work has been subsequently ignored and often written off entirely out of hand. Take, for instance, Andre Green's writings on Winnicott and Khan, cited above. Green asserts that Khan perverted Winnicott's thinking on play such that "play transgress[es] into "foul play" (as in Hamlet)" (Green, 2005, p. 30). Referring to the same paper of Masud Khan quoted above, Green comments that *"in [these] papers, he [Khan] reveals how he engaged in games of backgammon with some of his patients, thereby misusing them also [sic]"* (Green, 2005, emphases added).

It seems that for many Winnicottian practitioners, the backgammon board, card games, and the like, were summarily thrown out of the child psychotherapy room along with Masud Khan. Even today, such structured childhood games are all but absent from the discourse on psychoanalytic play technique in papers and books written by analytical therapists from the Independent tradition. In most textbooks coming from an Independent or eclectic perspective, guidelines on the subject of setting and technique still tend to recommend providing the child in psychotherapy only with toys suitable for pretend play or dramatic or "creative" expressive play and advise against the inclusion of board games in the child psychotherapy room. The chapter on child psychotherapy setting and process, written by the co-authors of *Winnicott's children* (Horne & Lanyado, 2012) Monica Lanyado and Ann Horne in their *Handbook of Child and Adolescent Psychotherapy* typifies this approach. They recommend equipping the room with a small number of communal toys such as a doll's house, lego, and a sandbox, and providing each child with their own box of simple toys which can be used by the child and therapist "as an aid to communication through play". They suggest toys such as "families of dolls, wild and domesticated animals, cars, ambulances, police cars, fire engines, soldiers, paper and pencils, felt tip pens, scissors, sellotape [and] string" (Lanyado & Horne, 2009, p. 158). Cards and board games, even marbles, are absent from this extensive list, and indeed, in both their books, even in the case vignettes, these games get only a passing and sporadic mention.

4.4   Anna Freud, mentalisation and ego psychology

Anna Freud's (1926) approach to child psychoanalysis differed significantly from both Kleinian and Winnicottian theory and technique. As discussed in Chapter 2, Anna Freud's thinking remained essentially Freudian, focused on the oedipal conflict, and associated intra-psychic ego defences. Her work has had considerable influence on modern-day child psychotherapy, especially in the US. Similar to her father's approach to adult psychoanalysis, the focus of child psychoanalysis in Anna Freud's eyes was to find ways to enable the child to *verbally* reveal their dreams, daydreams, anxieties, and feelings, thereby exposing unconscious conflicts, particularly surrounding the child's instinctual sexual/libidinal impulses and the defences against them. This point arises repeatedly in the *Discussions* (Sandler et al., 1980). She firmly believed that "[v]erbalization is the mode of expression which is ideally sought in the course of analysis" (Sandler et al., 1980, p. 118) and that the thrust of the analytic work is always towards "a shift from expression in direct action to expression in thought and words" (Sandler et al., 1980 p. 129):

> The ideally treatable child might be expected to be able eventually to enter into a dialogue with the therapist. The child may bring material verbally or in a nonverbal way that the therapist puts into words; either mode of expression may be suitable from the point of view of the analysis. What is necessary is that the child have the capacity *to talk about* what [s]he has produced *or think about* it when the appropriate words are provided by the therapist.
>
> (Sandler et al., 1980 pp. 118, emphases added)

In her initial papers on child psychoanalysis, Anna Freud recommended the psychoanalyst should gain the child's confidence by visiting the child in her home, slowly engaging the child and encouraging them to recognise their problems and confide in the analyst by telling stories, dreams, and daydreams so that together they could solve the child's neurosis, just as in adult analysis. In the younger child, Anna Freud advocated the use of drawings and creative art as well as storytelling to access unconscious conflicts and associated defence mechanisms.

Echoes of her father come across loud and clear in Anna Freud's own words:

> Verbalisation should be examined in the general context of ego tools and ego means, keeping in mind that thought and words are means of civilizing the individual, and that "putting into words" can be a substitute for action.
>
> (Sandler et al., 1980, p. 121)

And similarly: [T]he technique I have described... does not take us beyond the boundaries where the child's speech faculty begins – and so where [s/he] thinks in the same way as we do.

> (Freud, 1946b, p. 46)

Anna Freud's focus was on "analysing children's resistances and defences: [on] how children defended themselves rather than what they defended against" (Bleiberg et al., 1997, p. 3). She maintained that the aim of child psychoanalytic treatment is the "restoration of the ego to its integrity" (Freud, 1946a, p. 4, quoted in Ellman, 2010, p. 186): her clinical approach was from the surface of the mind down, since the ego is "so to speak, the medium through which we try to get a picture of the other two (id, superego) institutions" (Freud, 1946a, p. 8). Hinshelwood describes the crucial difference between classical Freudian theory and technique and Klein's approach clearly and succinctly:

> From a Kleinian point of view, therapeutic change comes from a deeper understanding and insight into the specific roles and relations exhibited and enacted in the transference...This contrasts with a theory that derives from Freud's interest in the structure of the ego... [T]he difference is this: one aim is the strengthening of the ego through better self-understanding, and the other aim is a strengthening of the ego through better organization of defences.
>
> (Hinshelwood, 2007, pp. 1483–1484)

4.4.1   Anna Freud, play and games

In accordance with this approach, Anna Freud initially viewed playing games, fantasy or otherwise, as serving little direct psychoanalytic purpose, but of use mostly in order to gain the child's confidence as preparation for the psychoanalytic work. In her early writings, she argued that Klein's fantasy play was invalid, maintaining that child's play is often just play and not symbolic of inner conflicts. Her reservation about material arising from play, dreams and drawings was that material in fact was too dominated by the child's id:

> [Children] reveal their id-tendencies in a more undisguised and accessible form than is usual in adults. ... There is therefore a risk that child-analysis may yield a wealth of information about the id, but a [too] meagre knowledge of the infantile ego.
>
> (Anna Freud 1936 [pp. 40–41], quoted in Midgely, 2012)

As summarised by Midgely (2012), "Anna Freud's concern, then, was that a focus on the unconscious phantasies that emerge through play would too easily bypass the child's immature ego" (Midgely, 2012, pp. 54–55).

Similarly, she continued to doubt the validity of the symbolic interpretation of children's play:

> No one really has confirmation of how far a symbolic interpretation matches a fantasy in the mind of a patient, or how far it represents a fantasy in the mind of the person who interprets. Because symbolic interpretation is so open to the influence of the analyst's speculations, I do not like it.
>
> (Sandler et al., 1980, p. 129)

These statements notwithstanding, as Anna Freud began to work increasingly with nursery-school-aged children, she realised that many of these children naturally brought material to analysis through various nonverbal modes of expression, ranging from different forms of play, drawing, and dramatisation, to changes in tone of voice, silences, and impulsive behaviour and acting out. Fuelled by this increasing interest in analysing younger children, Anna Freud developed a more flexible and integrated approach to play:

> From [Anna Freud's] perspective, the child analyst should be equally interested in the repressed instinctual drives (which play reveals very clearly) and the unconscious working of the ego (which, she believed, play mostly bypasses). Without such a dual focus, she argued, there was a danger of returning to the "pre-psychoanalytic" days when Sigmund Freud had used hypnosis to assist his patients to quickly access repressed memories, but without helping them integrate such memories into their whole personality.
>
> (Midgely, 2012, pp. 54–55)

As this extract from Midgley's paper shows, despite the emphasis on the therapeutic value of verbalisation, Anna Freud and her fellow practitioners at the Hampstead Clinic understood that many children also need access to certain toys, games, and creative materials in order to express themselves emotionally. Indeed, especially at the beginning of therapy, they proposed that it is often necessary to play actively with the child in order to reach out to them and engage them in the therapeutic work. According to Anna Freud and her colleagues, the number of toys should nevertheless be kept to a minimum, chosen judiciously and specifically to match each particular child's needs, and stored in the child's individual locker. Providing a wide range of toys and materials in the child psychotherapy room, they maintained, can encourage a defensive retreat to play in the service of gratification of infantile instincts and grandiose narcissistic fantasies (Sandler et al., 1980).

Anna Freud herself distinguished between play in the younger and the older child. Whilst she saw play as the natural form of expression in the younger pre-schooler, she tended to view play in the older child as a retreat to a defensive position:

> Fantasy play can reveal a great deal of material, but any kind of play can be used defensively. A serious obstacle in child analysis lies in the child's relative inability to remove the logical controls [s]he has to exercise over thought processes without at the same time removing the similar controls over action. The adult can do this relatively easily.
>
> (Anna Freud, quoted in Sandler et al., 1980, p. 125)

This general scepticism towards the therapeutic value of play, particularly in the older, latency-aged, child, can be detected throughout Anna Freud's writings. As she famously made clear in the *Discussions*, she did not see toys and games as central to the psychotherapeutic process:

> ...toys... can be used by the child to express his fantasies [but can also be] used in quite different ways. They may express ideas of value, feelings of exclusiveness, or rivalry with others. They may, for instance, serve as missiles. *The role of the toy as a therapeutic agent has been greatly overrated...*[W]hat is really important is what the patient and analyst say and how they relate to each other, what the child reveals, and so on.
>
> (Sandler et al., 1980, p. 127, emphases added)

By the end of her life, Anna Freud's technique and theory of child psychoanalysis had shifted considerably. Interpretation of transference and of play had become important tools in her psychoanalytic work with children, though she still regarded them as secondary to thinking about and talking about what has been interpreted and about the analytic relationship as a whole:

> The use of toys cannot be contrasted with the analysis of the transference. It is not one or the other, but one helps the other. That which is really important is what the analyst says and how the analyst and patient relate to each other.
>
> (Anna Freud, quoted in Sandler et al., 1980, p. 39)

Like Klein, however, board games and other formal games remained off limits in Anna Freud's eyes. She held that such games are used primarily defensively by the child as "they [involve]... logical sequences dominated by the rules and needs of the particular activity" (Sandler et al., 1980, p. 125). This statement is surprising or even paradoxical, given Anna Freud's special interest in the workings of the ego in this age group and her oft-quoted developmental descriptions of the latency-aged child's natural preference for competitive rule-bound games (Peller, 1954). Indeed, in the very same chapter, *Bringing in Material* (Sandler et al., 1980, pp. 117–136), in the *Discussions*, the authors suggest that in practice games in general and formal games in particular may occasionally be the only way for certain material to emerge. They cite just such a case of a child who insisted on playing chess with the therapist and ended up it seems throwing the chess set on the floor when he lost, and thus conveyed to the therapist how his father had behaved towards him in similar games at home. This vignette, I would suggest, calls into question two of Anna Freud's suppositions concerning play referred to earlier: one that the child's controls over action and controls over thoughts necessarily go hand in hand; and second that the child's expression of unconscious content and f/ph/ antasies is in fact necessarily inhibited when playing formal structured games. This point is critical to the theory and technique of child psychoanalytic psychotherapy in general and the therapeutic use of structured games in particular, and will be examined in more detail in the coming chapters.

This vignette of the child playing chess is also interesting in that it brings us indirectly to the additional question of treating "difficult to handle", disorganised, and deeply traumatised children who tend to express their emotional distress and pain through action and acting out, rather than through words. This is an issue on which Anna Freud also expressed her doubts:

> Special problems are presented by children in analysis who are difficult to handle and who bring in material predominantly in a nonverbal way. ... Their inability to contain their feelings and impulses in words and in verbal symbols poses many difficulties in their treatment and raises the question whether they can be treated at all. The question of treatability is bound up with the question of the capacity of the child to bring his[her] material in a way that is suitable for the analytic work and which allows communication between the therapist and the patient.
>
> (Sandler et al., 1980, p. 118)

4.4.2   Mentalisation-based approaches to child psychoanalytic therapy

Similar to the forces for change that caused the radical shift in Kleinian and post-Kleinian thinking towards a focus on projective and introjective identifications and transference–countertransference communications, the challenge of treating children with severe disturbances led to equally significant theoretical and clinical shifts in child psychoanalytic theory and technique in the Anna Freud Centre and beyond. The long-term outcome and process research into psychodynamic and psychoanalytic treatments for children through the years at the Anna Freud Centre revealed that intensive treatment was in fact most effective and most needed in cases of the more severely disturbed and deprived children, whom Anna Freud had deemed unsuitable for psychoanalysis (Fonagy & Target, 1997, 1998). However, these authors also found that these very children were mostly unable to benefit from classical "Anna Freudian" psychoanalytic interpretations because they lack the emotional mental apparatus to do so: that is to say that these children lack or are limited in their capacity to be aware of their own and other people's mental states (Bleiberg et al., 1997). From this research was born the theory of mentalisation and mentalisation-based techniques of psychotherapy for both children and adults were developed (see Section 7.2.2 in Chapter 7 for a more detailed discussion of mentalisation theory and technique). Suffice it to say that the aim here is to strengthen the children's capacity to recognise and monitor their own mental states, which in turn, the authors maintain, helps the child manage their own behaviour and recognise and understand the words and actions of others.

In sharp contrast to the post-Kleinian emphasis on process and the non-verbal, these "post-Anna Freudian" approaches emphasise more conscious verbal processes and "thinking about thinking". Play is nevertheless regarded as central to the mentalisation process, and recent developmental and psychotherapy empirical research supports this view:

> [Research has shown that] symbolic play facilitates processing emotions, providing a safer pretend platform to experience emotions from a representational distance and experiment with several types of tentative mental states [(Gergely et al., 2002)]. By using symbolic expression via play, children may feel safer to express difficult feelings and experience subsequent affect regulation [(Chazan, 2000)].
>
> (Halfon et al., 2019, p. 563)

In solitary play, the child creates characters and fantasy worlds from their own inner world in external reality, using real external "phenomena", to borrow Winnicott's terminology. For Fonagy and Target, the emphasis is on the mental space that play enables: through play the child literally and metaphorically can view and explore their inner world from different perspectives. Just as important is play with a reflective, benevolent, and playful other: the ability and willingness of adults or older siblings and playmates to join in and play along with the fantasies of the child, whilst simultaneously holding the boundaries of external reality in their own mind is critical. To develop mentalising capacities and begin to integrate internal and external realities, the child needs to experience their thoughts and feelings represented in the secure base of the other's mind and equally they need to be able to internalise the experience of the stable secure "frame" of the other's reality-oriented perspective (Fonagy & Target, 1996). Play is the natural medium through which this process takes place and good-enough experience of play with the other is developmentally crucial and is therefore also an integral part of mentalising based therapies with children:

> Thus, the analyst's play with the child has an important development-enhancing function. Not only is it his sole route to engaging the child's representational system, but it is also a developmental opportunity for the child to gain better understanding of the nature of mental states. In [the child's] play, all the characters ... feel, think, believe, wish and desire,[1] and their shared world (the consulting room) brings into sharp contrast their different perceptions, [and]

their sometimes painfully incongruent experiences of the world. Naturally their conflicts, worries and relationships provide a rich source of material for interpretation as well as insight into [the child's] perceptions and feelings about the transference. But there is something else. [The child] uses her play with the analyst to test out her ideas about how her own mind and the mind of others functioned. The analyst must begin by acknowledging the compelling reality of the child's experience, entering into the pretend world, only gradually showing her through contact with his mental experience that it is a set of representations that can be shared, played with and changed.

(Fonagy & Target, 1996, p. 231)

Surprisingly, throughout the literature on mentalisation-based child psychotherapy, the emphasis is once again on pretend play with dolls and simple toys, even when the articles focus on school-aged children and their difficulties in play (e.g., Midgley & Vrouva, 2013; Muller & Midgley, 2020) Games such as *Frustration/Trouble, Monopoly,* and *War and Cheat,* whose names alone bear witness to their potential to arouse intense emotions and interpersonal friction are mentioned sparsely, and only incidentally, in the literature. The mentalisation theory and clinical approach focus on self and other representations and understanding interpersonal interactions, and yet the possible therapeutic benefit of using inherently interactive board games and card games has scarcely been investigated in the literature.

4.5   Ego psychology and the beginnings of the therapeutic use of board games

Whilst Klein's model of child psychoanalysis grew to dominate the field in the UK and South America in the second half of the 20th century, Anna Freud's psychoanalytic theory and practice had immense and long-term influence on psychoanalysis in the US. Through Anna Freud's work and teaching and that of her fellow European emigrés, Heinz Hartmann, Ernst Kris, and Hans Lowenthal, ego psychology become the main psychoanalytic paradigm in the US in the first three decades following the Second World War years. Hartmann and other ego psychologists of this period stressed the analysis of the interaction of ego functions with the stresses of reality and the environment over analysis of ego defences in the face of internal conflict (Ellman, 2010). Over time, a growing recognition of the formative role of the environment nudged many theorists and clinicians in the field of ego psychology in the US to include object relations theory and attachment theory in their clinical and theoretical work (Wallerstein, 2001). The thrust of psychoanalytic work with adult and child patients became increasingly multifaceted, with a simultaneous focus on ego defences and adaptive capacities; on identifying, understanding and working through self and object representations (Kernberg, 1995); and on themes connected with the separation–individuation process (Mahler et al., 1975); and on the influence of the environment and on peer and family relations.

Coming from this integrated ego psychology perspective, one of the most influential and prolific US psychoanalytic writers of this period on child psychopathology and child psychoanalytic therapy, was Paulina Kernberg. Kernberg advocated strongly for psychotherapy with traumatised and deprived children across the range of emotional problems and psychiatric disorders, calibrating the work with these children in accordance with the depth and breadth of their psychic disturbance (Kernberg et al., 2008). Dramatic and "creative" play and work in the transference are all central tools in Kernberg's psychotherapeutic work with children across the range of pathologies (Kernberg et al., 2008). In her book *Forms of Play* (Kernberg, 2000), she describes "normal" play as:

[A]n activity which is age-appropriate, gender-appropriate, initiated spontaneously, developed and carried to a smooth conclusion. The child can portray his creativity and fantasy, which engages him in an absorbing, fun, enjoyable experience, which includes a fantasised or real interaction with people, with both adults as well as peers, and provides the child with an ongoing source of self-esteem and mastery.

(Kernberg, 2000, p. 26)

She describes different forms of play characteristic of different psychopathologies and advocates awareness of these different forms in order to guide both diagnosis and techniques in treatment. In the autistic child, the play tends to be repetitive, non-symbolic, joyless, and non-reciprocal, whereas in the psychotic child, the play has a nightmarish, bizarre, chaotic quality to it. The borderline child is often addicted to pretend play according to Kernberg, often with a primitive fantasy level characteristic of a much younger child. Aggressive and sexual impulses, accompanied by powerful anxieties, pervade the play and the "space of make believe" collapses (Kernberg, 2000; Kernberg et al., 2008). Accordingly, pertinent to this discussion, Kernberg recommends that "play materials with more disturbed and deprived children should be simple and lend themselves to gross motor activities – sponge balls and bowling equipment- or to fantasy play – dolls, soldiers, puppets, superheroes and rubber monsters of all kinds" (Kernberg et al., 2008, p. 169). In her many papers and books on child psychotherapy, Kernberg makes only passing reference to any sort of board games and card games, although video games she singles out as eminently unsuitable. However, as in the example of chess play in the *Discussions with Anna Freud* mentioned above, here too, just two pages after this statement, Kernberg and her fellow authors give an example of the therapeutic use of "pick-up sticks" in promoting superego integration in the treatment of a borderline child. (As a sign of the times, a more recent review paper by Kernberg and her colleagues (2012) mentions board games and their therapeutic use directly, albeit only briefly.)

As noted in the introduction, it appears that Kernberg and her colleagues were in fact not alone in such de facto use of formal games at the time. Despite the repeated and widespread explicit censuring of playing board games in the consulting room that appears in the literature, several papers advocating using structured board games for a variety of therapeutic and diagnostic ends were nevertheless published during the 70s, 80s, and 90s in the US. The authors of these papers usually focused on specific therapeutic uses of these games: to address issues around competition, self-esteem, and impulse control (Beiser, 1979; Fried, 1992; Levinson, 1972); to help overcome resistances (Loomis, 1976); as diagnostic assessment tools (Beiser, 1979); or for their symbolic meaning (Coriat, 1941; Fried, 1992).

Some of these authors describe the special therapeutic power of using board games with particularly challenging and resistant "latency-aged" children. For instance, Green (1978) described using "structured latency games" to strengthen ego functions in psychotherapeutic work with severely abused and deprived children:

> The therapist actively mobilizes the healthy areas of the child's personality and cognitive apparatus. He encourages verbalization and containment of impulse and action and helps the child increase his tolerance for frustration. *He assists the child with reality testing, promotes sublimation, and encourages participation in the typical structured latency games.* One major goal in this area is the establishment of more adaptive controls and defenses so the child can finally experience a latency period relatively free from excessive external and internal stimulation.
>
> (Green, 1978, p. 362, emphases added)

Writing from an ego psychology object relationship perspective, Helen Beiser emphasises the developmental-educational aspects of playing board games. She suggests that "[t]he game is a projection of the relationship between the players to which each brings his own abilities, personality, and problems to bear, and agrees that 'the rules' will hold for both" (Beiser, 1979, p. 487). Thus, diagnostically, Beiser suggests that observation of how the child plays board games can be very informative and playing these games in a therapeutically informed way can often be more effective than pretend play with the latency-aged child. She recommends using formal games to bolster self-esteem, to help the child learn to cope with the frustrations and narcissistic hurt of losing, and to moderate their omnipotent fantasies and impulse to control. Like most of the authors quoted above, Beiser takes a strong line against allowing rules to be bent or re-invented. In her view, allowing the child to cheat in this way encourages infantile omnipotent fantasies and regression. For this reason, although she recommends board games that allow for a mixture of strategy and chance, rather surprisingly, she discourages having a deck of cards available in the therapy room because "the number of games is endless, and the child knows more than most therapists. This opens up opportunities for cheating" (Beiser, 1979 p. 484–5). For Beiser, "[t]he essence of latency development is to understand that rules apply to all for the benefit of all, putting games in a general social context" (Beiser, 1979 p. 486), and therefore, the thrust of the therapeutic work should be in the direction of learning to respect the rules and developing the skills required to win and the ability to withstand frustration of waiting turns and give and take.

A highly unusual and somewhat controversial exception to this mainstream "ego psychology" rather strict and rigid approach to rules, competition, and cheating is to be found in John Meeks' (1970) paper "Children who cheat at games". In this paper, Meeks (1970) highlighted the wider therapeutic importance of playing structured competitive games in psychotherapy with children. Contrary to many other authors, Meeks suggested that allowing children to cheat and bend the rules is in fact therapeutically useful and enables them to play out, test, and work through their omnipotent fantasies. However, until recently, this paper was very rarely cited and it was regarded as so contentious at the time that it was published only on condition that Meeks allow a discussion/rebuttal, written by Beiser (1970), to be added to the paper and published with it (Meeks, 2000). In this discussion, Beiser argues strongly for reinforcing play according to the rules of the game with latency-aged children and doubts the therapeutic wisdom of indulging the child patient's infantile fantasies through allowing cheating and made-up rules.

4.6   Entering the 21st century

Tracing the history of child psychotherapy through the second half of the 20th century, it can thus be seen that, in spite of ongoing developments in technique and theory, the field nonetheless remained largely bound to the historical paradigm of the playroom of early childhood: the world of childhood fantasy, of make-believe stories, of dressing up and play acting and of play with dolls, animals, paints, and crayons. Klein and Anna Freud's legacy of clear strictures vis-à-vis technique and the concrete "tools of the trade" continued to exert a powerful influence on practitioners on both sides of the Atlantic. Bar the few papers cited above, structured games were regarded by most child psychotherapy authors and practitioners as obstructive to the therapeutic process. Opposition to their use was particularly strong in psychoanalytic circles where fantasy play was regarded as critical to the psychoanalytic process, on a par with adult dreaming (Caruth, 1988).

The closing words of the discussion of Meeks' (1970) paper, written by Beiser, are telling. Despite her deep reservations regarding Meeks' approach to cheating, Beiser nevertheless concludes by throwing down the gauntlet to other therapists to rethink their views on the practice and theory of playing structured games:

> I am sure other child therapists could add much to the meaning and technique of playing games as a part of therapy, and I hope Meeks's paper will stimulate them to share their experiences, as well as giving therapists who have objected to games a new insight into their potentialities.
>
> (Beiser, 1970, pp. 173–174)

But in fact, it took another thirty years for this discussion to be brought to the fore and taken up in earnest in the child psychoanalytic literature (Bellinson, 2000; Herman, 2000; Krimendahl, 2000), and still this discussion has been confined almost exclusively to the US.

4.6.1 Intersubjective and relational developments in child psychoanalytic psychotherapy and the increasing use of structured games in the 21st century

The deeper understanding of the potential developmental benefits and ego-strengthening aspects of playing formal games in the consulting room, combined with the shift in emphasis in psychoanalytic theory and practice from content to process, and from a one-person to two-person psychology, has opened the way for new thinking on the subject well beyond the sphere of ego psychology. In recent decades, a spate of clinical papers on board games has been published in leading child psychotherapy journals. Notably, Oren (2008) and Bellinson (2002, 2013) have described in detail how playing games like *Monopoly, Cluedo,* and even *Snakes and Ladders* can not only provide insights into the child's emotional state and difficulties and access to unconscious fantasies and drives, but they can also be a powerful tool through which the child can express and work through issues such as narcissistic frustrations and rage, emotional regulation, self-image and self-esteem, splitting and cohesion of the self and conflicts around separation individuation. Oren, Bellinson and others, especially Meeks (1970, 2000), Herman (2000) and Krimendahl (2000), have emphasised the importance of allowing flexibility and creativity in playing board games, letting the child "cheat" and bend and break the rules (Saar et al., 2017). These authors advocate "indulging" or challenging the child in psychotherapy as necessary, understanding these issues psychodynamically and, where possible, reflecting and interpreting at a suitable level. They suggest that the language of the board game – like the fantasy play of the pre-schooler or the dreams and verbal material of an adult patient – is a psychodynamic language like any other to be intuited, interpreted, and worked through with the child.

In this context, the intersubjective understanding of psychic development has been very usefully applied to the use of structured games in child psychotherapy and particularly to the issue of rule bending and cheating. Pertinent here is Caruth's (1988) ground-breaking paper "How you play the game: On game as play and play as game in the psychoanalytic process", in which the author differentiates between the modes or axes of "playing" and "gaming" in both child and adult psychoanalytic psychotherapy. In the "playing" mode, defined by Caruth as playing in health in the Winnicottian sense of the word, the adult or child patient is able to spontaneously and freely associate, verbally or through fantasy play, and thereby do therapeutic work symbolically in the transitional space, with little "need" to resort to projection into and onto the therapist. By contrast, in the "gaming" mode, the patient's observing ego functions are barely available, splitting is rife, and the unconscious fantasies and conflicts are projected, re-enacted, re-experienced, and worked through almost entirely within the framework of the transference–countertransference and with the intense involvement of the therapist. Caruth argues that "gaming" – that is, the child-therapist interaction inherent in structured games – actually facilitates the emergence within the transference of aggressive and libidinal content and fantasies from the child's inner world. She suggests that many therapists avoid playing games with children precisely because of the intense infantile emotions they arouse in the countertransference:

"[J]ust as games may ward off the frightening aspects of play, namely, the unconscious infantile fantasy life", (Solnit, 1993; Winnicott, 1971, 1980), so "play [often serves to] ward off the frightening aspects of the game, namely the conscious experience of transference [CM and especially in the countertransference]".

(Caruth, 1988, p. 186)

Similarly, Levy (2008) has approached the subject from a relational view of psychotherapy and stresses process and therapist–client interaction, both of which are inherent in play with a child in psychotherapy. He quotes contemporary relational theorists as emphasising that "clients must be encountered – that is therapists must do something more than listen and interpret" (p. 285). Play, especially interactive play including game-play, is, in his view, an ideal vehicle for this encounter to take place. Levy continues:

Play demands the participation of therapists in ways that are unimaginable in more verbally oriented therapies. As a result, the roles of child therapists are necessarily more active and they find themselves in situations that allow little time to reflect upon the meaning of what transpires in treatment prior to their actions.

(Levy, 2008, p. 285)

Play treatment affords children with a unique opportunity to enact their difficulties with an adult who understands the therapeutic efficacy of play, and to develop new patterns of relating and experiencing self and others.

(Levy, 2008, p. 288)

4.6.2   Work in the countertransference: thinking, dreaming, playing, and game-play in the post-Kleinian and post-Bionian child and adolescent psychotherapy room

The emphasis on projection, splitting, and projective identification in Kleinian and post-Kleinian thinking noted above (Section 4.2.1), and the more recent exploration of dreaming and thinking in Bionian and post-Bionian theory and technique (see Chapter 8), has also contributed much to liberating the field of child psychoanalytic psychotherapy from the strictures of interpretation of conflict, repression, and resistance. This shift to the unconscious inter-psychic container-contained levels of communication has allowed practitioners to work outside the paradigm of the traditional Anna Freudian, Winnicottian, and Kleinian child psychotherapy playroom and to follow the child (and indeed adolescent) patient's lead in playing more interactive age-appropriate competitive games. Rosenfeld's (2016) moving description of his deep intense psychoanalytic work with a psychotic adolescent addicted to video games is a case in point. Rosenfeld was an analysand of Klein and went on to be one of the leading British post-Kleinian thinkers of his time. In this case, he describes his intuitive, but unconventional and non-conformist, decision in his first meeting with the 17-year-old Lorenzo to reverse the prohibition of video games imposed by the previous treating psychiatrist. Instead, Rosenfeld promises his patient to literally follow his lead and go together to the video arcade:

> In fact, it was clinically vital that I learned what happened to the patient while he played, so I decided to go with him to a video-game arcade and get to know the characters he played with, and those he identified with me and with the psychiatrist on my team. The patient projected my attributes on to some of these characters. He wanted to play a game called "Street Killer", and another one called "Street Fighter", both of which are extremely violent: you have to kill the characters with a sword, cut their throats, or hit them very aggressively. When he played with me, Lorenzo won most of the time, and he experienced his triumph omnipotently. But after winning at the games, he came to his session terrified because he had won—as though he had killed me and cut my throat. The same theme was projected onto many external objects; ...
>
> (Rosenfeld, 2016, p. 122)

Alvarez (2010), also from within the post-Kleinian milieu, has similarly challenged the conventional Kleinian wisdom on the primacy of interpretation of infantile impulses and defences, especially denial and splitting, in child psychoanalytic treatment. In her thought-provoking paper *"Beyond the unpleasure principle"* (Alvarez, 1988), she underlines the importance of the positive aspects of play, but with a post-Kleinian twist:

> The child development and Winnicottian question, "What can I do with this object?" is so fundamentally different from what seems to have been the question in the early years of psychoanalysis, "what can I no longer do with this object", or "what can I not do that I previously imagined I could do", or "what can I not do that my mother or father can do", that it is hard to imagine they are both talking about a thing called children's play. And yet the idea that play is denial of more fundamental and painful truths dies hard.
>
> (Alvarez, 1988, p. 9)

Alvarez argues that whilst for some children, interpreting play in terms of defensive denial of suffering, pain, and loss brings relief and psychic growth, for others such interpretations can be soul-destroying. She suggests that children, whose "story of their life is often filled with feelings of loss, impotence, shame and terror", need first to gain some perspective from the often excessive and chronic trauma before they can symbolise it and metabolise it through the therapist's interpretations. This, she believes, the child can achieve through "anticipatory" play, in "phantasies of gain, potency and trust", a form of play that has often been interpreted as manic defence by classical Kleinian analysts:

> Little two-year-olds put a cowboy hat on and nobody tells them, "Now don't forget, you're not daddy yet!" The mother says "Wow, what a tough guy you are today!" She "contains", not only his disappointments, but also his aspirations. She plays the game.
>
> (Alvarez, 1988, p. 11)

She brings a poignant example from her own work with a little boy whose treatment was about to be curtailed due to unforeseen changing family circumstances:

> [A] little boy patient of mine came into a session with a mask, a sort of Marine Serjeant's mask with a big square jaw … and he put it on straightaway. I said that he seemed to want me to see him as strong and powerful today. I then added that I thought that we both knew this was because he was actually scared to death because his treatment was ending prematurely at Christmas… When I implied, however, that the mask was a defence against his anxieties and fears of weakness, he simply shouted "no" in terrible desperation…a few minutes later, when he put on the mask again, I repeated that it was clear that I was to see him as a very strong brave tough fellow today. But this time, I left the second bit out — I did not add that underneath he was really terrified. He listened tensely, and then said slowly and with great relief — "yesss". [Often a child needs] his object, not to remind him of the current sad frightening pathetic reality, but of the potential possibility of being strong one day.
>
> (Alvarez, 1988, p. 10)

In her later writings, Alvarez develops these ideas and focuses on the need to work at a safe distance from the painful, traumatic, and terrifying themes that often overwhelm deprived and abused children, who are grappling with very disturbed states of mind. For these children, their play is often an attempt to build safe fences and boundaries around benign thoughts and imaginings and to keep the menacing "wolves" at bay. Such splitting and denial are often a sign of a child trying to overcome the turmoil and terror within and as such should be respected and even encouraged. She likens psychotherapeutic work with borderline and psychotic patients to that of a chemist working with explosive and inflammable materials,[2] and recommends that psychoanalytic work should take place, step by step, and at a safe distance from the violent and persecutory elements within the patient's mind (Alvarez, 1989, 1996, 2010a, see Chapters 7 and 8 for further development of these ideas).

And yet, for all the emphasis Alvarez places on the importance of structuring in the mind in middle childhood, and of approaching emotionally charged and threatening material with caution and from a distance, under cover and through the language of the game if possible, structured games are nowhere to be found in her writings. As we shall see in Chapters 7 and 8, this omission by Alvarez and by other leading Kleinian and post-Kleinian child analytic psychotherapists has more to do with the deep-seated Kleinian preconceptions on what constitutes "analysable" play and what does not, than the inherent unsuitability of childhood board and card games for analytic psychotherapy: old beliefs indeed "die hard"!

The Italian and South American psychoanalytic schools, also heavily influenced by Kleinian and Bionian thinking, seem to have had fewer preconceptions and proscriptions regarding the analytic playroom and what constitutes therapeutically meaningful play. In this spirit, contemporary thinkers, such as Ferro and before him Baranger and Baranger, have extended Winnicott's ideas on play and the transitional space and Bion's theory of dreaming and thinking, to develop new ways of using play in analytic treatment in general (Baranger, 2012; Baranger & Baranger, 2008) and child analytic treatment in particular (Ferro, 2003; Ferro & Nicoli, 2017; Molinari, 2017b, 2017a). More recently, these ideas have been applied, albeit only in passing, to board games (Brady et al, 2012) and even to the internet and mobile phones (Molinari, 2017a). Ferro has suggested that psychoanalytic work takes place through "transformations in dreaming" and "transformations in game". For Ferro and Molinari, when children play, they in effect "narrate" and try to metabolise and solve what is going on inside them, using whatever "characters" are available at the time (toy animals and cars, blocks, and paper and pencils). This process becomes creative and therapeutically transformative through the mental presence of another person – be they parent, babysitter, or therapist–who is receptive to and capable of containing and digesting anxieties that may arise in the child's play. The therapeutic power of play in child psychotherapy in this context can therefore be seen to be not only in its role as the child's natural form of communication and expression, but also, and even more significantly, in its location in the transitional space, or in what Ferro terms the "bi-personal field": the area of interaction and mutual creative construction, transformation and psychological growth between parent and child, analyst and patient. Like Alvarez, Ferro (2003) stresses that it is essential in our therapeutic work to "use same level of communication as that used by the patient" (Ferro (2003), p. 159) and suggests we do this by joining in with the child's game, creating a jointly narrated story and intuitively moving and playing with the "pawns" (Ferro's own term) or characters appropriate to that game.

Viewed in this light, the specific toys available and games played in the psychotherapy playroom become a side issue. Molinari's writings on the matter are particularly refreshing in the common sense and playfulness underlying her words:

Some analysts think that too many games may distract and disperse the attention and that some types of games will encourage symbolic expression more than others (animals, buildings, a doll's house with family members etc.). Others think that the analyst should feel free to equip his room in the way that suits him best because shared pleasure is not just an ingredient of the game but also a factor in expanding the game itself.

(Molinari, 2017b, p. 177)

...Many children wonder why there are no electronic games [in the analytic playroom] and explicitly ask why not. The usual reason analysts do not offer such games is that they make children passive and think less. However, on the occasions when children have brought some electronic game to the session or some pre-adolescent has asked to be able to watch a music video or clips from a movie together, none of the things we used to dread have actually happened. My personal opinion is that play is more of a mental function than an actual game, and the analyst will keep his role whether he plays a video game or reads a story or chases a real live hamster the child has brought along to the session and let out of its cage.

(Molinari, 2017b, p. 178)

4.7 Conclusion

This chapter has traced the evolution of play and playing over the last hundred years in the field of child analytic treatment. In particular, I have highlighted the often-puzzling controversy surrounding the place of structured games in child analytic treatment, and the increasingly widespread use of these games de facto in the child psychotherapy playroom today. Developing and applying general psychoanalytic theory to playing these traditional board games and card games is in its infancy. The gap between clinical theoretical discourse and practice remains vast. Even today, in supervisions, seminars, and training institutes alike, discussion of the clinical use of games such as Monopoly or UNO is limited, and papers on the subject are few and far between (Krimendahl, 2000). A survey of online papers in the field over the last ten years reveals that there are still relatively few proponents in the literature of the use of card games and board games in the analytic playroom and those articles that have been published are rarely included in the curriculum in child psychoanalytic psychotherapy training programmes. The attitude of many child analytic therapists to this day is still heavily coloured by the traditional view that the rules of competitive structured games restrict and stunt emotional expression and are useful only for psychoeducation, assessment, and strengthening ego functions. As Krimendahl (2000) puts it:

Analysts who work entirely within the metaphor of pretend play instead of linking interpretations to the child's "real" life feel uncomfortable enough, playing board games may seem even more disreputable, making us feel more like overpaid babysitters than analysts.

(Krimendahl 2000, p. 44)

The literature survey presented in this chapter revealed several recent, potentially complementary, developments in thinking on play and games in the field. On the one hand, the last 30 years have seen a burgeoning of contemporary psychoanalytic papers on the therapeutic use of board games and card games as "the therapy itself", emanating mostly from ego psychology and from the relational and intersubjective schools in the US. In parallel, contemporary post-Kleinian, post-Bionian and Winnicottian theory has radically transformed psychoanalytic thinking on therapist–child inter*play* in child analytic treatment. Furthermore, new psychotherapeutic approaches to children who are "difficult to treat" have been developed, from the Kleinian, the Independent/Winnicottian and the Anna Freudian schools of child psychoanalysis. All these have a common thrust towards enlarging intra-psychic and inter-psychic space, with an emphasis on handling explosive and threatening themes from a safe psychic distance, and at an attuned pace, tolerable to the child.

Drawing these strands in theory and technique together with the detailed developmental picture of middle childhood constructed in Chapters 2 and 3, I would suggest it is theoretically and clinically vital to recognise the therapeutic potential inherent in game-play in child psychotherapy. Board games, ball games, and card games are not only the natural arena of play and communication in middle childhood, but their omission from the child analytic playroom seems to have been based more on unfounded preconceptions about play and playing, than on carefully researched analytic developmental and clinical theory. Moreover, it can be seen from the findings presented so far in these chapters that these games are also the natural conduit for intra-psychic and inter-psychic communication in child analytic treatment for children of this age, and contemporary child psychoanalytic thinking has the potential to fit like a glove to the theory and technique of game-play in the analytic playroom. However, whilst these are indeed strong and valid justifications for a reappraisal of the use of these games in the analytic playroom, they are not by themselves sufficient as proof of the worth and the power of game-play as a psychoanalytic language. To this end, the next chapter will be devoted to the theoretical exploration of the concepts of play, playing, games, and game-play, both from the standpoint of child psychoanalytic theory and in the context of 20th-century philosophical enquiry into play and games. The chapters that follow (in part III) will build on this next chapter and further elaborate on such issues of technique and clinical theoretical understanding of game-play in child analytic treatment, whilst considering the developmental picture of middle childhood outlined in Chapter 3. The "proof of the pudding" will be "in the eating": in the clinical theoretical formulation developed, and most tangibly in the clinical vignettes presented alongside the clinical theory in these later chapters.

But first to the basic ingredients of the "pudding", to the conceptual question of game-play as a *bona fide* form of the psychoanalytic language of play, fundamental to the clinical theory building that is the major aim of this research.

Notes

1   The tense of this quote has been changed from past to present tense for the sake of clarity.
2   With reference to Primo Levi's descriptions in his book *The Search for Roots* (Levi, 2001).

Bibliography

Alvarez, A. (1988). Beyond the unpleasure principle: Some preconditions for thinking through play. *Journal of Child Psychotherapy, 14*(2), 1–13.

Alvarez, A. (1989). Development toward the latency period: Splitting and the need to forget in borderline children. *Journal of Child Psychotherapy, 15*(2), 71–83.

Alvarez, A. (1993). Making the thought thinkable: On introjection and projection. *Psychoanalytic Inquiry, 13*(1), 103–122.

Alvarez, A. (1996). Addressing the element of deficit in children with autism: Psychotherapy which is both psychoanalytically and developmentally informed. *Clinical Child Psychology and Psychiatry, 1*(4), 525–537.

Alvarez, A. (2010). Levels of analytic work and levels of pathology: The work of calibration. *The International Journal of Psychoanalysis, 91*(4), 859–878.

Alvarez, A. (2012). *The thinking heart: Three levels of psychoanalytic therapy with disturbed children.* Routledge.

Alvarez, A., & Phillips, A. (1998). The importance of play: A child psychotherapist's view. *Child Psychology and Psychiatry Review, 3*(3), 99–103.

Baranger, M. (2012). The intrapsychic and the intersubjective in contemporary psychoanalysis. *International Forum of Psychoanalysis, 21*(3-4), 130–135.

Baranger, M., & Baranger, W. (2008). The analytic situation as a dynamic field. *The International Journal of Psychoanalysis, 89*(4), 795–826.

Beiser, H. R. (1970). Discussion of children who cheat at games. *Journal of the American Academy of Child Psychiatry, 9*(1), 171.

Beiser, H. R. (1979). Formal games in diagnosis and therapy. *Journal of the American Academy of Child Psychiatry, 18*(3), 480–491.

Bellinson, J. (2000). Shut up and move: The uses of board games in child psychotherapy. *Journal of Infant, Child, and Adolescent Psychotherapy, 1*(2), 23–41.

Bellinson, J. (2002). *Children's Use of Board Games in Psychotherapy.* Jason Aronson.

Bellinson, J. (2013). Games children play: Board games in psychodynamic psychotherapy. *Child and Adolescent Psychiatric Clinics of North America, 22*(2), 283–293.

Bion, W. R. (1962). *Learning from Experience.* Tavistock.

Blake, P. (2011). *Child and Adolescent Psychotherapy.* Karnac Books.

Bleiberg, E., Fonagy, P., & Target, M. (1997). Child psychoanalysis: Critical overview and a proposed reconsideration. *Child and Adolescent Psychiatric Clinics of North America, 6*(1), 1–38.

Caruth, E. G. (1988). How you play the game: On game as play and play as game in the psychoanalytic process. *Psychoanalytic Psychology, 5*(2), 179–192.

Chazan, S. E. (2000). Using the children's play therapy instrument (CPTI) to measure the development of play in simultaneous treatment: A case study. *Infant Mental Health Journal: Official Publication of The World Association for Infant Mental Health, 21*(3), 211–221.

Coriat, I. (1941). The unconscious motives of interest in chess. *The Psychoanalytic Review (1913–1957), 28*, 30.

Eagle, M. N. (2013). *Attachment and Psychoanalysis: Theory, Research, and Clinical Implications.* Guilford Press.

Eigen, M. (1981). The area of faith in Winnicott, Lacan and Bion. *The International Journal of Psychoanalysis, 62*(4), 413–433.

Ellman, S. J. (2010). *When Theories Touch: A Historical and Theoretical Integration of Psychoanalytic Thought.* Karnac Books.

Ferro, A. (2003). *The Bi-Personal Field: Experiences in Child Analysis.* Routledge.

Ferro, A., & Nicoli, L. (2017). *The New Analyst's Guide to the Galaxy: Questions about Contemporary Psychoanalysis.* Karnac Books.

Fonagy, P., Cooper, A., & Wallerstein, R. (Eds.). (1999). *Psychoanalysis on the Move: The Work of Joseph Sandler.* Psychology Press.

Fonagy, P., Steele, M., Steele, H., Moran, G. S., & Higgitt, A. C. (1991). The capacity for understanding mental states: The reflective self in parent and child and its significance for security of attachment. *Infant Mental Health Journal, 12*(3), 201–218.

Fonagy, P., & Target, M. (1996). Playing with reality: I. Theory of mind and the normal development of psychic reality. *International Journal of Psycho-Analysis, 77*, 217–233.

Fonagy, P., & Target, M. (1997). The problem of outcome in child psychoanalysis: Contributions from the Anna Freud Centre. *Psychoanalytic Inquiry, 17*(S1), 58–73.

Fonagy, P., & Target, M. (1998). Mentalization and the changing aims of child psychoanalysis. *Psychoanalytic Dialogues, 8*(1), 87–114.

Freud, A. (1946a). *The Ego and the Mechanisms of Defence.* Univ. Press.

Freud, A. (1946b). *The Psychoanalytical Treatment of Children.* Imago.

Freud, S. (1908). Creative writers and day-dreaming. In J. Strachey (Ed and Trans): *The Standard Edition of the Complete Psychological Works of Sigmund Freud, Volume IX (1906–1908)* (pp. 141–153). Hogarth Press.

Freud, S. (1909). Analysis of a phobia in a five-year-old boy. In J. Strachey (ed and Trans.): *The Standard Edition of the Complete Psychological Works of Sigmund Freud, Volume X* (Vol. 10). Hogarth Press, 1955.

Fried, S. (1992). Chess: A psychoanalytic tool in the treatment of children. *International Journal of Play Therapy, 1*(1), 43.

Geissman, C., & Geissmann, P. (1998). *A History of Child Psychoanalysis.* Psychology Press.

Gergely, G., Fonagy, P., Jurist, E., & Target, M. (Eds.). (2002). *Affect Regulation, Mentalization, and the Development of the Self.* Karnac Books.

Green, A. (2005). *Play and Reflection in Donald Winnicott's Writings.* Karnac Books.

Green, A. H. (1978). Psychiatric treatment of abused children. *Journal of the American Academy of Child & Adolescent Psychiatry, 17*(2), 356–371.

Grunbaum, L., & Mortensen, K. V. (2018). *Psychodynamic Child and Adolescent Psychotherapy: Theories and Methods.* Karnac Books.

Halfon, S., Yılmaz, M., & Çavdar, A. (2019). Mentalization, session-to-session negative emotion expression, symbolic play, and affect regulation in psychodynamic child psychotherapy. *Psychotherapy, 56*(4), 555.

Heimann, P. (1950). On counter-transference. *International Journal of Psycho-Analysis, 31*, 81–84.

Heimann, P. (1977). Further observations on the analyst's cognitive process. *Journal of American Psychoanalytic Association, 25*, 313–333.

Herman, J. L. (2000). Treating the cheater: An ego and self psychological approach to working through of the cheating syndrome in the treatment of latency children. *Journal of Infant, Child, and Adolescent Psychotherapy, 1*(2), 59–70.

Hinshelwood, R. D. (2007). The Kleinian theory of therapeutic action. *The Psychoanalytic Quarterly, 76 Suppl*, 1479–1498.

Horne, A., & Lanyado, M. (2012). *Winnicott's Children: Independent Psychoanalytic Approaches with Children and Adolescents.* Routledge.

Joseph, B. (1985). Transference: The total situation. *International Journal of Psycho-Analysis, 66,* 447–454.

Joseph, B. (1998). Thinking about a playroom. *Journal of Child Psychotherapy, 24*(3), 359–366.

Kegerreis, S. (2009). *Psychodynamic Counselling with Children and Young People: An Introduction.* Palgrave Macmillan.

Kernberg, O. F. (1995). *Object Relations Theory and Clinical Psychoanalysis.* Jason Aronson.

Kernberg, P. F. (2000). The forms of play. In K. von Klitzing, P. Tyson, & D. Burgin (Eds.), *Psychoanalysis in Childhood and Adolescence* (pp. 25–41). Karger Publishers.

Kernberg, P. F., Ritvo, R., Keable, H., & of Child, T. A. A. (2012). Practice parameter for psychodynamic psychotherapy with children. *Journal of the American Academy of Child & Adolescent Psychiatry, 51*(5), 541–557.

Kernberg, P. F., Weiner, A. S., & Bardenstein, K. K. (2008). *Personality Disorders in Children and Adolescents.* Basic Books.

Khan, M. (2012). *Hidden Selves: Between Theory and Practice in Psychoanalysis.* Karnac Books.

Klein, M. (1927). The psychological principles of infant analysis. *The International Journal of Psycho-Analysis, 8,* 25.

Klein, M. (1932). The technique of analysis in the latency period. In M. Klein, *The Psychoanalysis of Children.* Hogarth Press.

Klein, M. (1975). Personification in the play of children. In Klein, M., *Love, Guilt and Reparation and other works 1921–1945* (pp. 199–209). Hogarth Press.

Klein, M. (1980). The psycho-analytic play technique: Its history and significance: 1955. In Klein, M., *Envy and gratitude and other works: 1946–1963* (pp. 122–140). Hogarth Press.

Klein, M. (2011). The technique of analysis in the latency period. In Klein, M., *The Psycho-Analysis of Children* (pp. 58–79). Random House.

Krimendahl, E. (2000). "Did you see that?": A relational perspective on children who cheat in analysis. *Journal of Infant, Child, and Adolescent Psychotherapy, 1*(2), 43–58.

Lanyado, M., & Horne, A. (2009). *The Handbook of Child and Adolescent Psychotherapy: Psychoanalytic Approaches.* Routledge.

Levinson, B. M. (1972). Use of checkers in therapy. *Psychological Reports, 30*(3), 846–846.

Levy, A. J. (2008). The therapeutic action of play in the psychodynamic treatment of children: A critical analysis. *Clinical Social Work Journal, 36*(3), 281–291.

Loomis, E. A. (1976). Use of checkers in handling resistance. In C. E. Schaefer (Ed.), *The Therapeutic Use of Child's Play* (p. 385). Jason Aronson.

Mahler, M. S., Pine, F., & Bergman, A. (1975). *The Psychological Birth of the Human Infant.* Symbiosis and Individuation.

Meeks, J. E. (1970). Children who cheat at games. *Journal of the American Academy of Child Psychiatry, 9*(1), 157–170.

Meeks, J. E. (2000). Reflections on children who cheat at games: A commentary. *Journal of Infant, Child, and Adolescent Psychotherapy, 1*(2), 71–75.

Midgley, N. (2012). Peter Heller's child analysis with Anna Freud: The significance of the case for the history of child psychoanalysis. *Journal of the American Psychoanalytic Association, 60*(1), 45–70.

Midgley, N., & Vrouva, I. (2013). *Minding the Child: Mentalization-Based Interventions with Children, Young People and their Families*. Routledge.

Molinari, E. (2017a). *Field Theory in Child and Adolescent Psychoanalysis: Understanding and Reacting to Unexpected Developments*. Taylor & Francis.

Molinari, E. (2017b). Variations on a theme: Child and adolescent analysis. In Ferro, A., (Ed.), *Contemporary Bionian Theory and Technique in Psychoanalysis* (pp. 176–216). Routledge.

Muller, N., & Midgley, N. (2020). The clinical challenge of mentalization-based therapy with children who are in "pretend mode." *Journal of Infant, Child, and Adolescent Psychotherapy, 19*(1), 16–24.

Oren, A. (2008). The use of board games in child psychotherapy. *Journal of Child Psychotherapy, 34*(3), 364–383.

O'Shaughnessy, E. (1981). A commemorative essay on W.R. Bion's theory of thinking. *Journal of Child Psychotherapy, 7*(2), 181–192.

Peller, L. E. (1954). Libidinal phases, ego development, and play. *The Psychoanalytic Study of the Child, 9*, 178–198.

Rosenfeld, D. (2016). "Lorenzo": Psychotic addiction to video games. In Marzi, A., (Ed.), *Psychoanalysis, Identity, and the Internet*, pp. 135–165. Routledge.

Saar, N., Bar, M., & Gothelf, D. (2017). Understanding cheating in board games play therapy with children. *Sihot/Dialogue: Israel Journal of Psychotherapy, 31*(3), 211–217.

Sandler, J., Kennedy, H., & Tyson, R. L. (1980). *Technique of Child Psychoanalysis: Discussions with Anna Freud*. Harvard University Press.

Sandler, J., & Rosenblatt, B. (1962). The concept of the representational world. *The Psychoanalytic Study of the Child, 17*, 128–145.

Segal, H. (1989). *Melanie Klein*. Karnac Books.

von Hug-Hellmuth, H. (1921). On the technique of child-analysis. *The International Journal of Psycho-Analysis, 2*, 287.

von Hug-Hellmuth, H., Putnam, J. J., & Stevens, M. (1919). A study of the mental life of the child. *Psychoanalytic Review, 6*(1), 65–88.

Wallerstein, R. S. (2001). The growth and transformation of American ego psychology. *Journal of the American Psychoanalytic Association, 50*(1), 135–168.

Winnicott, D. W. (1971a). Playing: A theoretical statement. In Winnicott, D.W., *Playing and Reality* (pp. 38–52). Penguin Books.

Winnicott, D. W. (1971b). The use of an object and relating through identifications. In Winnicott, D.W., *Playing and Reality* (pp. 101–111). Penguin Books.

Winnicott, D. W. (1989). Notes on play. In C. Winnicott, R. Shepherd, & M. Davis (Eds.), *Psychoanalytic Explorations* (pp. 59–63). Karnac Books.

Chapter 5

Questions of play, playing, and game-play

5.1 A question of technique: communication, play, and structured games in the analytic playroom

Thanks to Klein and Winnicott's innovations in theory and technique, play has in many ways usurped the more traditional Freudian verbal techniques in the field of child psychotherapy as the royal road to the child's unconscious (it seems it was Erikson (1940) who first coined this phrase). It is pretend and creative play, and verbal interpretation of such play, that has been hallowed and revered in the kingdom of child psychoanalysis. As we have seen, the criticisms aimed most often against structured games are that they neither constitute pretend play nor are they a product of the imagination. Historically, these games have been perceived more as a therapeutic dead end leading to a solid brick wall of defences rather than a royal road leading to the palace of the unconscious. But I would contend that this argument misses the point on a fundamental level. Just as the analytic play technique with young children is regarded as a valid psychoanalytic technique despite its very different form compared to verbal technique with adults, so there should be no reason to predicate validity of technique on similarity of form vis-à-vis game-play. Playing structured games is certainly not pure pretend play per se, but this still does not mean that these games do not enable access to the inner world of the older child. I would even go as far as to suggest that the space for imagination and pretence in these games is in fact far greater than is generally accepted (a point that will be taken up in detail in part III).

Klein's analytic play technique and Anna Freud's therapeutic use of children's drawings, imaginary stories, and daydreams were devised as adaptations of Freud's techniques to the needs and capacities of young children. The central question of validity of Klein and Anna Freud's approaches was not whether these techniques constitute play, but whether they allow access and interpretation of unconscious material. Likewise, it is theoretically and clinically imperative not to confound the question of whether game-play is a valid form of play, analytically and philosophically speaking, with the question of whether structured games constitute a royal road to the unconscious and a valid psychoanalytic mode of communication for the average school-aged child.

DOI: 10.4324/9781003425229-7

These two questions of access to the unconscious and of play are, as it happens, closely connected, but this need not necessarily be the case. Just as Ogden writes of his verbal discussions of literature or films with his patients as examples of Winnicottian playing (and Bionian dreaming) (Ogden, 2008), it could equally be said that structured games are not play as defined philosophically, but could be used for playing, dreaming, and communicating the Winnicottian and Bionian sense in child psychodynamic treatment. Or, conversely, these games might be regarded as play philosophically, but might not be useful psychoanalytically. Or they might be defined as play philosophically, but not constitute Winnicottian creative play, and yet still serve as a language of communication in the psychotherapeutic context. This latter issue has been discussed in depth by Green (1997, 2005), Lenormand (2018), amongst others, who have contended that some forms of play are in fact the antithesis of Winnicottian playing, but are central to the analytic process. I shall return to this last point in Chapter 6.

5.2 Game-play: the royal road to the unconscious of the wave-particle child?

Melanie Klein turned to play with young children because she realised that this was the child's natural mode of communication and she saw children's play as a projection of their inner world and phantasies. Later, as we have seen, play was reformulated by Winnicott as a therapeutic end in and of itself. Notwithstanding, Klein invented the psychoanalytic play technique first and foremost as a method of "understanding the patient's mind and conveying to him what goes on in it" (Klein, 1975, p. 129). This aspect of child's play, "simply" as a useful psychoanalytic tool for accessing the child's unconscious and communicating with it, is still relevant today, as reflected in the following representative statements of principle on child analytic technique and practice:

> Throughout a child analysis, play remains a primary means of communication, revealing the child's coping strategies and, especially, serving as the primary medium for the playing out of interactions among the child's unconscious, the object world, and the transference relationship.
>
> (Lang, 2007, pp. 937–938, excerpt from summary of
> APA panel on Play in the Psychoanalytic Situation)

> In the psychoanalysis of children, it is children's play that offers us the easiest access to the inner world of the child. At the same time, children's play and playing with children have caused the most headaches over the question of what is correct therapeutic technique. We often experience play as getting out of hand, as breaking the bounds of norms and rules.... Children's play can ... also get lost in narcissistic over-inflation of self-importance, which blanks out the disturbing reality of others and of triangulating thought, or which in obsessive repetition acts as defence against all forms of threatening inner objects.

Nevertheless it is play that allows us to come into contact with children and their unconscious inner world.

(Günter, 2018, p. 1, from textbook on Technique in Child and Adolescent Analysis)

Psychoanalytic technique has always been established clinically and theoretically in spiral fashion: first, the clinical problem encountered (how to reach the unconscious and communicate with the patient's psyche in particular states of mind or in a particular clinical situation); then the suggestion of new technique premised on a combination of theory and clinical experience; and then the application of the new clinical technique suggested, exploration through clinical examples leading finally to a deepening and expansion of clinical-theoretical understanding. The clinical theoretical premise that I shall now put forward for examination and discussion in this chapter is in essence a restatement of what has been established vis-à-vis game-play in the literature critique up to now: *Game-play as we have seen in chapters 2 and 3 is the vernacular of middle childhood and therefore should be regarded as the language to learn and the tongue to speak in child analytic psychotherapies, if therapists are to meet children of this age on their terms and on their level.*

Just as Freud used dreams and verbal associations to access spontaneity and "sincerity" (Freud, 1905), and to circumvent defences in adults; and Klein used the imaginary play of younger children because she observed that play is where children frankly and freely express themselves; it follows logically that the key to working psychoanalytically with school-aged children should lie in finding the most natural channel of communication, where defences are least rigid and least active. As discussed in Chapters 2 and 3, for most wave-particle children, this frank and free channel of communication is the arena of game-play: the traditional games of middle childhood, games such as *War, Cheat, Monopoly*, football, and basketball. Even if these games are not the pure spontaneous product of the child's imagination as Klein would perhaps have preferred, and even if they have structure and rules and also a marked tendency to get out of hand (to paraphrase Günter's words above), I would argue that they are nonetheless most likely to facilitate "contact with children and their unconscious world". This is probably true to a greater extent than if we listen to the verbal narrative ramblings of their minds, or if we offer these same children creative materials and dolls and cars to play with. For now, this statement of technique can only be proposed as a strong supposition, based on literature critique presented in chapters 2 and 3, everyday observational evidence, and common sense. The theoretical "proof" and the clinical discussion and evidence will occupy the remaining chapters of this book.

School-aged children are only verbal beings in theory: their speech is often superficial, monosyllabic, monotonic, and artificial, a somewhat stilted imitation of adult verbal communication. So play is the logical place to look if the unconscious is to be accessed. For children who talk and draw freely, who use dolls and cars for imaginary projective play, child psychoanalytic theory and practice, as it stands today might be sufficient. I would nevertheless reiterate, in line with Bellinson (2000, 2002), Beiser (1979), Krimendahl (2000), Meeks (1970, 2000), Oren (2008), and others, that it is often developmentally important for older children to engage in age-appropriate game-play in the therapeutic setting, whatever their capacity for imaginary and creative play (as shall be seen in the next three chapters). However, for many children, the issue of access to and communication with their unconscious is both more urgent and more of a challenge. Most boys aged 9+ refuse point-blank to engage in free imaginary or creative play at all, inside and outside the therapy room, and there are a large number of older children whose seemingly imaginative and creative play is in reality just as monotonic, monosyllabic, and anchored in their false selves as their verbal communications. Such difficulties in analytic treatment are alluded to by Günter above – play lost in "narcissistic over-inflation" or in psychic deadness – and have been well documented elsewhere, particularly for more disorganised, prerepresentational, and disturbed children (Alvarez, 2012; Bellinson, 2002; Ferro, 2003; Molinari, 2017; Slade, 1994). It is for these children or in these clinical situations that I believe game-play is not only useful, but becomes essential in analytic treatment for the school-aged child. This is precisely because game-play constitutes the natural language of communication in middle childhood, the dialect of play that is found ubiquitously in school playgrounds, back gardens, and on the streets across the globe, a language that I contend belongs equally to the child psychotherapy room.

The long-standing argument of psychoanalytic theorists and clinicians against the use of structured games in the analytic playroom is that these games are used by the child more often than not to "ward off, disguise, or hide the fantasies... [and] serve to defend against the behavioural dramatization of play" (Solnit, 1987, p. 215). But experience inside and outside the therapy room tells us differently: game-play is in fact where spontaneity, libido, rage, and envy often come to the fore in middle childhood, as any child knows intuitively and as any parent or educator learns viscerally when watching children of this age engaged in game-play inside and outside the home. Some psychoanalytic writers recognise this natural shift towards structured games in older children, but still maintain that the therapeutic work can only take place in so-called imaginative and creative "free" play and it is only in the framework of such "pretend play" that the child can project their inner world into the play and into the transference (Blake, 2011; Gilmore & Meersand, 2013; Meersand, 2009).

I bring here the following quote, representative of many more recent papers published on the subject, both as evidence of a change in attitudes towards game-play in child analytic treatment, and as evidence of the ongoing lacuna regarding the elements of play in game-play. This extract comes from a seminal paper on the subject, based on the work of a long-standing study group at the Anna Freud Centre and entitled *Play: Its role in child analysis* (Gavshon, 1989):

> With the establishment of the repression barrier, latency activities become more ego orientated. Competitive games requiring rules and skills, drawing and building models, provide the forum for analytic work. *The play as such is not "the*

thing". It is the defensive and affective expression surrounding the preoccupation in the activity that provides the material for analysis. The fear of success and failure, the urgency to triumph, the rage or despair on losing and the wish to cheat and humiliate the therapist are related to feelings which are linked with the past.

(Gavshon, 1989, p. 48, emphases added)

Gavshon recognises the therapeutic power of competitive games in rekindling feelings and conflicts related to the past, a very significant step in the adaptation of analytic treatment to middle childhood, and yet she dismisses game-play itself as "not the thing", not play. It is this latter statement that I wish to contend.

In this context, the arguments against the use of structured games in analytic treatment can be restated in the form of two major criticisms: the first that the rules and structure of these games preclude free play, by definition, and likewise bar access to the unconscious; and the second, that there is little to interpret in structured games by dint of their predetermined content, and therefore limited analytic work can be done. The first criticism, I contend, is illusory; the second falls away with the changing emphasis in psychoanalytic treatment from content to process and from one-person to two-person psychology.

5.3   Psychoanalysis as a structured game

Clear structure and predefined settings and roles have been part and parcel of analytic work almost since the inception of psychoanalysis, as has the flexibility and changing nature of the very rules. It is an illusion that psychoanalytic treatment has no rules: it has many, and for good reason. Psychoanalysis in fact relies on its own rules and clear well-defined framework and structure to enable patients and analysts alike to explore the wilds and uncharted territories of the unconscious, each according to their preassigned and mutually agreed roles. It is these very rules that allow analytic work to take place through the security they confer: safety and stability that endow the patient with the confidence, the freedom, and the courage to give freer rein to their unconscious and to communicate with it more authentically, with sincerity, in Freud's words (Freud, 1905). It follows, therefore, that to discount structured games as invalid as a tool for psychoanalytic work precisely because these games are rule-bound and have some predetermined parameters is a somewhat self-contradictory argument. As discussed in detail in Sections 5.6 and 6.2, I would even argue that in many ways the rules and preconditions in the games of middle childhood serve the same function as in psychoanalysis itself: to act as a protective container in which phantasies, drives, and impulses can be expressed safely, relatively freely, and sincerely. Freud himself referred to the "game" of psychoanalysis and the associated "rules of the game" recommended to ensure efficacy of treatment (Freud, 1913):

In what follows I shall endeavour to collect together for the use of practising analysts some of the rules for the beginning of the treatment...Their justification is that they are *simply rules of the game* which acquire their importance from their relation to the general plan of the game.

(Freud, 1913, p. 123, emphases added)

But even Freud did not always adhere to the rules he himself prescribed: it is apparent from his own case histories and from much that has been written since, that Freud was anything but a *tabula rasa* for most of his patients, and he also chatted more spontaneously and interactively than one would expect during analytic sessions. Some rules were established purely and simply as a consequence of Freud's personal preferences: he himself explained the origins of the analyst's position behind the couch in his discomfort in "being stared at by other people for eight hours a day (or more)" (Freud, 1913, p. 134). The "rules of the game" instituted by Freud have also changed with time. Some have been modified, others newly formulated and subsequently carved in stone, even though they were not originally fundamental tenets of psychoanalysis as dictated by Freud. The rules of Kleinian child psychoanalysis, as presented by Klein herself and by such Kleinian figures as Hannah Segal and Betty Joseph, appear very stringent: a separate box of very specific toys for each child; analyst as observer of the child's play rather than as joint player in interaction with the child; and the injunction to "interpret, interpret, interpret". Like Freud, Klein herself did not always adhere to these rules: she was known to have gone outside to her garden with the child when she felt it expedient (Klein, 1961) and she frequently took active interactive roles in the child's make-believe games (see Chapter 4), in addition to "pure" observational and interpretative work. Winnicott, too, adapted technique to meet the needs and capacities of his patients. Although he unequivocally dismissed the use of traditional childhood games with rules and boundaries as unsuitable for use in psychotherapy, he invented the squiggle *game* (sic), stipulated various rules around the game (taking turns, use of pencil and plain paper, closed eyes when initiating the squiggle), interpreted psychoanalytically what emerged from the game, and promoted the game as a recommended technique for children who were less inclined or able to play freely (Claman, 1980; Winnicott, 2018).

For Freud, the rules he laid down were recommendations, guidelines to be followed not unconditionally, but flexibly and with wisdom, as determined by the "constellation" of the particular patient's psyche and the course of their analysis:

> I think I am well advised, however, to call these rules "recommendations" and not to claim any unconditional acceptance for them. The extraordinary diversity of the psychical constellations concerned, *the plasticity of all mental processes and the wealth of determining factors oppose any mechanization of the technique*; and they bring it about that a course of action that is as a rule justified may at times prove ineffective, whilst one that is usually mistaken may once in

a while lead to the desired end. These circumstances however do not prevent us from laying down a procedure for the physician which is effective on the average.

(Freud, 1913, p. 123, emphases added)

...the various forms of disease [and by corollary the various age groups too CM] treated by us cannot be all dealt with by the same technique.

(Freud, 1955, p. 165, quoted in Gunter (2018))

These lines embody two critical aspects of rules in the psychoanalytic game: First the necessity for rules and setting as container and as reference point and grounding for both patient and therapist (to use modern-day terminology); and second, the counterpoint to the necessity of rules–flexibility when implementing rules, imposing limits and bounded frameworks. There should be "no mechanisation of technique", one size most definitely does not fit all ages and all "forms of disease". Nevertheless, in the field of child psychoanalysis, especially, these words of counsel from the founder of psychoanalysis were frequently forgotten out of overzealous devotion to the founding fathers and mothers of psychoanalysis, giving rise to the conflicting and often confounding prescriptions and proscriptions around child and adult psychoanalytic technique that still abound today. The majority of textbooks on child psychodynamic psychotherapy and child analysis advise against the use of structured games of any sort, as noted in the foregoing literature critique. And yet many of the textbooks published today include chapters on analytic work where the internet or electronic devices and games play a central role in the treatment (Blake, 2011; Meersand & Gilmore, 2017). Likewise, case presentations at conferences and papers in journals very rarely refer to board games and card games in psychoanalytically oriented work with children, but increasingly cases where online games and social network platforms feature significantly in the work with the child and adolescent patient appear in the literature and in conference programmes. As if what was chastised in structured games is acceptable in electronic form, perhaps because when the child chooses to bring their mobile phone into the session, it is the child's spontaneous gesture and the game or video clip shared can be viewed as an extension of the child's inner world. Furthermore, de facto, the therapist has little say today in whether the child arrives with or without their phone. Whereas the decision of whether to have structured competitive games in the therapy room, and if so which ones, belongs more to the therapist or to the public clinic directorship, than to the child.

This broadening in attitude to different forms of games and play is refreshing and in effect acts as indirect support of psychodynamic play with structured games, even if direct references to such casework are still few and far between:

Play occurs in whatever playground contemporary culture provides. If child patients resist playing with the toys of yesteryear and prefer contemporary ones, they are in sync with their time. Because children inevitably express their inner life through the iconic elements— heroes, narratives, media, and modalities— that their culture provides, it is the obligation of child clinicians to keep pace with their patients in order to understand them...Clinicians must change too and must learn the contemporary language of childhood.

(Meersand & Gilmore, 2017, p. 115)

Günter (2018) maintains that this tension between the "correct application of psychoanalysis and the necessity of handling it flexibly in terms of technique" has occupied the field of psychoanalysis since its inception. And indeed, in line with the more eclectic psychoanalytic thinking of recent decades, this emphasis on elasticity and adaptation of technique has increasingly been echoed by writers from many different psychoanalytic schools of thought, also in the child analytic field (Alvarez, 2012; Blake, 2011; Günter, 2018; Meersand & Gilmore, 2017; Molinari, 2017; Slade, 1994). Furthermore, I would add that treating the rules of games flexibly and creatively is, as we shall see, at the root of the therapeutic power and plasticity of structured games as such.

5.4 Content interpretation versus interpretative intervention and process

The second major argument against rule-bound games as outlined above has its origins in the Freudian–Kleinian emphasis on interpretation of content. This argument can best be stated thus: structured games have predetermined content and "plot" and therefore interpretation of content is of little consequence. When a child kills off the mother doll in the midst of a dramatisation of a make-believe story of their own invention, such play begs interpretation of its unconscious meanings; when a child captures the queen in a game of chess, interpreting this as a sign of unconscious murderous rage against the internal maternal object has less clinical-theoretical validity. This criticism of structured games is not easily refuted, albeit the space for imaginative and projective use of many board games, ball games, and card games is broader and deeper than appears at first glance. Which game is chosen, what character within the game is adopted, and the meaning with which the child infuses the game all have therapeutic and interpretative significance. Many of the early papers on game-play concentrated on the symbolic aspects, particularly in games of checkers and chess (Coriat, 1941; Fried, 1992; Levinson, 1972; Loomis, 1976). Nevertheless, content interpretation can never constitute the therapeutic backbone of structured games, precisely because the content is at least partially predetermined.

I believe that the crux of the counterargument to the criticism of a dearth of analysable narrative content in game-play lies elsewhere: in the change in technique and approach to interpretative work in child and adult analytic treatment over the last thirty years. The field has moved on from the days of the analyst as a *tabula rasa*, neutral observer and interpreter of unconscious projected and repressed content. A shift has taken place in many psychoanalytic schools of thought away from interpretation of the content of the child's play, fantasies, and daydreams in terms of Kleinian paranoid-schizoid anxieties and themes or Freudian oedipal themes of rivalry, patricide, castration, and masturbatory obsessions. The emphasis for practitioners from these schools is no longer on insights and interpretation of the transference, but on understanding the transference–countertransference matrix, on the therapeutic relationship itself, and on the therapist as container for the intra-psychic pain and distress of the patient. It is the unconscious *dynamics* as opposed to unconscious *content* that has taken centre stage. As shall be seen, these are aspects of the psychoanalytic encounter that all naturally come to the fore when playing the competitive, interactive games of middle childhood.

Contemporary papers from many different psychoanalytic authors abound with comments relating to children's impatience with therapist's verbal comments and their tendency to reject even the most simple observation of their psyche out of hand. "Don't yak – let's play" (Günter, 2018, p. 17), "Shut up and move" (Bellinson, 2000), and "No talking... let's get on with playing!" (Slade, 1994, p. 90) are common utterances in child analytic treatment. Slade, amusingly, continues her description of this last interaction with the child thus: "When I suggested that we could play *and* talk, she [a little girl, just five years old] said, quite emphatically, Naaaahhhh!" (Slade, 1994, p. 90). Slade here is referring to treatment of pre-schoolers: even children as young as her patients, with all their oedipal exhibitionism and lack of inhibitions, shy away from "saying it as it is" or indeed even just hearing "it as it is":

> In many instances, I found myself left with no choice but to simply play with the child and—for the time being—to abandon my own need to deduce the meaning of the play and somehow communicate it to my little patient. Often this left me with the uneasy feeling that I somehow wasn't acting like a therapist, nor was what I was doing really therapy.
>
> (Slade, 1994, p. 81)

It seems to be that the field of child psychotherapy is at times at odds with itself over attitudes towards the role of play and playing, per se, in the analytic playroom. On the one hand, the therapeutic and developmental value of playing with children, as described here by Slade, has been understood de facto since time immemorial. This is therapist "as an organizing, enhancing, and engaged play partner...; in many instances... of enormous value clinically and developmentally [in and of itself]" (Slade, 1994, p. 90, p. 81), and a view of playing "in health and for health" understood and conceptualised to new depths by Winnicott (1971, as outlined in the previous chapter). And yet, as in society at large so in the psychoanalytic world, play has often been frowned upon and juxtaposed with productive work and "deep and meaningful" verbal interpretations. Birch has voiced this view of therapeutic play beautifully in a case study of a three-year-old published in 1997. Her thoughts on the subject are equally applicable to game-play with older children as to pretend play with younger children:

> The high value our culture places on rational, logical, scientific thought often leaves me, like many other child therapists, feeling vaguely guilty when our time with children is spent "just playing." And yet, in case after case, although the so-called real issues that led the child's family to bring her to therapy are rarely addressed directly, and although we spend our working hours unprofessionally crawling around on all fours, growling, or hiding under tables, [or likewise kicking around a football, and playing irreverent games of War and Cheat CM], the child gets better. There is genuine communication going on, in a medium native to the child, though all but forgotten by most adults.
>
> (Birch, 1997, p. 58)

Here Birch is describing much more than "just playing". Reading such case studies, it is clear that therapist "enactments" in play, be it "growling on all fours" or "hiding under the table" in pretend fear of a scary monster function therapeutically as *bona fide* interpretative interventions and speak to the child's aggressions and anxieties as loud and clear as any classical Kleinian verbal interpretation. This aspect of playing with the child in psychotherapy goes well beyond "simply playing" and can be understood as content and process interpretation through action, "interpretation in game". I would argue that what is true for make-believe play with pre-schoolers is as true for game-play with school-aged children. By entering the game and responding to the child's play through the game itself, in a manner that communicates to the child something of their inner world: whether via a slight change in narrative in the imaginative role play or doll play; or through an attuned response to cheating in a game of *War*; through actions and interventions in the play itself; we can reach the child at a level that they can understand and internalise, often unconsciously or preconsciously. Like many similar recently published books on the subject, Blake's (2011) textbook *Child and Adolescent Psychotherapy* is full of clinical illustrations of these contemporary "psychoanalytic techniques of play". He describes how "taking the material out of the metaphor [of play]" can be "disruptive and detrimental to the [therapeutic] work" with children and suggests joining in the play and speaking as the character, or even as the object at play:

> If a child is cutting a piece of plasticine one can speak as the plasticine: 'Oh no, I don't want to be cut up; I need to stay together.'
>
> ...Still playful, but a little more observational, is the comment, 'I think the plasticine doesn't like being cut up, I think it wants to stay together'.
>
> ...An even more removed position, although still staying in the play, is to become more 'technical' about the properties of plasticine. This level of entry may require a comment such as, 'Plasticine is interesting, isn't it. It is all soft

and easily cut up, but it can hold its shape when it is put back together. It's as if it has never been cut up'.

(Blake, 2011, pp. 221–222)

This technique is particularly useful in treating more disturbed, pre-representational children, as Hezi Cohen (1995) has observed. Cohen argues that children in borderline states of mind cannot relate to or refer to the therapist as a transformative separate object, but instead need the therapist as self-object (Kohut, 1977) or subjective object (Winnicott, 1971). The therapist is conceived of by the child as part of their own inner psychic reality, and therefore "has to address the child's psychic reality through a total immersion in the interaction" (Cohen, 1995, p. 36), preferably expressing therapeutic interventions through the voice of whatever play object is centre stage in the game, be it a ping pong ball, a toy soldier, or the football goal itself. Viewed in this light, "the totality of the intervention is the essence of the treatment" (Cohen, 1995, p. 36).

This form of interpretation in game can be conceived of as consisting of two intrinsically connected psychoanalytic techniques: the play itself and the metabolism and transmuting interpretations, verbal and non-verbal. The therapist cannot be an "organising and enhancing" agent in the child's play without interpretations in play and game that serve to voice (not necessarily verbally or explicitly) and metabolise the child's unconscious and preconscious feelings, impulses, conflicts, and anxieties. For it is the metabolism of the anxieties that lead to an expansion of the area of play. But likewise, it is the area of play itself, the transitional space, however restricted, that allows the interpretations in game to take place, often where verbal interpretations fall flat or are summarily dismissed by the child ("Shut up, Dr Slade!").

If then it is recommended child analytic practice to talk and interpret within the framework and narrative of the child's play, even as a piece of plasticine, then surely responding through the game-play – by capturing or not capturing the vulnerable pawn in a game of chess or by negotiating the rights and wrongs of a penalty called in a game of football – is an equally valid form of therapeutic interlocution? Children do not like being observed (maybe few of us do, no matter how old we are), nor do children appreciate comments on their behaviour and feelings, and they take even less kindly to interpretations relating to their home life and family relations. But children can hear comments and actions made within the language of make-believe play or game-play, and they can relate to these in the game, respond and absorb them at different levels of consciousness.

Therapeutically speaking, Winnicott emphasises that it is "only when [play] is 'experienced' by the subject and then 'reflected back' in a shared area, that playing is liable to bring about a subjective mutation" (Lenormand, 2018, p. 86). I would suggest that the corollary is also true: if a game, any game, with dolls, toy cars, or playing cards, is experienced by the child and reflected back, then it can be regarded as therapeutic playing, which can bring about subjective mutation in the child's psyche.

And "at the same time and on another level", I would argue that since today the therapeutic relationship and the transference–countertransference matrix (see Chapter 8) are recognised by most as at the focus of analytic work today (Ferro, 1992; Joseph, 1985; Slade, 1994), then the fact that structured games do not lend themselves easily to narrative content interpretation becomes fairly irrelevant. On the contrary, given the raw and powerful emotional reactions to competition and rivalry, losing and winning, cheating and playing by the rules, aroused by games such as *War, UNO,* draughts/chequers, or basketball and football, and their visceral interactive nature, these games can in actuality be a useful, even vital, therapeutic tool through which to access and work through transference–countertransference issues, in a child-friendly, non-threatening manner.

5.5   But is this really play?

Many writers on the subject of play have differentiated between the Latin word for play, *ludere*, which refers to play in the context of sports, games with rules, but also poetic, often eroticised, play with words; and the Greek *paidia*, the frolicking of children and animals, which emphasises free expression, and absence of external constraints (Lenormand, 2018). The English language has two words to describe these activities: *game* (which most likely has its roots in the Viking-Norse languages) and *play* (from the Old English word *plegan, plegian* for engaging oneself, making music, exercising, and rejoicing), words which are used sometimes interchangeably and sometimes to denote distinct but related concepts. In many languages however, the concepts of play, playing and games, are denoted by a single word (jeu-jouer in French; משחק-לשחק in Hebrew; spielen-Spiel in German) with multiple related meanings combining the concepts of action, engagement, pleasure, and joyous movement. Some philosophers have drawn a conceptual distinction between "play" and "games" and have suggested that competition, rules, and the drive to win necessarily stand in opposition to the imaginative and creative aspects of play (for discussion and review of this topic see: Caillois, 2001; Deakin & Tiellet Nunes, 2009; Feezell, 2010; Malaby, 2007; Nguyen, 2017; Ridge, 2019). In child psychoanalytic psychotherapy and child development in particular, this distinction has been widely accepted and has become entrenched. I believe that this distinction between play and game is misplaced and even conceptually and clinically unhelpful. The child, like the adult, plays within the framework of their cognitive, physical, and social abilities. The toddler plays, building towers with wooden blocks and knocking them down, because that is the form and level of play possible, in accordance with their cognitive, physical, and social development. The school-aged child builds houses with Lego, or metaphorically destroys the parents' houses in a game of *Monopoly*, precisely because at this age they have developed the capacity to play at these higher levels of cognitive, physical, and social complexity. But this increasing complexity does not, I believe, change the essence of play and potential for playfulness inherent in the game. In fact, observation reveals that the creativity and imagination employed by the school-aged child is far greater than that of the toddler building and knocking down towers. And this is as it should be, developmentally speaking (Malberg & Raphael-Leff, 2012; Plaut, 1979). The greater element of reality and rules in the schoolagers' *games* does not preclude per se creativity and spontaneity. The make-believe element – "it is only a game" – remains as central to the child's game of *Lego* or *Ludo* as to the toddler's game. Play, like work, has its own developmental line. Infants play and (re)create differently from school-aged children, who play differently from adolescents and then again from adults.

Caillois' (2001) definition of play in terms of six core features is useful here:

1 *Free: in which playing is not obligatory; if it were, it would at once lose its attractive and joyous quality as diversion;*
2 *Separate: circumscribed within limits of space and time, defined and fixed in advance; [though these boundaries are permeable CM]*
3 *Uncertain: the course of which cannot be determined, nor the result attained beforehand, and some latitude for innovations being left to the player's initiative;*
4 *Unproductive: creating neither goods, nor wealth, nor new elements of any kind; and, except for the exchange of property among the players, ending in a situation identical to that prevailing at the beginning of the game;*
5 *Governed by rules: under conventions that suspend ordinary laws, and for the moment establish new legislation, which alone counts;*
6 *Make-believe: accompanied by a special awareness of a second reality or of a free unreality, as against real life.*

(Caillois, 2001, pp. 9–10)

Lenormand (2018) follows Caillois' thinking in her learned discussion on play and playing in child psychoanalysis. She points out that rules do not automatically block or interfere with play: on the contrary, according to Caillois' definition, rules can be seen to be a prerequisite for play:

However operational Winnicott's distinction between play and game may be, it needs to be nuanced. I want to suggest that the "separate" space of play, to use the metaphor of Caillois (1958), is nothing other than the fruit *of rules (however minimal they may be) that are capable of opening up the "potential space" that Winnicott has described* so brilliantly.

This has two consequences: first, the presence of rules is not enough in itself to create a real obstacle to the emergence of something new and, thus, to any form of playing, since all play, on the contrary, implies at least one rule. As Winnicott's work strives to show with the squiggle game and the spatula game (note here the use of the word game), innovation and the discovery of the self remain possible within the framework of a game that is sufficiently open.

(Caillois (1958, p. 96, emphases added)

Thus, the rules of the game can once again be seen to be a red herring when it comes to distinguishing between play and not-play. Rather the creativity and playfulness of play are determined by the openness of the game itself; by its nature as a "moving target" (Malaby, 2007, p. 103, quoted in Nyugen (2017, p. 20)), involving the suspension of reality and a different mode of interaction with the self and with others; by its separation from the routine tasks of life, often accompanied by a different consciousness and level of absorption; all these are the factors that determine whether a particular game constitutes play, philosophically speaking. And so, according to these broad-based criteria of play, most children's games, including organised sports and certainly informal sporting games, are viewed as play by the majority of philosophers of play and games (Caillois, 2001; Feezell, 2010; Greif, 2010; Huizinga, 1949). It follows therefore that Caillois' attributes of play listed above can be attributed equally to game-play in particular as to play in general and can now be seen to be perfectly compatible with the features of play deemed crucial in the child psychotherapy setting as outlined in the literature over the last century, summarised here by Meersand and Gilmore (2017):

- A unique combination of both mental fantasy and physical action
- An inherent "as-if" quality
- The capacity to inhabit the playful while maintaining awareness of pretending
- The inherently safe and nonconsequential nature of the playing situation (Meersand and Gilmore, 2017, p. 9).

Clearly, like pretend play, the extent to which the child plays in this "as-if", totally immersed, manner varies greatly with their changing states of mind, as shall be discussed in more detail directly and indirectly in the remaining chapters.

5.6   Game-play as Milnerian creativity and Winnicottian playing

It is in playing and only in playing that the individual child or adult is able to be creative and to use the whole personality, and it is only in being creative that the individual discovers the self.

(Winnicott, 1971, p. 54)

I would speak of a distinctive attitude toward playful activities. They are not "serious," yet they can be wholly absorbing and engaged in quite seriously. I have called such an attitude "serious nonseriousness".

(Feezell, 2010, p. 14)

Having established game-play as a bona fide form of play on the conceptual-philosophical-social level, we are now ready to examine the question of the creative and playful aspects of structured competitive games in the transitional space, in the Milnerian and Winnicottian sense of these terms. I turn first to the work of Marion Milner, Winnicott's close colleague for over four decades. It is her key concepts of the *framed gap*, *reverie*, and *absent-mindedness* (Milner, 2005) that I believe can contribute especially to illuminating questions of creativity, playfulness, alive experience, and psychic growth in structured games. Ahead of her time, Milner understood how, when the need for knowledge and certainty is laid aside, a space emerges for intuition and for creation of the new and the surprising, often out of the depths of the unconscious. In her 1950 volume *On Not Being Able to Paint* (Milner, 1957a), she applied insights from her personal struggles to find her own authentic style and "voice" as a painter to the understanding of the creative process:

> Observations of problems to do with painting had all led to the idea that awareness of the external world is itself a creative process, an immensely complex creative interchange between what comes from inside and what comes from the outside, a complex alternation of fusing and separation.
>
> (Milner, 1957a, p. 171)

For Milner, true creativity necessarily involves a process of re-creation, of experiencing the outside world from within and re-creating it anew as an alive experience (Caldwell, 2000; Raab, 2000; Spelman & Raphael-Leff, 2022; Stefana, 2019). Crucial to this process is the benign regression from two-ness (separation between me and not-me, inside and outside, self and other) to an illusion of one-ness with the outside world. This benign regression to fusion of external and internal reality allows the artist, or indeed the child playing, to re-create the outside world anew, shaped by their own inner experience, but not deluded or overwhelmed by it. The experience is imaginative and creative, but not psychotic: discrimination between the inner and outer world is simultaneously both maintained and blurred, a paradox that is at the core of creativity (Milner, 2005).

The key to such re-creation is what Milner playfully termed *absentmindedness* (literally absenting the mind to allow for "undirected thinking" to emerge from the inner world) or *reverie* (Milner, 1952b, 1957a). Interestingly, Milner used the term reverie well before Bion appropriated this term for his theory of thinking and dreaming. This is a state of mind or phase of thinking, in which there is a "fusing or con-fusing [of] subject and object, seer and seen" – the re-creation is in "making a new division of these. By suffusing the not-me objective material with me-subjective psychic content, it makes the not me real 'realisable'" and recreates outside reality anew (Milner, 1957b, p. 228).

Already in her 1952 paper, "Aspects of symbolism in comprehension of the not-self", Milner located play as originating in this same space of creativity, the space between internal and external reality, between me and not-me, something "half-way between daydreaming and purposeful instinctive or expedient action"

(Milner, 1952a, p. 186). In a similar vein, Winnicott's definition of creativity is intrinsically linked to his theory of playing. He links both play and re-creation to living and being alive and therefore to mental health:

> Creativity is then the *doing* that arises out of being.
>
> (Winnicott, 1986, p. 39)

> By creative living I mean not getting killed or annihilated all the time by compliance or by reacting to the world that impinges; I mean seeing everything afresh all the time.
>
> (Winnicott, 1986, p. 41)

The central aspect of creativity for Winnicott is the freedom from compliance, from impingement, the freedom to destroy (a blank canvas for instance) and create something new, afresh (a painting where blank canvas was before).

As discussed in chapter 4, Winnicott (1971) describes play as the infusing of "external phenomena", outside objects discovered in reality, with the colours and phantasies of the inner world and manipulation of these outside objects in accordance with inner reality. For both Milner and Winnicott, play, creativity, and re-creation take place between the subjective and the objective, at the intersection between imagination and reality. The movement of play and creativity is outwards and inwards simultaneously, thereby creating psychic space (Green, 1997, 2005; Lenormand, 2018), and it is in this space of playing that the individual also discovers themselves as other, as *not*-me.

Many parents, educators, and therapists alike are confounded by the superficially not-me, reality-bound, and rule-bound quality of the traditional games of middle childhood and overlook the "being-ness", the me-ness, that is within. Children's literature abounds with descriptions of the creativity of the games of middle childhood: Mark Twain's Huckleberry Finn and Tom Sawyer were experts in marbles and tag and creating elaborate hide-outs in the woods; whilst Enid Blyton's *Famous Five* and *Secret Seven* and J.M. Barrrie's "betwixt-and-between" *Peter Pan* and his faithful band of lost children could all be described as being involved in a series of intricate collaborative games in fictional external reality. Modern-day children's books are similarly full of games, rules, and creative ingenuity. Take for example the climactic chapter from *Harry Potter and the Philosopher's [Sorcerer's] Stone* (Rowling, 2015), in which the rescue of the powerful magic stone relies on a combination of Harry's extraordinary Quidditch skills, Ron's creative and insightful chess playing, and Hermione's logic and didactic approach. The very solution of the riddle relies on the threesome's sheer grit and determination, and an unbeatable admixture of powerful emotion and daring (personified by Harry); creativity, impishness, and flare (personified by Ron); and fierce intellect, logic, and rules (personified by Hermione), all within the context of real-live magical game-play. Together, Harry, Ron, and Hermione are the epitome of the multi-faceted wave-particle child: a wondrous mixture of physical skill, emotions seething beneath the surface, spontaneity, resourcefulness, and creative thinking, along with a bubbling over of energy and enthusiasm (at times mitigated with perhaps a little too much self-righteousness). The "doing that comes from the being" in the literature for middle childhood is almost always to be found in the imaginative games children play, bounded by rules, competition and purpose, and the adventures they embark on, defined by clear goals, and multiple obstacles to be surmounted by physical skill, creative problem solving, peppered with a healthy dose of mischief and disobedience.

Superficially, the rules and predetermined contents of structured games could be thought to preclude the element of apperception and creation of something new, the playfulness that lies in the transitional space between me and not-me. But a few moments of contemplation both of these children's stories and of the traditional structured games children play, from football to jacks (five-stones)[1] to skipping games to chess, reveal the creative and playful elements of these games immediately. The beauty of a novel football trick, whether executed by an eight-year-old enthusiast or a football great; the endless variations in jacks and skipping games; or the unpredictable and surprising moves in a chess game: all these involve the apperception and creation of something surprising and novel. As in all play, this is true only provided the child is in a healthy secure enough state of mind to absent their mind and let their inner self meet the not-self, merge with it, and re-create anew. Each time the child plays their turn, they choose afresh how to play, they create an imaginary fortune on the *Monopoly* board or an invincible army on the chess board, they become a fearless giant or roguish thief on the *Talisman*[2] board, or a newly discovered Lionel Messi on the tiny improvised 6 square metre carpet-cum-football pitch in the therapy room. This is the very same pretend, as-if, quality of play mentioned above in Meersand and Gilmore's list (2017), but which for schoolagers is often more accessible in their favourite board games and modern-day console games than in the "free" pretend play of early childhood.

5.7   Statement of position: game-play as psychoanalytic play

I contend that the philosophical understanding of competitive games, as belonging unequivocally to the realm of play, together with the evidence collected here so far from the fields of child development and child psychoanalysis, places the traditional game-play of middle childhood fairly and squarely in the psychoanalytic play space. It is now possible to identify four separate justifications for this statement:

1   *Game-play is the natural language of intra-psychic and interpersonal communication of the wave-particle child and therefore is the most suitable, easily accessible, and intuitive candidate for the language of psychoanalytic/psychotherapeutic engagement with school-aged children.*
2   *Texts on psychoanalytic child psychotherapy emphasise the dual purpose of play in the analytic setting, both as a channel for communication with the unconscious and as enabling cognitive, emotional, social, and physical development. As discussed at*

length in Chapter 3, the traditional game-play of middle childhood in all its many forms (board games and card games, sports, hobbies, and collections) is vital to all these aspects of the child's development during the post-oedipal pre-pubertal years.

3   *Games, like play in general, occupy a peculiar position in life: they take place in a separate space, in a permeable "magic circle", suspended between reality and the make-believe. They have undetermined and unpredictable outcomes; they involve complex engagement and interaction with the self and other; and are a matter of "serious nonseriousness". The corollary of these peculiar and distinct features is that game-play provides a natural outlet for the projection and expression of the unconscious from middle childhood through to adulthood. Game-play is after all only play, "only a game", and by dint of being "only a game", it can serve as a powerful and immediate, age appropriate, medium through which and into which the child can project and enact their inner world, their anxieties, fantasies, creative and destructive urges, into the separate space of "plausible deniability" (Levy, 2008).*

4   *Similarly, the position of structured games as having one foot in the real world and one foot in fantasy and make-believe, as being simultaneously "of the utmost consequence and of no consequence at all", as pleasurable and creative, all define game-play as taking place in the Milnerian area of creativity and the Winnicottian transitional space, and therefore as a natural and appropriate tool for psychotherapeutic work towards psychic health.*

5.8   Unanswered questions

This statement of position throws up new clinical-technical-theoretical questions. *How* do the languages of middle childhood and of play with structured games fit into, and indeed enrich, the grammar and vocabulary of child psychoanalytic theory as it stands today? And at a higher resolution: *Can* these games be used as transitional space for both free and structured "wave-particle" play at one and the same time, and if so, *how? What* is happening on the intra-psychic and inter-psychic level when the child and therapist play games such as *War, Monopoly,* or basketball in the psychotherapy session? *When* should we use *which* games and *how? How* do the balls, bats, dice, and boards of these structured games become a psychoanalytic *tabula rasa* onto and into which the child can project their inner world and phantasies? *When* should we insist the child patient abide by the rules of the game and *when* should we turn a blind (yet wide open) eye to cheating?

Having so far addressed the questions "whether" and "why" (*whether* middle childhood constitutes a differentiated and significant developmental stage? *why* structured games should be considered as an essential part of child psychotherapy toolbox?) in parts I and II of this volume, I shall now go on to address these clinical conceptual questions of *how, what, which and when* regarding the therapeutic use of game-play in child analytic treatment in Part III.

Notes

1 For explanation of the game of Jacks/five stones, see https://www.mastersofgames.com/rules/jacks-rules.htm.
2 For description of the board game *Talisman*, see: https://en.wikipedia.org/wiki/Talisman_(board_game).

Bibliography

Alvarez, A. (2012). The thinking heart: Three levels of psychoanalytic therapy with disturbed children. Routledge.

Beiser, H. R. (1979). Formal games in diagnosis and therapy. *Journal of the American Academy of Child Psychiatry, 18*(3), 480–491.

Bellinson, J. (2000). Shut up and move: The uses of board games in child psychotherapy. *Journal of Infant, Child, and Adolescent Psychotherapy, 1*(2), 23–41.

Bellinson, J. (2002). *Children's Use of Board Games in Psychotherapy*. Jason Aronson.

Ben-Ari Smira, K. (2015). *The Hidden Father: Reintroducing the Father into Psychoanalytic Discourse*. Reisling.

Birch, M. (1997). In the land of counterpane: Travels in the realm of play. *Psychoanalytic Study of the Child, 52*, 057–075.

Blake, P. (2011). *Child and Adolescent Psychotherapy*. Karnac Books.

Bohleber, W., Fonagy, P., Jiménez, J. P., Scarfone, D., Varvin, S., & Zysman, S. (2013). Towards a better use of psychoanalytic concepts: A model illustrated using the concept of enactment. *The International Journal of Psychoanalysis, 94*(3), 501–530.

Caillois, R. ([1958] 1961). *Man, Play and Games* [Les jeux et les hommes]. New York: The Free Press of Glencoe.

Caillois, R. (2001). *Man, Play, and Games*. University of Illinois Press.

Claman, L. (1980). The squiggle-drawing game in child psychotherapy. *American Journal of Psychotherapy, 34*(3), 414.

Cohen, Y. (1995). Addressing the psychic reality of the borderline child. *International Journal of Psycho-Analysis, 76*, 35–38.

Coriat, I. (1941). The unconscious motives of interest in chess. *The Psychoanalytic Review (1913–1957), 28*, 30.

Deakin, E. K., & Tiellet Nunes, M. L. (2009). Effectiveness of child psychoanalytic psychotherapy in a clinical outpatient setting. *Journal of Child Psychotherapy, 35*(3), 290–301.

Erikson, E. H. (1940). *Studies in the Interpretation of Play: Clinical Observation of Play Disruption in Young Children*. Genetic Psychology Monographs.

Feezell, R. (2010). A pluralist conception of play. *Journal of the Philosophy of Sport, 37*(2), 147–165.

Ferro, A. (1992). Two authors in search of characters: The relationship, the field, the story. *Rivista Di Psicoanalisi, 38*(1), 44–90.

Ferro, A. (2003). *The Bi-Personal Field: Experiences in Child Analysis*. Routledge.

Freud, S. (1905). On psychotherapy (1905 [1904]). In J. Strachey (Ed. and trans), *The Standard Edition of the Complete Psychological Works of Sigmund Freud Volume VII (1901–1905): A Case of Hysteria, Three Essays on Sexuality and Other Works*, pp. 64–145. Hogarth Press.

Freud, S. (1913). On beginning the treatment. In J. Strachey (Ed. and trans), *The Standard Edition of the Complete Psychological Works of Sigmund Freud Volume XII (1911–1913): The Case of Schreber, Papers on Technique and Other Works 121–144*. Hogarth Press.

Freud, S. (1955). Lines of advance in psycho-analytic therapy. In J. Strachey (Ed. and trans), *The Standard Edition of the Complete Psychological Works of Sigmund Freud, Volume XVII (1917–1919): An Infantile Neurosis and Other Works* (pp. 157–168). Hogarth Press.

Fried, S. (1992). Chess: A psychoanalytic tool in the treatment of children. *International Journal of Play Therapy, 1*(1), 43-51.

Gavshon, A. (1989). Playing: Its role in child analysis. *Journal of Child Psychotherapy, 15*(1), 47–62.

Gilmore, K., & Meersand, P. (2013). *Normal Child and Adolescent Development: A Psychodynamic Primer*. American Psychiatric Pub.

Green, A. (1997). The intuition of the negative in playing and reality. *International Journal of Psycho-Analysis, 78*, 1071–1084.

Green, A. (2005). *Play and Reflection in Donald Winnicott's Writings*. Karnac Books.

Greif, D. (2010). Revaluing sports. *Contemporary Psychoanalysis, 46*(4), 550–561.

Günter, M. (2018). Problems of technique in analysis of children and adolescents: Transference—interpretation—play. In H. Hasenclever & M. Günter (Eds.), *Technique in Child and Adolescent Analysis* (pp. 1–12). Routledge.

Huizinga, J. (1949). *Homo Ludens: A Study of the Play-Element in Our Culture*. Routledge & Kegan Paul.

Joseph, B. (1985). Transference: The total situation. *International Journal of Psycho-Analysis, 66*, 447–454.

Klein, M. (1961). *Narrative of a Child Analysis: The Conduct of the Psycho-Analysis of Children as seen in the Treatment of a Ten year old Boy*. Random House (No 55).

Klein, M. (1975). *Envy and Gratitude and Other Works 1946–1963: Edited By: M. Masud R. Khan*. Hogarth Press.

Kohut, H. (1977). *The Restoration of the Self*. International Universities Press.

Krimendahl, E. (2000). "Did you see that?": A relational perspective on children who cheat in analysis. *Journal of Infant, Child, and Adolescent Psychotherapy, 1*(2), 43–58.

Kuhn, T. S. (1962). *The Structure of Scientific Revolutions*. University of Chicago Press.

Lang, F. (2007). Play in the psychoanalytic situation. *Journal of the American Psychoanalytic Association, 55*(3), 937–948.

Laplanche, J. (1992). Interpretation between determinism and hermeneutics: A restatement of the problem. *International Journal of Psycho-Analysis, 73*, 429–445.

Lenormand, M. (2018). Winnicott's theory of playing: A reconsideration. *The International Journal of Psychoanalysis, 99*(1), 82–102.

Lesley Caldwell. (2000). *Art. Creativity, Living*. Routledge.

Levinson, B. M. (1972). Use of checkers in therapy. *Psychological Reports, 30*(3), 846–846.

Levy, A. J. (2008). The therapeutic action of play in the psychodynamic treatment of children: A critical analysis. *Clinical Social Work Journal, 36*(3), 281–291.

Loomis, E. A. (1976). Use of checkers in handling resistance. In C. E. Schaefer (Ed.), *The Therapeutic Use of Child's Play* (p. 385). Jason Aronson.

Malaby, T. M. (2007). Beyond play: A new approach to games. *Games and Culture, 2*(2), 95–113.

Malberg, N. T., & Raphael-Leff, J. (2012). *The Anna Freud Tradition: Lines of Development - Evolution and Theory and Practice Over the Decades*. Karnac Books.

Meeks, J. E. (1970). Children who cheat at games. *Journal of the American Academy of Child Psychiatry, 9*(1), 157–170.

Meeks, J. E. (2000). Reflections on children who cheat at games: A commentary. *Journal of Infant, Child, and Adolescent Psychotherapy, 1*(2), 71–75.

Meersand, P. (2009). Play and the older child: Developmental and clinical opportunities. *The Psychoanalytic Study of the Child, 64*(1), 112–130.

Meersand, P., & Gilmore, K. (2017). *Play Therapy: A Psychodynamic Primer for the Treatment of Young Children*. American Psychiatric Pub.

Milner, M. (1952a). Aspects of symbolism in comprehension of the not-self. *International Journal of Psycho-Analysis, 33*, 181–194.

Milner, M. (1952b). The Framed Gap. In M. Milner, *The Suppressed Madness of Sane Men* (pp. 79–82). Routledge/Taylor & Francis Group.

Milner, M. (1957a). *On Not Being Able To Paint*. Heinemann.

Milner, M. (1957b). The ordering of chaos. In *The Suppressed Madness of Sane Men: Forty-Four Years of Exploring Psychoanalysis* (pp. 216–233). Routledge/Taylor & Francis Group.

Milner, M. (2005). *The Suppressed Madness of Sane Men: Forty-Four Years of Exploring Psychoanalysis*. Routledge.

Molinari, E. (2017). Variations on a theme: Child and adolescent analysis. In A. Ferro (Ed.), *Contemporary Bionian Theory and Technique in Psychoanalysis* (pp. 176–216). Routledge.

Nguyen, C. T. (2017). Philosophy of games. *Philosophy Compass, 12*(8).

Ogden, T. H. (2008). *Rediscovering Psychoanalysis: Thinking and Dreaming, Learning and Forgetting*. Taylor & Francis.

Oren, A. (2008). The use of board games in child psychotherapy. *Journal of Child Psychotherapy, 34*(3), 364–383.

Palgi-Hecker, A. (2005). *Mother in Psychoanalysis: A Feminist View*. Am Oved.

Plaut, E. A. (1979). Definition of play. *Psychoanalytic Study of the Child, 34*, 217–232.

Raab, K. A. (2000). Creativity and transcendence in the work of Marion Milner. *American Imago, 57*(2), 185–214.

Ridge, M. (2019). Play and games: An opinionated introduction. *Philosophy Compass, 14*(4), e12573.

Rowling, J. K. (2015). *Harry Potter and the Philosopher's Stone (Vol. 1)*. Bloomsbury Publishing.

Scarfone, D. (2013). A brief introduction to the work of Jean Laplanche. *International Journal of Psycho-Analysis, 94*(3), 545–566.

Slade, A. (1994). Making meaning and making believe: Their role in the clinical process. In *Children at play: Clinical and Developmental Approaches to Meaning and Representation* (pp. 81–107). Oxford University Press.

Solnit, A. J. (1987). A psychoanalytic view of play. *Psychoanalytic Study of the Child, 42*, 205–219.

Spelman, M. B., & Raphael-Leff, J. (2022). *The Marion Milner Tradition: Lines of Development: Evolution of Theory and Practice over the Decades*. Taylor & Francis.

Stefana, A. (2019). Revisiting Marion Milner's work on creativity and art. *The International Journal of Psychoanalysis, 100*(1), 128–147.

Stein, Y. (2005). *The Psychoanalysis of Science: The Role of Metaphor, Paraplax, Lacunae, and Myth*. Sussex Academic Press.

Winnicott, D. W. (1971). The use of an object and relating through identifications. In D.W. Winnicott, *Playing and Reality* (pp. 101–111). Penguin Books.

Winnicott, D. W. (1986). *Home is Where We Start From: Essays by a Psychoanalyst*. WW Norton & Company.

Winnicott, D. W. (2018). The Squiggle Game: An amalgamation of two papers: one, unpublished, written in 1964, the other published 1968 1. In C. Winnicott, R. Shepherd, M. Davis (Eds.), *Psycho-Analytic Explorations* (pp. 299–317). Routledge.

PART III

Clinical theoretical formulation of game-play in the psychoanalytic playroom

Chapter 6

50 shades of game-play

Man plays when he is in the full sense of the word a man, and he is only wholly Man when he is playing – Friedrich Schiller

(From: *On the Aesthetic Education of Man*, Schiller, 1795, quoted in Lenormand, 2018, p. 87)

This chapter examines questions of playing and "negative playing" (Green, 2005) in game-play in the analytic playroom. The chapters that follow in this section (III) build on this chapter and further elaborate issues of technique and clinical theoretical understanding of game-play in child psychotherapy. These chapters together comprise a clinical reconceptualisation of structured competitive childhood games as a rich and varied world of play, fantasy, and dreaming, a natural medium for conscious and unconscious intra-psychic and intersubjective communication in middle childhood inside and outside of the child psychotherapy playroom. These issues will be explored and developed to the length and depth, sometimes "top-down", sometimes "inside-out", first with reference to play in the transitional space per se (Chapter 6), then to contemporary theory of the maternal, the paternal, triangular space and mentalisation (Chapter 7); and thence to the transference–countertransference matrix, the container-contained, and the post-Bionian bi-personal analytic "playing" field (Chapter 8). Clearly, these various aspects of psychoanalytic theory are interconnected and will be applied in sequence and in parallel, as appropriate, all interwoven into the fabric of the theoretical formulation and accompanied by clinical illustrations.

First, to matters of game-play per se, as a vehicle for expanding psychic space in the transitional space.

6.1   Playing structured games in the transitional space

Play should be introduced under proper regulation as medicine – Aristotle

(Quoted in *Tustin, 1988*, p. 93)

Despite Winnicott's repeated written objections to what he perceived as the restrictive structure of the rule-bound games of middle childhood, his ideas on play,

DOI: 10.4324/9781003425229-9

playing, and the transitional space (detailed in Chapter 5) are crucial to understanding the psychodynamic processes underpinning game-play in child psychotherapy.

As noted in Chapter 5, in his writings on playing in psychotherapy, Winnicott stressed that the "external phenomena" we present to the child or adult patient for their and our "manipulation" should feel safe and familiar, words and play materials that can, in the language of Bion (1967) and Ogden (2014), "be dreamed with" easily.[1] Ogden (1985, 2001) points out that adults naturally play with words. Analytic therapists use words, dialogue, even mundane conversation about anything and everything, to expand the transitional space and the overlap of playing between therapist and patient. But for children, words are not the external phenomena to which they instinctively turn: dolls, toys, creative materials, ball games, card games, and board games fulfil this function instead.

Many children can play and "dream" relatively easily with dolls, toy animals and cars, pencils, paints, and paper. But there are others, particularly school-aged children, who feel precarious in themselves and mistrustful of the outside world, and tend to balk at the regressive pull of dolls and creative materials, fearful of being overwhelmed by more infantile impulses and needs. These children often need toys and games that are more age appropriate and more acceptable to their own self-image, that are more "user-friendly" and familiar and at a "safe" psychic distance from their inner private selves. Winnicott (1971, 1980) believed that playing structured games serves as a defence against the psychic dangers involved in creative play and therefore should be avoided in child psychotherapy. However, it is my clinical experience that the reverse can equally often be true. Precisely because of the safe boundaries provided by structured games, school-aged children can and do use these very games for creative play or at least for their sincere desperate attempts at creating a Winnicottian transitional play space for themselves. As we have seen, child psychoanalytic writers, even those who have cautioned against the use of structured games in child psychotherapy, including Anna Freud herself, often note the older child's natural tendency to play these games (Blake, 2011; Gilmore & Meersand, 2013; Lanyado & Horne, 2009; Meersand, 2009; Solnit, 1993, 1997). The balls, cards, pawns, and boards of these games are, I believe, naturally experienced by the wave-particle child as "safe enough" external phenomena, through which they can communicate with themselves and others and in which they spontaneously and easily invest "dream meaning and feeling".

As Lenormand (2018) points out, and as discussed briefly in chapter 5, rules are more often than not a prerequisite for play and for creativity. Indeed, structure and predetermined form were integral to poetry and the visual arts for many centuries. The strictures of the 14-line rhyme scheme of the classical sonnet or the demands of the iambic pentameter rhythmic form of verse can hardly be said to be reasons for discounting Shakespeare's creativity. The same can be said of the rules of perspective and balance in Renaissance art and architecture. These rules of form and structure neither negate nor serve as a dictate for play and creativity. A sonnet, a painting, and also children's play, can be alive and creative even though bounded by rules and form, or conversely can be unbounded and "free", without predetermined structure, and nevertheless be lifeless and empty. (For further of this discussion of the question of when play is not creative, not alive, not Winnicottian playing, and therefore not belonging to health as such, see below, Section 6.4.) For many school-aged children, adolescents and adults alike, it is easier to be creative and playful when building with *Lego* bricks, playing a card game, inventing *Scrabble* words, or aiming a basketball into a net, than when applying paints to a blank canvas, or doodling on a sheet of A4 paper. It is the safe-enough distance from the game and its pawns (of whatever shape and form) that gives the child or adult the space in which to create afresh and to play out the themes of their inner world through the metaphor or under cover of the game.

Clearly, I do not mean to imply that all games of *Monopoly*, football, Chess, or UNO/TAKI are acts of alive creation, but they can be, depending on the individual player-creators themselves, the transitional space created between them, and also between each individual and the game itself. Within the rules and structure, when "standing [and moving] in the spaces" (Bromberg, 1998), lie the opportunities for the unknown and the non-sense that is playing, as well as for drives and their vicissitudes that are also part and parcel of play (Green, 2005) (see Section 6.4). Even in the simplest and most prosaic of card games play can thus come alive, as can be seen in the following clinical vignette:

VIGNETTE A   Clare – The perfect patient turned cheat

Clare was a highly gifted and intelligent 10-year-old girl referred to psychotherapy because of depressive symptoms and suicidal thoughts. Precociously mature and articulate, Clare would sit there, session after session, recounting her worries and her troubles, especially the problems she had with her divorced parents and their new partners. But the sessions were lifeless and stilted. Eventually, she took some coloured pencils and pieces of paper and began to draw, and we wrote some stories together about what she drew. I was encouraged, but only momentarily. Her talent was evident, but she drew perfect girls, beautiful flowers, fairies, and idyllic landscapes and her stories were stilted and predictable. Her "false self" (Winnicott, 1971) was tyrannically stifling the sessions. Eventually, I decided, somewhat counter-intuitively, to insist on playing simple, "frivolous" card games. She scorned my suggestion at first as being childish, but eventually she took up the gauntlet and I, in turn, got more than I bargained for.

Clare decided that if we were to play cards, then it had to be the game of *War*. My heart sank. I have to admit that of all the card games that I know, *War* is one of the few games I try to avoid; I usually find playing it unutterably tedious. But what ensued surprised both of us. I dealt out the cards evenly and to my and Clare's dismay, I began to win hands down as ace after ace and royalty after royalty appeared in my pack. Clare found it intolerable and, encouraged by me, began to cheat, searching before her turn for her high cards to trump mine and choosing her lowest cards to give me when I won a round. She even resorted to openly stealing my aces and jokers. I responded by playfully resisting and complaining that she wasn't playing fair, whilst simultaneously joining in with her glee at her own naughtiness and childlike compulsion to win. For the first time in the many months of therapy, we were at last playing spontaneously, her needy and healthy, greedy and selfish "true self" emerged and her hidden yearning for infantile omnipotence took centre stage. "I've never played like this before, are you sure it's allowed?! Don't tell anybody!"

Paradoxically, Clare had come alive and creatively playful in the Milnerian-Winnicottian sense only when she agreed to leave the pseudo-creative world of her own drawings and stories and enter the rule-bound framed world of structured games. Clare, as Klein put it, seemed instinctively to know that she could use me and the therapy in a different, special way to "overcome [her] resistances against experiencing and expressing thoughts, feelings and desires, which are incompatible with convention" (Klein, 1955, p. 125). As we progressed from *War* to full-blown games of *Cheat*, Clare talked less and less about home life and became more spontaneously playful, and the therapeutic space began to expand. Clare ended therapy when she felt that she had achieved her therapeutic goal, defined in her own words, "I'm not a nerd anymore!".

When Clare had been in the phase of sitting in the armchair, talking and crying, drawing and storytelling, she had indeed been very nerd-like and emotionally shut down. To use more psychodynamic terms, her false-self and strict superego had dominated. When we played card games together, the strictures and boundaries, imposed not by Clare's superego, but by the framing structure embodied by the cards themselves and the rules of the game, had allowed Clare to express her infantile, greedy, spontaneous, naughty self and work through the feelings and needs she had kept neatly and studiously hidden behind a world of pseudo-creativity, pseudo-maturity, and school achievements.

6.2   Play, the frame, and the "work of the negative"[2]

So, what is going on here? Why do structured games frequently enable more creativity and freedom of access to the psyche for many school-agers than pretend play or drawing and painting, not less? Logic tells us that the very structure and rules of these games demand mindedness. I turn again to the work of Marion Milner to point us in the direction of a solution to this conundrum. Through her struggles as an artist with anxieties that forestalled and interfered with her creativity, Milner came to realise that mindedness and absent-mindedness must go hand in hand, that a setting "both physical and mental" is a prerequisite for absent-mindedness and thus for re-creation (Milner, 1957a, 2005). As discussed in chapter 5, according to Milner, there can be no blank mental space, no reverie, no transitional space, without a frame. The gap in which creativity takes place is always a "framed gap":

> It requires a physical setting in which we are freed, for the time being, from the need for immediate practical expedient action; and it requires a mental seeing, and attitude, both in the people around and in oneself, to tolerate what may at moments look very like madness.
>
> (Milner, 1957b, p. 231)

Prescient to Green (1999), Milner understood that this framed gap that enables creativity and reverie has its origins in the primary carer's reliable, safe, benign hold, and that impediments to creativity "are a result of a failure of the child's environment to provide the necessary setting for such absent-mindedness" (Milner, 1957b, p. 231).

Taking these ideas one step further, this concept of the framing gap, and Green's (1997, 1999) allied concept of the framing structure of the (internalised) holding parent, can be applied to the *structure* inherent in the traditional competitive games of middle childhood. The scaffolding of rules, dice, cards, the box itself, and the playing board and pawns it contains can all be seen to serve as framing the gap and enabling absent-mindedness and creativity to emerge. In Milner and Green's terminology, they serve together as the frame symbolising the security of parental holding, or as a substitute for a framing structure that has not yet been securely internalised. I believe that it is by dint of the external organising frame inherent to these games that the child can allow themselves not to know, to absent their minds and re-create, in the knowledge that they can always fall back on the holding structure of the squares marked out on the playing board, of the predetermined metaphor of the narrative of the game, of the rules of the game and the numbers on the dice or cards they hold in their hand.

Lenormand (2018) suggests that "framing" rules are in fact a *sine qua non* of play, and that compliance with pre-established rules most certainly does not preclude play per se (see the discussion in Chapter 5). As noted above, the iambic pentameter and the rhyming structure of the sonnet by no means impaired Shakespeare's creativity nor his playfulness. And, similarly, the rules Winnicott invented in the squiggle game served to provide a framework in which non-sense could be accessed in children who were "non-compliant" in pretend play. This I believe was precisely because the anxiety of free play, without a protective structure, was overwhelming for these children and led to compulsive and repetitive play, or no play, which Winnicott responded to intuitively by providing a structured and yet playful solution in the form of the squiggle game. The unintegration in a board game or even in a game of ping pong or football is certainly less than when painting, or sculpting, or composing music, where the framing structure is less rigid and predetermined. But therein also lies the power of structured games as a therapeutic tool: it is the very sturdiness and clarity of the frame of these games, which paradoxically allow the child to let go and allows uncertainty and chance to enter their psychic experience. This, I believe, is the natural area of transitional space of middle childhood, however constricted or fragile it may be for some children.

Early in her writings, Milner linked absent-mindedness, reverie, and creativity to the child's capacity to doubt (Milner, 1942) and to Keats' (1925) notion of negative capability "when a man is capable of being in uncertainties, Mysteries, doubts, without any irritable reaching after fact and reason" (quoted in Spelman & Raphael-Leff, 2022, p. 174). It is worth remembering that this notion of the "work of the negative" or "negative capability" and its role in originality of thinking, and aesthetics holds true not just for the literary greats, but for all forms of creativity, not only in the arts, but also in mathematics and the sciences. Many of the critical scientific discoveries and mathematical solutions have occurred only when "irritable reaching after fact and reason" has been abandoned and the thinker has had the courage to let go of the familiar, safe, facts and modes of thinking (see McLeish, 2019, for a fascinating discussion of creativity in art, music, and science). And equally, negative capability is central to creativity and playing on the micro, everyday level: whether for the adult amateur artist or musician, the physicist, teacher, or psychotherapist; or for the child playing on the seashore, discovering the beauty and wonder of the sand, the sea and the myriads of shells at their feet; and no less for the child playing a game of five stones, perfecting their cartwheels or football moves in the school playground, or planning their next move on the chess board

Like Milner, Winnicott writes about playing as involving a "relaxation" which has "no aim", an openness to *non*-sense and to form-*less*-ness, to the *un*-integrated personality. Connected to this is the acceptance of the paradox of the transitional object as *not*-me, but also *not*-other, a paradox which involves tolerating the *un*-known and the *un*-predictable (Winnicott, 1971). Building on these ideas, Green (1997) points out that since playing involves a recognition of the area of *not*-me and the related capacity to reside in the space between the subject and the object, play should be conceived of as movement in a space that has been created by an absence. Like Milner, Green emphasises the space, the frame, the absence of a presence in play – absent-mindedness in Milner's language. This is what Green calls the "work of the negative", the ability of the psyche to tolerate space, separation and absence, and the unknown: akin to Keats' negative capability and Milner's capacity to doubt, not to know.

Playing cards or a game of five stones is a far cry indeed from the "language of achievement" of Shakespeare and Virginia Wolff, Lisa Meitner,[3] and Albert Einstein, but nevertheless, playfulness in structured games, like Winnicottian and Milnerian creating and playing in general, relies no less on being able to withstand uncertainties and doubts. The game player does not know what card they will be dealt, what number will appear on the dice, where the opponent will bat the ball, or even whether the ball will go where their foot intended. Such a capacity to tolerate not knowing is indeed not trivial, and many a session in child psychotherapy is spent helping a child gradually allow chance, doubt, and uncertainty to creep into the space between them and the therapist, between their omnipotent wish for a double six and the numbers appearing on the dice, between their dream goal and the shot they produce, between the ace they wanted so desperately and the seven they are dealt from the pack. In essence, these "normal" "healthy" aspects of the negative are to be found in the spaces between the rules, in the uncertainty inherent in games of chance, in the creativity in the strategic and aesthetic decisions to be made. These childhood games evolved naturally through the ages precisely to engage the child's imagination and drive for playing and creativity as well as their need for sublimation and for frameworks in which to test out and develop their cognitive, physical, and social skills. Winnicott maintained that the organisational aspects of games "forestall the frightening aspect of playing" (Winnicott, 1971, p. 50) and protect "against the anxiety that might be aroused by the experience of formlessness" (Lenormand, 2018, p. 89). But this statement can in fact be interpreted in both directions. It is my clinical experience that games like *Monopoly* or *War* often act to contain the child's anxiety and thereby enable, rather than prevent, play and communication.

6.3   In sickness and in health – game-play as a vital psychotherapeutic tool in work with children in borderline states of mind

For children in borderline states of mind, who have suffered trauma and abuse, the protection proffered by the clear form and structure of childhood games and the psychic distancing from toys and creative materials and from the regressive pull of the primary parental transference in psychotherapy becomes critical. Alvarez (1989, 2010) elaborates on the existential need such "damaged" children have for creating inner mental and psychic space. She suggests these children have a "need to forget", to distance themselves from the traumas that have scorched their psyche. Spontaneous play and verbal "explanatory" interpretations are often experienced as a threat to their fragile structure of defences. Alvarez likens psychotherapeutic work with borderline and psychotic patients to that of a chemist working with explosive and inflammable materials. She quotes Ludwig Gatterman's instructions to organic chemists cited by Primo Levi in his autobiography *The Search for Roots* (Levi, 2003):

> Work with explosive substances should never be done without wearing goggles...Care must invariably be taken with ether and other volatile, readily inflammable liquids that no flame is burning in the neighbourhood. If a fire occurs, everything which may ignite must immediately be removed. The fire should then be extinguished with moist towels or by pouring on carbon tetrachloride, but not water.
>
> (Alvarez, 1989, p. 75)

These simple words from the far-removed world of chemistry serve as a vivid metaphor for the desperate, raw, necessity of keeping a safe distance from threatening and anxiety-provoking psychic material in psychotherapy when working with children (and also adults) in such "borderline" states of mind. It is my clinical experience that creative and expressive play materials, such as dolls and paints, can and often do act as a spark to the tinderbox that is the traumatised child's psyche. Drawing and fantasy play can all too easily lose their symbolic meaning for the child, and become the "thing itself" (Bion, 1962), instantaneously engulfed in the flames of destructive rage and envy that the child struggles to contain. Or alternatively, the child senses catastrophic danger hidden in these regressive play materials and immediately evacuates all meaning and life from the situation; play is left lifeless and empty. Too close and the child's psyche ignites, too far and it turns to ice.

Despite the considerable obstacles that we encounter in psychotherapy with these children even when playing structured board games, I would contend that where free expressive play is too threatening, traditional board games, card games, and ball games can serve as suitable and familiar safety gear that enable the child to begin to explore their own inner emotional world and the interpersonal sphere, all from a safe psychic distance. As Levy (2008) puts it in his paper on "The therapeutic action of play":

> ...[Play allows a] 'plausible deniability' concerning troubling material, i.e. it permits the parties to suspend and if necessary, to disavow its reality. After all it's really only a game. Play therefore frees the participants to express and explore these issues [the troubling material] in ways that would be far more difficult if one was to pursue a more exclusively verbal means of communication.
>
> (Levi, 2008, pp. 284–285)

This is as true for game-play as it is for imaginary play. The more so for the older child, who is no longer comfortable to play with toy animals and dolls, but is accustomed to express their frustrations, anxieties, psychic pain, and phantasies naturally and freely through the metaphor or under cover of their favourite board game or ball game. They gleefully murder us again and again as we stand weak and helpless on the *Talisman* board; they score countless goals against us and fantasise they are Messi or Ronaldinho in the World Cup final; the race car and battleship *Monopoly* figurines take on a life of their own on the playing board. The therapist answers in the same language of plausible deniability, so as to meet the child in the overlap between the two areas of playing, mindful to respond in the game at the child's level and at moderated attuned intensity so as not to engulf the child in what can inadvertently become an overextended and overbearing area of play on the therapist's part.

I would contend therefore that game-play can be not only useful but often vital in the psychotherapeutic process, enabling psychic development and the expansion of the transitional space for many children.

Game-play, like interactive dramatic play with younger children, acts as the vehicle for psychic change in and of itself, and not just an "activity that provides the material for analysis", important though this is (cf. Gavshon, 1989, quoted above in Chapter 5). It is the conscious and unconscious manipulation by therapist and patient alike of the "external phenomena" in the analytic playroom – whether in the form of words, toys and play materials, pawns on the board, or balls in the air – that introduces "surprising enough", but not too surprising, elements into the transitional space. It is these "surprising-enough elements" introduced into the transitional space which in turn provide possibilities of new and challenging self-experiences and self-other experiences to emerge. The area of play expands, and so too the intra-psychic, and also the inter-psychic space (see in particular Chapter 8).

Alvarez (2010, 2012) regards the "calibration" of the level and distance of psychotherapeutic work with the patient's level of pathology and degree of traumatisation as crucial. As shall be discussed in the forthcoming chapters, it is through good-enough, flexible, and playful manipulation of the rules and steps of the game that we can regulate the pace and the area of overlap, challenging and frustrating the child just enough, not too much and not too little, like Goldilocks and the three bears. The area of play grows and expands to allow spontaneity and healthy greed and destruction to creep in or be curtailed as necessary, at the right time and in the right place. For the borderline, disorganised, or chronically traumatised child, we can offer them a new world, characterised neither by psychotic chaos, nor by authoritarian dictatorship and bullying, but by a calm clear containing structure, where competition and aggression, greed and pleasure, can be expressed, lived through together, and survived, without fear of cruel retribution, abandonment, or traumatising impingement.

6.4   When is play not Milnerian/Winnicottian playing? And what purpose does game-play serve in situations of "negative play" and "anti-play"?

Play in health is an ever-evolving process of creation and re-creation. Being able to play creatively and with an aliveness and joy is predicated on a level of psychic maturity in its many different facets: separation from the object and the achievement of unit status in Winnicott's terminology (Winnicott, 1971); an ability to take repeated leaps of faith (Eigen, 1981) and tolerate the anxiety of the unpredictable and the unknown; the capacity to mourn the road not taken; and equally to mourn the healthy destruction of the object or of the blank board or canvas as metaphor for the object. For all these reasons, as Winnicott writes, playing in the transitional space is not trivial and is a sign of health: the corollary to this, however, is that much of play inside and outside the analytic playroom is neither Winnicottian playing nor does it belong to health. Winnicott himself listed various forms of what he called the psychopathology of play:

A *The loss of the capacity associated with lack of trust, anxiety associated with insecurity*

B *Stereotypy in play patterns (anxiety re free fantasy)*
C *Flight into daydreaming (a manipulated state halfway between true dream and play)*
D *Sensualisation – instinct appearing in crude form along with failure of symbolisation*
E *Domination – one child only able to play his own game but involving other children who must comply*
F *Failure to play a game (restless, deprived children) unless dominated by strict rules and a games-officer*
G *Flight to physical exercise from calisthenics right up to a need to be drilled*

(Winnicott, 1989, p. 61)

And elsewhere, he highlighted the anxiety underlying these forms of non-playful play:

> Anxiety is always a factor in a child's play, and often it is a major factor. Threat of excess of anxiety leads to compulsive play, or to repetitive play, or to an exaggerated seeking for the pleasures that belong to play; and, if anxiety is too great, play breaks down into pure exploitation of sensual gratification.
>
> (Winnicott, 1987, p. 144, quoted in Lenormand (2018), p. 91)

Winnicott also pointed out that many works of art, even if seemingly free form external constraints, are often pseudo-creations, originating from places of deep pathology, compliance, and impingement (Winnicott, 1971).[4] However, throughout his writings, Winnicott's focus was always towards "health" (in his words), rather than further exploring the psychoanalytic meaning of these pathological forms of play. It was left to later psychoanalytic thinkers, notably Green and his colleagues, to develop understanding of "anti-play", in all its many guises (Green, 1997, 2005; Lenormand, 2018). These authors repeatedly point out that these latter forms of play very much belong to psychotherapy and are integral to intra-psychic and inter-psychic communication in analytic treatments with children especially. In his critique of Winnicott, Green highlights the many and varied negative aspects of play, in all its variants, and the involvement of the drives:

> My conclusion, therefore, is that play, this universal activity, belongs to an innate attribute of the mind that takes different shapes, not only in various groups, but also for different individuals. Winnicott was too stuck in the mother–baby relationship to interpret its universality in relationship to the characteristics of the mind. I am not even sure that play belongs to health. For example, I wonder how health can be integral to some kinds of play—such as the Roman games, or playing a kind of football with the heads of the defeated enemies in Latin America, or playing Russian roulette; today, even football matches may become

excuses for assassinations. On the other hand, I see a strong participation of the drives, both sexual and destructive.

(Green, 2005, p. 11)

Winnicott clearly would not have counted these grim examples of "play" as healthy playing in the transitional space, but this is not the main point of this passage. Here Green is deliberately drawing our attention to forms of play that work against psychic growth.

Lenormand (2018) highlights the widespread confusion that exists between the Winnicottian concepts of play and playing, which have often been used loosely and interchangeably in the literature, not least by Winnicott himself. This, Lenormand suggests, has led to a common misconception amongst many clinicians that all play is inherently creative, healthy, and self-curative, a view which she believes can all too easily lead to therapeutic "dead-ends". Green and Lenormand remind us that negative play and anti-play are often expressions of the child's attempts at self-cure. I would add that the corollary to this statement equally holds true: this overvaluation of pretend play and "creative" play in child psychotherapy and in child development has led directly to the long-standing lacuna regarding the therapeutic use of other forms of play which are not immediately and obviously identifiable as make-believe or creative play: game-play, play on smartphones or computer console games and sports, to name but a few.

Lenormand highlights the necessity and therapeutic benefit of paying attention to play in *all* its forms: be it impulse-driven, sublimatory, omnipotently narcissistic or "purely creative" play, healthy and not so healthy; and of understanding these different forms of play as psychodynamic communications at different levels and as serving different inter-psychic and intra-psychic purposes. She writes:

I suggest, therefore, that it is the way play is invested that seems clinically decisive. The unconscious logic that animates this or that form of play at one moment or another, particularly in the transference, might well serve as a more reliable guide for the clinician [than the form of play per se].

(Lenormand, 2018, p. 96)

Bringing these strands together, I think it would be true to say that Milnerian/Winnicottian playing, be it pretend play, "creative" play or game-play, is not defined by the rules, structure, or lack thereof, but by the "work of the negative" involved, the child's state of absent-mindedness, the experience of suspension of integration, of control, of saturated form, and the encounter with formlessness and unintegration combined with the aliveness of the drives, and basic physical and cognitive capacities of the individual playing. Formlessness, deconstruction, and unintegration should not be confused with disorganisation and disintegration: the former are features of playing, belong to the area of the healthy "work of the negative" and of negative capability; the latter belong to disturbed and destructive states of mind.

Green views the inability to play creatively and healthily as connected to the destructive and excessive aspects of the drives, to traumatic anxiety, and to the work of the negative and to negative hallucination in its pathological forms (Green, 1997, 2005). In his view, when the holding experience is not good enough *and* capacities of the infant's psyche are tilted towards the destructive elements of the negative, the absence of the parental holding becomes the driving psychic theme, and a blank hallucination fills, or rather wipes out, the space left by the holding frame.[5] He quotes Winnicott: "failure of the [external object] in some essential function indirectly leads to deadness or to a persecutory quality of the internal object" (Winnicott, 1971, p. 9) "and thus the transitional object becomes meaningless too" (Green, 1997, p. 1074). The evacuating and obliterating aspects of the negative then come to the fore, what Perelberg (2016) calls the "negative hallucination of thought", which "leaves holes and emptiness in the psyche", in which the destructive excessively persecutory aspects of the drives can run rife. This is where negative play dominates the game:

> And just as Bion created the symbol "K" for Knowledge, he also created "-K" as its complement. I believe that play, apart from its emotional value, is a form of thought (like the dream) or of knowledge that, according to some patients, is a form of not knowing. In the same way, just as treacherous, cruel, and destructive plays are forms of non-playing, they can also be seen as negative playing. Nothing is left to chance. The winner or the loser (as in the negative therapeutic reaction) is known in advance. Domination infiltrates the whole playing. It is difficult to extract oneself from these "foul plays".
>
> (Green, 2005, pp. 12–13)

Much of psychotherapy is spent in this area of treacherous and cruel "foul play", when play is not "the thing", it is not the vehicle for promoting health and creativity, but should be seen rather as the "activity that provides the material for analysis" (as quoted earlier, Gavshon, 1989). Winnicott describes this form of play as linked to a "denial of the inner world", contrasted with healthy play(ing), which he described as "a simple and enjoyable dramatisation of inner world life". In these disturbed states of mind, "The play is always compulsive, [repetitive], excited, anxiety driven, and more sense exploiting than happy" (Winnicott, 1975, p. 37, quoted in Lenormand, 2018, p. 91,). Just as play has been added to Freud's fundamental tenets of psychological health of work and love, so, in the light of Green's analysis of Winnicottian playing and of negative play, I think it could be useful to think of play in all its shades along the continuum from P to –P, alongside Bion's axes of L, H, and K. This raises the question of whether –P is always associated with –K or whether by dint of the fact that some forms of negative play (–P) are attempts at self-cure or at communication with a containing other, or are serving the drives, but not necessarily attacking psychic knowledge per se, these could be seen as attempts at +K or completely independent of K. This is a subject for discussion, in and of itself, beyond the scope of this book.

Over the last few decades, with the changing emphasis in child psychoanalytic psychotherapy towards deep work with children in more disturbed and traumatised states of mind, an increasing number of authors have described similar states of negative play, meaningless play, dissociated, perverse, dead, and disorganised play (Alvarez, 1988, 1989, 2010; Blake, 2011; Ferro, 2003; Kernberg, 2000; Molinari, 2017; Tustin, 1988). Each author has emphasised and described different manifestations of these states of negative play, each within their own psychoanalytic frame of reference, but all maintain that these forms of play, though not self-curative and not Winnicottian playing, are forms of unconscious and conscious communications that demand and deserve psychotherapeutic interventions.

Tustin described these states of communicative anti-play particularly clearly:

> [These children] are not hiding/repressing/disguising feelings and fantasies they cannot tolerate. They are living in a chaotic emotional universe that, by virtue of its very disorganization, precludes disguise because it precludes symbolization [...Their] play does not serve to hide or disguise; rather, their play is a manifestation of the failure to make meaning on any level.
>
> (Tustin, 1988, p. 89)

As discussed in the previous chapter, Slade, who wrote extensively on play in psychoanalytic work with young children, has called attention to these modes of negative play with a deep sensitivity for the disturbances and disorganisation she observed in her young patients' play:

> Sometimes their play was highly disorganized, vague, and primitive; at other times, they couldn't make-believe at all. Instead, they immersed themselves in barren, repetitive play that made any attempt at discussion or interpretation impossible.
>
> (Slade, 1994, p. 81)

She views these children "who cannot use the symbols of play and language to make sense of their emotional experiences, who cannot create narratives for their experiences" as possessing immature or developmentally compromised representational abilities (Slade, 1994, pp. 81–82). For Slade then, the aim of psychotherapy with these children is to make meaning through play, not via interpretation from the outside, but by joining in the play and by interpretations and movements in the play. I would suggest that techniques such as these and those described by Blake, quoted above, can be applied equally to game-play with older children who function at what Slade (1994, pp. 81–82) calls the prerepresentational level and whose play is similarly disorganised and compromised. (Such techniques shall be examined and elaborated upon in Chapters 7–8.) It is my clinical experience that for older children in these states of mind, it frequently happens that the only way to facilitate the beginnings of Winnicottian playing is by providing a "robust enough" framing structure in the form of a structured game with rules and boundaries, which enables the child to suspend their addiction to compliance or to destruction and obliteration. Paradoxically, in such cases, it is only by dint of the "organisational aspects" of these games do children dare to allow a modicum of formlessness and spontaneity to gradually enter their play.

Tustin also emphasised the nothingness and deadness that often takes over these forms of –P:

> This sense of 'nothingness', and its inhibiting effect on play, was well illustrated by a sad observation of a speaking child who was very isolated. ...[The little girl] would purposely select defective materials such as broken pencils, and then apathetically try to draw with them. The word 'nothing' stippled her conversation, both with herself and with the observer. For example, she drew 'snakes doing nothing'. She also drew something which she called 'nothing going very fast'. She picked up a fawn pencil crayon and said, 'It's not brown, it's a nothing colour'. After talking about a loaf of bread which had been obliterated by a shower of rain, Jane drew 'spots of nothing'.
>
> (Tustin, 1990, p. 103)

Developing Tustin's ideas, and weaving in Winnicott's thinking, Alvarez (2012) suggests that some play lacks meaning because the child's psychic development has been founded on an excess of *not-me* experiences, on an experience of remoteness and desolation that leaves a "symbolic emptiness", and identification with emptiness. She highlights the possibility that some objects are experienced by the infant child as entirely alien, entirely not me, empty of me, and that play for children in these states of mind has a quality of desolation. In these situations, it is the blankness and meaninglessness that takes over.[6] Other authors have suggested that anxieties of separation from the object, loss of the object or fragmentation and disintegration are the underlying causes of negative forms of play. Kleinian and post-Kleinian authors tend to stress the destructive aspects linked to envy, greed, and rage. Bionian and post Bionian authors such as Ferro and Molinari concentrate on failures of containment, excessive projective identification and malignant containment. Many authors place the origins of perversions of play in cumulative neglect, deprivation, and trauma. But all seem to agree that negative play, pseudo-play, drive-infused play, destructive play, meaningless play, all serve the purpose of communication in child psychotherapy. These forms of play can be understood in many ways: as a desperate attempt at self-cure; as a method of wreaking revenge on the persecutory and abusive world they have experienced; and/or as a defence against these cruelties and trauma. I would argue furthermore that such perversions of play appear equally in game-play as in pretend play and all demand different forms of therapeutic interventions, in tune with the underlying communication and state of mind of the child, as shall be discussed and illustrated in the following chapters.

6.5   Conclusions: 50 shades of game-play

I have ended this chapter with a discussion of perversions of play, forms of what I have suggested can be called–P. Now I would like to go back one step. I would like to emphasise here the many shades and forms of play, playing, and negative play across the spectrum of pretend play and game-play. Not only should–P and P be conceived of as lying on a continuum between dead, empty, "soul-destroying" play on the one end and alive creative Milnerian/Winnicottian play on the other, but these forms of play and perverse play can be coloured by the drives, anxieties, and unconscious phantasies as Klein (1927) understood a century ago, and they serve as rich and varied forms of intra-psychic and inter-psychic communication for the child inside and outside the psychotherapy playroom. The closing paragraphs of Lenormand's (2018) article summarise this approach clearly and concisely:

> …All these forms [of play] need, therefore, to be envisaged from the moment the clinician allows the child to play freely in the space of his or her consulting room. Only attentive listening to play, to the unconscious logic that animates it, and to the way that it fits into the transference and the demand will enable the clinician to know how to respond to it. *I suggest, therefore, that, rather than relying unconditionally on the virtues of playing, the emergence of which should of course never be excluded, it is by identifying how this or that form of play fits into the logic of the transference, according to this or that unconscious logic, and at a given moment in the analysis, that the clinician will have a chance of finding his or her bearings.*
>
> (Lenormand, 2018, pp. 99–100)

These ideas are equally relevant for game-play as for pretend make-believe play and the creative arts. The very names of children's games betray the passions of the psyche they can reveal: *Monopoly, War, Spit, Risk, Frustration,* and *Cheat.* Or take the game of darts for instance, and its many possible various forms: the child can throw a dart with elegance and flourish true to what Alvarez (1989) suggests is an expression of the aesthetic of the depressive position found in children's love of sports; they can throw the dart forcefully and with determination straight at the centre of the target as a sublimation of their sexual desires and aggressive urges; the game can become overwhelming and threatening and turn perverse, the dart aimed at the therapy room walls or at the therapist herself; or the game can be mechanical, dead, no joy, no drives, no movement, going nowhere, coming from blankness in the child's psyche. But all these are therapeutic communications "in game" (Ferro & Nicoli, 2017), to be responded to at the same level, calibrated to the child's age, state of mind, and stage in therapy (Alvarez, 2012). I would add that the intervention we choose not only depends on the particular inter-psychic and intra-psychic mechanism at hand, but also on the focus of the therapeutic work at that moment, as shall be seen.

In the next two chapters, I shall concentrate on identifying and describing how the drives, conflicts, and more archaic destructive and obliterative forces of the psyche, on the one hand, and formlessness, deconstruction, and unintegration, on the other, appear in structured games. My focus will be especially on the many and varied forms of -P in game-play and the critical question of how we can use the age appropriate and familiar language of game-play to enable the older child to gradually abandon negative play and develop "positive" Winnicottian/Milnerian playing. These issues will be addressed explicitly and implicitly in the following chapters, often "experientially" through the clinical vignettes described, as befits Winnicottian playing and Bionian "learning from experience", – first in the triangular and polygonal space (Chapter 7) and then in the playing field of the transference–countertransference matrix (Chapter 8).

Notes

1 See Chapter 8 for further discussion on using structured games to expand the Bionian capacities to think and to dream.
2 Green (1999).
3 Lise Meitner (1878 – 1968) was an Austrian-Swedish nuclear physicist who was the first to describe and explain the mechanism by which large atoms like Uranium split and release radioactive energy, the process which she named nuclear fission.
4 Take, for example, the exhibition of "Picasso's women" exhibited around the world in various configurations and under various titles, which bears witness to this phenomenon. Picasso's paintings are monumental and brilliant works of art, but reflect his deep pathological narcissistic attitudes to women, whom he viewed, by his own admission as either "goddesses" or "doormats" (Gilot et al., 2019). The experience of the viewer is one of impingement (one could say even traumatic impingement), not of expansion of the Winnicottian transitional space.
5 This is a highly simplified and abbreviated version of Green's critique of Winnicott's thinking. See Green (Abram, 2018; Green, 1999, 2005) and Perelberg (2016) for a full in-depth discussion of these points.
6 See Subchapter 7.4 for discussion of therapeutic game-play with children in such states of mind.

Bibliography

Abram, J. (2018). *Andre Green at the Squiggle Foundation*. Routledge.
Alvarez, A. (1988). Beyond the unpleasure principle: Some preconditions for thinking through play. *Journal of Child Psychotherapy, 14*(2), 1–13.
Alvarez, A. (1989). Development toward the latency period: Splitting and the need to forget in borderline children. *Journal of Child Psychotherapy, 15*(2), 71–83.
Alvarez, A. (2010). Levels of analytic work and levels of pathology: The work of calibration. *The International Journal of Psychoanalysis, 91*(4), 859–878.
Alvarez, A. (2012). *The Thinking Heart: Three Levels of Psychoanalytic Therapy with Disturbed Children*. Routledge.
Bion, W. R. (1962). *Learning from Experience*. Tavistock.
Blake, P. (2011). *Child and Adolescent Psychotherapy*. Karnac Books.

Bromberg, P. M. (1998). *Standing in the Spaces: Essays on Clinical Process, Trauma, and Dissociation*. Analytic Press.

Eigen, M. (1981). The area of faith in Winnicott, Lacan and Bion. *The International Journal of Psychoanalysis*, *62*(4), 413–433.

Ferro, A. (2003). *The Bi-Personal Field: Experiences in Child Analysis*. Routledge.

Ferro, A., & Nicoli, L. (2017). *The New Analyst's Guide to the Galaxy: Questions about Contemporary Psychoanalysis*. Karnac Books.

Gavshon, A. (1989). Playing: Its role in child analysis. *Journal of Child Psychotherapy*, *15*(1), 47–62.

Gilmore, K., & Meersand, P. (2013). *Normal Child and Adolescent Development: A Psychodynamic Primer*. American Psychiatric Pub.

Gilot, F., Lake, C., & Alther, L. (2019). *Life with Picasso (Reprint edition)*. NYRB Classics.

Green, A. (1997). The intuition of the negative in playing and reality. *International Journal of Psycho-Analysis*, *78*, 1071–1084.

Green, A. (1999). *The Work of the Negative*. Free Assn Books.

Green, A. (2005). *Play and Reflection in Donald Winnicott's Writings*. Karnac Books.

Keats, J. (1925). *Letters of John Keats to His Family and Friends (Si. Colvin, Ed.)*. Macmillan.

Kernberg, P. F. (2000). The forms of play. In K. von Klitzing, P. Tyson, & D. Burgin (Eds.), *Psychoanalysis in Childhood and Adolescence* (pp. 25–41). Karger Publishers.

Klein, M. (1927). The psychological principles of infant analysis. *The International Journal of Psycho-Analysis*, *8*, 25.

Lanyado, M., & Horne, A. (2009). *The Handbook of Child and Adolescent Psychotherapy: Psychoanalytic Approaches*. Routledge.

Lenormand, M. (2018). Winnicott's theory of playing: A reconsideration. *The International Journal of Psychoanalysis*, *99*(1), 82–102.

Levi, P. (2003). *The Search for Roots: A Personal Anthology (P. Forbes, Trans.)*. Ivan R Dee.

Levy, A. J. (2008). The therapeutic action of play in the psychodynamic treatment of children: A critical analysis. *Clinical Social Work Journal*, *36*(3), 281–291.

McLeish, T. (2019). *The Poetry and Music of Science: Comparing Creativity in Science and Art*. Oxford University Press.

Meersand, P. (2009). Play and the older child: Developmental and clinical opportunities. *The Psychoanalytic Study of the Child*, *64*(1), 112–130.

Milner, M. (1942). The child's capacity for doubt. In M. Milner, *The Suppressed Madness of Sane Men: Forty-Four years of Exploring Psychoanalysis* (pp. 9–11). Routledge.

Milner, M. (1957a). *On Not Being Able To Paint*. Heinemann.

Milner, M. (1957b). *The Ordering of Chaos. In the Suppressed Madness of Sane Men: Forty-Four Years of Exploring Psychoanalysis* (pp. 216–233). Routledge/Taylor & Francis Group.

Milner, M. (2005). *The Suppressed Madness of Sane Men: Forty-Four Years of Exploring Psychoanalysis*. Routledge.

Molinari, E. (2017). Variations on a theme: Child and adolescent analysis. In A. Ferro (Ed.), *Contemporary Bionian Theory and Technique in Psychoanalysis* (pp. 176–216). Routledge.

Ogden, T. H. (1985). On potential space. *International Journal of Psycho-Analysis*, *66*, 129–141.

Ogden, T. H. (2001). Reading Winnicott. *The Psychoanalytic Quarterly*, *70*(2), 299–323.

Perelberg, R. J. (2016). Negative hallucinations, dreams and hallucinations: The framing structure and its representation in the analytic setting. *International Journal of Psycho-Analysis*, 97(6), 1575–1590.

Schiller, F. von. (1795). *On the Aesthetic Education of Man, in a Series of Letters (R. Snell, Trans.)*. F. Ungar.

Slade, A. (1994). Making meaning and making believe: Their role in the clinical process. In Slade, A., & Wolf, D. (Eds.), *Children at Play: Clinical and Developmental Approaches to Meaning and Representation* (pp. 81–107). Oxford University Press.

Solnit, A. J. (1993). *The Many Meanings of Play: A Psychoanalytic Perspective*. ERIC.

Solnit, A. J. (1997). Beyond play and playfulness. *The Psychoanalytic Study of the Child*, *53*, 102–110.

Spelman, M. B., & Raphael-Leff, J. (2022). *The Marion Milner Tradition: Lines of Development: Evolution of Theory and Practice over the Decades*. Taylor & Francis.

Tustin, F. (1988). Psychotherapy with children who cannot play. *International Review of Psycho-Analysis*, *15*(1), 93–106.

Tustin, F. (1990). Psychotherapy with children who cannot play. In F. Tustin, *The Protective Shell in Children and Adults* (pp. 97–121). Karnac/Routledge.

Winnicott, D. W. (1971). The use of an object and relating through identifications. In D.W. Winnicott, *Playing and Reality* (pp. 101–111). Penguin Books.

Winnicott, D. W. (1975). *Through Paediatrics to Psycho-Analysis: Collected Papers*. The Hogarth Press and the Institute of Psycho-Analysis.

Winnicott, D. W. (1987). *Child, the Family, and the Outside World*. Addison-Wesley Pub. Co.

Winnicott, D. W. (1989). Notes on play. In C. Winnicott, R. Shepherd, & M. Davis (Eds.), *Psychoanalytic Explorations* (pp. 59–63). Karnac Books.

Chapter 7

Game-play and the dyadic, the triangular and the polygonal space in psychotherapy

Having established game-play as a bona fide form of play and potential psycho-therapeutic language, we are ready to investigate in detail questions of technique and goals: questions of when, and moreover how, to use the traditional game-speak of middle childhood in psychotherapy with school-aged children in different psychological states of mind.

This chapter will focus on therapeutic approaches using game-play to expand the triangular and polygonal psychic space in the psychotherapy room. I will use a "top-down" approach, psychodynamically speaking, with reference to three levels of psychoanalytic meaning and psychic functioning and therapeutic work. This division will be broadly in line with what are often defined as the neurotic, borderline, and psychotic levels of functioning, corresponding, respectively, to psychic integration, splitting, and fragmentation and psychic death. These levels of functioning and states of mind are, needless to say, always found on a continuum and do not appear as discrete categories, neither in different groups of patients nor in the individual psyche, but they are states of mind experienced by the individual to a different degree at different moments and in different circumstances. Notwithstanding, these distinctions serve as useful or even necessary concepts when thinking about psychotherapeutic work with different psychic states.[1] Many authors writing over the last half century advocate flexibility and careful attunement in psychoanalytic psychotherapy, adjusting the level of therapeutic work/intervention/interpretation to the level of the psychic functioning of the patient (Alvarez, 2010, 2012; Britton, 2004, 2006; Ferro, 2017; Fonagy & Target, 1998; Grotstein, 2018; Kernberg, 1979, 1995; Kernberg et al., 2008; Ogden, 2018; Roth, 2001; Steiner, 2003).

These three levels will be discussed, respectively, in the three subchapters that follow. The first of these, Subchapter 7.1, will focus on the more symbolic, explanatory, interpretative, and sexuated aspects of triangularity and polygonality. Many different terms have been used to define what was once called the neurotic oedipal state of mind or the Kleinian depressive position. In these states of mind, a more or less clear distinction exists between the self and the other, between fantasy and reality, and the psyche is free to tackle the more complex and nuanced issues connected to self and identity, autonomy and individuality, sexuality and gender, as a

DOI: 10.4324/9781003425229-10

whole and separate individual existing in connection with and in interaction with others in the family and in the outside world.

From this complex level of thought and psychic integration, I shall proceed to examining psychotherapeutic work through the medium of the game-play with school-aged children in "borderline" states of mind. Here, thinking and interaction are dyadic: this is the level equivalent to Klein's "schizoid-paranoid" level; Winnicottian "subjective-object/object-relating"; Mahler's "separation-individuation"; Rosenfeld's "thick and thin skinned" patients (Rosenfeld, 1987); and Britton's "hyper-subjective" and "hyper-objective" patients (Britton, 2004). At this level of analytic work, the movement is on the cusp between dyadic and triadic thinking, between splitting and integration, from relating dyadically, in parallel, discrete, disconnected dyads with internal parental and sibling objects to observing other internalised dyads from an outside perspective. This can be conceived as movement towards relating to the outside other, the third, or to the imagined other in the object, from within the dyadic relationship: Movement towards a vertex outside of the subject–subjective object dyad that creates a triangular psychic space. The complexities of a multiplicity of dyads and triads and the nuances of gender identities and identity integration are barely relevant at this level of work: indeed, it can even be detrimental if such issues are introduced when the child is functioning and interacting in this more "primitive" state of mind (see Alvarez 2010, 2012).

Lastly, I shall discuss therapeutic work with school-aged children when the most primitive states of mind are dominant. Such states can be divided roughly into two categories: states of fragmentation, chaos, symbiosis, and merger, on the one hand, akin to so-called psychotic states; and in a separate category, states of psychic deadness, anaclitic despair, autistic encapsulation, and catatonia. At these primitive and non-alive levels of functioning (or rather non-functioning), the issue is no longer triangularity, but an issue of space between the subject and the object at the most rudimentary "linear", "me/not-me", level. Psychotherapeutic work with children in these states of mind takes place at the fundamental level of facilitating primitive organisation and movement of the psyche, of turning fragmentary chaos into order and space per se, of breathing life and aliveness into the therapy itself, and so into the patient's psyche and inner world. These are levels of functioning where the emergence of splitting and splitting-off often signals a developmental advance for the child (Alvarez, 1989). And here, perhaps surprisingly, the age-old beloved games of middle childhood, with their inherent space and order, and their familiar age-appropriate content, combined with the inevitable element of contained surprise, can sometimes offer an escape from chaos on the one hand, and psychic impasse, deadness, on the other.

The discussion in this chapter will flow through the three subchapters that follow, from the more complex states of mind and psychic functioning to the more basic levels, from the metaphor of "polygonality" (see chapter 3 for explanation of this term), to "triangularity" to the basic linear dyadic level of linear movement between the psyche and the other.

7.1   The polygonal and the triangular space

When viewed through the polygonal prism of psychosexual and psychosocial development (as detailed in chapter 3), the psychotherapeutic paradigm based on the playroom of early childhood is weighted towards the sphere of what has been traditionally regarded as the maternal, the sphere of the mother–infant dyad, privileging boundlessness, receptivity, subjectivity and being over productivity, emancipation, cognition, and doing. I contend here that the simple addition to the child psychotherapy room of the traditional competitive structured games of middle childhood, symbolic of the "objective" and "exciting" outside world, bounded in time and place, a world of action, discovery, and adventure, naturally redresses this long-standing imbalance. By offering children of this age the full gamut of toys, dolls, creative materials, bats, balls, and structured games in the psychotherapy room, we can create the very "multi-gendered systems of operations" (Balsam, 2018) they need in which to explore the "maternal", the "paternal", the "paternal in the maternal", the "maternal in the paternal" (Ogden, 1987), and also the fraternal and the sororal, in all their polygonal shapes and forms.

It should be emphasised here that the dichotomies between maternal and paternal, being and doing, emotion and cognition, receptivity and competition, structured games, and imaginative creativity, are in and of themselves distortions and deceptive myths. The very names of many childhood games bear witness to the seething emotional world concealed within the framing structure of the game: *Cheat, War, Risk, Spit, Slam, Dungeons and Dragons, Battleships, Fox and Hounds, Frustration,* and *Snakes and Ladders*, to name but a few. Anyone who has ever played any of these games, whether therapist, educationalist, parent, teenager, or child, knows full well the visceral emotions that all too easily erupt at the mere throw of a six or a flip of an ace. And likewise, the creative imaginative world often relies on cognition, on unwritten rules or narrative, on skill and symbolic thinking. Conversely, fantasy and imaginative make-believe play can be stifled by ego-defensive elements as easily as a game of football or *Monopoly* can be disrupted and descend into chaos, under the influences of primal urges and anxieties. Cognition, emotion, creativity, and logical reasoning are not independent axes of mental functioning, nor are they associated with disconnected opposing hemispheres in the brain, as some theories and cultural myths have had us believe; in reality, throughout our lives, they act in tandem in the mind and in the psyche.

In this context, I would suggest that the multiplayer structure of many board games, such as *Frustration, Cluedo, Monopoly*, or *Talisman*, with choices of different pawns, player identities, or cards, immediately lays down a polygonal field of play and projection of internal objects onto the playing board. Themes of sibling rivalries and peer relations run through all such games. The game board with its four sides and multiple characters in the game; the football pitch with its inbuilt structure of teamplay; even a pack of cards with its symbolic hierarchical royal family; all embody horizontal as well as vertical (Mitchell, 2013) familial and social relations. Even if the child and therapist are but two in the room, imaginary rivals (symbolic of the parental or sibling internal and real life external objects) are built into many of these games, in the form of different player identities (in games such as *Monopoly, Cluedo,* and *Talisman*), in wild cards and taxation, or monsters, or magicians in *Talisman or Dungeon.* These are "rivals" to be captured or overcome in the game through cunning and bravery, or who conversely threaten to wipe the child right out of the game (echoing the themes from children's adventure books and films from *Peter Pan* to *Harry Potter* to *Frozen* and *Mulan*).

To recap the developmental formulation discussed in Chapter 3, it is at this polygonal level of psychic organisation and functioning that the child, or indeed the adult at different moments throughout the lifespan, examines the more nuanced issues and questions connected to identity, to the self, including the body self and the sexual and gendered self, also in relation to the other and the outside world. The child is on an unconscious and conscious quest to answer questions such as "Who am I?"; "What am I made of?"; "Am I boy, girl, a mixture, both or neither?"; "Am I still a baby or maybe already an adult?"; "Who are my parents? And my siblings?"; "With whom do I identify?"; "To whom am I similar?"; "In what ways am I different?"; "What are my likes, my dislikes, my strengths, my weaknesses?"; "How do I manage my emotions, my body, my impulses, and drives within the real world?" This is a multifaceted quest, encompassing questions of identity, identification and belonging, examination of questions of sexuality and gender that is, as we have seen above, often at the heart of children's literature and traditional children's games.

I turn here to two clinical vignettes to illustrate how a flexibly and diversely equipped child psychotherapy playroom can allow children to express and explore freely the complexities of issues of identity, gender identity and integration, the enigma of difference, and the fact of incompleteness, discussed in Chapter 3. I begin with a vignette where the issues of gender identity and identifications were clear and overtly expressed by a 10-year-old girl who almost exclusively dressed in boys clothes and would play nothing but football and volleyball in our sessions; and then proceed to the case of a small anxious boy who played repeated games of Flight 501 (a world flight travel board game) for weeks on end, in order to explore his ambivalent identifications with his father, who was loving and caring, but all too often away from the home on work trips abroad.

VIGNETTE A – "Monopoly is way too girly a game for me!"

Ella, a ten-year-old girl, one of four girls all very close in age, was referred for psychotherapy by her parents, who had noticed in her signs of unhappiness, even depression, alongside a tendency towards angry outbursts and destructive impulsivity. During the intake, it became clear that Ella came from a warm, caring, and intelligent family, but was having difficulty finding her niche as an individual in her female dominated family. She loved sports especially football, was always on the move, and had little patience for her schoolwork, though she was clearly quick thinking and intelligent. Ella felt she did not fit in, had never liked arts and crafts, nor playing with dolls, nor ballet and dresses, and found it hard to find a common language with her sisters and with the girls at school. She dressed exclusively in sweatpants and sweatshirts or shorts and T-shirts in the summer and shied away from any behaviour or activities she perceived as "girly". The girls at school played games that Ella said did not interest her, and the boys with whom Ella had played when younger were reticent to include her in their games now they were older, for fear they would be teased and ostracised by the more macho aggressive boys in the class.

In therapy, Ella talked about her negative feelings towards her sisters and her ambivalence about being a girl. But hers did not seem to me to be a classic case of gender dysphoria. Talking helped, but not enough. She seemed stuck in her anger, jealousy, and feelings of rejection. In time, I realised that she needed me not only to listen, but also to engage with her actively in the therapy, as "biological female" to "biological female", but through the gamut of gender identifications. At first, Ella stuck to football and volleyball, competing with me with all her skills and might, as if trying to prove to me she was as good, or better, than any boy I had ever played. I thoroughly enjoy ball games, but after a while, I felt that with Ella, these games were beginning to lack flexibility and spontaneity. Her emotional world was restricted and stifling: it seemed to me she had adopted a false-self solution, sticking rigidly, almost obsessively, to games and sports favoured by boys.

It became clear that Ella had become stuck in a rut in therapy, as in her emotional life, and I decided that it was time to challenge her in different directions. I thought it was worth suggesting a board game or a card game as a change from basketball and football. Ella reluctantly chose *Monopoly* off the shelf. She had mentioned that her sisters often played Monopoly, but she claimed it had never interested her and preferred practicing football outside on her own whilst they played together. I wondered whether Ella's reluctance to play was not in fact based on a lack of interest and curiosity in the game, but rather due to her anxiety lest her sisters reject her. Maybe she had chosen the "sour grapes approach" (the game's no fun anyway) rather than risk rejection, and her sisters for their part perhaps benefited from scapegoating her as the "annoying problem sister" who could not play without throwing a tantrum?

We set about playing. Ella covered her retreat at first, saying *Monopoly* was boring, a game for "sissies". It soon became apparent that she actually enjoyed the game, almost too much: she found it hard to know how to channel her aggression and her need to win, perceiving herself as destructive rather than competitive. As in our football games, she needed me to put up a fight, to take joy in her competitiveness, and to be able to handle her aggression, without retribution. From *Monopoly*, we progressed to the card game *Spit/ Speed*, where aggression and competitiveness are a must, and which had been labelled in Ella's mind as belonging to the girls' world. Ella needed me to be strong and competitive, to uphold the rules of the game, which she felt protected her from her own aggression. Equally, she needed me to express my own libido and aggression, freely, spontaneously, and without anxiety, all through the metaphor of the game. All of this allowed Ella to expand her paths of self-expression and begin to explore issues of gender identifications, through other structured games, through experiencing me as a female therapist taking on a range of stereotypically feminine and masculine roles in the games we played. In time, these explorations spilled over into Ella's relationships with her sisters at home, her mode of dress, and her more varied social interactions with her peers at school.

***

It is interesting to note in the context of this section, that Monopoly had become gendered in Ella's mind as a girls' game, so in this case and to my surprise, we played Monopoly, a game usually identified with the male world of commerce and finance, as a vehicle through which to enlarge the polygonal space in the direction of what Ella perceived as dangerous, out of bounds, femininity.

VIGNETTE B   My absent father the frequent flyer – from angst to anger and potency

Filip's father went on regular business trips, once every month for two weeks each time. Sometimes, on the rare occasions that Dad flew to Europe, the trip was foreshortened to only ten days, and these were the times Filip (aged 8) looked forward to. The most treasured times were at Christmas and the New Year when Dad did not travel at all and was at home for a whole month. Filip's parents were both adamant that these trips made no difference to home life and that Dad was an involved and active father, more than most stay-at-home Dads. Filip himself became fiercely defensive if I so much as hinted he might find these prolonged and repeated absences upsetting. So I desisted and quietly bided my time, but made sure that, alongside Monopoly and the packs of cards, the world travel game Flight 501[2] was on a lower shelf easily visible to this rather small patient of mine. After many sessions of darts and football, Filip decided he wanted to play a board game with me, and his eye fell on the picture of the aeroplane on the cover of Flight 501.

We sat down on the carpet together, opened the box, and laid out between us the map of the world we found inside. He asked me where Taiwan, China, Germany, and the US were on the map, all countries his father frequently visited. And Britain, where I had flown to recently on one of my family visits. We each took the requisite five cards, each card with a name of a different city, which we had to visit on our travels around the world before returning "home" to the country where Filip lived. Filip asked to see my cards and became almost visibly green with jealousy to discover that I had cities in the US and the Far East where his father had visited, even if only for a stopover. He had to have those cards himself, to hold them in his possession; it did not matter to him that these were cards that made his route longer and more tortuous and increased his likelihood of losing. The next game, he asked to choose the cards himself, to choose the cities whose names he knew from Dad's business trips. At this point, the game itself and the rules seemed to me to be of little importance, and I let Filip have his way, realising that he desperately needed to fly with his father to the same countries and cities to which his father flew. In essence, he needed to be his father, travelling across the globe, week after week, session after session. On occasion, he asked me to read to him what was written on the cards about the different cities, but his curiosity was very superficial. His need was not driven by curiosity about the places his father visited but was more visceral, almost like a "father hunger" (Herzog, 2013), a need to possess these names and places, and thereby both "become" his father (more through incorporation than through identification) and simultaneously and magically erase the gaps and holes created by his fathers' absences. My comments were limited in this period to comments on Filip's need to possess the cards and his fantasy of being his father.

As the weeks went by, the cards began to lose their primal visceral attraction as objects to be possessed and incorporated, and Filip seemed less sad and more alive in the sessions. His parents reported that he was less anxious and more joyful and playful at school. (His anxieties had played out more at school, probably because of his anxiety at separation from home). I wondered whether the time was now ripe to help Filip move to a more symbolic identification with his father and decided that I would try playing the game with him now more in line with the rules, dealing the cards out by chance, and encouraging him to discover the world and be competitive. Playing this way could help Filip explore being *like* his father *symbolically*, rather than magically incorporating the cards and fantasmatically, concretely, *being* his father. It took him time, but Filip began to enjoy the game more and more as a game, he focused on strategy and how to beat me and tried to cheat when I was in the lead. As he mastered the rules and the strategies of the game, he asked to deal out more cards to each of us so as to make the game more challenging. In tandem, his curiosity came alive: he avidly read the information on the cards about the different cities and asked me to tell him more about the different countries and continents in the world.

***

This level of work with Filip can be conceptualised as on the cusp between the level of symbolic formulation and true symbolic thinking and functioning (Segal, 1957, 1978). As such, it could be said to be more relevant to the dyadic–triadic level of work discussed in the next section. However, the vignette is included here both because Filip in therapy functioned in general at a polygonal integrated level, with a good-enough emotional primary parental base, and because Filip's use of the game *Flight 501* poignantly highlights the therapeutic power of board games in issues of identification with the father or what could be called the "realm of the father" (the third), and with the wider outside world (beyond the third, the polygonal space). As in the previous vignette, with Ella, where *Monopoly* was identified as associated with femininity and being girly, this game of Flight 501 could equally be used by a child to explore issues of concrete and symbolic identification with their globe-trotting "outside-world oriented" mother, rather than father. However, the mix of identificatory introjections of reproductive and productive aspects of the parental imago, of being and doing, activity and passivity, and matters of gender identification would of course all be different. It is upon the therapist to be flexible in their own polygonal psychic space and so enable the child–patient to explore their own gender and parental identifications freely and flexibly.

7.1.1 Potency, autonomy, mastery, and self-esteem, striving towards development and health

Perhaps, some of the most overarching issues at this level of individuation, autonomy, agency, and responsibility are those that largely come under the umbrella of potency, efficacy, mastery, and self-esteem. At this stage of development, the task for the child is gradually to learn to abandon mastery through omnipotent fantasy in favour of *real-world mastery and agency*:

> The acceptance of irrefutable and irresistible laws of reality is an essential precondition to successful adjustment to that reality....In other words, if one does not admit the existence of an objective reality, unaffected by one's wishes, skills in dealing with that reality are unlikely to develop.
>
> (Meeks, 1970, p. 161)

Much of the literature on structured games in child development in general, and in child psychotherapy in particular, centres around these issues (Beiser, 1979a,b; Bettelheim, 1972; Capell, 1968; Freud, 1966; Peller, 1954). Which perhaps is not surprising, given that so many childhood activities at home and at school, alone and with peers, are devoted towards mastery and agency (as detailed in Chapter 3). Beiser asserted that formal games can and should be used by psychotherapists to help the school-aged child work through issues surrounding infantile omnipotence and work towards "realistic mastery" (see Chapters 1 and 4).

In the psychotherapy room, it is my experience that activities that focus on issues of omnipotent versus realistic mastery, at this level of greater psychic integration and robustness, tend to be divided into four broad categories: (1) the practicing and honing of gross motor skills, be it sporting tricks, athletic feats, or ball games; (2) developing cognitive strategic tactical skills and knowledge that are, not by chance, an integral part of traditional card games and board games; and (3) perfecting fine motor skills often through building games such as Lego or through the latest craze in arts and crafts, such as rubber band bracelets or slime manufacture. A fourth category involves the fads and collections children of this age accrue and bring with pride to the therapy room: from football cards, to Magic and Fortnite cards, from the conkers of yesteryear to the worldwide slime craze of 20-teens.

As discussed above, this fourth category of fads and collections serves multiple psychological and social purposes and is integral to the transition from infantile omnipotence to real-world mastery. The child feels strong, powerful, and important when they own many collectibles, they entertain grandiose fantasies of possessing all the best items and being No. 1 collector in the class, the school (the world!). They learn to deal with the disappointment and hurt of being less wealthy and strong than their friends. Indeed, this category also frequently overlaps with the other three: many collections centre on themes of sports (football and baseball cards); or involve fine motor coordination skills like slime manufacture; and many informal "street" or "schoolyard" games with these collectibles have been invented by children themselves, based on motor skills like conkers or card flipping, or on cognitive skills such as with *Pokémon* and *Magic* cards (see reference in the preface to Francis Alÿs video art work of such children's games from around the world). Notwithstanding these more polygonal aspects, the obsessional and anal hoarding aspects of these collections speak for themselves. There is the endlessly repetitive "accounting and recounting" that typifies children's monologues around these collections. And then there are the tactile crazes like *Slime*, which offer the child opportunities to work through leftover issues associated with anality, challenging the therapist to confront their own issues around disgust, cleanliness, and order, often in directions where the parents in reality have difficulties in containing the mess involved.

During the course of this research, I found myself in a lengthy and surprising discussion on the merits of *Pokémon, Magic Attax* cards, and *Slime*, with two bright earnest primary school children,[3] both of whom spontaneously echoed the words of Canham and of Waddell on the subject, quoted in Chapter 3. Before elaborating further, by way of introduction to issues of meaning and significance of these childhood games in the psychotherapy room, I bring here a few of the thoughts they shared with me:

Why it is fun to collect and trade Pokémon cards (conversation with H, aged 10): I think it is fun to collect them because they teach you to trade with other people and the excitement of getting the cards that you need feels amazing. I also think it is interesting because on most types of cards there are normally some form of statistics which you can use to beat your opponents, very similar to the [classic] *Top Trumps*. Almost all cards have a picture and a group like a club or an element that they belong to.

The normal way to start trading is to show everyone your cards and then ask if anyone would like to trade for them. When you find someone who would like to trade with you, ask them what they would be willing to trade for it. If it feels like you are giving them more than they are giving you, ask them if they can put some more or better cards into the trade. The only problem in trading with your friends is that if you make a "bad" trade and you want your cards back, the other person has probably already realised this and is now taking advantage of your mistake. If they are a good friend, they will probably let you trade back but if they are greedy, they probably won't. The only way I have found around this is to get someone else involved for instance a friend of theirs or a teacher. The reason I think that teachers wanted to ban cards is that they cause a lot of trouble. I think that trading these cards will help me later on because it teaches me how to trade and gives me a chance to practice my techniques.

And what is fun about slime (conversation with G, aged 7)? It is interesting because it can come in any different sizes and colours and types, and there are so many things about slime like you can make your own slime and you don't have to ask someone to make it for you. I prefer to be playing with it with someone else because then we can each say how we like playing with it, and we can each give opinions on how we think it should be played with and how it feels and what it feels like.

It is fun to play with because it is sticky and stretchy, and it can be in all different types like water slime and cloud slime. Slime is interesting because you can explore what it is like, and it doesn't get boring because there are loads of different types. Every slime is unique, especially if you make your own. Water slime feels like it's really watery and cold, and it's really slimy and sticky, and it can easily slip out of your hand so it's really slippery like butter. Cloud slime feels like it's really really soft and puffy and you can poke it, and you can squeeze it and it's really really stretchy. You can make it into all different shapes and sizes.

******

At the polygonal level, many of these four categories of activities have benign interactional aspects to them (as opposed to the perverse or vindictive interactions that are the hallmark of borderline states of mind) which the child brings to the therapist–child relationship, whether at the level of the child's need for narcissistic encouragement and nourishment from the therapist *qua* therapist, or whether at the level of testing their own strength and mastery against the parental object or against their siblings and peers as embodied in the therapist. When the child involves the analytic therapist in these activities, multiple issues of technique arise which are complex to examine theoretically: clinical vignettes will be used to both demonstrate and illustrate the techniques discussed.

7.1.1.1 Athletic mastery and bodily self-esteem in the child psychotherapy room

Alvarez sees the activities focused on sporting skills and physical prowess as belonging to the "depressive level" and the child's developing sense of aesthetics for aesthetics' sake, independent of issues of competition, parricidal fantasies, or sublimated sexual drives (Alvarez, 1989). Many competitive ball games, and other traditional games based on motoric proficiency and skills, such as five stones or French skipping, challenge the player to advance to ever higher levels of skill and so foster an increased sense of competence and aesthetic satisfaction.

I would argue that these gross motor games of skill and sporting proficiency are especially important for boys in middle childhood. It is my clinical experience that the majority of 7–13-year-old boys entering the psychotherapy room instinctively and immediately look to kick a ball around or practice their basketball shooting skills, not as an escape from therapy but as a means of communicating safely, through the language of the back garden or local playing field they know best. Multiple surveys and behavioural and developmental research have documented a gender difference between girls and boys in patterns of play and choice of game in the years of middle childhood (Edwards et al., 2001; Kinzie & Joseph, 2008; Lever, 1976). These differences seem to be disappearing in recent years, particularly in North America and Western Europe (Van Rheenen, 2012), but are still particularly marked where games involving physical activity are involved (*Active Lives Survey*, 2018; Martínez-Andrés et al., 2017; Roud, 2010). The most common language of play for boys of this age in the school playground or local park, street, or backyard is the competitive ball game, be it basketball, football, baseball, or cricket depending on locality (Martínez-Andrés et al., 2017; Roud, 2010; Van Rheenen, 2012). This has been the case perhaps since time immemorial – there are records of games played by boys and young men involving kicking or hitting balls made of different materials dating back to ancient China, Greece, and Rome, through the Middle Ages to modern times. And boys who do not connect with their peers on the level of these nationally popular ball games often have a harder time socially, whereas for girls this is not the case. Even today, at a time when girls and women are more involved than ever before in these sports both on the amateur and professional level, social interaction between girls is still not predicated on ball game proficiency, as it often is for boys.

All this underlines the necessity, especially for boys, of options for ball games and for "sports sessions" in the analytic playroom. The more so since mental health problems are more frequently diagnosed in boys than in girls of this age group, and drop-out rates are significantly higher. It should be noted that the actual rates of occurrence of mental health problems are not necessarily higher amongst boys. Rather, the referral rates are most probably skewed by the tendency of boys to externalise mental health problems through acting out and disruptive behaviour, whereas girls of this age tend to internalise and withdraw and their emotional difficulties are consequently more likely to go undetected (Deakin et al., 2012, 2009; Hamblin, 2016; Midgley & Kennedy, 2011).

Different children, or the same child in different sessions and at different stages in the therapeutic process, use these games at many different levels of the therapeutic work. A more disturbed child, who may have experienced chronic deprivation, abuse, or cumulative trauma, whose inner world is peopled by persecutory and punitive part-objects, is likely to initiate a persecutory and punitive competitive ball game in which he will trap the therapist in a no-win situation, with every goal or basket being disqualified and every move declared a penalty. Another child might lose control and deliberately aim the ball to damage the room or hurt the therapist.[4] But these are not sufficient reasons to avoid ball games a priori, even if the situation is challenging. Such a deprived or abused child is just as likely to spray paint or throw felt tips and pencils or toy animals and sand around the room or at the therapist with equal venom. Or worse still, in the face of the regressive pull of the dolls, sand boxes, and creative materials, walk out of therapy and refuse to engage altogether (these issues are discussed in more detail below– Subchapter 8.3).

Self-esteem and self-confidence frequently take a severe hit in the transition from kindergarten to primary school, and many children referred to psychotherapy have come up against social and/or academic difficulties in primary school, often for a multiplicity of reasons, difficulties which frequently worsen as they move up through the school grades. At the level of psychic functioning under discussion in this section, where the child is in a more integrated state of mind, if the child chooses to play ball games or engage in other physical or sporting activities in the psychotherapy room, they often initially allocate to the therapist the role of "benevolent sports coach" or Kohutian, mirroring self-object (Kohut, 1977). This involves the therapist looking on and encouraging the child as they practice various skills, helping the child when they give up or are fearful to try, and containing the child's grandiose statements and narcissistic omnipotent attempts to hide their lack of belief in their abilities and their feelings of inadequacy. From here, as self-esteem and mastery become stronger and more stable, the child will usually gain the courage to challenge the therapist to interactive sporting games of football or basketball and the dilemmas as to how to play with the child become more complex.

Different therapeutic roles raise different therapeutic questions: to what extent does our mirroring strengthen the child's psyche and to what extent may we be reinforcing the child's pathological narcissism? Should you play your hardest or should you let the child win? To what extent is the frustration developmentally constructive and when is it harmful to the child's emerging self-esteem?

Beiser's (1979b) writing on the similarities between the term infantile omnipotence, grandiosity, ego ideal, narcissism, and self-esteem is relevant here. She maintains that healthy infantile omnipotence continues in different manifestations and to different levels of intensities from infancy through childhood and adolescence right up to young adulthood (and often beyond). She defines and distinguishes between infantile and pathological omnipotence thus:

> [I]nfantile omnipotence …is a feeling or fantasy of power… under the control of the self, which results in positive expectations before experience with reality has indicated otherwise. Pathological omnipotence is a defensive manoeuvre the ego may use to deal with a feeling of helplessness or angry frustration….[5]
>
> (Beiser, 1979b, p114)

To illustrate these points and add flesh to the theory, I present here two clinical vignettes[6] where ball games are central to the psychotherapy sessions, and from there, I will go on to tackle the question of self-esteem, agency, rules, and cheating in structured games in general.

VIGNETTE C   Mirroring and mastery: "See this trick, I'm going to be the next Lionel Messi!"

Alan, a slightly clumsy, shy, and, soft-spoken eight-year-old boy, short for his age and chubby, is referred to therapy for anxiety by his parents. In the initial assessment, it quickly became apparent that underlying his anxiety was considerable anger towards his siblings and aggressive fantasies alongside a "good-enough" home background and emotional base and higher than average cognitive abilities.

Alan certainly did not want to talk about what was troubling him, denied any worries and anxieties and shied away from all creative materials, dismissing them as "girly". But he loved football and immediately picked up on my English accent and quizzed me as to my knowledge of the ins and outs of the English football league, whilst making it very clear his allegiance was to *Real Madrid*. His eyes then fell on the football (full size, but made of sponge) I keep in the corner of my room, alongside ping pong bats and balls, a small rubber basketball and plastic net, elastic for French skipping, and a couple of small soft balls for throwing and catching. "May I?" Alan asked timidly and began to kick the ball around without waiting for an answer. He clearly didn't feel confident enough yet to play against me, but rather was intent on showing me every trick he had ever seen. It rapidly became painfully apparent that Alan's enthusiasm for the game far outweighed his talent. He tried unsuccessfully to bounce the ball from his knee to his foot and back again, he headed the ball in various directions, not those he had intended, and then showed me how he was "just like Lionel Messi" and could manoeuvre the ball from behind him and kick the ball straight in the makeshift goal we had made, all in one fell swoop. He promptly tripped over the ball and totally missed the goal, and then shot me a look as if to say: "you didn't see that!" In these initial stages of therapy, Alan clearly needed me to remain firmly inside his omnipotent fantasy of becoming the next all-time great footballer of the world. I was not to say a word, just look on and encourage him.

But it was not easy to go along with the falseness and grandiosity, nor to bear Alan's embarrassed and quite lame attempts to cover up his inadequacies. I felt he needed more from me than continuing merely to sit on the sidelines and try to act as mirroring self-object. Alan needed me to take on more of a role of idealised self-object and help foster his physical prowess in a safe environment and to help him confront and work through his feelings of frustration and anger at his shortcomings. After a few sessions playing "cheerleader" in this fashion, I decided he was ready to let me in a little and slowly edge towards letting go of the thin grandiose veneer. At this stage, I judged that he needed me neither reinforcing his grandiose fantasies nor challenging them.

And so began a series of sessions where Alan's potency and sense of agency in the real world became the focus of our work. We worked hard on his football skills, and I occasionally reflected back to him his increasing self-confidence and competence. Session after session, I passed the ball to Alan to practice headers, we counted together how many times he could bounce the ball on his foot and took mutual pleasure and pride in his progress. I encouraged Alan to shoot goals at me and instructed him gently and tactfully how to aim the ball and direct it more powerfully and assertively towards the goal. In tandem, Alan's parents reported that he was standing up to his siblings more and no longer cowering and crying in the face of their threats. However, at school, he was still quite reticent socially and avoided the playground at break time. It became clear to me that Alan needed to move to the next stage and risk a live interactive game with me. It was time for me to move from the role of parental self-object to polygonal rival and competitor.

Not all boys are so obsessively focused on football. Indeed, the very fact that football is the *lingua franca* of the school playground, back street, or local park across much of the world means that for some boys, the game can become the very symbol of their sporting inadequacies and sense of inferiority. For boys like these in particular, football can often be too tainted a game to play in psychotherapy. However, many will nevertheless still seek out the physical sporting channel of communication, rather than more sedentary creative activities or board games and card games. They might emphatically state their loathing of football, but instead, they are deeply passionate about basketball or volleyball. They ask that I set up the net as soon as they walk through the door, practice shooting the ball into a net again and again, keeping track of rates of success, and challenging themselves each session to shoot from further away or from a sharper angle. For others, it is ping pong to which they turn, practicing bouncing the ping pong ball on the bat session after session, ensuring I am assiduously counting their every attempt, following their every move, willing them on to progress and succeed. This may sound like avoiding the therapeutic challenge and work, but the countertransference such sessions arouse is tell-tale, as Beiser (1979b) has described. In cases where the child is working near the level of transition from omnipotent to realistic mastery, I find myself riveted as the child strives to learn and then perfect their skills, often physically willing the child along, with my whole body and soul. I am the adulating crowd, the referee, the coach, and the competitor all in one. When the same behaviour is being used as an escape or as avoidance (even in the same child), I can find myself bored, my mind wandering, sometimes almost falling asleep, as if the child is casting a spell on me to avoid any true therapeutic engagement.

Before continuing with another vignette from Alan's therapy, I wish to devote a few lines to consider the subject of girls and sporting games in the psychotherapy room. According to the studies cited above, even today girls are less likely than boys to be intent on perfecting sporting skills like football or basketball, and their self-esteem, social standing, and acceptance amongst their peers in general are less dependent on their physical and sporting prowess. Nevertheless, girls, like boys, often need to work through these same issues around physical prowess, confidence, agency, and competence through practicing and perfecting other games based on gross motor skills in the therapy room. In the analytic playroom, girls tend to turn more often to schoolyard games like ball games against the wall, jumping and hopping games such as French skipping, but the issues of self-esteem and agency and the psychotherapeutic approach are similar to those described above. However, where girls do seek out ball games traditionally played by boys, issues of gender bias often come into play in the therapy. Many girls (sadly) approach traditional boys' games like football and basketball with reticence and lack of confidence, assuming they cannot play or succeed, but they are curious and bring that curiosity, coupled with considerable hesitation and low expectations of themselves, to the therapy room. There are also the girls who are desperate to play and express themselves and their inner worlds through the medium of football or basketball and bring to the therapy room their frustrations at having had their natural sporting inclinations discouraged or ridiculed by their family and peers. Others, conversely, may express a compensatory pride in their "cross gender" abilities and behaviour, in an attempt to cope with the gender bias they encounter in the playground and at home (as in vignette A in the previous section).

VIGNETTE D   Playing the game: "You're Wayne Rooney and I'm Lionel Messi"

Like many boys of his age, football continued to be the focus of psychotherapy sessions for Alan throughout his treatment. As he grew more confident, less diffident, and less fearful of his own aggression, he dared to challenge me to competitive games, one against the other. We improvised makeshift goals at either end of my small clinic, moving tables and chairs aside, and defined the boundaries of the "pitch". In the summer months, when Alan appeared in flip flops for the session, I found myself having no choice but to remove my shoes so as not to hurt him accidentally, and we both ended up playing barefoot. The first dilemma I had was the comparative sizes of our goals and the associated question of how much I should hold back in my game. Alan was small in stature, quite weak, and not so proficient at football. If I played my hardest, I would be likely to beat him hollow and damage his still fragile self-esteem and pride in his newly honed skills. If I played too gently, he would sense I was "letting him win", and I would not be helping him develop real-world mastery and cope with losing and competition. I suggested that his goal be smaller than mine, explaining to Alan that this seemed to me to be a fairer deal, given our respective heights and my many years playing football (thanks to many hours spent in my youth in games of "three and in" in the garden with my elder brothers and their friends). The wording of such suggestions is often critical. Children, like all of us, are sensitive to any implication that they have inferior capabilities, and I therefore carefully word these explanations in terms of relative heights and age, rather than strength of kick or level of skill.

Despite these adjustments, Alan felt very threatened whenever I scored a goal, even if he was a few goals up on me. He would disqualify my goals with claims of offside, would demand penalties and free kicks at the drop of a hat, and my ball seemed to be constantly straying off the "pitch", whilst the boundaries of the pitch seem to stretch magically when the ball was in his possession. This did not feel like a vicious battle for survival in a persecutory world, as it might do with a more damaged and disturbed child, but rather it felt like playing with a younger child who needed to score most of the goals in the game in order to feel any sense of mastery.

The therapeutic aim was to enable Alan to develop a robust sense of mastery and potency, so that even when the score was 10–8 and not just 10–0, he could withstand the narcissistic blow and continue playing, and eventually, he would be able to lose to me without losing all self-esteem and self-worth. Such transformations do not happen overnight. To enable the child to accrue and solidify a sense of reality-based mastery, the therapist needs to become a real "strong enough" opponent in the game. In practical terms, this means gradually adjusting the goals to be of a more equal size, challenging the child with harder, more competitive play, and encouraging them to rely on their own developing skills rather than on omnipotent control of the game. It was clear to me that Alan was replaying with me scenes with his siblings where he felt weak and inferior and unable to fight on equal terms. As he fought me harder and more successfully on our miniature football field, so he began to better withstand the physical battles that are part and parcel of sibling rivalry at home and to show aggression and anger both towards his siblings and his parents. As is often the case in child psychotherapy, the parents found it hard to accept these changes in Alan from a golden-haired, malleable, albeit anxious, little child, to a forceful, assertive, less agreeable schoolboy: considerable parental work was required in tandem with the child psychotherapy sessions to help Alan on his way.

7.1.1.2   Winning, losing, and cheating and the issues of agency, self-confidence, and impulse control in board games

In line with the clinical thinking and examples presented here, Capell (1968), Nickerson and O'Laughlin (1980), Meeks (1970, 2000), and Crocker and Wroblewski (1975) similarly all attest to the benefits of playing traditional board games such as *Risk, Monopoly, and Chequers* in child psychotherapy in an age-appropriate and attuned manner. These different authors highlight in particular using game-play in the therapy room to address children's anxieties surrounding competency, weakness and helplessness, success and failure.

In addition, some authors also note the inherent creative and fantasy elements in these games and suggest that these very elements both encourage the child to explore their own areas of creativity and fantasy and also enable new and different behaviours to be tried and tested within the safe transitional space of the game, in preparation for real-world interactions. The overall focus of such therapeutic approaches is towards strengthening what is weak and nascent and needs developing in the child, rather than confronting and deconstructing conflicts and resistances (Bloch, 1981).

On the inter-psychic level, in these "polygonal" states of mind striving towards individuation and autonomy and triangular and polygonal symbolic psychic space, competitive board games and card games such as these enable, or even impose, a priori, a separation between the self and other(s).[7] Through the medium of the interactive competitive game, themes of possession and lack, of difference and similarity, of strengths and weaknesses can be explored within the safety of the psychotherapy room and through the metaphor of the game.

This having been said, the very set-up of the psychotherapeutic relationship between a skilled adult psychotherapist and a weaker, less experienced novice child often creates an inherent imbalance in skill, knowledge, and agency between child–patient and therapist. This being the case, I believe that calibrated adjustments in the therapist's game-play must be made to enable the child to explore freely and safely the issues surrounding competency, success and failure, and self-esteem. The therapist needs to be able and willing to adjust their own level of play to challenge the child at their particular level of competency, neither too much nor too little, but within the optimal "Goldilocks" levels of challenge and frustration with which the child can cope. This approach necessarily requires the therapist to have a flexible attitude towards cheating and bending of the rules. Going one step further, I suggest that given that the odds of winning in most structured games are not based solely on chance, but depend also on motoric and cognitive skills and knowledge, and on strategic and abstract thinking, the odds of winning are often necessarily stacked against the less experienced child. It is therefore usually therapeutically beneficial for the therapist to actively hold back in the game or "cheat in reverse" to avoid winning. Flexibility in game-play in child psychotherapy at this level, when seen in this light, facilitates a graduated modulated shift from pseudo-mastery founded on infantile omnipotence to more solid reality-based potency and agency.

VIGNETTE E   Calibrating the game

Mor – 11 years at referral.

Mor was a chubby, average height boy, who dressed fairly sloppily and did his best to present himself as unlikeable and stupid. He suffered from night terrors and severe psychosomatic anxieties, describing himself as a wimp and a failure at school. The beginning of therapy was hard for both of us: he was furious at being sent to a psychologist instead of a real doctor who would really cure his psychosomatic symptoms, which he regarded as real, and life-threatening. His rage at me, at his parents, at his whole family was intense and his anxiety overwhelming. I didn't argue with his symptoms, nor with the existential fear of illness and terror he associated with his symptoms, but only tried somehow to reassure him I would do everything I could to help him. The first few sessions, he screamed at his parents on the way to our sessions, he screamed at me outside on the stairs leading to the clinic, and in the sessions themselves. Mor's outbursts were generously peppered with a rich variety of obscenities, aimed mainly at his parents and the doctors: "Son of a bitch, idiots, it's all just a load of shit, fuck them all, assholes!" It was not easy to withstand this violence of his rage and anxieties, but equally I found it challenging to find meaning in the incessant "pooh/bum" talk and Mor's fixation on his Sony PlayStation, the only content which he brought in addition to these angry outbursts.

After around six weeks of meeting Mor for twice weekly sessions, I realised I need to change tack and draw us away from the pseudo-psychological talk about his terrors and his rage. I worked with his parents on the intergenerational aspects of his psychic distress, but it gradually became clear to me that equally, Mor's profound feelings of impotency, of failure, of being "stupid" and a "wimp", his complete lack of self-worth and self-esteem, were fuelling his anxieties and his rage. Touching these topics directly was impossible at this stage of the therapy. However, avoiding them and not engaging with them was also impeding progress. So, I began purposely to try to engage him in playing simple games, hoping to open a less emotionally loaded channel of communication through which to begin to digest what felt to be inaccessible through verbal channels. Mor readily accepted my suggestion and had no problem choosing which games to play, his favourites being TAKI (UNO) and football. At first, our play was far from spontaneous and joyful. Mor was sulky and lacking in libido, convinced he had no chance of winning and equally convinced of his inherent stupidity. However, in contrast to children with histories of deprivation and abuse, these feelings were communicated directly, without recourse to indirect channels of communication, through mechanisms of projective identification of humiliation and destructive envy directed towards me. He did not cheat or engage in underhand manipulations of the game, and my self-worth remained intact. But his feeling of impotence and lack of agency persisted, and his rage at his parents and his anxieties at home barely subsided. I understood I needed to find a different game that could perhaps defuse the situation. After a couple of months I suggested, almost insisted, that we switch from football to basketball, knowing that he played on the local junior basketball team, hoping that in basketball he could feel more secure in himself, less impotent, and we could begin to build up his sense of agency, his self-worth.

It was as if he had deliberately chosen to play with me games where he felt himself to be a "wimp and a failure" to bring the message home to me where the therapeutic work needed to be done.

And indeed, in our games of basketball, Mor became alive and joyful. He was a skilful player, whereas I barely had a clue, football being my game. He repeatedly beat me hands down, relished showing me tricks he learned in basketball practice and at last we both began to relax into the therapy. Eventually, these games began to be too predictable; it was too easy for Mor to beat me, I wasn't enough of a competition for him, and we both realised he needed more of a challenge in order to progress in therapy. The time was ripe to return to the games that had been too intimidating before. Mor suggested we play TAKI/UNO again and this simple, but highly versatile and quite addictive card game became the mainstay of our sessions for the next year or so, though in time we did venture into other modes of play and communication.

At this stage of the therapy, Mor's game was not sophisticated, his abilities to forward plan and delay gratification were limited, and I understood that I had to "calibrate" my game (to use Alvarez's (2012) terminology) and engage in "reverse cheating" in order to level the playing field. As discussed above, this is a technique I use often when playing competitive games, depending on the child's age, skill level, self-confidence, and what they need from me therapeutically. I held back on using my wild cards in the game, picked up extra cards when I didn't need to and at first let him win most of the time. (I should note here that TAKI/UNO is a particularly useful game when working with children who need us to let them win without them knowing – this being most children at the beginning of therapy. Since it is a card game where each player holds their cards in their hand, hidden from the opponent, the child has no idea what we have in our hand and usually cannot sense if we are manipulating the game in their favour.) As Mor amassed more wins, week after week, his self-confidence and his enjoyment of the game increased. At home too, his behaviour became less explosive, his anxieties lessened, and his confidence on the basketball court increased, though not yet in the classroom.

At this point, I introduced to Mor a longer form of the game, consisting of eight consecutive rounds of the game, starting from eight cards in a hand and working down to one. The tension involved in this longer form of the game would not have been possible for Mor to bear at the beginning of the therapy, but now I felt this variation could add spice and aliveness to our sessions and challenge Mor to dare to expand his psychic zone of comfort, his psychic space. I was still very careful to calibrate the game but allowed myself to win rounds within the long game, gauging all along the way how big a gap between us he could tolerate, without losing hope and faith in his own abilities. His game became more sophisticated, his theory of mind improved once he had the psychic space to dare to take risks and to think beyond what was in his hand to what might be in my mind and what I might be planning. Interestingly, when Mor returned to therapy in his late teens, we played TAKI again, in between talking openly and directly about his anxieties and issues of self-esteem and anger and frustration towards his parents. One day, it suddenly dawned on him that his games with me as a teenager were very different from what they once had been, and I was putting up a real fight against him and even beating him in some games. He wondered out loud how it was possible that when he had been 12 years old, he had almost always beaten me, but now I had become his equal in the game, though he knew he was now playing a much more sophisticated and challenging game. He pondered the question for a moment and then added: "Ahh I see", he said, "Back then I needed you to let me win, but now I need you to challenge me as much as you can!"

TWO VIGNETTES: "To cheat or not to cheat? that is the question!"

Younger or less emotionally mature children, and adults in times of stress and deprivation, find it difficult to deal with the caprices of luck and chance that are part and parcel of everyday life, and central elements in almost all board games. They find it hard to withstand the tension of the unknown and the lack of control over their fate and often cheat in order to counteract what they experience as the inherent unfairness of chance. Acceptance of the vagaries of chance and understanding the laws of probabilities governing chance (intuitively, not mathematically) are essential for coping and functioning well in the real world. This central developmental task of middle childhood is not a straightforward achievement and often involves painful and challenging processes along the way. What was interesting in Mor's therapy is that he never cheated. It didn't seem to occur to him. But, as Meeks put it, cheating is the route many "resort to … in order to escape the blind finality of chance" (Meeks, 1970, p. 161). Board games, with chance as their central feature, provide the ideal therapeutic tool for helping a child along this developmental path, where they have become stuck or are having difficulties negotiating the way forward. As I have said, I believe that as child psychotherapists we can be helpful only if we are attuned to the child's capacities to withstand lack of control, frustration, and disappointment. This means judging at every step along the way, to what extent the child "needs" to cheat in order to maintain their self-esteem and narcissistic pleasure and pride, even if omnipotently, and to what extent the child is able to risk abandoning their fate to chance, in the knowledge that "you win some, you lose some".

This issue is not without contention in the literature (as discussed in Chapter 4). Beiser (1970, 1979a), for example, vehemently opposes allowing children to cheat or bend the rules when engaged in playing structured games in psychotherapy. She sees allowing such behaviour as indulging pre-oedipal omnipotent fantasies and as undermining psychological development. Many contemporary authors (Bellinson, 2002, 2013; Caruth, 1988; Herman, 2000; Krimendahl, 2000; Meeks, 1970, 2000;

Oren, 2008), who advocate the use of formal games in child psychotherapy, today disagree with such a rigid and formalistic approach and suggest that therapeutic flexibility regarding the rules and regulations of structured games enables the child to test out and work through these very omnipotent fantasies. In his groundbreaking 1970 paper on cheating, referred to already in chapter 3, Meeks (1970) defines the therapeutic aims regarding cheating with child patients of this age as follows:

> The therapeutic aim in dealing with cheating at games is to increase the child's acceptance of his real capacities and limitations. This goal requires the therapist to deal tactfully with several aspects of the syndrome of cheating: (1) the child's fragile mechanism for maintenance of self-esteem; (2) the child's magical interpretation of successful performance, both in the therapist and himself; (3) the self-defeating characteristics of a reliance on cheating.
>
> (Meeks, 1970, p163)

Bellinson (2000) goes one step further and connects a flexible therapeutic attitude towards cheating to the creative and projective aspects of playing board games in psychotherapy:

> Consider the ways other playroom materials are used. One would never tell a child how those had to be used: "Don't put the toilet in the bedroom, it has to be in the bathroom"; "You can't draw an elephant today, you have to draw a dinosaur"; "You have to choose either a revolver or a laser gun, you can't have one in each hand"; "The soldiers have to be used on the battlefield, they can't come into the dollhouse." ...When children use toys or dolls or art supplies or other playroom materials, therapists watch to see what is created, used, and revealed in the play. *Structured games, too, can be highly informative if they are seen as projective material—regardless of what the box top says or how they are used in other contexts.*
>
> (Bellinson, 2000, p. 29, emphases added)

Herman (2000), writing from the perspective of ego and self-psychology, echoes these sentiments:

> Directly confronting and prohibiting the cheating is equivalent to forbidding the expression of a symptom, like saying to a depressed or anxious patient, "Stop being anxious or depressed!" Cheating is a symptom, the analysis of which provides an exquisite opportunity for significant therapeutic gain. Cheating can be understood as an effort to resolve complex conflicts between the desperate need for omnipotence and omniscience, the dread of painfully shameful and humiliating failure and disgrace, and the dawning, uneasy awareness of the necessity of facing the reality of constraints, limitations, and risks embodied in playing the game according to the rules in order to ensure fairness.
>
> (Herman, 2000, p. 63)

The following two vignettes illustrate what could be seen superficially as two opposing approaches to cheating: the first where a child with a strict and rigid superego is encouraged to cheat; and the second where the child is enabled to abandon cheating and omnipotent control and to dare trust to chance and their own skill and judgement in order to win. The guiding therapeutic principles, however, are the same—calibration to the individual child's emotional difficulties and developmental needs and flexibility in game-play.

VIGNETTE F   Uncovering the drive to win

Working with Fiona (aged nearly 12) was very different from most children I have worked with in all my years as a child psychotherapist. Albeit Fiona was visibly unhappy and having some difficulties in her relations with her peers, it soon became clear to me that here was a child with a basically balanced and healthy psyche who was ready and able to discuss with me openly and directly her problems at home with her siblings and with her peers. Her home environment was, psychologically speaking, a decidedly "good-enough" environment and her internal objects largely benevolent. However, like many older children in the last years of primary school, particularly girls, Fiona was struggling to deal with the complexities of peer relations. As we talked more in depth, we both understood that she was primarily anxious about expressing her own needs and preferences and losing friendships as a consequence. She knew she had outgrown certain friendships and that some of her so-called friends were abusing her goodwill and generosity, but she feared disappointing them or angering them and feared being a "bad friend" or indeed a "bad" person. Over the previous few months, Fiona had become unhappy at school and short-tempered and hyper-sensitive at home. She was in danger of disavowing whole swathes of her true self and of becoming stuck in "false-self" relationships with her girl-friends.

In the sessions, in some ways, this pattern repeated itself. Fiona was (even more than Clare described in Chapter 6) the ideal verbal cooperative patient who readily engaged in observing and verbally analysing her difficulties. I felt that whilst this work was important and helpful, we were nevertheless not engaging fully with her issues. A couple of months into the therapy, I began to question whether I had colluded with her false self and unwittingly skipped over the stage of game-play and more age-appropriate communication through game-play. The next time I noticed Fiona eyeing the toys and games in the room, I suggested that maybe for a change she would like to play and not just talk. She jumped at the opportunity and immediately took the Monopoly set down from the shelves and eagerly began to lay out the board, dealing us each our starting budget of money. She then asked me what figure I would like to be. I was struck by her insistence that I choose first but said nothing. The game continued in similar vein. Over the next few weeks, as we both amassed properties and began to build houses and hotels on those properties. I was astonished and somewhat concerned to discover that Fiona not only willingly paid me any debt she accrued, but also she was often uncomfortable receiving money from me and repeatedly offered to let me off the hook. Despite the fact that Fiona was not in a fragile psychic state, here too I was careful not to push for too rapid a change too soon. I let Fiona at least partially lead the way and set the pace. After winning a couple of games all too easily and enjoying my riches and my victories, I decided it was time to challenge Fiona on her "niceness" and generosity. I suggested that whilst it was fun for me to win, I suggested losing might not be so much fun (she insisted she didn't mind at all) and that she was missing out on the gleeful feeling of having lots of money and owning lots of properties, of feeling rich and powerful. I suggested that instead of politely letting each other off the hook, we both play to win and see how much money we can gain from each other. She readily cooperated, but her discomfort in openly enjoying her wealth and success was tangible. I was in the strange position of hoping she would land on my properties and she would have to pay me, so that the gap between her ever growing wealth and my lesser fortune would not be too intolerable for her – an unusual position indeed to be in for a child psychotherapist. Instead of interpreting her glee at her wins, I decided a better tack would be to express my emotions freely and honestly in the game. When I had to pay her, I moaned about it, when I landed on Go and was rewarded 400 dollars, I was happy but totally annoyed when I had to pay 200 in tax on my next go. When she landed on my properties, my relief was palpable and I shamelessly expressed my hope that it would happen again and allow me to close the gap between us. I hoped for doubles and for other particular numbers where needed and encouraged her to do the same.

Over the next few weeks, the games came alive, Fiona became freer and more spontaneous in her play. When she asked to throw the dice again so she would not land on my property again (albeit she did not dare let herself cheat on the sly), I knew our work was all but done. Being a child who was open and capable of verbal interpretive work, I connected these games with her wish to please her friends and the price she had paid for belittling herself and hiding her feelings and her needs, and to the ambivalent feelings and even jealousy, anger, and frustration she felt towards her siblings (all benign, but hard for her to cope with). Therapy finished not long after, once she had practised winning a good few more times and had learned to ask me freely for leniencies and even began to cheat playfully and with glee (albeit with my permission) when throwing the dice. She intuitively understood exactly the intra-psychic and inter-psychic movement she needed to make away from an overstrict superego and an overdeveloped need to please, and her relations with her peers and with her siblings improved dramatically.

VIGNETTE G   Discovering the thrills and spills of games of luck

Hila, a short, skinny nine-year-old, was referred to psychotherapy because of crippling separation anxiety combined with a tendency to violent temper tantrums. A highly intelligent, talented, and articulate little girl, she was very willing to come to therapy and happy to spend the time together chatting non-stop and busying herself in arts and crafts, but it was hard to get at the real issues troubling her. Here was a child who was clearly functioning on many levels, with parts of her psyche stuck in infantile omnipotence and object relating, and others (or at other moments) functioning on the cusp between the triangular and the polygonal with an ability for insight, and complexity of thought and relations.

In the therapy sessions, Hila was highly cooperative, creative, and a joy to work with. The child who lost control on a daily basis and was a terror at home was nowhere to be seen. Like Clare in the vignette in Chapter 6, I felt Hila was hiding behind her creative talents and judged it was time to suggest playing board games with her. Hila's mother had inadvertently thrown down the gauntlet to me in one of the parental sessions, on spying the shelf with board games in my clinic:

> You should know that it's impossible to play any game with Hila, she always *has* to win and she *absolutely refuses* to play by any rules. Nobody ever agrees to play board games with her. Neither us, nor her siblings, nor even her friends. Good luck to you!

When I suggested Hila choose a game to play, she, like Clare, immediately chose *War* ...but unlike Clare, Hila needed absolutely no encouragement to cheat. She let rip immediately. She looked at all her cards ahead of time, chose her Aces and Jokers as she pleased, and stole mine at will, and the game was over in a few short minutes. For the first few rounds, I let Hila play as she wished and barely imposed any order to the game, which became increasingly disorganised and manic. After each win, Hila was triumphant, but her triumph began to have a false ring to it. Like Mor, the absence of shades of humiliation, torment, or perversion towards me signalled to me a more triangular/polygonal level of therapeutic work. Here was an intelligent, insightful child who developmentally should have been able to play by the rules by now and enjoy such games with her siblings and peers. It seemed to me that Hila also felt her victory to be hollow, but did not dare to play any other way for fear of losing her omnipotent control. She did not know how to cope flexibly and creatively with the uncertainty of randomly dealt cards and a real, live opponent, nor with externally imposed boundaries and rules. Her game-play lacked vitality, curiosity, and true joy.

Unlike Mor in vignette E, Hila's self-esteem, her self-confidence, and sense of agency were not at stake. I judged that to tread too carefully in our games was to give her the wrong therapeutic message. It would be signalling to her that her psyche was still fragile, which I did not intuit to be the case. She did not seem to know that her psyche was strong enough and the environment stable enough to feel secure enough in the game, in the framing gap that was the game, to withstand the vagaries of chance. Within a couple of meetings of these games of War, I suggested to her that playing in this fashion was rather boring, even for her, and perhaps real competition might be more exciting. I was careful nevertheless to calibrate the game. This is not so easy to achieve in a game like *War* where the outcome depends purely on chance. I too had no control over the cards she or I had, so instead I opted for a different strategy of play. In the next few games, I suggested to Hila that she choose between her top three cards once I had placed my top card face up. I then progressed to allowing Hila to choose her card before she knew my card, except in a *War* situation, where the narcissistic risk of losing several cards at once was too threatening for her. Eventually, we were able to play more or less by the book, despite her being only nine years old and the early stage of the therapy, I let her win most of the time, and if I won, I made sure the margin of my win was not too large, and it was not the last game in the session. For both of us, the games became joyful and exciting, and Hila could finally experience the joys and thrills of discovering our unknown cards and of real competition and rivalry. From these games of *War*, we soon progressed to Monopoly (see vignette H).

7.1.2   Ego functions and impulse control

As discussed in Chapter 4, much of the literature on structured games in child psychotherapy until recently focused on classic "oedipal" and "latency" aspects of ego functions in these games. Many authors, mostly from North America, emphasised the beneficial role of structured games in strengthening areas of ego functioning such as sublimation, reality testing, and impulse control. Similar to the clinical illustrations in vignette E with Mor and with Hila in vignette F, these authors describe using board games (mentions of ball games and card games are few and far between in these early papers) in various ways to help the child learn to accept and tolerate frustrations and disappointments; to manage their own and their peers' aggressive tendencies and hostilities; and to cope with the vicissitudes of successes and failures in their daily lives (Beiser, 1979a; Chused, 1982; Collier & Robles, 2004; Gavshon, 1989; Green, 1978; Meeks, 1970; Nickerson & O'Laughlin, 1980; Oren, 2008).

Nickerson and O'Laughlin (1980) in their review paper highlight some interesting points regarding game-play in psychotherapy, in particular: the use of specific games such as *Risk*, *Monopoly*, and *Frustration* for specific psychological conflicts; the importance of learning and abiding by the rules as "an analogy for living responsibly by acceptable norms of society and seeing one's rights and privileges in relation to those of others" (Nickerson and O'Laughlin, 1980, p. 79). Several authors have described the therapeutic power of using board games with more disturbed and resistant children in the area of ego functioning and defences (Collier & Robles, 2004; Gavshon, 1989; Green, 1978; Nilsson, 2009; Oren, 2008). In her detailed and innovative paper "The use of board games in child psychotherapy", Oren (2008) advocates flexibility when playing games in child psychotherapy and presents a useful and clear schema for calibration of therapeutic approach to different developmental levels when tackling such issues of ego functioning and defences; superego rigidity and flexibility; frustration and anxiety; and aggression and impulse control.[8] Similarly, Green (1978) suggests that in playing age-appropriate structured board games with abused or traumatised children, the therapist mobilises "healthy areas of the child's personality and cognitive apparatus" to promote "more adaptive controls and defences" (Green, 1978, p. 362). These ideas regarding the role of playing structured games in psychotherapy with children in more disturbed states of mind bring the discussion naturally to questions of theory and technique with school-aged children when working on issues associated with dyadic and more primitive triadic states of mind, the subject of the next section in this chapter.

7.2   From the dyad to the triad: board games, the missing link, and the triangular space

Whilst middle childhood is theoretically a period of development where triadic relations have already been well established, alongside symbolic thinking and an integrated sense of self and other, in reality even for the most psychologically healthy children of this age group, "work is still in progress" in all these areas. As discussed in Chapters 2 and 3, even well-functioning school-aged children often struggle to function and to relate on the triangular level, let alone on the polygonal level. Many aspects of triadic and symbolic thinking and relating can still be a challenge for the child: to imagine another's point of view (cognitive or emotional); to think symbolically and ward off projections and distortions; and perhaps the hardest emotional challenge of all, to cope with exclusion from the quintessential parental couple in all its forms, be it the parent–parent couple, the parent–sibling couple, or even the parent–outside world or parent–parent's mind couple. Traditionally, in psychoanalytic theory, this triangular level of development has been conceived of in terms of movement from the mother–infant dyad to the oedipal mother–father–toddler triad. I will touch here only briefly on a few central ideas and concepts in psychoanalytic thinking post-Freud (though not necessarily post-Freudian). most relevant to these issues of dyadic and triadic thinking and relating, before elaborating on how these issues appear and can be approached and worked through in psychotherapy with the wave-particle school-aged child.

Early in her writings, Melanie Klein formulated the early shift from mother–infant dyad to oedipal triad as a developmental progression from the paranoid schizoid position to the depressive position: the former associated with dyadic relations, distortions in thinking influenced by infantile omnipotence, splitting, envy, and rage; and the latter associated with triangular relations, relinquishing omnipotent control, recognition of the other as separate, and guilt and sadness, coupled with an urge towards creative reparation and symbolisation. Hanna Segal, on the one hand, and Lacan, the radical French post-Freudian philosopher-psychoanalyst, on the other, though coming from very different theoretical standpoints, have both emphasised the relationship between the father, triangulation, the real world, language, culture, and society, and the symbolic function. Segal (1957, 1978) differentiated between symbolic formulations that dominate thinking in the more primitive paranoid schizoid sates of mind (the symbol is equated with the "thing itself" (Bion, 1967)) and the symbolic function, attained in the depressive position, a product of separation from the object, of the creation of psychic space, the basis of abstract thinking and creativity. Lacan's theories, by contrast, focus heavily on the father whom he sees as the castrating prohibiting figure who introduces the child into the "Symbolic" order and system of language, through what he termed both the "Non" (No) and the "Nom" (Name) of the Father[9] (Davies & Eagle, 2013; Etchegoyen & Trowell, 2005; Hamburg, 1999). For Winnicott (1971), for Kohut (1977), and for Mahler (2000) on the other side of the Atlantic, the focus was, by contrast, on separation and the development of a cohesive integrated sense of self, not on language and symbolism. All these authors emphasised the role of the father in protecting the developing infant against the regressive pull of the symbiotic engulfing primal mother and in encouraging exploration of the exciting outside world, part and parcel of the process of separation and individuation (Abelin, 1975, 1980; Mahler et al., 1975; Winnicott, 1971).

As discussed above, many contemporary thinkers view this move from the dyadic to the triadic level of internal and external space in less gender defined terms. The mother–infant dyad is neither exclusive nor is the father the sole interlocutor or ambassador of the outside world. Fathers today partake in much of the holding and handling in early infancy. Many mothers work outside of the home, mothers have always talked copiously to their infants and been at least as responsible as fathers for laying down the law, introducing the infant to the outside and acting as mediator between the infant and reality (Ben-Ari Smira, 2015; Davies & Eagle, 2013; Etchegoyen & Trowell, 2005). Likewise, mothers have (and always have had!) minds, relationships, and metaphorical if not physical "rooms of their own", outside of the infant-mother dyad.

But this is not to say that the infant relates triadically from birth. Rather, I would suggest that the infant should be conceived of as progressing developmentally from dyadic relationships with a restricted number of significant others at the beginning of life, to multiple dyadic relations experienced first discretely in series and then in parallel (for instance, relating to the one parent whilst being held by the other) (Ben-Ari Smira, 2015); and then being able eventually to hold the other in mind and observe the other. It is important to emphasise that we are talking here about dyadic, then triadic, and later polygonal relations not *only* with the parents, but also with an increasing multiplicity of other significant others such as caretakers, grandparents, and siblings, right from infancy. From this perspective, it can be said that it is not the father per se, *but the third vertex, the other outside of the dyad* (Davies &

Eagle, 2013), that is necessary to create this space for the capacity for thinking, for symbolisation, play, and creativity, for mentalisation and the ability to formulate self and other representations, and for language to grow and develop.

This movement towards the other, that is the third, the outside world, is plain to see at the physical, concrete level during toddlerhood: in the movement of a young toddler, taking their first steps away from one parent and towards the other parent awaiting with open arms to catch and embrace the toddler; in the magical moment when the toddler lets go of the safety of the table and sets off, in trepidation and with eager anticipation, on a journey of discovery across the wilds of the sitting room, intoxicated by the excitement of their newfound powers. Likewise, language and symbolic thinking become necessary to denote what is outside the dyad. The acquisition of language is often accompanied by infant and parent pointing at objects outside of the dyad: "look, there's a cat!"–"Meow" responds the toddler; "Woof, woof" says the toddler "Yes, that's right, it's a dog!" responds the parent. This creation of the triangular space via the third, whether a concrete, tangible other, or the third within the other's mind, is vital in psychological development, cognitively, emotionally, and socially.

7.2.1   Structured games as a metaphor for the missing parental link

Britton (1989, 1998, 2004) has written in detail and with great insight on this process of triangulation and the creation of psychic space. His understanding of the distortions and disruptions in psychic triangulation is particularly pertinent to the discussion here and is therefore explored in some detail.

In his seminal paper, "The missing link: Parental sexuality in the Oedipus complex" Britton (1989) describes adult patients who have severe difficulties in thinking in the triangular space, and for whom "being in analysis is a problem" (Britton, 2004), and doing analysis with these patients becomes a problem for the analyst. He divides these patients into two distinct groups – the "thin-skinned" and the "thick-skinned" patients (after Rosenfeld, 1987). "Thin-skinned" patients are characteristically locked into an "archaic", "hyper-subjective", and primal dyadic mode of thinking, behaving, and relating. They adhere compulsively to what would traditionally be regarded as the maternal vertex. Such patients cannot bear points of view, thoughts, or feelings, different from their own. "Thick-skinned" patients, by contrast, dare not veer from a detached, pseudo-intellectual, didactic, fact based, "hyper-objective" modes of thinking and behaving – the traditionally paternal, emotionally distant, "rational" vertex. Talk of feelings, personal experiences, or childhood memories is usually anathema to such patients. With neither the hyper-subjective nor the hyper-objective patient is the therapist allowed to think, to have a mind of their own. Britton sees malignant primary parental containment, what Winnicott would call not good-enough primary caretaking, as a major root cause of psychic hyper-subjectivity or hyper-objectivity in the developing psyche. However,

Britton regards the influence of the parent-parent dyadic link as no less seminal. When this latter relationship is highly distorted or missing, the couple dyad link remains unimaginable for the infant and toddler and, paradoxically, exclusion from the couple is unbearable. The developing oedipal triangle is thus tragically flattened or non-existent, and the young child has little psychic space within which to develop triangular symbolic thinking.

It is useful at this point to introduce Jessica Benjamin's thinking on thirdness. Akin to Britton's ideas on maternal containment as a foundation for the triangular space, so Benjamin suggests that the primary parent's ability "to hold in tension her subjectivity/desire/awareness and the needs of the child", what she calls the "third in the one" (Benjamin, 2004, p. 13), enables in turn a co-created thirdness between infant and parent, "a shared third". Benjamin likens this intersubjective relationship as a joint dance based on resonance between two separate beings, a "cooperative endeavour" typical of early infant-parent mutual babbling. These early forms of thirdness are precursors of triangular thirdness, symbolic thirdness, and imagining the other's mind, "the one in the third", based on mutual recognition as separate minds, intersubjectivity, the ability to recognise and negotiate difference and connect with the other as a separate subject (Benjamin, 2004, p. 13).

If we think of the wave-particle characteristics of the psyche in middle childhood, these hyper-subjective and hyper-objective states of mind can be seen to be but normal modes of intra-psychic and inter-psychic relating in this period of development. As discussed in Chapter 3, the internal "oedipal" triangle of the wave-particle child is far from firmly established: separation from the primary dyad, from the subjective world of omnipotent fantasy, and from the safety and familiarity of the home is exciting and often liberating at this developmental stage, but simultaneously, it is threatening and frightening. Supposedly rational, thinking human beings, children of this age actually find it extraordinarily difficult to accept different points of view, even cognitively. Being excluded from another's mind, from another dyad, can be well-nigh unbearable for a child who does not yet have a secure and firmly bounded sense of self and identity. The developing school child still often instinctively clings to their own subjective experience and knowledge to maintain their pseudo-autonomous independent sense of self. Or, as a defence against the regressive pull towards the primal-subjective dyad, children often adopt a form of non-pathological developmentally appropriate "false-self" based on the opinions of their peers, the "solid secure facts" they have accrued in class, books, or on knowledge they have gleaned on the internet from "Professor Google". Similarly, these schoolagers tend to take refuge in strict adherence to the rules and regulations of the school, sports, or scouts club into which they have been inducted (hence the peculiar attraction in children of this age have for the uniforms, badges, and plethora of rules in Scout and Guide clubs). Like the borderline adult, free and spontaneous movement between these two realms of subjectivity and objectivity is often difficult and confusing, particularly for the younger wave-particle child and can even be experienced as threatening and destabilising to the child's nascent psychic equilibrium, separateness, and autonomy.

As children grow through middle childhood, so too their freedom of movement within the triangular space and their ability to combine objective reality with their subjective inner world and become intersubjective beings develop. At a gradual pace, children learn to observe and tolerate being observed, to imagine the mind of the other and their mind in the mind of the other, and to bear the pain and relish the emancipation and newfound opportunities that are in the separation and independence from the mind of the primary object and from the parental couple. With this freedom comes the ability to negotiate between different parental figures, between home and school, between the pretend world and the real world outside their minds, between their emotions and their burgeoning cognitive faculties and acquired knowledge, and between rules and regulations and impulses and urges.

Many children negotiate this developmental trajectory "well-enough", but some need an outside third, a psychotherapeutic third, to help them on the way. This is where the therapeutic use of structured games comes into play. The element of "thirdness" inherent in these games can act as this much needed therapeutic third vertex in therapies with children of this age. The games we play with our child patients enable this developmental progression to take place towards the triangular in the potentially intersubjective space these games naturally provide. This is especially true of board games and card games with predetermined, clearly defined contents and rules, such as Monopoly or TAKI/UNO, but the same thirdness is at play in less structured games, as illustrated in the football games in the "Lionel Messi" vignette D (Section 7.1.1). Oren (2008) makes this point in the discussion of the case of Nathaniel in her paper quoted above (Section 7.1.2):

> In addition to having to relate to me as a separate person, Nathaniel had to relate to the game as an independent third element in the triangle (him, me and the game) ... An example of this relationship was seen when Nathaniel would 'talk' to the dice to convince them to fall favourably, knowing that he would have to 'obey their decision'. When feeling omnipotent, Nathaniel would negate the independent existence of the game entity by disregarding the rules and in the same way also ignore my subjectivity.
>
> (Oren, 2008, p. 380)

In this same paper, Oren highlights tension between three different forces that can be identified as acting on the child, the therapist, and the game. These are: the rules of the game; the child's schizoid paranoid needs for omnipotent control and their low self-esteem, which make losing hard to bear and lead to difficulties in impulse control; and the maturational impetus towards agency, individuation, and playing the "real game" and functioning in the "real world".

The game board, the pawns, the dice, the cards, the goalposts, and the football are all real tangible objects but take on specific playful meanings, roles, and purposes within the game. The game takes place in the realm between the pretend and the real, between subjectivity and objectivity, in Winnicott's transitional space,[10] in the triangular space: *Monopoly* money is not real money, taxes not real taxes, the child who loses all their cards in *War*, or has their queen's "head chopped off" in chess, can always play again. These events are, on a certain level, pretend, like events in a play on a theatre stage, belonging both to the child's subjective, fantasy world of play, and to external reality. The meaning the pawns of the game take on is both infused by the child's fantasy world and has mutually agreed upon, a priori, meaning in the realm of the objective. The rules and structure of the game act as the link to reality, as an incarnation of the third, the "other" parental figure, within the game. *Therefore, I would argue that for older, school-aged children, the combination of a playful therapist and structured ball games, board games, and card games can usefully and effectively function as a bridge between the subjective and the objective, "the parental link" emphasised by Britton in the developing child's oedipal triangle.*

VIGNETTE H

I return to Hila from vignette F, this time to the games of *Monopoly*, which followed our games of *War* described above, and which enabled work on this very level of subjectivity, objectivity, and the internal parental link. This internal parent–parent link was weak indeed in Hila's case and characterised in reality also by hyper-objectivity on the part of her father and hyper-subjectivity on the part of her mother. Since *Monopoly* is a game that usually lasts well beyond 50 minutes, five minutes before the end of the session, I suggested to Hila, as I usually do with my child patients, to record our positions on the board, the money we each had, the properties, houses, and hotels we own. This allows continuity between sessions and the game to run its course to its full length and breadth. And Hila, like most children, eagerly took me up on the suggestion. Children seem to appreciate the chance to be taken seriously in their wish to have "proper game", and like the drawings and toys they place in their personal box in the therapy room, the act of writing down the names of the streets we have purchased and the money we have gained and lost from week to week serves to hold and contain the session-to-session narrative of the goings-on of their psyche.

Initially there was, as Hila had warned me, "one big mess". She behaved almost manically and simply took all the money and all the properties for herself. In effect, there was no game. The next game I took charge, dealt out the money evenly, made sure we each threw the dice in turn and bought properties and built houses as we were able. However, the first time we played in this way, I did not manage to get the balance right between objectivity and subjectivity, between boundaries and omnipotence and infantile greed, and between the pretend mode and reality: Hila lost patience half way through, stole all the money from the bank once again, and broke out into a manic victory dance, all of which left her feeling empty, unprotected, and out of control. It was clear I needed to make more adjustments. The next week, I dealt us each more money at the beginning than required by the rules, kept an eye to ensure the game was even, and removed the building repairs cards, which I judged would be very difficult for Hila to tolerate.

It should be noted that playing *Monopoly* with only two players means that there is little initial capital in the game. This means that the game naturally progresses slowly, which can be too frustrating for younger patients, especially given children's generally low levels of patience and the constraints of fifty-minute sessions. Thus, when playing with children in psychotherapy or with young children one on one as a parent, aunt, or babysitter, I frequently inject extra money initially into the game, as I did in these games with Hila.

As we moved around the board and acquired properties, paid fines, received bonuses and eventually also made property deals and built houses, it felt as though this was a new experience for Hila: playing more or less according to the rules, with an adult who put boundaries on her and on the game, whilst at the same time recognising Hila's infantile need to win and her limited ability to deal with the inbuilt frustrations of the game. Playing in this way allows the boundaries imposed by the rules of the game, calibrated and modified by the therapist, to be experienced by the child as protective and benevolent, rather than as deprivation. It could be said we were striking a balance in the way we played the game between her overly strict father and overly soft mother. This was a novel experience for Hila of free though measured movements in the game between subjectivity and objectivity. I held her emotional needs, her frustrations, and her anxieties in my mind and gave voice to them, sometimes in-game, through the metaphor of the game, and sometimes verbally and more directly. If I sensed Hila needed to feel and experience the boundary of my presence in the game, I insisted she paid me; when it was clear it was too much for her, I would let her off payment; in general, I insisted we follow the dice, but occasionally, when Hila's luck was out, I would let her throw the dice again. This in turn allowed Hila some space to begin to let go of her omnipotent hold on the world and feel the relief and the release that comes from relinquishing that control and to begin to think about her own actions and feelings in the game and about mine. My verbalisations were aimed at this expanding psychic space:

"When you have all the money in the world it's wonderful, but then the game's not interesting any more".

"You feel so strong when you have all the money, but then there's nobody left strong to play with, and that's not such a good feeling".

"You're in control of all the rules, which is such fun, but suddenly the game's got very confusing and is one big mess".

These interventions are both complex and direct. They worked well for Hila, but would be inappropriate for a more disturbed and deprived child, who is likely to experience the "you" as a narcissistic blow, as a persecutory attack, and the complexity of the intervention as confusing or threatening (see Section 7.3.3 for discussion of interventions with children in these more fragile states of mind).

In tandem, I worked with Hila's parents on boundaries and especially on coordinated parental limits between father's classically tough, rigid, almost punitive discipline, and mother's haphazard, overly understanding, and soft ways. Interestingly, not long into the therapy, I had decided to carry out some traditional psychological testing in order to try and understand more of the dynamics underlying her symptoms and to provide me with some solid, "objective" facts pertaining to Hila's cognitive and emotional functioning, which I could use to help the parents think about Hila differently. Since Hila loved drawing, I began with the Bender-Gestalt[11] test, which, if used judiciously, I often find surprisingly revealing with this age group both as an indicator of graphomotoric and organisational difficulties and sometimes also on the psychodynamic level. Hila copied the first three geometric shapes somewhat impulsively, but with confidence and accuracy. As I presented her with additional cards, she became more anxious and drew borders around the previous shapes and each subsequent shape as she finished it. She then explained herself: "You know, without boundaries [her word, not mine] between the shapes everything would be one big mess". She thought a little, looked at me again, and remarked, with a mixture of glee and anxiety in her voice:

> It's really like that, also at home. My parents don't know how to put down limits, so we eat whatever and whenever we want, and do whatever we like at home. I love making a huge mess, especially in the kitchen… and in my bedroom!

Her expression suddenly clouded over and she added quietly, "… But actually, I don't always like it, things can get really out of hand, especially with my younger brothers and then it's really scary". (It is noteworthy that here too, it was essentially the inherent structure of the Bender-Gestalt test that is reality-oriented and has clear rules and instructions that prompted Hila to express some of her more hidden fears and feelings.) I found it hard to believe my ears. Here was a nine-year-old child telling me exactly what she needed from me and from her parents and explaining to me why she was so scared to be left alone to the devices of her own and her siblings, potentially destructive and chaotic impulses. This work on the parental link was vital and enabled Hila to feel more safe and secure to move more freely in the triangular space between her and her parents in reality, and in her internal triangular space between the primal dyadic subjective world of omnipotent fantasies and her growing inner objective world of cognition, knowledge, and rules and regulations. Feeling more safe and secure allowed her to relinquish her separation anxiety and venture out into the real world with confidence and playfulness.[12]

It is of note how these themes strongly echo Alvarez' (1989) thinking on the developmental need for structuring, compartmentalisation, and boundaries in middle childhood.[13] It was almost as if Hila had read and internalised Alvarez' very words and acted them out line by line, to bring the message home to me loud and clear:

> Such splitting has an important developmental function, which is by no means purely defensive.
>
> The difficulty is, one's experience in the consulting room with [such] patients does make one feel their reaction is terribly defensive, it *feels* defensive. But, of course, if a farmer encloses a field so that his "sheep may safely graze", the hungry wolves outside may see the fence as defensive; the sheep also, may feel - in their anxious moments – that the fence is for their defence. But in their safer moments, they may feel protected by it so that the flock may graze peacefully and flourish.
>
> (Alvarez, 1989, p. 75)

7.2.2   Game-play as practice ground for developing mentalisation

At this point, I wish to turn in detail once more to the theory of mentalisation born out of the Anna Freudian, rather than the Kleinian, vertex of child psychoanalytic psychotherapy. Mentalisation, as discussed in Chapters 3 and 4, has been defined as the ability to form mental representations of the thoughts and feelings of the self and the other and is crucial for the formation of a cohesive sense of self and perception of the other, and for stable, mature, and healthy interpersonal relations in adulthood (Bateman et al., 2009; Bateman & Fonagy, 2013):

> Mentalization or reflective function is the developmental acquisition that permits children to respond not only to another person's behavior, but to the child's conception of others' attitudes, intentions, or plans. Mentalization enables children to "read" other people's minds. By attributing mental states to others, children make people's behavior meaningful and predictable... Exploring the meaning of others' actions, in turn, is crucially linked with the child's ability to label and find meaningful his own psychic experiences, an ability that we suggest underlies affect regulation, impulse control, self-monitoring, and the experience of self-agency.
>
> (Fonagy & Target, 1998, p. 92)

The focus of therapeutic work according to mentalisation-based theory and technique is on understanding the basics of give and take in interpersonal relationships, on developing a tolerance for frustration, understanding limit setting, and separating reality and fantasy. Fonagy and his team list several primary therapeutic goals when working with "difficult to treat" children whose mentalisation is damaged or underdeveloped:

- Verbalisation of internal states and differentiation of feelings
- Facilitating understanding of cause and effect within relationships

- Helping the child separate internal from external, real from unreal
- Setting limits, explaining the limits provided
- Establishing reciprocity of giving and taking
- Developing frustration tolerance and the capacity to delay gratification
- Gradually confronting the child with opposing (conflicting) ideas, widening the scope for change

(Bleiberg et al., 1997, p. 21)

It is interesting to note that these authors suggest that the capacity to mentalise develops throughout the period of infancy and toddlerhood, towards the end of the "oedipal stage", or of Piaget's stage of egocentric thinking. Given the developmental picture formulated in Chapter 4, I would suggest that the capacity for mentalisation in fact continues developing well into middle childhood and is often still shaky, especially in the earlier years of this developmental stage. Studies have shown that younger school-aged children (6–8-year olds) in particular find it difficult to imagine/represent in their mind either their own thoughts and feelings or those of their peers, parents, or siblings (Diem-Wille, 2018).

Similar to Britton, but couched in different language, Fonagy and Target also stress the importance of the integration of thoughts and feelings as part and parcel of development of the capacity for mentalisation:

In a serious frame of mind [that is a reality-oriented frame of mind], the child expects the internal world in himself and others to correspond to external reality, and subjective experience will often be distorted to match information coming from outside (psychic equivalence mode). While involved in play, the child knows that internal experience may not reflect external reality, but then the internal state is thought to have no relationship to the outside world and to have no implications for it (pretend mode).

(Fonagy & Target, 1998, p. 96)

As described in Chapter 4 (Section 4.4.2), play facilitated or mediated by an adult or older child capable of "mature" mentalisation is central to this process of integration of inner and outer reality, of the pretend mode and the psychic equivalence mode:

[When] children learn to play with objects, another person, and, ultimately, with ideas, [they gradually discover] that all may not be as it seems, [that an "alternative perspective exists"], and that [their] habitual thoughts and feelings are not the only way of seeing the world or necessarily the way that others see the world.

(Bleiberg et al., 1997, p. 29)

This "alternative perspective", so important for the development of mentalisation, is akin to the third, the "other" outside the dyad, to Britton's vertex of objectivity. Here too, it seems to me that the traditional games of childhood play an important role:

with their combination of the pretend and the real, conceived naturally as they were to match the developing cognitive, physical, emotional, and social abilities of school-aged children, these games serve as an ideal practice ground for developing mentalisation. *The interactive nature of these games and the structure of the game induce the child to "mind" the other, to imagine the other players' cards sitting across from the child, to mentalise strategies, and imagine future fortunes and misfortunes. Seen from this perspective, it becomes clear that these games lend themselves perfectly to the above list of therapeutic goals of mentalisation, whether on the level of learning give and take, opposite the other (literally) competitor-player-therapist, or working on impulse control, or understanding cause and effect in relations, or in actions and reactions, concrete, and emotional, per se.* The metaphor of the game, the story behind the game, the fantasy characters of the game, and imagery of the cards and the board serve as the "pretend" element, the element of "playfulness" and subjectivity that was originally the parents' function, opposite the rigidity of reality as interpreted by the child. The mediating other, the "alternative perspective", the outside world, resides in the rules, the content, and the structure of the game. Learning to play these structured games, especially board games and card games, without excessive anxiety or overwhelming anger and frustration, requires an integration of these two modes of functioning of fantasy and reality. Without this integration, the game either descends into chaos or is joyless and lifeless. And it is the integration of these two modes that is the foundation of mentalising, of triadic relations, and the symbolic function.

Drawing all these strands together, playing board games and card games can now be conceptualised as involving a combination of Britton's subjectivity and objectivity, of Fonagy and Target's "pretend mode" and "psychic equivalence mode", and of inner and outer reality. As such I would argue that these games can and should serve as an essential element in the child psychotherapy toolbox, especially with children in borderline states of mind for whom the integration of these elements of psychic experience is particularly challenging.

VIGNETTE I   "When you win the game and I don't throw a temper tantrum, then it will be time to finish therapy!"

David had been with me in therapy already for a year and a half, having been referred by his sibling's therapist on account of social difficulties and severe lack of self-confidence. He was nearly eight-years old, small, wiry, and full of rage. His self-esteem was very low, and I had to tread very carefully along the way. As he became stronger in the therapy and his existential fears of annihilation and his experiences of physical and emotional abuse at the hands of his siblings had been partially worked through, his rage subsided, and we were able to begin to work on issues of infantile omnipotence and relinquishing his hyper-subjective paranoid schizoid view of the world, and developing a more mature theory of mind.

David and I played *Monopoly* regularly in the sessions. He found it very difficult to leave things to luck in the beginning and cheated blatantly in order to "escape" the "blind finality" of chance (cf. Meeks, 1970, p. 161, quoted above). He controlled the dice absolutely: for many months, he refused to let me even roll the dice myself. He could not bear to let me buy any streets or properties and likewise he would not let me advise him how to build up his strength prudently in the game. His only focus was on the most expensive streets and properties, nothing else mattered to him. He therefore won all the games hands down, but they were over quickly and the element of surprise, chance, and spontaneity were missing. This is precisely what Green meant when he described "foul play", when "nothing is left to chance. The winner or the loser is known in advance" (Green, 2005, pp. 12–13, quoted above in Chapter 6). No "alternative perspective" existed for David. There was no space for a mediating other, reality had to coincide with his inner subjective reality, with the pretend mode, and when it didn't, he found it intolerable.

Realising David felt he could not survive otherwise, initially I went along with these idiosyncratic rules based on David's intense need for infantile omnipotence and a fear of abandoning the pseudo-safety of this magically controlled world. But I also knew that if I continued playing his way, I would not be helping him along the road to triangular thinking and mature mentalisation. As I gained his trust and his envy, rage, and paranoia abated (points that will be expounded upon below in subsequent chapters), I judged that I could begin to challenge David to let me and external reality play more of a role in the game. In contrast to the example of the games of *War* with Clare, I began to insist that we played at least partially by the rules, as a representative of the "alternative perspective", the other that is vital to the development of theory of mind. I insisted on my rights as an external other, a player that is outside of his control (at this stage only partially) to roll the dice myself and purchase a few of the less valuable properties. Tangibly, physically, he learnt to tolerate my holding and throwing the dice and moving my pawn myself, making my own decisions on what to buy and not to buy. He could see the cards accruing in my area of the board, a visual physical aid to mentalising me as other, sitting opposite him, holding different cards from him in a reality that did not match his inner reality, his omnipotent inner world. But David still could not tolerate too large a mismatch between his inner reality, his subjectivity, the pretend mode, and outer objectivity, the external predetermined rules of the game, and the outer world as represented by me. The idea that I might land on the most expensive streets and "steal" them from him was unbearable. So we agreed to share out the towns and cities between us, depending on who lands where first, with the exception of the dark green and dark blue, the two most valuable sets, to which David had exclusive rights. He was not yet ready for deals and could not really understand the concept of negotiation on an emotional level, although cognitively he was more than able.

Gradually, David learnt to tolerate me owning more properties and even demanding payment where due. In the sessions, it was hard for him when he landed on my properties. I could see him taking deep breaths to cope with the anger at having to pay me, and then he would reassure himself, words that I had said to him in the past, part adopted mantra, part voiced as his own thoughts about the game, chance, and risk. Just as in the passage by Bleiberg quoted above, David was able to mentalise to himself an alternative reality he had already experienced over and over again, through me, mediated by me, within the game, where "all may not be as it seems [in his internal reality]": "It's OK", he would say to himself, "Soon you'll land on my properties and pay me even more". This worked most of the time, and David's new-found joy of me landing on his properties by chance, and not at his behest, and handing him hefty sums was unmistakable. However, I still needed to be carefully attuned to his emotional resilience, or lack thereof. One session, I pushed the boundaries too far: he landed on my more expensive properties three times and paid me a good few thousand pounds. He still had many thousands left but became visibly threatened by my increased wealth. I threw the dice and, for the third round of the board in a row, I miraculously escaped landing on any of his properties. David had been banking (literally!) on me to land on the dark blue properties on which he had built hotels, and I missed yet again. His face went red, he could barely breathe for anger, and his eyes filled with tears. I could almost see the smoke coming it of his ears, he looked as if he would explode and I knew I had to interfere with "the banality of chance". I gently suggested that it felt intolerably unfair, and that maybe I should throw the dice again. His relief was tangible. I threw the dice (several times in fact) until I landed on his most prized hotel and paid him the requisite 2,000 pounds.

Meanwhile, I sensed David was becoming less guarded in his relationship with me and willing to talk more directly about his hurt. A few weeks later, during a game that was going David's way, I noticed that David nevertheless looked sad and I commented on the fact. He responded by telling me he had decided to leave the afternoon programme he was going to because the kids were being mean to him. Then he added that he had invited some other kids for a pizza at his house that day, but only two girls were coming. I decided he was ready for more direct interpretations, and I connected what was happening in the afternoon programme to what was happening in our games. That perhaps he finds it hard to play with the other children, that it is always hard to withstand losing, to part with money and give it to our rivals, or to concede the goals scored against us. Despite David's increased psychic strength, I still avoided direct "you find, you feel, you think" interpretations, deeming it would be too threatening for him and would most likely cause emotional shutdown or meltdown. In the next round on the *Monopoly* board, David missed all my properties, and then I landed again on the most lucrative property on the board, owned by him. "You really never do manage to win any games", he gloated, and insisted I pay immediately, though I had let him off countless times. I was very aware that I felt hard done by and felt that he was being unjust, especially given how "magnanimous" I had just been to him, but I realised that is exactly what he needed to happen, therapeutically speaking. I let myself feel the injustice and the hurt of his comment, realised this was projective identification at its most potent (see Chapter 8), but decided to leave these matters of humiliation and powerlessness to a later date. Nonetheless, I judged the time was ripe to risk a direct interpretation in a different direction, in the direction of mentalisation, of perception of the real world, free from his paranoid schizoid view of himself as maligned and hard done by victim. I pointed out that when we play, he often seems to forget how many properties he has and how much money he has and seems to always feel that he is weaker than me. I wondered out loud if maybe his siblings and his peers sometimes make him feel weak and stupid, and he forgets how clever and strong he is. His response was immediate: "Yes, they do. They're stupid idiots. They always call me the stupid idiot." This was a giant step for David. It is worth noting the polygonal relational aspects of this clinical example, where David used the game of *Monopoly*[14] not only to work through painful issues of inadequacy and impotence, but also for the first time he was able broach directly the hurt he had suffered at the hands of his siblings and peers at school.

Notwithstanding his progress, I knew that David was still not yet ready for me to win the game. David knew it too. And after a few more weeks wiping me out in our games of *Monopoly*, he looked me in the eye at the end of one session and said: "Now I understand…the day when you win and I don't throw a tantrum, then it will be time to finish therapy…But not yet!!"

7.2.3 Working with difficult and "damaged" children in the triangular space

Up to this point, I have concentrated on psychotherapeutic work with children functioning at higher levels of psychic integration, on the cusp between dyadic and triadic functioning. However, for many children, such as those who have suffered from deprivation, abuse, illness, repeated traumatic disruptions to family life, or those suffering from far-reaching learning difficulties or problems of impulse control and emotional regulation, this is not the case. In these children, fragile, brittle, and disorganised states of mind dominate. They show a marked tendency to chronic severe splitting, denial and to primitive levels of projection, and concrete thinking, rigidity, and distortions in reality-testing abound. Their symbolic function is defective and highly inconsistent, "links" (Bion, 1967) within and without are constantly under attack, they are prone to overwhelming and destructive emotions, and their impulse control is severely lacking. Their internal object relations and their real relations are often coloured by paranoid thinking, a basic mistrust in others, primal envy and narcissistic vulnerability, and rage. Children struggling at these more archaic states of mind are in dire need of psychotherapy in order to help them reorganise their inner private selves quietly, safely, at their own pace, but their ability to communicate their distress, anxieties, and psychic pain directly is all but blocked both in the therapy room and outside. The challenges they present in child psychotherapy are formidable.

These children fit Britton's description of patients where hyper-subjective and hyper-objective states of mind tyrannically dominate their psyche and their psychotherapy.[15] It can be said that the internal link between the parental couple in these children is highly distorted or all but missing, and there is little or no triangular space in the psyche within which to roam and develop symbolic thinking. These children remain psychically entrenched in the hyper-subjective or hyper-objective states of mind, able to move only in separate parallel lines, either along the primal-subjective dyad or along the objective-other dyad. Moving between the two is too threatening and involves inexorable psychic pain and danger. Development towards triangular and polygonal thinking and relating has become derailed or even arrested. Exclusive dyadic relations coloured by infantile omnipotence are often experienced as vital for survival and must be ferociously defended against the threat of any intrusion by another.

Britton vividly describes the considerable problems encountered when treating such patients, a description I find applicable to child patients as to adults:

> ... Being in analysis is a problem—i.e., being in the same room, the same mental space. Instead of there being two connected, independent minds, there are either two separate people unable to connect or two people with only one mind.
>
> ...In one group, the other is treated as of no significance; in the second group, the patient cannot commune without making the significant other an extension of him- or herself. In the first situation, the analyst cannot find a place within the psychic reality of the patient, while in the second, the analyst cannot find a place outside it.
>
> (Britton, 2004, p. 52)

Bateman and Fonagy (2013) identified similar polarities in borderline patients to these described by Britton, but which they describe in terms of deficits in the capacity for mentalisation and distortions in patterns of attachment. At one pole, there are patients who tend to strategies of "deactivation" of attachment, such as excessive detachment in interpersonal connections and over-rationalisation in thinking. At the other pole are those who tend to inappropriately intense attachment, hypersensitivity to rejection and frustration, and volatile behaviour (all consequences of what Bateman and Fonagy term "hyperactivation" [of attachment] strategies). The origins of these patterns are believed to be in the failure of the primary caretaker to build and hold undistorted representations of the child's mind in their own mind

(Fonagy & Target, 1998, p. 93). In infancy, parents, and caregivers respond to their infant's affects and emotions with "affective displays of their own," and it is this contingent mirroring of the infant's mind and affect states that enables the infant to develop their own capacity for regulation, and in time the representation of their own mind (Fonagy et al., 2018).

"Not good-enough" (Winnicott, 1971) or "malignant" (Britton, 1989, 1998) parental mental representations and non-contingent mirroring of the child's feelings and thoughts can be characterised as falling at two poles: hyper-accurate mirroring with no space between the child's feelings and the parental representation of these feelings; and parental mirroring that is contaminated, detached, or absent:

> If the mirroring is too accurate, the perception itself can become a source of fear, and it loses its symbolic potential. If it is frequently absent, reluctant, or contaminated with the mother's own preoccupation, the process of self-development is profoundly compromised.
>
> (Fonagy & Target, 1998, p. 94)

Such dysfunctional parenting rarely tends only to one pole but usually oscillates unpredictably between these modes of distorted mirroring. Likewise, most borderline children and adults tend to have mixed disturbed patterns of attachment, oscillating between hyperactivation and deactivation strategies. At both these poles of patterns of attachment and of mentalisation, the link between feelings and thoughts, between inner and outer reality, and between subjective and objective is weakened or even attacked, and patterns of attachment and mentalisation are distorted.

The aim of psychotherapy with children in borderline states of mind is to enable them to "find [themselves] in the mind of the analyst as thinking and feeling being[s]"[16] (Fonagy & Target, 1998, p. 109):

> For the abused child, the adult's mental world is too real a threat to permit play and is thus shunned and avoided. The analyst's attitude and verbalization permit the opening of a window on the mental world of self and other, but the child has to find the courage to use this, to look through it and find his own feelings and ideas—something that has never before felt safe. In other words, the therapeutic intent is to facilitate the establishment of a beachhead, an area of self-other relatedness.
>
> …Gradually, children are nudged to introduce small modifications in their play to better encompass the complexities, limitations, conflicts, and frustrations of reality. The transitional space of play and fantasy offers borderline children the magic of anonymity in which to attempt to bring together split-off representations of the self and others.
>
> (Fonagy & Target, 1998, pp. 107–108)

The implication is that mentalisation, the transitional space, and playing are all intrinsically interconnected with one another, and by corollary therefore also with the triangular space. This is not so surprising, given that the infant clearly can only explore the parents' mind if there is some degree of separation, of potential space (physical and psychic) between infant and parent. Winnicott often referred to the reflection of infant in the eyes of the parent and the "minding" of the infant in the primary parent's mind (for Winnicott, this was the mother's mind) and the curiosity of the infant to explore the mother's mind. Much of Winnicott's imagery also implicitly involves triangulation between the holding parent, the infant, and the other (be it the other parent, or the transitional object, or the outside world/reality/ the "not-me"). Indeed, Green (2000/[1997]) makes this connection between Winnicott's transitional space, the triangular space, and the "third object" explicit:

> To distinguish between the first object and the first 'not me possession', as Winnicott does, extends our thinking, especially if this is located in an intermediate area between two parts of two bodies, mouth and breast, which will create some third object in between them, not only in the actual space that separates them, but in the potential space of their reunion after their separation.
>
> (Green, 2000/[1997], p. 87)

Over the course of my clinical work over many years, I have met many children who fit these two poles of psychic disorganisation. There are the hyper-objective children, whose play is dead, where no creative chink of light can enter, who spend hours arranging the dolls' house or the soldiers for battle, and then nothing happens, no story, no battle, and no life. Many scorn dolls and creative materials altogether, avoid them like the plague, and insist instead on playing the most lifeless and boring board games and card games. It is strictly forbidden to stray from the set rules of the game and games that involve an element of luck or surprise that could be experienced as unbearable. However, under these thick walls of defence, we can often sense a hyper subjective child, seething with rage, primal anxieties, and burning psychic pain.

Then there are the hyper-subjective children who ignite and explode at the very sight of the dolls, soldiers, crayons, and paints. Whose inner envy and almost cannibalistic rage is so near the surface that when they paint, they can only drown the paper in oozing layers of every colour, usually culminating in an orgy of thick black slime. In play with dolls, these children repeatedly enact mass murder and rape or stage endless battles with toy soldiers that inevitably end in indiscriminate torture and slaughter week after week. Like their hyper-objective counterparts, many of these children also run a mile from creative materials and toy animals and dolls and ask to play ball games or board games instead. But these children, by contrast, are almost incapable of playing by the rules; they lie and cheat mercilessly. They invent their own idiosyncratic rules, which they change indiscriminately, usually with neither warning nor explanation. Playing "structured" games with such children often feels anything but structured. The experience is far from playful and feels more like a cruel and hopeless struggle for survival than a harmless game. The therapist often feels helpless and useless, imprisoned under the child's tyrannical rule, subject to their cruel whims and fancies, forbidden even to score a single goal, or throw the dice independently, let alone buy a street or capture a pawn.

The choice these often highly disorganised and severely damaged children make when they enter the analytic playroom, of choosing to play the developmentally appropriate "normal" "benign" games of childhood, often seemed strange to me. But I came to understand, through years of clinical work with these children, that these games in fact offer the child a safe and familiar framing structure they so sorely lack, within which they can begin to explore and express their terrifying persecutory inner worlds. I suggest that the presence in the therapy room of structured games with rules and boundaries, in addition to dolls and creative materials, allows us as child psychotherapists to offer a potentially triangular space, even to children who seem atrophied in the linear hyper-subjective or hyper-objective modes, and who cannot initially utilise that space. I would liken therapeutic work with such psychically fragile children to moving the vertices of subjectivity and objectivity, inner and outer reality, the pretend world and the real world, slowly and gradually, outwards and upwards, from a skewed, oblique-angled paranoid schizoid triangle towards a more balanced and spacious, more equilateral, triangular transitional psychic space.

The child sits on one vertex, we at another, holding their mind in our mind, and the games, toys, and creative materials act as the third vertex to form the triangular potential space in which to roam and psychically grow and develop. Triangles within triangles within triangles: the therapist, their mind and psychoanalytic theory, and the child; the child, the rules and structure of the game, and their raw emotions and seething inner world; the child and the therapist, the "objective" structured competitive games of the "other", the outside world, and the "subjective" creative materials and dolls of fantasy play. The symbolic and psychic triangular and transitional space grows, and with it, the therapist's and the child's ability to touch the child's highly flammable and explosive inner world, safely, carefully, and without injury. In this way, hyper-subjective children can begin to slowly separate from the subjective tyrannical world of archaic omnipotent fantasies and dare to taste and experience the objective world of written rules, of a benign order of the benevolent external third. And conversely, with hyper-objective children, by careful calibration of the game, we can gradually soften and relax their obsessive adherence to the rules and encourage them to express archaic narcissistic needs and wishes, to bend the rules, to cheat, and to win with glee. *The very framing structure, the narrative of the games, the pawns and the cards, together confer the "magic of anonymity" in the game-play with the child, "in which to attempt to bring together split-off representations of the self and others" (Green, 2000/[1997]). At this level of psychic functioning, the game is used less as a metaphor and more as a cover, a container, a window into which to project the split-off and the threatening.*

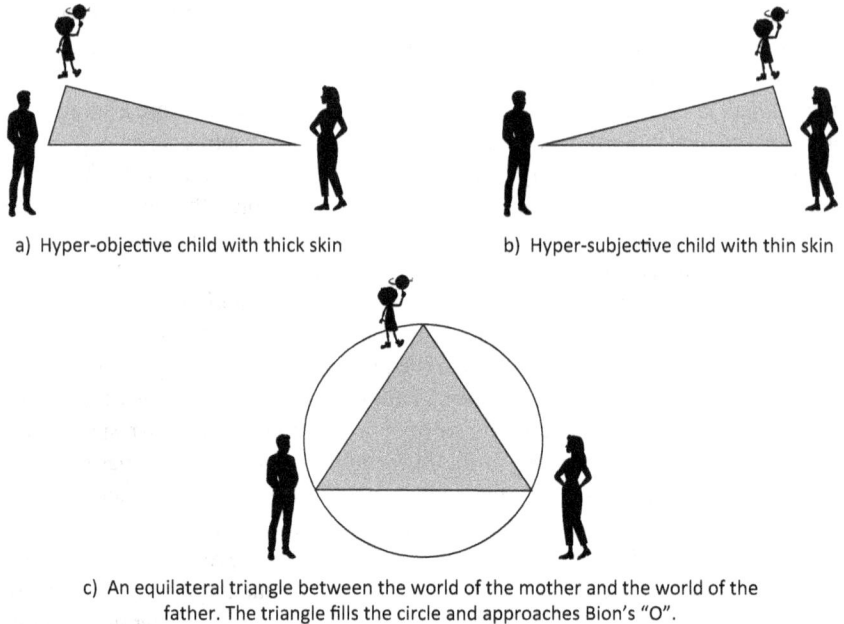

a) Hyper-objective child with thick skin   b) Hyper-subjective child with thin skin

c) An equilateral triangle between the world of the mother and the world of the
father. The triangle fills the circle and approaches Bion's "O".

Figure 7.1 Depictions of the transition from hyper-objectivity or hyper-subjectivity
into the broader triangular space.

VIGNETTE J – A fateful game of chess

Jane was a highly traumatised nine-year-old, whose mother had died in a terrible self-inflicted car crash some years before. She was preoccupied with grown-up matters and hated playing with her peers, focused almost exclusively on her intellectual capacities, and prided herself on her academic achievements. At first, I tried offering *Playmobile* and *Lego*, Winnicott's Squiggle game, and drawing with paints and markers. She would engage for a couple of minutes and then lose interest and become frozen. Jane was willing only to play board games: *Monopoly*, *Cops and Robbers*, and *Guess Who*. All ostensibly benign games with clear rules and goals, but the games we played together were infused with tyranny, terror, and helplessness. In *Cops and Robbers,* she would trap me in a one-way street with barriers at each end and refuse to move them, even when the rules dictated it was time for my release. In *Monopoly*, she built expensive hotels while in debt to me for thousands of dollars.

With Jane, deciding how to handle issues of cheating and winning and losing was tough. Her narcissistic, almost vindictive, pleasure in her wins and tyrannical control in the games we played seemed neither healthy nor constructive developmentally. On the one hand, I feared that letting her bankrupt me in a game of *Monopoly* when she had £20,000 in hand, when earlier she had been indebted to me by the same amount, would only serve to further impair her reality testing and foster her grandiosity and arrogance in Bion's (1958) psychotic sense of the word. On the other hand, Jane's sense of self and the cohesion of her psyche were so fragile that I felt it would be catastrophically destructive to point out the realities of her dire financial situation. Such an intervention would, I judged, serve only to make her prematurely and traumatically aware of her tragically limited power to control her environment.

Jane had an interesting way of changing the rules surreptitiously, of persuading herself and me that her rules did not constitute shifts from the conventional rules but were the "rules themselves". Only gradually did I begin to insist on some safeguarding, a return to the "common sense" (Bion, 1967) rules of the game. I Wondered aloud about houses and towns built without foundations, of mortal fear and anxiety in the face of the danger of their imminent catastrophic collapse. Closer to home, I talked of my own confusion and hopelessness in the knowledge I could never win. I gradually set caps on our debts, waived her payments to me less often, or insisted on reciprocal leniency when I could not pay her. In *Cops and Robbers,* after describing the helplessness and desperation I felt, like a mouse in a maze with no exit, I invoked the rule that releases the roadblocks after three turns. And I began to play all our games with more skill and determination to win. As therapy progressed, I could see that Jane could see me more as a real, live opponent with an active presence in the game, who was beyond the reach of her "omnipotent intellectual powers", with my own strengths and weaknesses, mental strategies, capacity to win, and resilience to survive losing.

From time to time, Jane would ask to play chess, a game I usually try to avoid because the chance element is heavily biased towards the cognitive and the intellectual, the calculated and the objective, and the opportunities for the therapist to introduce new or surprising elements and playfulness are more limited. About two years into therapy, I finally relented and agreed to her request to play what she called a "marathon tournament". For six weeks in a row, I lost repeatedly, game after game, to Jane's almost sadistic satisfaction. And then I cracked. In the seventh week, I lost my therapeutic neutrality; the instinctual urge to win, for revenge, overcame me. In an unplanned move that appeared out of nowhere as if straight from my unconscious, I found myself in one fell swoop capturing her queen and entrapping her king in checkmate. We were both in shock, tears filled her eyes, and I had trouble digesting my terrible, almost murderous empathic failure. But simultaneously, I realised this was a scene we had to re-enact between us, a re-enactment I had been avoiding session after session, ever since the first meeting with Jane. It was the game of chess, by dint of its strict rules and intellectual challenge, the "father of all" board games, that finally allowed the therapeutic space to be created in which Jane's psychic catastrophe of her mother's tragic death/suicide and her own terrible guilt could be relived and survived by us both. The game ended, and the session soon after. I knew the experience had been a visceral shock to us both, this, albeit metaphorical, reenactment of Jane's mother's catastrophic death, and I sensed the working through had to take place at first through the game of chess itself. We continued to play for the next few weeks, at first full of fear and trepidation, both stepping lightly, without the cutting aggression and existential urgency that had coloured the earlier games. Instead, it was sadness and a sense of hopelessness and helplessness that dominated our games. Once I felt Jane had been given the chance to let these feelings settle and work through the shock by playing more games, to win and lose again (mostly win) but not catastrophically, to feel her intellectual powers and abilities restored, we moved on. I think we were both relieved to leave the chessboard in the cupboard, ghosts exorcised from it. I will return to this clinical example and to the transference countertransference aspects I have left out here for the sake of clarity of discussion in Chapter 8.

7.3   Petrification, chaos, and the reclamatory power of game-play

In Chapter 12 of *The Thinking Heart*, Alvarez (2012) describes her sensitive work with a nine-year-old boy with quite severe autism, work which to her surprise involved "the intensified use of some infantile, maternal *and paternal* countertransferences" (2012, p. 163, emphases added). Like many children with autism, Joseph had little speech, rarely engaged in eye-to-eye contact or in direct verbal communication and was addicted to private repetitive idiosyncratic pseudo-play and speech. Faced with this monotony and non-aliveness in the sessions, Alvarez "came to use a kind of 'motherese' when [she] begged him to pay attention to [her] rather than to his autistic figures" (2012, p. 163), but with little success. Eventually she realised she had begun to introduce a new "other" voice to the therapy room, to surprise Joseph out of his autistic comfort zone without alarming him: "a kind of 'fatherese' …[which] amplified on, and invited him to take note of, the strength and assertiveness that were buried in some of his autistic repetitive movements" (Alvarez, 2012, p. 163).

Developing these ideas further, Alvarez stresses the importance of attributing an albeit very primitive proto-theory of the mind to the autistic child and going beyond their encapsulated psyche towards proto dyadic and triadic relations.

I think he [Joseph] needed *both* the more receptive coaxing 'motherese' from me *and* the more challenging 'fatherese'. There seems to have been two aspects to the father's voice in the room: first, a father who declines to indulge omnipotence, makes demands on his child to learn and to grow, and makes it clear that the child is not the same as the grown-ups; and, second, the father who invites and permits identification (with [a] strong voice and [physical] potency).… Some identification with a father certainly aids the tolerance of Oedipal rivalries and enables omnipotent methods to be replaced by a more realistic sense of agency and potency.

(Alvarez, 2012, p. 172)

This use of oedipal terminology is perhaps surprising when talking of work with children in autistic states of mind. However, as Maria Rhode (2011, 2022[2023]) has pointed out, this clinical understanding of holding in mind both female and male elements of the child's psyche and of the containing function of the parent/analyst when working with primitive states of mind is not entirely new. In Freudian and Kleinian thinking, the role of the paternal element is viewed as responsible for establishing distance and 3-d psychic functioning away from primary adhesive skin-to-skin relationships. Bion (1967) conceptualised the female element of the containing function as that responsible for taking in the patient's unconscious communications and the male element as responsible for giving back the unconscious communication transformed and digested through the analyst's reverie. Elaborating on this line of thought and combining these ideas with his and Anzieu's ideas of the psychic envelope, Houzel (2001) has suggested an inherent bisexuality in the infant's/child's/patient's psychic envelope as an internalisation of the bisexuality of the parental container. Rhode (2011) herself has likewise proposed that the infantile psychic skin combines the "female" element of permeability to inter-psychic communication and the "male" element of solidity to enable a separate sense of self to develop.

Having now introduced terminology connected to Oedipal themes, the maternal, and the paternal, I would like to digress slightly for a moment to add a caveat in this discussion and call this gender stereotypically couched terminology into question. I believe that the terms maternal and paternal countertransference and "motherese" and "fatherese" as used here by Alvarez, whilst useful clinically, are also restrictive and as such potentially misleading. Mothers frequently make "demands on their infants and children to learn and to grow" and fathers know how to coax and be receptive. I would therefore like to propose here an alternative non-gendered terminology and suggest using more developmentally accurate alternative terms of "primarese" and "otherese", instead of the restrictively gendered terms "mother-ese" and "father-ese". It is these latter terms that I shall use in the discussion from here on.

This having been said, the crux of the matter of Alvarez and Rhode's clinical conceptualisations remains the same. Children with deep developmental and emotional disturbances often need the therapist to hold in their mind a two- and three-person psychology, however rudimentary, and to use the voice of the limiting, demanding, potent, and yet attuned "other", as well as the patient, containing, receptive, indulgent "primary" voice. This "other-ese", the voice of reclamation towards reality, introduces the rules and regulations and demands of reality, but also the excitement of discovery of the real world outside the primary dyad, at the right developmental moment, not too soon, not too late.[17] Both Alvarez and Rhode reiterate that the demand coming from the parental "other"/the therapeutic "other" of the child to grow and develop is an expression of the fact that time is not limitless and has crucial meaning for the child's developmental path. Clinical experience has taught me that these clinical axioms hold just as true for the child who is in a chronic state of psychotic fragmentation and disorganisation, as for children in autistic encapsulated states of mind. It is true that for very long periods of time, children in such psychotic states of mind need the therapist to use a "primary" holding containing therapeutic stance to withstand their bizarre, terrifying, and chaotic inner world, but I have found that eventually there comes a time in treatment when such children also need the therapist to take a stand in the face of the all-engulfing chaos, boundlessness, and timelessness, and "demand" of the child a more age-appropriate, reality-oriented level of functioning and psychic order.

In her paper "On a knife-edge: Looking for the right distance in work with children on the autism spectrum",[18] Rhode (2022[2023]) describes the extreme hyper-subjectivity and hyper-objectivity of autistic children. Following Meltzer, Rhode categorises two modes of being in autistic children: those who are terrified of "falling off" and being pushed into space forever by a "hostile father element" and those who are terrified of losing themselves and "falling into the adult" and being swallowed up by an all-engulfing mother element. These children experience a chronic and "catastrophic instability … of the body as well as of space and relationships". Alvarez has long stressed the importance of calibrating the psychic distance of therapeutic intervention in accordance with the explosiveness and fragility of the child's mental state (Alvarez, 1989, 2010, 2012). Like Alvarez, Rhode emphasises the therapeutic and developmental necessity for triangular space for these children:

> It is essential to have the concept of a stable father element that structures the experience of space and the distance between child and mother if the child is to feel stable himself and to be able to communicate symbolically (by means of drawings, for example, rather than bodily actions).
>
> (Rhode, 2022, English translation [2023] p. 6)

She concludes her paper using oedipal terminology in surprising fashion:

> I suggest that working at maintaining a stance that embodies a three-person, Oedipal constellation, in terms of the therapist's mental positioning as well as in terms of the phrasing of comments, is central if the child is not to feel unduly threatened by the twin dangers of being pushed too far away, out into space, or, conversely, of being sucked in by the therapist and losing what sense of self they may have.
>
> (Rhode, 2022, English translation [2023], p. 10)

7.3.1 Primarese and otherese in game-play with children in primitive states of mind

Over the years I have found that, when working with school-aged children functioning on these levels of psychic encapsulation or fragmentation, but whose cognitive faculties are relatively intact, age-appropriate familiar board games and card games can sometimes fulfil the therapeutic function that I have termed here "otherese". These children see their siblings and peers play these traditional childhood games at home and at school, games they often yearn to join in on, but do not dare to, or find themselves unable to do so. In the child psychotherapy room, however, these children often ask specifically to play these very games, perhaps understanding instinctively that therapy offers opportunities to "learn from experience" new modes of being and interpsychic interaction. I have learned from these clinical encounters that these games can indeed serve to cajole the child "upwards and onwards" towards development, even at the most basic of levels of psychic functioning, as Alvarez describes in her work with Joseph. The very act of suggesting a board game, an interactive age-appropriate game, can be an organising developmental challenge for the child functioning at the psychotic level. Similarly, for the child on the autistic spectrum, playing a board game can be a form of "reclamation" and a call to aliveness. This is an act that surprises and challenges the child, but it is an act that can only be made therapeutically when in response to our sense that the child has begun to experiment in more developmentally appropriate activities that demand joint play and joint attention, even on the most rudimentary level.

Alvarez (2012) describes this stage in Joseph's therapy when she began to challenge him to venture out of his comfort zone of interminable private, unintelligible, uncommunicative conversations:

> I also persisted with the idea that his talk was not real, and *that I knew he was yearning to talk in a real way* (2012, p. 170, emphases added)....to be brought onto firmer ground where there were other real people.
>
> (Alvarez, 2012, p. 171)

When the therapist insists on playing an interactive developmentally appropriate board game with a child who is chronically using repetitive mechanical autistic pseudo-play with dolls and small objects to prevent psychic movement and space, they are effectively saying to the child: "I know your play is pseudo play, but I know you are yearning to play in a real way with a real other person and I know you are ready to try it out".

Conversely, board games themselves can of course also be used by the child on the spectrum as a form of autistic shape, as a force preserving stasis, against development, against movement.[19] Their play is robotic and lifeless. In fact, the word play does not really describe the activity. They turn to board games as a rigid, unbending, un-alive framework that acts as a protective shell or armour against the vagaries of the outside world. The rhythm and rhyme of board games can, as we have seen, be containing and paradoxically liberating for the wave-particle child, but they can be deadening when in the hands of a child who has never experienced their own wave-like qualities and lives in terror of any wave that may come their way and engulf them in its wild, unpredictable swirl.

At the opposite pole are "psychotic" children, who themselves exist in a timeless wild swirling unbounded psychic universe, for whom the rules and structure of the board game are unintelligible or even experienced as a persecutory threat to their omnipotent, often megalomaniac, phantasy world. These children tend to avoid board games in the child therapy room like the plague, but their pretend fantasy play lacks all rhyme and reason, and as such is as monotonous and deadening as the "autistic" child's deadly dull ritualistic doll play or game-play. Whether board games are consistently avoided, or used as an autistic defence by the child, it is upon the therapist to bide to wait for the time to ripen when the child is ready to dare to take the developmental step forward towards psychic movement and space that game-play can offer.

Bion's concept of the two poles of psychic functioning of the "Establishment" and the "Messianic" can be of help in conceptualising these two extreme "autistic" and "psychotic" poles of –P, as I have termed such anti-play or non-play above. According to Bion, the "Establishment" in the psyche is that which is stable and invariant; it has a chronicity and a directionality, whereas the "Messianic" or the "mystic" denotes the elements in psychic functioning that are explosive, expansive, and unbounded in time and place (Amir, 2015; Bion, 1962; Britton, 1992). In a sense, one can think of the Establishment as having its roots in conscious reality, and the Messianic in the unconscious. The combination of these elements leads to what Bion called binocular vision (Bion, 1962), which enables the perception of depth and perspective and the creation and growth of psychic space. In his paper "Keeping things in mind" Britton (1992) refers to Bion's unpublished paper "Catastrophic change" and explains these fundamental elements of the psyche in the more intuitive and communicative terms of the "continuous" and the "emergent":

> Bion, in a description of the 'container' in an unpublished paper entitled *'Catastrophic change'*(Bion, 1967), says that 'some aspect of the personality is stable and constant, and that this is maintained as the only force likely to contain emergent ideas which express new awareness of reality of the self or the world.' If the relationship between this continuous self and the recurrently changing emergent self is mutually enhancing, development takes place.
>
> (Britton, 1992, pp. 111–112)

When there is a fundamental failure of containment, on the level of handling and holding, the psyche experiences the threat of disintegration and fragmentation. In the extreme, where the "establishment" or the "continuous" is in tyrannical control of the psyche, autistic adhesion to order, petrification, and robotic repetition result. Where the messianic rules, all is chaos. Amir (2015, 2018) draws an intriguing link between the "continuous" and the "emergent" with Freud's concept of the "uncanny", *Unheimlich*: "Without the 'continuous' one cannot build up a sense of familiarity. But in the absence of the 'emergent' one will be unable to accumulate enough unfamiliarity, enough *Unheimlich*, to enable desire" (Amir, 2018, p. 206).

For the child on the autism spectrum, who is addicted to lifeless petrified game-"play", it is upon the therapist to find the element of *Unheimlich* within the game. To find the reclamatory call to life, the call to face-to-face (in Alvarez' terms) interaction, that is strong enough and close enough to surprise the child out into the real interpersonal world, but not too unfamiliar, too unsettling, and too disconcerting to send the child retreating further back into the depths of their autistic shell. It is my experience that when the "Establishment" in the child's psyche is too well rooted and tyrannically controlling, the element of chance inherent in all board games, if carefully managed and titrated by the therapist, can act as this "emergent" element, the challenge towards movement.

And conversely, for the child in a chronically psychotic state of mind who is similarly addicted to non-thinking and meaningless behaviour, but of the chaotic variety, the structure, and rules of the board game, can act as an organising, bounded, stable, and resilient container. This is provided that the game is offered to the child in an attuned and calibrated manner, within the child's own frame of reference, reeled in from somewhere in the outer reaches of their familiar chaotic world and not as an outside, persecutory, threatening, imprisoning force.

To illustrate the therapeutic power of such clinical interventions, I bring two clinical examples, the first of work with a child on the autism spectrum and the second of work with a child in a psychotic state of mind. The first was shared with me generously by my late colleague, Anna Iofan, to whom I am indebted for this example and our many enlightening discussions concerning work through the medium of game-play with children in highly disturbed states of mind.

VIGNETTE K – What does it mean "give and take"?[20]

Kim, aged 10, a child who seemed chronically ill at ease in his own skin, rigidly obsessive in his behaviour, and socially isolated, was diagnosed during the course of treatment as functioning on the autism spectrum. In the psychotherapy sessions, he was addicted to playing Monopoly: in all the year and a half of treatment, he had hardly ever agreed to play anything else and certainly never initiated playing any other game. The games followed the same script, week in, week out. He bought some properties, his therapist bought some properties, but Kim insisted on sticking to the rules so rigidly that these games never progressed very far. In any case, he could not bear to part with his money and build enough houses and hotels to bring the game to life. Almost every game ended in stalemate with half the properties owned by Kim, half owned by the therapist and both with very little money in their possession. The bank, the Establishment, had absolute control over the game.

Then came the day that the therapist had had enough. Something had to budge, it was time to let a breath of fresh air into the game, to break the monotony of the sessions, but without shocking Kim right out of his skin. The properties had as usual been evenly divided between them and they each dutifully paid their few shekels of taxes to each other round after round. No one was ever going to win, and no one was ever going to lose. All nice and safe, and predictable and lifeless. About 20 minutes before the end of the session, the therapist turned to Kim and suggested they strike a deal and swap property cards between them. [The words she actually used were the Hebrew words for negotiation משא

ומתן – literally "give and take".] "No!" was the immediate reply. They continued playing as if nothing had happened, a good few minutes passed, and then Kim, who was an intelligent boy with a wide if stilted vocabulary, looked at the therapist a little abashed and asked: "What does that mean, a deal? What are negotiations?" Kim looked as surprised as the therapist by his question. "Well, it means giving and taking, I give you something and you give me something that we both agree is fair to both of us". She let her words sink in and then added:

> It works like this: I suggest what I want to give you and then you tell me what you what you are willing to give me. If we both think the deal fair, we agree and exchange cards and then we can make sets of properties.

Kim looked thoughtful, hesitant, anxious, and excited all at once. These were not emotions that were usually discernible in him. It was already the end of the session and, despite the fragility of the moment, the therapist had no option but to suggest they write down the properties they each had in their possession and continue the discussion in the following session.

The next session, Kim marched into the room ahead of the therapist, took the *Monopoly* set down off the shelf and almost without taking a breath said: "So, I want to do a deal today. I want to do a...*negotiation*." Kim used the word awkwardly, as if testing the temperature of the waters, carefully, gingerly. Perhaps the week's break had enabled the temperature in the therapist-child interaction to cool down to a bearable temperature, but not to freeze, and had given Kim time to digest the new concept slowly, at his own pace. The therapist responded in tune and again explained the meaning of the word negotiation, "give and take", and what it meant to make a deal. It is interesting to recall here that Benjamin links the negotiation of meaning with a sense of agency, psychic space, and thirdness: "Thirdness is felt as mental space to negotiate meaning. I am free to confer meaning, I respond out of my own sense of agency and authorship, rather than feeling myself merely acted upon, impinged upon, having to react*"* (Benjamin, 2007, p. 6).

The therapist and Kim set about exchanging cards; each step of the way the therapist explained the relative values of the cards to Kim and why some deals were reasonable and some unfair. His curiosity had been piqued; and the game came alive. It was a lot to take in at once and the therapist limited the deals to two exchanges, although there were many more possible options. Now Kim had in his hands two full sets of properties, and for the first time ever he decided to part with his money and build some houses. The therapist did the same, but built no more houses than Kim so as not to bankrupt him if he landed on her properties. They played a few rounds until finally the therapist landed on Kim's property and had to hand him a pile of notes. He was almost overwhelmed by his riches and seemed astonished that the game could be played this way. The game was alive, but the anxiety was also palpable, for therapist as well as patient. The movement towards psychic space and the experience of thirdness, "otherese" and "primarese" (motherese) together was palpable. Kim was almost intoxicated by his newfound sense of agency to create new meanings in the give and take with the therapist-other.

Two more rounds and Kim landed on the therapist's prize property. It is no wonder it had taken almost two years to get to this point that Kim could risk so much in the session, could allow himself to explore so far from his comfort zone. He had to pay the therapist a sizeable fee and he seemed torn between acquiescing and quitting, between moving forward towards interpersonal interaction, towards the region of interpersonal give and take and negotiation, and disappearing back into his shell like a startled mollusc. With a little coaxing, encouragement, and a few words in "primarese" from the therapist reflecting to him just how new and scary, but also exciting, this all was, Kim eventually managed to part with the money, to risk being in uncharted, unpredictable waters. Play, and this was rudimentary alive play at last, continued and to the therapist's relief she soon landed on Kim's prize property and had to pay him her dues, which more than replaced the money she had taken from him. His relief was visceral, physical. And hers. As the session ended, Kim got up suddenly and shot out the door in the direction of the toilets: in all the tension and the rush of excitement in the game, he had wet himself through and through. It had almost been too much for him; his anxiety was almost overwhelming, but he had indeed crossed the Rubicon, the die had been cast, and playing *Monopoly* would never be the same again.

VIGNETTE L   From "atonality" to the "tonality"

Lee, nine years old, was referred to me for intensive psychotherapy because of severe difficulties with emotional regulation, impulse control, behavioural issues at school and at home, and learning difficulties in some areas. Notwithstanding, his cognitive abilities were above average, and he was gifted linguistically and musically.

In therapy, Lee talked loud and fast, characterised by an intense pressure of speech and loose associations. He was often on the point of losing control and throwing a temper tantrum, which could last only a matter of minutes or the entirety of the session and beyond. He talked incessantly about his nightmares and his anxieties about monsters and zombies, his rage at anything and anyone, his obsessions with Fortnite, and his megalomanic plans to fly to Europe to play drums with his favourite boy band. The sessions were often manic, overwhelming, and very noisy. It was hard work for both of us. At the beginning, it seemed that we were making progress, the therapeutic bond strengthened, Lee's psychotic anxieties lessened, the content of his speech became less idiosyncratic and more cohesive, and his rage and general behaviour became more controlled.

Then we hit therapeutic impasse. Nothing interested Lee except talk of Fortnite or his drums; he would hide behind his mobile phone watching endless nonsensical (to me) clips and fight me over anything and everything. In the first year of therapy, these battles had seemed therapeutically meaningful and had served to strengthen trust and work through Lee's existential anxieties and destructiveness. But now that destructiveness and rage had become hollow and meaningless, as if Lee had become addicted to destruction for destruction's sake, all meaning was being emptied out of the sessions and all psychic links attacked, time after time. The messianic, the nihilistic mystic, to use this same Bionian terminology, had usurped control over Lee's psyche, and the Establishment had absented itself completely. The sandbox, paints, animals, and Lego all led to chaos; all paintbrushes, pencils, paper, balls, dinosaurs, and toy cars turned to weapons of mass destruction and self-destruction.

There had to be another way. I felt I had to bring Lee back to the realm of therapeutic communication, to insist on links and meaning, however short lived, and to break this cycle of nihilistic rageful attacks. For a time, talk of music, of different rock bands, and working out complicated rhythms together on improvised drums in the room served as a channel of meaningful and even creative communication in the sessions. But as the weeks passed, the "jam sessions" themselves came under attack, Lee felt impelled to destroy these few fragile links we had managed to create, he would quickly become derailed and the drumming would lead time and again to uncontrolled outbursts of destructive senseless banging against the wall or the table, which I struggled to limit and contain. Eventually I realised the makeshift drums and drumsticks we had created had been hijacked into Lee's chaotic volcanic world and I took the difficult unilateral decision to remove them for a while from the therapy room to protect both of us and the therapy.

I understood I had to find another medium through which to reach Lee. I had to try using the language of "other-ese". And it struck me that a structured card or board game might just be the form of "other-ese" to which Lee might respond. The language of the Establishment that might counter and contain the megalomanic expansiveness had engulfed Lee's psyche and the therapy itself. I thought of all the games I usually play with children Lee's age, and nothing seemed appropriate or feasible. Playing *War* would result in just that, a concrete barrage of cards, it would not hold his attention, playing *Monopoly* was too long and involved, the rewards too remote, playing *Cheat* or *Mastermind (Code-Breaker),* involved a theory of mind well beyond Lee's capabilities, and playing football was far too dangerous physically in his present volatile state.

My eyes fell on the game of *Set,* a game that involves looking for similarities in patterns in cards of three different shapes, shadings, and colours laid out in rows of three. Only 12 cards at each round. No sharing of cards, no need to hold any in his hand as potential missiles. Lee had great visual acuity and was mathematically talented, and I thought this game might just do the trick. Challenging enough to grab his attention, but each round short enough not to lose him to his own chaotic inner world. His response was not encouraging: "What are you doing, you're mad! It's a stupid game". He almost spat at me. But I stood my ground, putting firm limits on his destructive urges, I took the cards in my hands and began to lay them out between us. I played and talked with insistence, with urgency and enthusiasm, using what could be called a "reclamatory" voice (to borrow and paraphrase Alvarez's term) in order to grab Lee's attention and bring him into connection with the real world, with me in the real world. I looked for patterns and order in the cards, and hoped to bring benign reality and calming organising order into the session itself and so into Lee's psyche.

Gradually, I aroused Lee's curiosity. I talked him slowly through my thinking, and almost against his own will, he joined in, pointed out to me what I "couldn't see", he helped me find the third card to complete whatever set I was looking for. Then he began to look earnestly for sets himself, and I became his assistant in finding a set. Here at last was a game with joint attention and with joint play, and the urge to pillage and burn everything in his path dissipated, at least temporarily. This session opened Lee's eyes to a new language and a new world: it was as if he was allowing himself to acknowledge that maybe he was capable of joining in the interpersonal dialogue that was the game, that he could eat from the fruit of this other world outside of himself, rather than destroy it out of blind rage precisely because it was other. In the sessions that followed, Lee asked to learn other games he had seen his siblings and his friends at school play. *Mastermind, UNO (TAKI), Speed (Spit), Rat-a-Cat-Tat.*[21] We played the games at a level of a very young child, despite Lee's intelligence. His theory of mind was very rudimentary, and it was vital to keep frustrations and complexity to a minimum if I was to succeed in keeping Lee on "board".

This is not to say that we were out of the woods. Lee had not magically become grounded, and his addiction to psychotic rage and destruction had by no means dissipated. But we had found a way to create psychic and therapeutic space and to experience short stretches of time of communication, of joint attention, and joint play without being engulfed in the swirling stormy seas of his inner world. And throughout the therapy, these games with rules and boundaries, and "common sense" (Bion, 1962) continued to function as a therapeutic tool through which I could create a benign link with Lee, a step towards establishing psychic continuity and order, when he had become entrenched and trapped in the chronic megalomania and the meaningless expansiveness of his inner world.

7.3.2   The musicology of game-play

Elaborating on Bion's concepts of the continuous and the emergent, Amir's (2017) ideas on "tonality" and "atonality" of the psychic space are particularly apposite here. Amir borrows the terms tonality and atonality from musicology and applies them innovatively to the psyche. Tonal music, which follows the expected rules and laws of harmony, instils in the listener a sense of order and centredness. And yet, too much predictability and regularity leave the listener unmoved, bored, even stupefied. Atonality,' on the other hand, abandons classical harmonics and rhythms and undermines the very centredness of the music itself. The tonal centre vanishes, and tonality and order itself are disrupted by an unexpected, unfamiliar, or even alien element, leaving the listener unsettled, disquieted.

According to Amir, the human psyche can similarly be understood in terms of tonality and atonality, for it senses security in the familiar, the ordered and the predictable, in the tonal, and is unnerved by the unfamiliar, the alien and the uncanny, the atonal. Excessive tonality results in stasis and even fixation; atonality, in its extreme, results in fragmentation and disintegration. But atonality, the uncanny, the surprising, is also a vital force in creativity, imagination, and aliveness (in the psychoanalytic sense of these words). Tonality can thus be seen to be akin to Bion's concept of the Establishment, the continuous and atonality to the Messianic and the Mystic, the emergent (Amir, 2017).

Viewed from this perspective, Kim's adherence to order and predictability in the endless games of *Monopoly* with his therapist can be thought of as an addiction to rigid tonality. His deep terror of the unfamiliar, the atonal, was such that the game became fixated in its unchanging tonal form. Round after round, Kim and the therapist were trapped in the same repetitive rhythm of the throwing of the dice, the predictable movement of the pawns, the exchange of the bank notes, the inevitable pass "GO" and collect 200, the cyclical return to the tonal centre, only to repeat the same familiar tune all over again. No development, no new tonality, not even a shift to a different set of harmonics and time signature, what Amir (2017) terms "modulation", the "transposition from one region [of tonality of familiar psychic space] to another". The therapist's daring suggestion to make a deal, to introduce the inter-psychic and interpersonal concept of "give and take," was a courageous and intuitive "act of freedom" (Symington, 1983). It served as a crucial moment of atonality, which jolted Kim's psyche towards movement and life. An act of reclamation (Alvarez, 1992), a call to Kim to face-to-face, psyche to psyche interaction, that which by definition instils both deep discomfort and deep yearning in the autistic child (as in Alvarez' (2012) description quoted above of Joseph's reaction to her use of "fatherese"). This was no mere modulation or transposition, but what Amir (2017) defines as a moment of "transcendence" of Kim's inner static tonality, of transcendence of the therapist–child interaction up to that point, a moment of disequilibrium that propelled Kim towards psychic change:

> The deviation from the entire tonal center, in contrast, does not generate a search for a new center but a state in which the center as such is relinquished, enabling the lingering in a state of no-center while listening to the new possibilities it generates. This clearly comes at the expense of familiarity and satisfaction; it will

probably cause a sense of alienation, not just from the external world but also from one's inner experience of continuity…Yet, exactly because of its alien nature, this moment also gives rise to an unparalleled intimate encounter with ourselves.

(Amir, 2017, p. 172)

The experience with Lee on the other hand was of non-thinking of a diametrically opposite nature. A cacophony of sounds with no harmonic envelope to contain and give sense to the chaotic sessions. Strident, jarring sounds, no rhyme, and no reason to the shifts between one sound byte and another. All at a level of intensity that effected a relentless attack on the very fabric of the therapy. In this same paper, Amir describes Schoenberg's[22] employment of "negative rules" in his music, negations of tonality and existing musical genres. Sessions with Lee felt to me like listening to Schoenberg on an old distorting malfunctioning tape-player with no stop button, day in, day out, at full volume in a closed room, with no door through which to escape.

Continuity, boundaries, the room itself, were under constant attack and at times it seemed like we were living together in some kind of megalomanic, "messianic", timeless world of destruction and chaos. Lee seemed to experience the objective, the Establishment, the tonal, as an attack on his very being and needed tonality to be introduced in measured, assertive, safe, and secure doses. My insistence on playing *Set* as Lee bombarded me with insults and threatened attacks on me and the room, acted as a stabilising organising dose of "fatherese"/"other-ese", a call to order, to developmentally appropriate interaction. This was an instinctive move on my part to ground Lee and envelop him with the containing rhythm and harmony of the patterns of the cards themselves. An appropriate metaphor for a child so pre-occupied with his drums and rock music. The tonality of the visual patterns of the cards themselves and the rhythmicity of the placement of the cards in regular rows of 3 × 4 acted as a concrete introduction of temporal and emotional order into Lee's chronically atonal, fragmented world. It created, if only for a few short minutes, some measure of benign space and the rudiments of continuity in his inner psyche, in mine, and in the inter-psychic space between us.

I conclude this chapter with a slightly whimsical thought. Rereading the above clinical examples, I was suddenly struck by the triangular theme running through these two games, Monopoly and SET: in both, the aim is essentially to collect sets/families of three cards. I could not help but wonder whether this rhythmicity of three, found also in Rummy, tic-tac-toe, rock-scissors-paper, is merely coincidental or whether such triangulation has become naturally embedded in the language of many childhood games and songs as an intuitive, playful impetus towards development and mental space.

Notes

1 The outline given in this section is necessarily brief and superficial: for a more detailed understanding of these three levels of therapeutic work, see the references cited here especially Alvarez (1989, 2010, 2012).

2 Flight 501 is a board game in which players contest as pilots of commercial airliners to be the first to reach their final destination (Ben-Gurion Airport in Tel Aviv) after visiting all their designated destinations along the way. Players are dealt a set of five destination cards before play begins. They progress in turns according to a spun dial, which selects whether they advance, go back, stop to refuel, add a bonus turn, etc. The board depicts a map of the world, with possible flight paths marked on it. Players learn about the destinations and the geography of the world (https://www.kodkod.co.il/product/%D7%94% D7%A8%D7%9E%D7%96-1).

3 My grateful thanks to H and G from London for sharing with me these wonderful insights, and to their very special Mum Karen, for generously and dutifully typing up their every word!

4 It might be pertinent to point out at this point that these sporting games can be played in a surprisingly small space, even when the child is hyperactive and quite wild, but it is wise to take precautions to equip the therapy room in accordance: with soft balls of sponge or soft rubber rather than standard footballs and basketballs; with simple chairs that can be used easily to hold elastic rope for French skipping or double as goal posts; to leave one wall blank for games against the wall (though these games can be problematic if sessions are going on in neighbouring rooms); with a basketball hoop and matching ball (even if small and removable); and with ping pong balls and bats (no table and net needed) – often a hit with non-verbal teenagers.

5 This distinction is important vis-à-vis issues concerning countertransference and board games in psychotherapy and will be discussed in depth in Chapter 8.

6 Clearly, these vignettes are presented to illustrated particular points in theory and technique. It goes without saying that clinical material is always multi-layered and can be interpreted in different ways and on many different intra-psychic and inter-psychic levels. I have chosen here to concentrate only on the aspects of the clinical material relevant to the particular theoretical issues under discussion.

7 As discussed below (Section 8.4), at the schizoid paranoid state, subjective object state of mind, such a separation between self and other, subject and object, is often omnipotently blurred or denied by the child; in autistic and psychotic states of mind the separation is all but obliterated.

8 In this same paper, Oren also examines the use of board games with reference to issues of self-esteem and self-cohesion, existential anxiety, rage, envy and greed, and associated transference and countertransference themes, which shall be discussed in the relevant sections below and in Subchapter 7.2 and Chapter 8.

9 Though salient to the discussion, a detailed overview of Lacan's theory of the Imaginary, the Symbolic, and the Real, is well beyond the scope of this chapter. For a detailed explanation of Lacan's theories in accessible language, see Burgoyne and Sullivan (2015) and Julien (1995).

10 The subject of board games and Winnicottian play and the transitional space will be discussed more fully in the next section, which focuses on issues of expanding the psychic space with children who can barely play. This is for the sake of brevity and clarity, although clearly these Winnicottian concepts are relevant to this present discussion too.

11 The Bender-Gestalt test consists of nine cards picturing different geometric designs, which are presented in turn to the subject, who is asked to copy the design to the best of their ability, before the next card is shown.

12 Though critical to work with children, I have not detailed the parental work in any of the clinical examples given. This is both to protect confidentiality and because discussion of therapeutic work with parents on parenting is beyond the scope of this book.

13 Discussed in Chapters 5 and 6, Sections 5.1.2 and 6.6.

14 For explanation of the game of Monopoly, see https://www.britannica.com/sports/Monopoly-board-game or https://en.wikipedia.org/wiki/Monopoly_(game).

15 This is in contrast to Hila, in the above example, who was able to function well at school and in afternoon activities, where the boundaries were clear, and where she felt the "wolves" were being kept safely at bay. Likewise, most of the time, Hila could hear and make use of my fairly direct interventions and interpretation and communicate her response directly and even playfully. This cannot be said of children fixated in these rigid hyper-subjective and hyper-objective states of mind, whose functioning is affected in all areas of their life, and whose tendency is towards splitting and envious destructive attacks on the therapist and on the therapy itself.

16 These issues of being found in the analyst's mind "as a thinking and feeling being" are profoundly connected to Bion's ideas on containing, dreaming, and thinking, to be discussed in depth in the next chapter.

17 Knowing when the time is opportune often demands sensitivity to cues in the transference–countertransference interactions (see Chapter 8).

18 Published in German (Rhode, 2022). I am indebted to Prof Maria Rhode for kindly giving me permission to quote here from the English version of the paper, delivered on June 25th, 2023, as an online lecture organized by The Frances Tustin Memorial Trust.

19 Clearly, I am talking here about children on the spectrum whose cognitive faculties are fairly intact and who co-opt these faculties in order to shore up their rigid autistic defences and turn to board games (the more structured the better) as part of that defence strategy.

20 I am deeply indebted to my dear late colleague Anna Iofan, who shared this vignette with me during one of our many discussions on the subject, and generously gave me permission to use it in my PhD dissertation and publications.

21 For rules of these games, see: https://www.thesprucecrafts.com/spit-speed-slam-card-game-rules-412496; https://en.wikipedia.org/wiki/Spit_(card_game); https://en.wikipedia.org/wiki/Mastermind_(board_game); https://officialgamerules.org/game-rules/rat-a-tat-cat/; https://en.wikipedia.org/wiki/Taki_(card_game); https://en.wikipedia.org/wiki/Uno_(card_game)

22 Arnold Schoenberg (1874–1951) was an Austrian-born composer, music theorist, teacher, writer, and painter. He was a pioneer in innovations in music in atonality and experimented in a variety of ways with the absence of traditional keys or tonal centres in many of his later works.

Bibliography

Abelin, L. (1975). Some further observations and comments on the earliest role of the father. *International Journal of Psycho-Analysis*, *56*, 293–302.

Abelin, L. (1980). Triangulation, the role of the father and the origins of core gender identity during the rapprochement subphase. *Rapprochement*, 151–170.

Active Lives Survey. (2018, September 24). Living Sport. https://www.sportengland.org/research-and-data/data/active-lives/active-lives-data-tables

Alvarez, A. (1989). Development toward the latency period: Splitting and the need to forget in borderline children. *Journal of Child Psychotherapy*, *15*(2), 71–83.

Alvarez, A. (1992). *Live Company: Psychoanalytic Psychotherapy with Autistic, Borderline, Deprived, and Abused Children*. Psychology Press.

Alvarez, A. (2010). Levels of analytic work and levels of pathology: The work of calibra-tion. *The International Journal of Psychoanalysis*, *91*(4), 859–878.

Alvarez, A. (2012). *The Thinking Heart: Three Levels of Psychoanalytic Therapy with Dis-turbed Children*. Routledge.

Amir, D. (2015). *On the Lyricism of the Mind: Psychoanalysis and Literature*. Routledge.

Amir, D. (2017). Tonality and atonality in the psychic space. *Journal of Poetry Therapy*, *30*(3), 166–174.

Amir, D. (2018). The other as an object of conquest versus the other as horizon: A reading in Stephen Mitchell and Clarice Lispector. *Psychoanalytic Perspectives*, *15*(2), 199–208.

Balsam, R. H. (2018). Castration anxiety" revisited: Especially "female castration anxiety. *Psychoanalytic Inquiry*, *38*(1), 11–22.

Bateman, A., & Fonagy, P. (2013). Mentalization-based treatment. *Psychoanalytic Inquiry*, *33*(6), 595–613.

Bateman, A., Fonagy, P., & Allen, J. G. (2009). Theory and practice of mentalization-based therapy. In G.O. Gabbard (Ed.), *Textbook of Psychotherapeutic Treatments* (pp. 757–780). APA Inc.

Beiser, H. R. (1970). Discussion of children who cheat at games. *Journal of the American Academy of Child Psychiatry*, *9*(1), 171.

Beiser, H. R. (1979a). Formal games in diagnosis and therapy. *Journal of the American Academy of Child Psychiatry*, *18*(3), 480–491.

Beiser, H. R. (1979b). The problem of infantile omnipotence. *Annual of Psychoanalysis*, *7*, 113–132.

Bellinson, J. (2000). Shut up and move: The uses of board games in child psychotherapy. *Journal of Infant, Child, and Adolescent Psychotherapy*, *1*(2), 23–41.

Bellinson, J. (2002). *Children's Use of Board Games in Psychotherapy*. Jason Aronson.

Bellinson, J. (2013). Games children play: Board games in psychodynamic psychotherapy. *Child and Adolescent Psychiatric Clinics of North America*, *22*(2), 283–293.

Ben-Ari Smira, K. (2015). *The Hidden Father: Reintroducing the Father into Psychoana-lytic Discourse*. Reisling.

Benjamin, J. (2004). Beyond doer and done to: An intersubjective view of thirdness. *The Psychoanalytic Quarterly*, *73*(1), 5–46.

Benjamin, J. (2007). Intersubjectivity, thirdness, and mutual recognition. *A Talk given at the Institute for Contemporary Psychoanalysis, Los Angeles, CA*.

Bettelheim, B. (1972). Play and education. *The School Review*, *81*(1), 1–13. JSTOR.

Bion, W. R. (1958). On arrogance. *International Journal of Psycho-Analysis*, *39*, 144–146.

Bion, W. R. (1962). *Learning from Experience*. Tavistock.

Bion, W. R. (1967). *Second Thoughts: Selected Papers on Psychonalysis*. Heinemann.

Bleiberg, E., Fonagy, P., & Target, M. (1997). Child psychoanalysis: Critical overview and a proposed reconsideration. *Child and Adolescent Psychiatric Clinics of North America*, *6*(1), 1–38.

Bloch, H. S. (1981). The role of strivings to complete development in the therapeutic pro-cess of child analysis. *International Review of Psycho-Analysis*, *8*, 203–218.

Bollas, C. (1999). Dead mother, dead child. In G. Kohon (Ed.), *The Dead Mother: The Work of André Green*. (pp. 87–108). Psychology Press.

Britton, R. (1989). The missing link: Parental sexuality in the Oedipus complex. In R. Brit-ton, M. Feldman & E. O'Shaughnessy (Eds.), *The Oedipus Complex Today Clinical Implications*. Karnac.

Britton, R. (1992). Keeping things in mind. In R. Anderson (Ed.), *Clinical lectures on Klein and Bion* (pp. 102–113). Tavistock/Routledge.

Britton, R. (1998). *Belief and Imagination*. Routledge.

Britton, R. (2004). Subjectivity, objectivity, and triangular space. *The Psychoanalytic Quarterly*, *73*(1), 47–61.

Britton, R. (2006). Panel I: Contemporary Views on Stages versus Positions. *Journal of Infant, Child, and Adolescent Psychotherapy*, 5(3), 268–281.

Burgoyne, B., & Sullivan, M. (2015). *The Klein-Lacan Dialogues*. Karnac Books.

Capell, M. D. (1968). Passive mastery of helplessness in games. *American Imago*, *25*(4), 309–332.

Caruth, E. G. (1988). How you play the game: On game as play and play as game in the psychoanalytic process. *Psychoanalytic Psychology*, *5*(2), 179–192.

Chused, J. F. (1982). The role of analytic neutrality in the use of the child analyst as a new object. *Journal of the American Psychoanalytic Association*, *30*(1), 3–28.

Collier, T., & Robles, V. (2004). Issues of disruptive attachment and countertransference in the treatment of a young boy infected with HIV. *Journal of Infant, Child, and Adolescent Psychotherapy*, *3*(1), 47–63.

Crocker, J. W., & Wroblewski, M. (1975). Using recreational games in counseling. *Personnel & Guidance Journal*, *53*(6), 453–457.

Davies, N., & Eagle, G. (2013). Conceptualizing the paternal function: Maleness, masculinity, or thirdness? *Contemporary Psychoanalysis*, *49*(4), 559–585.

Deakin, E. K., Gastaud, M., & Nunes, M. L. T. (2012). Child psychotherapy dropout: An empirical research review. *Journal of Child Psychotherapy*, *38*(2), 199–209.

Deakin, E. K., & Tiellet Nunes, M. L. (2009). Effectiveness of child psychoanalytic psychotherapy in a clinical outpatient setting. *Journal of Child Psychotherapy*, *35*(3), 290–301.

Diem-Wille, G. (2018). *Latency: The Golden Age of Childhood*. Routledge.

Edwards, C., Knoche, L., & Kumru, A. (2001). Play patterns and gender. In J. Worell (Ed.), *Encyclopedia of Women and Gender: Sex Similarities and Differences and the Impact of Society on Gender*. Academic Press.

Etchegoyen, A., & Trowell, J. (Eds.). (2005). *The Importance of Fathers: A Psychoanalytic Re-Evaluation*. Routledge.

Ferro, A. (Ed.). (2017). *Contemporary Bionian Theory and Technique in Psychoanalysis* (1 edition). Routledge.

Fonagy, P., Gergely, G., & Jurist, E. (Eds.). (2018). *Affect Regulation, Mentalization and the Development of the Self*. Routledge.

Fonagy, P., & Target, M. (1998). Mentalization and the changing aims of child psychoanalysis. *Psychoanalytic Dialogues*, *8*(1), 87–114.

Freud, A. (1966). *Normality and Pathology in Childhood*. Wiley.

Gavshon, A. (1989). Playing: Its role in child analysis. *Journal of Child Psychotherapy*, *15*(1), 47–62.

Green, A. (2000). The intuition of the negative in Playing and Reality. In J. Abram (Ed.), *Andre Green at the Squiggle Foundation*. Routledge.

Green, A. (2005). *Play and Reflection in Donald Winnicott's Writings*. Karnac Books.

Green, A. H. (1978). Psychiatric treatment of abused children. *Journal of the American Academy of Child & Adolescent Psychiatry*, *17*(2), 356–371.

Grotstein, J. S. (2018). *But at the Same Time and on Another Level: Psychoanalytic Theory and Technique in the Kleinian/Bionian Mode*. Routledge.

Hamblin, E. (2016). Gender and children and young people's emotional and mental health: Manifestations and responses. *National Children's Bureau, 20*(2), 51.

Hamburg, P. (1999). The lie: Anorexia and the paternal metaphor. *Psychoanalytic Review,* 86(5), 745–769.

Herman, J. L. (2000). Treating the cheater: An ego and self psychological approach to working through of the cheating syndrome in the treatment of latency children. *Journal of Infant, Child, and Adolescent Psychotherapy, 1*(2), 59–70.

Herzog, J. (2013). *Father Hunger: Explorations with Adults and Children.* Routledge.

Houzel, D. (2001). New psychoanalytic views on bisexuality. In Guimón, J., & de Filc, S. Z. (Eds.), *Challenges of Psychoanalysis in the 21st Century: Psychoanalysis, Health, and Psychosexuality in the Era of Virtual Reality* (pp. 45–53). Springer.

Julien, P. (1995). *Jacques Lacan's Return to Freud: The Real, the Symbolic, and the Imaginary.* NYU Press.

Kernberg, O. F. (1979). Some implications of object relations theory for psychoanalytic technique. *Journal of the American Psychoanalytic Association, 27*, 207–239.

Kernberg, O. F. (1995). *Object Relations Theory and Clinical Psychoanalysis.* Jason Aronson.

Kernberg, P. F., Weiner, A. S., & Bardenstein, K. K. (2008). *Personality Disorders in Children and Adolescents.* Basic Books.

Kinzie, M. B., & Joseph, D. R. (2008). Gender differences in game activity preferences of middle school children: Implications for educational game design. *Educational Technology Research and Development, 56*(5–6), 643–663.

Kohut, H. (1977). *The Restoration of the Self.* International Universities Press.

Krimendahl, E. (2000). "Did you see that?": A relational perspective on children who cheat in analysis. *Journal of Infant, Child, and Adolescent Psychotherapy, 1*(2), 43–58.

Lever, J. (1976). Sex differences in the games children play. *Social Problems, 23*(4), 478–487.

Mahler, M. S., Pine, F., & Bergman, A. (1975). *The Psychological Birth of the Human Infant.* Symbiosis and Individuation.

Mahler, M. S., Pine, F., & Bergman, A. (2000). *The Psychological Birth of the Human Infant Symbiosis and Individuation.* Basic Books.

Martínez-Andrés, M., Bartolomé-Gutiérrez, R., Rodríguez-Martín, B., Pardo-Guijarro, M. J., & Martínez-Vizcaíno, V. (2017). "Football is a boys' game": Children's perceptions about barriers for physical activity during recess time. *International Journal of Qualitative Studies on Health and Well-Being, 12*(sup2), 1379338.

Meeks, J. E. (1970). Children who cheat at games. *Journal of the American Academy of Child Psychiatry, 9*(1), 157–170.

Meeks, J. E. (2000). Reflections on children who cheat at games: A commentary. *Journal of Infant, Child, and Adolescent Psychotherapy, 1*(2), 71–75.

Midgley, N., & Kennedy, E. (2011). Psychodynamic psychotherapy for children and adolescents: A critical review of the evidence base. *Journal of Child Psychotherapy, 37*(3), 232–260.

Mitchell, J. (2013). Siblings: Thinking theory. *The Psychoanalytic Study of the Child, 67*(1), 14–34.

Nickerson, E. T., & O'Laughlin, K. B. (1980). *It's fun—But will it work?: The use of games as a therapeutic medium for children and adolescents.*

Nilsson, M. (2009). Table hockey: Attack or linking? Psychoanalytic psychotherapy with an autistic boy. *Journal of Child Psychotherapy,* 131–141.

Ogden, T. H. (1987). The transitional oedipal relationship in female development. *International Journal of Psycho-Analysis*, *68*, 485–498.

Ogden, T. H. (2018). *The Matrix of the Mind: Object Relations and the Psychoanalytic Dialogue*. Routledge.

Oren, A. (2008). The use of board games in child psychotherapy. *Journal of Child Psychotherapy*, *34*(3), 364–383.

Peller, L. E. (1954). Libidinal phases, ego development, and play. *The Psychoanalytic Study of the Child*, *9*, 178–198.

Rhode, M. (2011). The 'autistic' level of the Oedipus complex. *Psychoanalytic Psychotherapy*, *25*(3), 262–276.

Rhode, M. (2022[2023]). Auf Messers Schneide: Die Suche nach dem richtigen Abstand in der Arbeit mit Kindern aus dem Autismus-Spektrum. *Jahrbuch Der Psychoanalyse*, *85*, 17–35. (English Lecture delivered on June 25th, 2023, in an online event organized by The Frances Tustin Memorial Trust.)

Rosenfeld, H. A. (1987). *Impasse and interpretation: Therapeutic and anti-therapeutic factors in the psychoanalytical treatment of psychotic, borderline and neurotic patients*. Tavistock.

Roth, P. (2001). Mapping the landscape: Levels of transference interpretation. *International Journal of Psycho-Analysis*, 82(3), 533–543.

Roud, S. (2010). *The Lore of the Playground: One Hundred Years of Children's Games, Rhymes and Traditions*. Random House.

Segal, H. (1957). Notes on symbol formation. *International Journal of Psycho-Analysis*, *38*, 391–397.

Segal, H. (1978). On symbolism. *The International Journal of Psychoanalysis*, *59*, 315–319.

Steiner, J. (2003). *Psychic Retreats: Pathological Organizations in Psychotic, Neurotic and Borderline Patients*. Routledge.

Symington, N. (1983). The analyst's act of freedom as agent of therapeutic change. *International Review of Psycho-Analysis*, *10*, 283–291.

Van Rheenen, D. (2012). A century of historical change in the game preferences of American children. *The Journal of American Folklore*, *125*(498), 411–443.

Winnicott, D. W. (1971). The use of an object and relating through identifications. In D.W. Winnicott, *Playing and Reality* (pp. 101–111). Penguin Books.

Chapter 8

The playing field

The transference–countertransference matrix and transformations in game

Bion describes real contact between any two people as like a storm – capturing how unsettling it is to sense that the other person in the consulting room is completely different from oneself. For adults treating children, an added level of the foreign intensifies the storm. Ogden says that in order to read early Bion, "the reader must be able to tolerate not knowing, getting lost, being confused and pressing ahead anyway" (2004a, p. 286). This uncertain state of mind is analogous to what a child therapist needs to sustain. Even more than with adult patients, we can lose our bearings. There is less secondary process thought. There is less of the veneer of shared social conventions. There is more action and, often, more commotion: the girl won't come into the building for her session; the boy is throwing paper aeroplanes at his therapist's head; the teenager's parents call to say she organised a party where Ecstasy was taken; a boy brings his boa constrictor unannounced to meet his therapist.

(Brady et al., 2012, p. 302)

As Brady, Tyminski, and Carey describe here with penetrating accuracy and a healthy dose of humour, child psychotherapy indeed can often feel like a never-ending series of intense, interpersonal storms, mitigated here and there by a few welcome bright and calm interludes. But it is precisely these highly charged, intersubjective encounters that constitute the crux of child psychotherapy, particularly when treating disturbed and traumatised children. Moreover, if handled with care and with due respect for the explosive potential of the material at hand, these "emotionally turbulent" (Bion, 2019) encounters can serve as a powerful catalyst for psychic growth. In the previous chapters, the focus was on the third, "other" vertex of the triangular space. The form of the chapter mirrored the content. Perhaps not coincidentally technique and theory were discussed from the observational vantage point of the triangle, as if the therapeutic techniques and interventions exist without reference to the intersubjective field. Specifically, the discussion of the transference–countertransference matrix was glossed over for the sake of simplification and clarity. Clearly, the intersubjective and the intra-psychic are always inexorably linked, but at the polygonal level of therapeutic intervention, the transference–countertransference issues are less stormy and less urgent,

DOI: 10.4324/9781003425229-11

more easily understood and interpreted. Not so at deeper levels of work with children in more disturbed states of mind: in these situations, we have to think and play under fire and on the fly. This is challenging at the best of times, but well-nigh impossible while being trounced by our young patients in a lawless game of football or *Monopoly*.

When playing with children who time and again resort to blatant and manipulative cheating and experience the game as a desperate fight for survival rather than friendly competition (Oren, 2008), transference–countertransference issues take centre stage and acquire an immediate, intense, and impassioned, even visceral, quality. This can be a disturbing and threatening experience for the therapist also: it is almost undoubtedly one of the major contributing factors to the widespread lack of enthusiasm for playing board games amongst child psychotherapists. An open and incisive discussion of the subject of cheating and countertransference has largely been absent in the literature, as Krimendahl (2000), Meeks (1970, 2000), Herman (2000), Saar et al. (2017), and others have pointed out:

> I believe that one important reason cheating is such a little discussed aspect of child therapy and analysis is that it provokes countertransference reactions that are less than noble. At best, we may feel useless and unanalytic; less salubriously, we may feel guilty and ashamed about our competitive feelings, angry at being manipulated by a cheater, and so forth.
>
> (Krimendahl, 2000, p. 44)

It is these vicissitudes of the transference–countertransference matrix in game-playing and their transformational power that I wish to explore and develop in this chapter.

When the child patient chooses to play games like *UNO*, ping pong, chess, *Frustration,* or *Mastermind/Code Breaker,* the therapist is placed fairly and squarely in an active participatory position (Caruth, 1988). The child bats the ball towards us or throws the dice, and we are thrust instantaneously into an intense inter-psychic mode of psychotherapeutic interaction with the child. The pawn must be taken or relinquished, the card must be played, the rent paid, or the goal saved. These acts are anything but neutral; the therapist cannot remain a blank screen, but rather she has to think and act on her feet, calibrating her every move on the board according to the child's emotional needs and functioning at that moment. Klein (1932), Joseph (1998), and many others expressly state in their writings that involvement as a partner in the child's play is "undesirable" in psychoanalytic terms, and should be regarded as one of the "unfortunate" adaptations needed in analyses with latency aged children. In theory perhaps, but not so much in practice. As noted in Chapter 4, Klein's own vignettes from her child analyses reveal that she herself was wont to enter into interactive role play in her analyses with small children when she deemed it therapeutically expedient: to the point of crawling around on the playroom floor variously pretending to be the "miscreant boy", the "cruel lioness", and the "helpful fairy mamma", all according to the dictates of her young patient (Klein, 1975). Similarly, and in line with Caruth (1988) and other authors mentioned above, I would argue that with school-aged children therapist participation in the child's game is not an unfortunate constraint in the therapeutic work, but rather an essential and powerful tool through which to enter and grapple with the emotional turbulence of a child's inner world. With the wave-particle child, this therapist–child interaction tends to take place in the make-believe world of competitive structured games, using the language of dice, cards, goals, and penalties, rather than in the realm of the imaginary pretend play of lion cubs, wicked witches, sword brandishing warriors and fairy godmothers.

Going one step further, I would suggest that such interactive game-play with the child in the psychotherapy playroom can be seen as an example of the Kleinian total transference situation par excellence. The child enters the therapy room, chooses a game, and challenges us to enter with them into the fray of their inner psyche, played out between the goalposts or across the wilds of the *Monopoly* board. The child's choice of game, the way they play and moreover the way they cheat, their attitude towards the therapist, whether as benign competitive opponent or as existential threat, all these are reflections and projections of the child's deepest anxieties and phantasies. This level of psychotherapeutic interaction is indeed a far cry from the objective neutral Freudian and Kleinian interpretative stance, and it presents its own particular and even peculiar challenges to the child therapist. Caruth (1988) astutely describes these complexities in her paper (quoted in Chapter 7) on "gaming" and "playing" in psychotherapy:

> Playing games immensely complicates the therapeutic task of maintaining an optimal balance between the experiencing ego and the observing ego... The requisite activity in playing games threatens the therapist's ability to maintain the appropriate distance of becoming involved but not overinvolved in the game and in the "gaming." In "gaming," the therapist must participate in the motoric and seemingly interpersonal activity of playing the game, even as he or she must simultaneously maintain the interpretative stance and the freely suspended attention that allows for the empathic and intuitive comprehension of the patient's communications.
>
> (Caruth, 1988, p. 185)

It is my clinical experience that the heart of therapeutic work when "gaming" lies in the powerful projective identifications that board games almost universally arouse in our child patients and in the intense countertransference reactions therapists experience in response. In the fierce battle to dominate and win the game, the therapist naturally becomes the direct transference object of the child's envious greed and the "victim" of the child's tyrannical infantile urges. Paranoid-schizoid phantasies run rife and projective identifications abound. The child repeatedly and blatantly cheats and bends the rules, and the therapist's own infantile helplessness, rage, and unresolved childhood rivalries are inescapably awakened in the countertransference. In these situations, recognising and working through these powerful negative countertransference feelings is of paramount importance to the therapeutic work, as emphasised by Winnicott over 70 years ago in his prescient paper, "Hate in the counter-transference":

> If the analyst is going to have crude feelings imputed to him he is best fore-warned and so forearmed, for he must tolerate being placed in that position. Above all he must not deny hate that really exists in himself. Hate *that is justi-fied* in the present setting has to be sorted out and kept in storage and available for eventual interpretation.
>
> (Winnicott, 1977, p. 196, emphases in the original)

These kinds of powerful transference–countertransference phenomena propelled psychoanalysts from the Independent Group and Kleinian and post-Kleinian think-ing in the last century towards new theory on projection, projective identification, and the use of countertransference as a central therapeutic tool. This new theory eventually led to the gradual shift in emphasis in psychoanalysis from one-person to two-person psychology and from what Ogden calls the epistemological – "per-taining to knowing and understanding" – to the ontological – "pertaining to being and becoming" – in psychoanalysis (Ogden, 2019). I believe it is these very areas of clinical theory and technique that can contribute significantly to our understand-ing of therapeutic game-play, and expand our capacity to withstand and to harness the power of these inter-psychic and intra-psychic storms in the direction of psy-chic growth.

8.1 Countertransference, projective identification, and the game as container-contained

In his 1957 paper on countertransference, Racker was one of the first to point out the connection between what he termed complementary countertransference, the patients' projections of disavowed emotions, phantasies, and impulses, and the analyst's unconscious identification with the analysand's internal objects. As Alvarez puts it: "… a patient may project so powerfully that not only may he feel his analyst is frightened or depressed, he may make the analyst *become* fright-ened or depressed" (Alvarez, 1997, p. 758). Like Paula Heimann (1950) before him, Racker realised that countertransference constituted not only a danger and an impediment to psychoanalytic work as Freud had maintained, but also a potentially powerful tool for understanding the deeper and more obfuscated workings of the patient's psyche:

> …These countertransference situations may be repressed or emotionally blocked but probably they cannot be avoided; certainly they should not be avoided if full understanding is to be achieved.
>
> (Racker, 1957, p. 315)

Racker's words are equally applicable to psychoanalytic game-play with children today as to adult verbally-based Kleinian analysis 60 years ago. Under pressure of the urgent countertransference feelings that are all too easily aroused by the child's ruthless, even persecutory, survival tactics in the game, many therapists get inexorably drawn into the web of the child's powerful projective identifications. Under the guise of promoting ego functions, the therapist may get caught up in their own countertransference and call the child out for cheating, invoke the rules of fair play, insist on claiming their just rewards in terms of goals scored or cards won, or *Monopoly* money gained. Alternatively, the therapist may unconsciously "retaliate" in the form of ostensibly well-intentioned, but cutting, interpretations. Herman (2000) describes these very same transference–countertransference themes in his recent paper *Treating the Cheater*:

> In therapy, cheating children are often drawn to board games and other competitive activities that they engage in with murderous, vindictive intent, and cheat "like mad." ... To add insult to injury, their thoroughly demeaned opponent [the therapist] is scorned, ridiculed, taunted, and excoriated as an incompetent, stupid idiot for losing, often accompanied by gales of derisive, mocking laughter at the humiliated therapist. Their reaction clearly reveals, via projective identification, what losing means to them. In turn, the frustrated, shamed therapist, infuriated by such blatant cheating, mockery, and illegal control, may be unable to refrain from chastising and moralizing to the child, rationalizing the admonishment as a needed effort to provide social learning of appropriate game-playing attitudes.
>
> (Herman, 2000, p. 62)

Ahead of her time, Heimann pointed out in her 1950 (Heimann, 2005, [1950]) paper that the complexities of the transference–countertransference matrix are an integral and inseparable part of the dyadic psychoanalytic relationship:

> ...[My] impression is that it has not been sufficiently stressed that it [the psychoanalytic situation] is a *relationship* between two persons...The aim of the analyst's own analysis, from this point of view, is ... to enable him, to *sustain* the feelings which are stirred in him, as opposed to discharging them (as does the patient), in order to *subordinate* them to the analytic task in which he functions as the patient's mirror reflection.
>
> (Heimann, 2005, p. 56, [1950])

According to Heimann, the therapeutic task vis-à-vis countertransference in this situation is threefold: it is upon the therapist first to identify the emotions and impulses as countertransference, as "ego-alien", as an "unconscious introjection of his patient, and an unconscious identification with [the patient]", in Heimann's (1977, p. 318) words; secondly to undertake a quick on the spot "self-analysis" (1977, p. 318) and understand the origins of this complementary countertransference (Racker, 1957), what we would call today projective identification; and thirdly to find an attuned form of therapeutic response.

This third step, finding a calibrated response born out of the "decoding" of the trans-ference–countertransference interplay, is perhaps the most difficult to formulate *in vivo* in the analytic playroom in the heat of the moment, but it is also the most critical. All the more so, because the most attuned interpretative intervention is in fact often "sim-ply" to sit still and "do nothing": to accept and attempt to decipher and understand the origins of the child's provocative and manipulative behaviour, without explicitly com-municating any of these insights directly to the patient. Although this might appear to the onlooker as therapeutic "inaction", given the often tormenting and humiliat-ing nature of the adult of child's behaviour, *not* interpreting and *not* responding ver-bally in fact demand considerable thought and effort, forms of therapeutic "negative capability", in the words of Keats, Milner, Bion, and Grotstein (see Chapter 6).

Bion's (1962) ideas on the container and the contained and Alvarez's (1983, 1997) distinction between the grammar of imperatives and the grammar of wishes in children's projective identifications are indispensable to the discussion in this context. Building on Klein's concept of projective identification and Racker and Heimann's perception of countertransference as a powerful analytic tool, Bion postulated that projective identification did not always originate in destructive unconscious forces or in psychopathology, but serves also, even primarily, as a form of nonverbal communication through which the therapist/parent experiences viscerally and forcefully what is unbearable and indigestible for the patient/infant/ child (what Bion termed "β (beta)-elements"). The primary object/therapist's role in this context is not to interpret, but to act as receptacle, and to digest and give rudi-mentary form and meaning to the unbearable and the unthinkable: that is to trans-form "β (beta)-elements" into digestible "α (alpha) bytes", available for safe and non-toxic communication back to the infant/child/patient.[1] (I use the term "α bytes" here rather than Bion's term, "α elements", to indicate the rudimentary level of pro-cessing encoded into the α bytes, absent in the formless anxiety-laden β elements.)

Brady et al. (2012) capture this parent-infant container-contained relationship vividly:

> The infant conveys [their] fears [β-elements] to the parent by projecting them into the parent for [them] to receive and know. The parent receives the fears and thinks about them, struggling to contain them by giving them meaning. The parent then conveys the results of [their] struggles and thinking by projecting them back into the infant, who introjects [their] metabolised thinking. Thus, the child's ability gradually to know [him or herself] is facilitated by being taken in and known in their parent's mind.
>
> (Brady et al., 2012, p. 304, the term "mother" has been replaced by "parent" to avoid gender bias and the pronouns for both the infant and the mother have been replaced accordingly)

This is containment, Bionian "reverie": an active, sometimes painful and taxing, largely unconscious psychic function, essential in the formation and registering of emotional experiences in the infant. The development of the capacity for emotional processing and thinking, the very growth of the human psyche, is for Bion an inherently intersubjective process between primary caretaker and infant. This is the essence of the birth of human experience, as Ogden writes:

> …The circumstances of the beginning of life, for "early Bion," involve two people … living/dreaming experiences together. It must be borne in mind that the work of the [parent] in a state of receptive reverie is highly demanding, and includes being inhabited by the infant's "violence of emotion".
>
> (Ogden, 2020, p. 237)

Viewed in this context, the analytic encounter as a whole can be reformulated as the interplay between what Bion termed the container and the contained (Bion, 1962). It is this reformulation, along with Winnicott's thinking on play and the transitional space, that positioned much of contemporary psychoanalysis on both sides of the Atlantic firmly in the intersubjective realm (Ferro, 2017; Grotstein, 2018b; Ogden, 2019), even if many classical Freudians, Kleinians, and post-Kleinians frequently eschew the term. Applying this model of the container ↔ contained to game-play in the child therapy room, the game becomes the conduit for the child's projective identifications, for the contained, more often than not through the language of cheating in its many forms. When working with children in borderline and psychotic states of mind, I find this model invaluable when struggling to contain the powerful and often destructive force of the child's raw projective identifications. A single snapshot from the psychotherapy playroom is worth a thousand words of theory.

VIGNETTE M   When a goal is not a goal

I am playing football with Michael, an aggressive boy of 11, with severe behavioural problems at home and at school, the son of a tyrannical father and a chronically depressed and emotionally absent mother. He has placed my goal at one end of the room and his at the other, but my goal is four feet wide and his is only two. We start the game, I score quickly, but Michael calls out offside – we are only two players, how can I not be offside most of the time? He shoots wide, but celebrates his goal wildly. And before I have time to gather myself together, he scores twice more; I don't even realise the ball is in play again. I breathe deeply and go gently, realising Michael needs to be well ahead in the goal count. I let him amass a few more goals and then try scoring again. This time he calls out a penalty just as I am about to score. In fact, for the rest of the session, every time I gain possession of the ball, I am stopped in my tracks by some arbitrary ruling of offside, penalty, or corner by Michael, self-appointed referee. This might have been just about bearable if Michael had not added insult to injury and accompanied my efforts with a non-stop barrage of derogatory comments and gleeful scorn on his part.

We end up at 15-0, and I suggest we call it a day. I realise I just want the game to end, but he insists on continuing to 25. My heart sinks. I know I am only in for more frustration and denigration and will not be allowed to score a single goal. I should be able to keep my calm: I am the adult, Michael is only 11 years old. But years of frustration in my own childhood at the hands and feet of two football-crazy stronger athletic elder brothers feed my anger and hopelessness: the projective identification fits like a glove to my goalkeeping hand. I sense I am in danger of retaliating, either by upping my game beyond my patient's footballing capabilities, or via some (veiled but potentially damaging) interpretation of his feelings of inadequacy and his rage. This is the same child who has kept me in jail mercilessly in *Monopoly,* whilst he collects fees on all his properties round after round and pays me nothing. (According to Michael's rules, I had to get three doubles in a row to get out of jail, and if *he* landed on one of *my* properties while I was in jail I had to pay *him* – he of course was sure never to be sent to jail.)

What to do, what to say, how to act in such a situation? Perhaps the first rule of thumb, as noted above, should be *not* to act and *not* to utter a word until the sentences and game-actions formulated in our mind feel contained, seem attuned to the child and their state of mind. A therapeutic form of the age-old injunction "if you don't have anything constructive to say, it's better to say nothing!" Alvarez (1997, 2012), quoting Betty Joseph's life-long work, stresses that the *"borderline patient in their psychotic state"* may need us to contain the projective identification and explore it only in our own psyche, often for a long time. It is in many cases therapeutically most prudent not to *"shove [the projection] back too prematurely at the patient"* (1997, 2012). As Ferro (2006) writes: "such interventions…may provoke intolerance in the patient's acceptance of the analyst's contribution" (p. 1000).

At such times, patients, and indeed infants and young children in general outside the therapy room, desperately *need* us to maintain the splitting and their phantasies of omnipotence, so as not to be crushed by their own deep despair, feelings of insignificance, or be torn apart by their inner rage or dreaded anxieties. Unlike the child functioning in the polygonal space, where symbolic function is fairly intact, and external and internal reality can be observed and relatively easily accepted, children in such borderline and psychotic states of mind are overwhelmed by what Alvarez (1989, 1997) calls the "imperatives" of their concrete "single-tracked" state of mind. Referring to children with autistic and psychotic disturbances, but equally relevant to the discussion here, Alvarez writes poignantly of the luxury of dual (or multiple) track thinking, compared to the vital necessity of the single-track descriptive level of interpretative intervention in cases of psychic deficit:

Bion's concept of alpha function (1962a) … suggests that the thought may have to be thinkable long before the therapist can or should concern himself with luxurious questions about who is having it. … [A] *psychoanalysis of description rather than of explanation* may be necessary for patients who cannot think, and certainly cannot think two thoughts at a time. One thought at a time may be enough for them.

(Alvarez, 1998, p. 217, emphases added)

Alvarez holds that it is imperative we respect these children's needs for splitting, that we first hold and detoxify within our own psychic space the child's massive, often poisoned, projections, the product of what Britton calls malignant containment. Only then should we form our interpretative (in the broadest sense of the word) interventions. Furthermore, as Steiner (2003) has pointed out, interpretations/interventions are frequently only tolerable to the patient when couched in terms of our own feelings and experience that he termed "analyst-centred", or even in the language of generalisations ("it is so hard/enraging/scary/annoying/upsetting when…") that cannot be misunderstood by the patient as accusations or devastating criticism. Interestingly, Alvarez (1989) suggests that the projections the child needs us to hold for them are not always negative. The child may be equally unable to assimilate good feelings, feelings of worth, and potency, for fear of their own self-destructive rage or external annihilation.

Viewed in this light, it becomes clear that in the vignette described above, Michael needed me to understand that the humiliation and helplessness I felt were in fact split-off feelings of his. It was I, the adult, whom he experienced as threatening and potentially denigrating, and he, the vulnerable child. He needed me to surrender (though not masochistically submit (Ghent, 1990)) to his need to park these intolerable feelings in me until they could be metabolised, goal by goal, penalty by penalty. He, like other children who compulsively play this way (in my experience, they form the majority of children who come to psychotherapy), uses the game to communicate what is for them unbearable, indigestible, existentially threatening, and traumatic. They need the therapist to contain, digest, metabolise, and then transform these intense visceral beta elements of anxiety, rage, inadequacy, and despair into bite-sized words and actions-in-game that can be tolerated and slowly internalised.

Changing the odds and becoming a subject: At first, I surrendered myself in the sessions with Michael to being "slaughtered" in the game, goal after goal, week after week, and then I began, slowly and in measured doses, to talk in general terms of how humiliating, even enraging, it is to lose. Subsequently, I ventured to talk of my own feelings of inadequacy and frustration when I lost so badly. Eventually, I insisted on more fairly placed goalposts and less draconian rules and penalties. Only towards the end of therapy, and even then, very rarely, did we talk directly about Michael's life outside of therapy. Nevertheless, the transformations in game occurred and both the quality of our sessions and Michael's experience of himself and his interactions with his peers and teachers at school turned benign, alive, even "joyful", to use "Alvareze" terminology (Alvarez, 2012). Or in the words of Winnicott or Benjamin, Michael and I had survived his tyranny, his need for omnipotent control over my every move, and the imperative to deny me all subjectivity and agency. He had discovered his own subjectivity and agency and recognised me as a separate and different, benign, subject in his newly discovered intersubjective world.

8.2   From object relating to object usage in game-play

At this point, following directly on from this description of Michael's move from tyrannical omnipotent control of our games to competitive playfulness, I wish to weave into the discussion Winnicott's distinction between "object relating" and "object usage" and issues of intersubjectivity (Atwood & Stolorow, 2014; Benjamin, 1988, 1995, 2007; Stolorow & Atwood, 1984). In his revolutionary paper, "The use of the object" (Winnicott, 1971), Winnicott described and formulated the basic tension in development between two modes of relating, between "object relating", where the object is conceived subjectively (the subjective object) and as subject to phantasies of omnipotent control and projective identifications (Winnicott himself largely avoided this inherently Kleinian term) and "using the object", where the object is conceived objectively in reality as outside the self (the objective object). Fundamental to these approaches is the understanding that although psychic development is towards object usage, this tension between the object relating (intra-psychic) and object usage (intersubjective) modalities continues throughout life (Benjamin, 1995). Viewed from this perspective, fiercely competitive, relatively chance-based games such as *Monopoly*, *Cheat*, or even football or basketball, can be seen to facilitate the emergence of an intense, intra-psychic object-relating mode of child-therapist interaction. The child's urge to win, to be the "King of the Castle" (Winnicott, 1971), to cheat and openly or surreptitiously change the rules, quickly takes over from the restrained, law-abiding "false-self"/ reality-oriented, mode of interaction. Aggressive and libidinal content and phantasies from the child's true-self dominate, and the therapist quickly becomes the "subjective-object" object of greed, envy, and destruction.

The stage between object relating and object usage according to Winnicott is "the most difficult thing, perhaps, in human development; or, the most irksome of all the early failures that come for mending [in psychotherapy]" (Winnicott, 1971, p. 105). The developmental task for the infant/child/patient is to repeatedly destroy the object (in phantasy) and thereby repeatedly experience the object's survival (in reality), leading to the perception of the object as a separate entity outside of the subject's omnipotent control, an inherent part of reality testing and of "mature" intersubjective (Benjamin, 1990) interpersonal relations. Many analyses and psychotherapies reside in this "irksome" area for long, very long, periods of time: it is upon the therapist to contain the urge to retaliate over and over again, and to survive the destructive phantasies of our patients (Winnicott, 1971):

In psychoanalytic practice the positive changes that come about in this area can be profound. They do not depend on interpretative work. They depend on the analyst's survival of the attacks, which involves and includes the idea of the absence of a quality change to retaliation. These attacks may be very difficult for the analyst to stand, especially when they are expressed in terms of delusion, or through manipulation which makes the analyst actually do things that are technically bad.

(Winnicott, 1971, p. 108)

These remarks of Winnicott aptly and accurately describe the vicissitudes of my work with Michael described in the previous vignette and echo the discussion so far, which has focussed on containing the "violent" and forceful omnipotent projective identifications of the patient for as long as it takes. Relevant here is Caruth's (1988) paper "How you play the game" cited previously, in which she differentiates between two modes of playing games in psychotherapy:

"playing", [characterised by] symbolic play with thoughts and fantasies, occurring during moments of free association and fantasy play with toys…[when] the transference [towards the therapist as objective object, CM] appears relatively positive and sublimated; and "gaming" [characterised by periods of] highly intensified responses to the therapist [as subjective object, CM] with whom and around whom fantasies and conflicts…are reexperienced, [these] frequently expressed through action including structured games with children, acting in, and acting out.

(Caruth, 1988, p. 179, excerpt from the abstract)

Developing this line of thinking, I would suggest that a very useful parallel can clearly be drawn between the "playing mode" and object usage and the intersubjective modality, and between the "gaming mode" (Caruth's term) and object relating and the intra-psychic modality. As such, playing structured games in child psychotherapy (gaming) can, I believe, serve as a powerful and immediate tool for psychotherapeutic work on the intra-psychic subjective-object level of object relating. The more fragile the child's psyche, the more quickly the "gaming" object-relating mode tends to emerge, the more massive the child's projections, and the more persecutory their play. Many children cling with all their might to intra-psychic fantasy control of the games they play, of the rules, of the therapist, session after session. As described in Chapter 7, for months on end, they may not let us throw the dice or accrue any money in *Monopoly*, nor score a single goal in football, and agree to part only with their lowest value cards in a game of *War*. These are children in states of mind where they dare not let a sliver of omnipotent control out of their grasp, children who in reality have had so little agency and control over their lives and have suffered repeated and painful impingements on their existence and interruptions to their "going on being" (Winnicott, 1965). Under these intra-psychic forces, play becomes a projection in the here and now of the maelstrom of the child's subjective persecutory inner world, distorted by trauma, helplessness, abandonment, and impingement. Winning is symbolically equated to survival (Oren, 2008), and the merest whiff of danger of losing the game can create mayhem in the child's psyche.

For the child, maintaining the therapist as a subjective-object serves to leave nothing to chance: winning and survival are thereby assured. Reality is far too unreliable and fraught with danger to relinquish control; the child cannot yet use us as an object in the real world. Tragically, it is when the child feels at their most psychically vulnerable to annihilation through the game that their attacks on the therapist are at their most vicious and scorching, and for the therapist, containing the urge to retaliate is often a constant struggle. Likewise, at this stage of the game, the child is also usually at their most resolute in their refusal of help and advice on how to gain strength and insight, even in the language of the game. Ironically, it is when the child treats the therapist as an omnipotently manipulated subjective-object in their existential intra-psychic battle for survival that it may well be hardest for the therapist to surrender in generosity to the child. This, precisely because there is so little intersubjectivity (in the sense that Benjamin uses the term – little or no recognition in the child of the therapist as a separate experiencing feeling subject) in the game.

It is my thesis that herein also lies the transmutative power of gaming: the threatened destruction seems all but real and tangible to both child and therapist: the survival of the therapist is therefore equally tangible in reality and fundamentally formative for the child's psyche. Children who are chronically trapped in the subjective-object mode of relating, need us to collaborate with their fantasy subjective intra-psychic world without challenge, maybe for many months, without us losing sight of hope towards movement, intersubjectivity, and psychic growth. In such periods, the therapist is called upon to recognise and keep in mind the subjectivity of the patient, in Benjamin's words, holding the third in the one (cf. Section 7.3.1). Michael needed me to survive as his subjective object, to survive his repeated attempts to destroy me as the object, to survive his onslaughts against me, his derogatory comments, the humiliating unjust defeats I experienced at his hands, again and again, until he could dare to let me play as a real goal-scoring subject in the game. It takes countless repeated such destructive attacks for the child to dare to loosen their omnipotent control over the game and over the therapist, and to begin to test the waters of playing inter-subjectively within the bounds of reality.

8.2.1   Surviving the game

From this perspective, the therapist's flexible and calibrated approach to the rules and regulations of the game can be envisaged as varying along the intra-psychic-intersubjective continuum, as moving from object relating to object usage (as concretely exemplified in the gradual adjustment of the goalposts in my games with Michael). As we survive the child's destructive attacks and despotic rule of the game, so their projections become less massive, the need for omnipotent control driven by the child's inner world and persecutory anxieties lessens, and the child moves towards the intersubjective realm in the land of real objects. The more real an object we become in the game, the more bearable and benevolent our countertransference. Voicing to the child our own fears of annihilation in the game, *our* helplessness, worthlessness, and hopelessness when we cannot even score a single goal, and *our* anger and frustration at *our* bad luck (even if the bad luck is in reality of the child's making and not really chance at all) enables the child to work through their own split-off projected feelings of helplessness and worthlessness, and facilitates the move away from the intra-psychic object-relating pole. *It is essential for the child's psychic growth to keep the pace of change slow and attuned*, from a position of surrender to the child's omnipotent tyrannical idiosyncratic rules of the game to playing according to mutually agreed upon "common sense" (Bion, 1967) rules of reality, however challenging and wearing this waiting game might be.

There eventually comes a time when the thrill and the glow of the predictable predetermined win begin to dull for the child, and they and we become bored in the sessions: these wins are after all a foregone conclusion, a form of action (or inaction) replay, week after week. This is the moment we can begin to show our faces as real objective objects, as separate subjects, and suggest or even demand that we throw our own dice, that our goals in football be recognised or that we can win a round or two in a game of cards. The game comes alive with the healthy destructive and constructive urges of creativity and the buzz and joy of joint intersubjective play. The transitional space grows in tandem. But this, as we have seen, can happen only after we and the game have been engulfed in flames of fury and survived, time after time. It is then that the child begins, perhaps for the first time in their life, to experience the joy and excitement of learning how to play, of discovering the thrills and spills of luck and chance, and even beat a real object, fairly and squarely. It is my clinical experience that the aliveness the therapist feels in the game is an indicator of where the therapist-child dyad is on the spectrum between the subjective object and the objective object, between the intra-psychic and the intersubjective.

All of this brings me to the somewhat surprising proposition, given the bad press structured games have always had as reality-based, rigid, and stultifying, that it is the very transitional space these games offer of playful destruction and creative construction that confer their therapeutic power. And it is this "window of magical anonymity" (Fonagy & Target, 1998), *in combination with the safe clear rule-bounded structure, that enables this calibrated move from object relating towards object usage and intersubjectivity.*

8.3 Dreaming, thinking, and playing

We have now arrived at the point where game-play in child psychotherapy can be seen to be not merely as a therapeutic tool, but as the therapy itself (Bellinson, 2000, 2002; Meeks, 1970, 2000; Oren, 2008): as the transitional space of overlap between the therapist's area of playing and the child's; as the arena of the total transference situation; as the conduit and the container for the child's projective identifications; and as the catalyst for work on the intra-psychic level of Winnicottian object relating and development towards object usage. I would now like to take the next step into the 21st century of contemporary psychoanalytic theory, and suggest that game-play in a child psychotherapy session can be treated as a Bionian dream, to be dreamed by the analytic therapist with the child, just as Ferro and others see children's pretend dramatic play and drawing in child psychoanalysis (Brady et al., 2012; Ferro, 2003; Molinari, 2017a, 2018).

Grotstein (2018a,b), Ogden (2004a, 2019), and Civitarese (2019), amongst others, have all emphasised the continuity between Kleinian and post-Kleinian thinking and Bion's theories on thinking and dreaming:

> … [Bion's] new theory of dreaming, unconscious, and affects, directly stems from Klein's formulation *dreaming = play = activity-of-symbolization*, from her view of the mind as the never closing theatre where meaning is constantly shaped by the interplay of unconscious phantasies, from her emphasis on the key role of the emergent anxieties in the here and now of the session; from the original and very fertile concept of projective identification…
>
> (Civitarese, 2019, p. 390, emphases added)

> The analytic session in its totality obligatorily constitutes: *transference ↔ countertransference ↔ reverie* … More than that, however, the concept of the analytic session as the "total situation" implies yet another important derivative hypothesis: an idea derived both from Freud and from Bion, as well [as] from Klein and Joseph: *that every analytic session constitutes a dream and should be analytically treated as an ongoing dream.*
>
> (Grotstein, 2018b, p. 56, emphases added)

These two formulations are critical: "dreaming=play=activity of symbolisation", and what I would write as "(transference ↔ countertransference ↔ reverie) + *total situation* = dreaming and play". The term dreaming is deceptive: ordinarily, outside of psychoanalysis, we think of dreaming as a calm, almost passive, state of mind, occurring mostly in our sleep. Bionian dream work takes place both in the waking hours (in the unconscious and in the preconscious, in the back rooms of the psyche as it were) and when asleep, and involves the transformation and processing of events or rather sense impressions (β-elements) which the psyche has as yet been unable to digest or digest fully.

Ogden (2020) likens β-elements to Poe's description of *"unthought-like thoughts that are the souls of thoughts"* (Poe, 1927, p. 8):

> These sense impressions are "unthought-like" in that they cannot be linked in the process of thinking—they are yet to be organized raw sensory data. At the same time, they are "the souls of thoughts" in that they are the only direct connection with our lived experience, and as such, they are the living core (the "soul") of every thought and feeling that results from the processing of this raw data. The infant's sense-impressions are all [she/] he has of the experience of being alive, and this continues to be the case throughout life.
>
> (Ogden, 2020, p. 237)

It is these β-elements, the "souls of thoughts" that are both the "stuff of life", and also the "stuff of trauma": if overwhelming and uncontained, or malignantly contained, they remain as raw elements, "unthought-like thoughts", the source of nameless dread and unthinkable terror. When contained and processed via reverie, via the mind's α-function, a process Ferro (1992) calls *alphabetisation*, the products become the basis for transformative dreaming and thinking. The concepts of α-function, reverie, and dreaming overlap somewhat: α-function, which can be thought of as a rudimentary form of unconscious thinking/dreaming, is necessary to transform raw primal fears, unthought-like thoughts, sense impressions – all β-elements – into pictographs, α-bytes, suitable for dreaming/phantasising and producing dream thoughts and *"emotions as thinkable thoughts"* (Grotstein, 2008), which in turn are the basis for conscious symbolic thinking and thoughts (Grotstein, 2008). When we observe our own dreams or thoughts, this is already at the level of conscious, even symbolic, whole dream or thought sequences.

Many patients, children and adults alike, arrive at therapy having had very limited or largely malignant experiences of parental reverie and containment. They barely know that raw emotional impressions can be mitigated and transformed into thoughts and emotions by a containing other, and their own internal containing α-function is often damaged and inadequate. Seen in this light, the aim of analytic psychotherapy is not to enable the patient to understand and think about their present and past emotional experiences, but rather to enable patients to develop a greater capacity to "think and dream themselves into being" and so experience themselves as "alive and real" (to use the language of Ogden and Grotstein). This occurs via the process of the patient and the therapist being immersed in the experience together, "living the experience together", the therapist leading the way in alphabetisation: translating and transforming the raw sensory impressions and primal anxieties of the experience into digestible, dream-bytes, which can be dreamed and become thinkable thoughts and emotions, first for the analytic therapist and then for the patient, just as the parent leads the way for the infant and young child.

This process of "dreaming the dream together" (Grotstein, 2018a,b; Ogden, 2004b) is the *sine qua non* of child psychotherapy. Unlike adults, children, especially traumatised and deprived children, usually do not even attempt a veneer of "rational" thinking and communication. For Klein (1932), play was the externalisation of the child's dream: as quoted previously, *"the small child is still under the immediate and powerful influence of its instinctual experiences and phantasies and puts them in front of us straight away"* (Klein, 1932, 94). Quoting again from Brady et al.'s paper, written from a post-Bionian perspective, *"Psychoanalytic treatment of children immerses us in a dreamscene brought to life in play, art, imaginary roles, action and words"* (Brady et al., 2012, p. 303). I would add that *this is true for older children playing structured games no less than for the pre-schooler playing with dolls*. Albeit usually under the cover of their favourite ball game or board game, the dream scene is brought viscerally to life in the fierce fight for survival they wage against us on the makeshift football pitch in our clinic or across the battleground of the chessboard. *The role of the child analytic therapist is to "play the dream" together with the child:*

> The play in play therapy allows the child a dream-like expression of her inner world, and allows the analyst a participation in the meanings of the child's inner world that become shared meanings. In play therapy, we become interpreters of dreams in the form of play. Unmetabolised raw emotions, such as Elizabeth's [a seven year old girl in weekly analytic therapy] competitiveness and angry desire to throw the playing pieces in her analyst's face, are dreams in the hour. *The analyst interprets dreams in the form of comments on and participation in the play.*
>
> (Brady et al., 2012, p. 308, emphases added)

Dreaming and living the terror of chess together with Jane (Vignette J – Chapter 7)

These aspects of containing, detoxifying, and dreaming in the game can clearly be seen also in the clinical illustration from Jane's therapy in Chapter 7, Vignette J above. With Jane, I described the tyrannical domination and name-less dread that infused our games of *Monopoly* and *Cops and Robbers*. Her only way of communicating her unconscious anguish and rage was through her almost vindictive control over the game and over me. Before and during our sessions, I frequently felt an overwhelming sense of despair combined with unspeakable undefined anxiety. Jane's internal container was so limited and even distorted that to interpret these feelings directly I believe would have been intolerable for her and would have been experienced as persecutory attacks. Week after week, I grappled with my dread of the sessions, which was in essence Jane's inner but disowned and split-off inner torment. I regis-tered these intense feelings as projective identifications, defused them as far as I was able, and interpreted to myself possible links between these emotions and Jane's personal history. The interpretative interventions and transforma-tions in the therapy took place in a multiplicity of ways: through my lack of retaliation; through negotiating Jane's debts and mine in *Monopoly*; through my insistence that Jane eventually release me from the cruelly cordoned off roads in the board game *Cops and Robbers*; through a gradual equalising of the value of our hotels and houses in *Monopoly* such that I could breathe and move. And occasionally I verbalised comments about the helplessness of my trapped police car in *Cops and Robbers* or my existential anxiety in the face of an ever-mounting debt and shaky foundations in *Monopoly*.

Not responding, *not* insisting Jane play by the rules, *not* acting on my feel-ings of injustice, humiliation, deep anxiety, and outrage proved challenging, far more challenging than formulating a verbal reflection or interpretation of the situation in the session.

Only in retrospect did I understand that for the first year or more of therapy, I had avoided playing chess with Jane because for her chess was not merely a metaphor, but "the thing itself". On some level, she saw the game as about omnipotently defending and protecting her mother-queen in reality. Intuitively, playing the game felt too dangerous in the context of the therapy. We had had to bide our time until the overwhelming "violence of emotion" (Bion, 1962; Civitarese, 2012; Ogden, 2004a) that had flooded our sessions had been partially mitigated through the endless rounds of projective identification, alphabetisation, and transformation in our tortured games of *Monopoly* and *Cops and Robbers*.

When we did eventually venture into the emotional minefield that was the chessboard, Jane's interrupted (Ogden, 2004b) nightmare was reawakened and could at last be dreamed together, terrible for both of us as that was. In my capture of her queen and simultaneous move to checkmate, I unconsciously re-enacted Jane's mother's fateful violent car accident. Jane's helplessness, hopelessness and visceral shock became mine too, an experience lived together. I wish to stress this was not a magical therapeutic moment that led to a happily ever after ending. The shock of the capture of the queen was literally terrible, instilled us both with terror and horror, and it took weeks of gentle tactful working through, also with Jane's father, to carry through the process of transformation from the nameless dread to a dread that could take name, shape and form. With Jane herself the work was almost always only on the implicit level: most of the times, explanation and interpretation at the explicit level felt neither helpful nor necessary (as is often the case with traumatised children in borderline states of mind (Alvarez, 1989, 2010, 2012)).

8.4   The playing field

8.4.1   Transformations in game

As numerous psychoanalytic writers and theorists point out, there are many parallels to be drawn between Bion's ontological view of psychoanalysis and Winnicott's.

As we have seen, Bion linked psychoanalysis with dreaming and thinking, whilst Winnicott conceived of psychoanalysis as a "highly specialised form of playing" (cf. Chapters 1, 4, and 6). For both, the goal of psychoanalysis is to expand and deepen "communication with oneself and others" (Winnicott, 1971, p. 48). Winnicott's playing and Bion's dreaming can be seen to be closely related, overlapping human (and mammalian) states of being. Both are crucial to psychic health and growth, both have their origin in the parent–infant relationship. As Ferro and Molinari put it, in Winnicott's view, "[t]he analytic couple are at work not to reveal something buried in the depths of the unconscious, but to create something together that had never previously existed" (Ferro & Molinari, 2018, wording differs slightly; Molinari, 2017b, p. 181).

Winnicottian playing and Bionian dreaming and thinking are often seen as interchangeable. If one looks at dreaming through the prism of its function to process events in the real world, both could be said to take place in the space between reality and the inner world or as a binocular product of both the conscious and the unconscious, the processed and the unprocessed (Ferro & Nicoli, 2017; Grotstein, 2018b; Molinari, 2017a; Ogden, 2004a, 2019; Schneider, 2010). However, it seems to me, in line with Ferro and Molinari, that Bion's dreaming should be seen rather as a psychic precursor to Winnicottian playing, rather than as its equivalent. Further to their description of the Winnicottian analyst quoted above, Ferro and Molinari define the role of the Bionian analyst in a similar fashion, but the focus is on the co-processing of raw sense impressions rather than on co-creation:

> The analyst is not the holder of knowledge that will help discover conscious or unconscious repressed memories, but is called upon to perform the function of co-builder of a capacity to process feelings and raw emotions by dreaming them.
> (Ferro & Molinari, 2018; Molinari, 2017b, pp. 182–183)

These authors hold that play, mixes unconscious and conscious processes and serves as an attempt to narrate and metabolise the *products* of unconscious dream work. The difference between dreaming and playing is very subtle, but I think it is important to differentiate between the two when deciphering the processes underlying game-play in this context. Molinari (2018) writes:

> However, *play* is something more than dreaming because *it includes real experience*. So it can be said that, if dreaming is knowing oneself as directly triggered by relations with the other, playing is knowing oneself together with the other.
> (Molinari, 2018, p. 91, emphases added)

For Ferro, when children play, they in effect "narrate" and try to metabolise and solve what is going on inside them, using whatever "characters" are available at the time, including the toy animals and cars, blocks, paper, and pencils present in the psychoanalytic playroom. This process becomes creative and therapeutically transformative through the mental presence of another person, parent or therapist, who is receptive to and capable of containing and digesting anxieties that may arise in the child's play in psychotherapy and then reflecting and interpreting these back to the child through the game – interpretative interventions and "transformations in game" (Ferro, 2003; Ferro & Molinari, 2018).

The play of a child, or indeed the narrations of an adult, are what Ferro and Civitarese (2018) call the narrative derivatives of the reverie and the α function. The raw β-elements, the excess sense impressions and feelings that have not been metabolised, and cannot as yet be metabolised by the child, are expelled into the intersubjective space between the child and the therapist. These proto-emotions and "unthought-like thoughts", the stuff of life, have first to be contained and digested and processed into α-bytes and thence to pictographs (alphabetisation), before they can eventually be communicated back to the child through the game-play. It is only through dreaming that the pictographs, Bion's α-elements, become dream sequences and thinkable thoughts, which the therapist introduces more or less consciously into the intersubjective patient–child space, as narrative derivatives in play and game, be it in the form of words, actions, facial expressions, drawings, narrative play, or moves in a competitive game.

As discussed above, for children playing in the therapeutic setting, especially for those functioning on borderline and psychotic levels, not using words, communicating through narrative derivatives and interpretative interventions in game, is often critical to the process, and sometimes the sole mode of therapeutic intervention. This nonverbal approach, leading to "transformations in dream" or "transformations in game" (Ferro & Nicoli, 2017, p. 133), is closely allied with and indeed influenced by Ogden's concept of the interpretation-in-action or interpretative action:

> By "interpretive action" (or "interpretation-in-action") I mean the analyst's communication of his or her understanding of an aspect of the transference-countertransference to the analysand by means of *activity other than that of verbal symbolization*. At times such activity is disconnected from words (e.g., the facial expression of the analyst as a patient lingers at the consulting room door); at times the analyst's activity (as medium for interpretation) takes the form of "verbal action," (e.g., the setting of the fee, the announcement of the ending of the hour, or the insistence that the analysand put a stop to a given form of acting in or acting out); at times interpretive action involves the voice, but not words (e.g., the analyst's laughter).
>
> (Ogden, 1994, p. 219, emphases added)

8.4.2 The board game as post-Bionian playing field

Ferro, Civitarese, Molinari (Civitarese & Ferro, 2018; Molinari, 2017a), and other psychoanalytic thinkers (mostly based in Italy) have combined these ideas with bi-personal field theory developed by Baranger and Baranger (2012, 2008) in South America, to formulate what they have called a *Bionian Bi-personal Field Theory (BFT)*. The Barangers' analytic field theory defines the analytic situation afresh as a complex bi-personal field. It is based on a conglomerate of ideas: from Bionian group theory, Kleinian and Bionian ideas on projective identification; and electromagnetic field theory and sociological field theory. The BFT can be visualised as a complex field of interactional "force lines" stretching out between the therapist and the child or adult patient and indeed between other family members (Molinari, 2017b) or characters in the patient's life, as if in an electromagnetic field with two and sometimes more poles with different and constantly varying strengths and positions.

The BFT combines the complexities of Bion's concepts of reverie, β-elements, and α-function, dreaming and thinking, and Winnicottian ideas on playing into the analytic bi-personal field. As a true Italian, Ferro likens the role of the analyst in the BFT to the art of cookery:

> The field permits us to describe, gather and group these emotions, clarifying and putting them into focus, using the characters as 'pot holders' which allow us to get close to the burning hot content…These emotions can be 'cooked' through their narrative transformation, with unsaturated interventions and always 'sampling' the patient's answer, to know which ingredients we need to add to enrich or lighten the dish … of course, it is a story of jealousy, abandonment, anger, fury, tenderness and rejection. Some of these narrative-emotional elements are already 'cooked', already utterable, … employing peripheral interventions which further cook, sort and create links with what the patient expresses. But sometimes there is a small amount of food which remains frozen and which needs to become thinkable [β-elements, proto emotions, that need to be alphabetised by the therapist and then presented to the patient at some point as narremes or pictographs in the game or dialogue].
>
> (Ferro, 2006, p. 999)

I have described this bi-personal field approach in depth here because it seems to be a conceptual framework that fits therapeutic play with structured games like a glove, both as a rationale for interpretations-in-game, as I have described throughout these last chapters, and on the explicatory level. The therapeutic process is like a spiral of recurring, but ever-changing and evolving metabolisations of β-elements, producing α-bytes and dream thoughts, which in time, through dreaming and thinking, present themselves as narrative derivatives played out via the multiplicity of characters in the bi-personal field. It is important to stress that although co-constructed, the role of the therapist in the field is nevertheless crucially different from that of the patient. As Ferro notes, most of the flow of the β-elements is, or should hopefully be from patient to therapist, and the narrative derivatives produced by the therapist are at a more conscious level, directed towards emotional experiencing and self-discovery in the patient, and to expanding the patient's container and the capacity to dream, play and think. At various points along the way, when the therapist senses the patient can tolerate it, the therapist/analyst's interventions will be more deliberately interpretative and transformative, rather than "merely" reflective and holding.

Viewed in this way, the therapeutic power of play in child psychotherapy can be seen not only in its role as the child's natural form of communication and expression, but also, and even more significantly, in its location not just in the transitional space, but in this wider "bi-personal field". Ferro (2003) and Molinari (2017a) propose that the child not only uses play to represent and metabolise their inner phantasies and anxieties, or to communicate inter-subjectively with the parent/analyst, but also uses play to narrate the *entire web* of projective identifications active at that moment in their intra-psychic and intersubjective environment.

This is the area of interaction and mutual creative construction, transforma-tion, and psychological growth between parent and child, analytical therapist and patient.

To my mind, the notion of multiple characters in the therapy room all participat-ing in the narration of the child's inner world beautifully captures the complexity of the manifold levels and strands of play and interaction in the child therapy room. This is true whether the child chooses to play *Cheat* or chess, tosses a football in the air, paints our portrait, or organises a doll's tea party. The kings, queens, aces, and twos in a game of *War,* and the pawns and knights on a chessboard, are as full of character as any toy soldier or angry lioness, as Lewis Carroll has amply dem-onstrated in his fantasy books *Alice's Adventures in Wonderland* and *Alice Through the Looking Glass* (Carroll, 1999). And likewise, the murderer, thief, and sorceress in a game of *Talisman* are experienced by the child playing in the analytic play-room as key characters in their inner world, as illustrated in the following vignette.

VIGNETTE N   "You'll be the fortune teller and I'll be the thief"

Noam, a slight ten-year-old boy, as fiercely competitive as he was intelligent, was referred to psychotherapy for behavioural problems, low self-esteem, and occasional suicidal thoughts. He played games body and soul as if his life depended on winning. Fun did not seem to be relevant to the playing experi-ence for him, neither inside nor outside the therapy room. He had learnt to play *Talisman*[2] at home, but was often cruelly bullied and taunted by his siblings during such games. Noam therefore jumped at the chance to wreak his revenge on me when he spied the box on my shelves.

Talisman is a complex lengthy board game (based on the role play game "Dungeons and Dragons"), which I keep on the shelves in my clinic precisely for boys like Noam – boys who are highly intelligent and slightly geeky, who need both intellectual challenge in the therapy in the form of board games they identify as oriented towards boys, but which serve as an alternative to football and basketball from which many such boys shy way. The game of *Talisman* is laden with monsters, wizards and sorceresses, ghouls and dwarves, and the constructive and destructive powers of magic and of the sword. With some children, the Tolkien-like backdrop becomes an integral part of the creative force in the therapy and can serve as a container and metaphor for all kinds of fantasies and fears. For Noam, this allegorical aspect was at first lost in the heat of the existential battle for domination and survival. Each player has to choose at random a card that determines the identity of their character in the game. For Noam, this did not feel like an "as if" experience: his entire being would become the ogre, the wizard, or even the sorceress, for the dura-tion of the game over many sessions. Especially when he played the thief or the murderer, the transitional space seemed to shrink, and it could feel palpably, existentially threatening to play with him. Actually, these feelings could become so concrete and real – no longer mere symbols but symbolic formulations (Segal, 1957, 1978) – that I felt the presence of these particular cards was counterproductive for Noam. Recalling Alvarez' warning about safety gear and explosive materials, I decided to remove these particular cards of thief and murderer from the pack for a time, stating my reasons as I did so, explaining that the cards felt too overwhelming and powerfully destructive. (Nevertheless, this behaviour was not a sign of pervasive psychotic thinking in Noam; outside of the game, he shed his assumed character and remained Noam).

In these games of *Talisman*, Noam did not leave anything to chance. In each game he chose which character we would each play, making sure he was the strongest character and I the weakest. We would then embark on our epic task to survive the dangers of the outer reaches of the board, and battle dragons, ghosts, and goblins, all in order to accrue physical strength and magic powers. I often felt caught up in Noam's fight for survival, struggling myself to remember this was only a game, cruelly caught in traps he set for me with ruthless glee. Sometimes I would resist when I felt he was strong enough to withstand the battle (both in his psyche and in the game in the powers he had amassed). Sometimes I had to submit passively (Ghent, 1990), sometimes I would surrender to his omnipotent control of the game. Noam was used to the harsh cutthroat games, which he played at home. In our game I tried to introduce compassion and elasticity. When Noam was about to "lose a life" and could not bear it, I suggested he roll the dice again or, conversely, when he did not dare to advance to the next stage, I pointed out he had the strength to do so (interpretation-in-action/in game). When I could not bear it, and felt taunted and trapped, I held in mind the bullying he had experienced in the game at the hands at home and did nothing and said nothing, until I could find the right phraseology to convey how weak and helpless I felt, to convey the desperation and rage I felt at being trapped, the temptation to retaliate and the dangers involved. (This was an intervention that was neither patient-centred nor therapist-centred, but a general statement of human feeling and experience, what Alvarez (2012) calls a descriptive level of interpretation, of ascribing and amplifying meaning.) These were proto-emotions that Noam could only expel and evacuate, and it was up to me to identify, metabolise and return them processed and given meaning through the game. But I also made sure gradually to challenge Noam's omnipotent control and to offer real opposition and contest in the game, slowly and surely, at his pace, as his anxieties lessened and his knowledge of his own capacities grew. And Noam, in turn, gradually began to try out the different characters in the game, investigating how it felt to have more magical powers as a sorceress or a wizard, but less strength in the sword, how it felt to take risks and let chance take its course.

8.4.3   Narrations of the psyche and transmutations in the game-play

When we allow the child to dominate the game omnipotently, cheat, and wipe the floor with us in an "innocent" game of *War, UNO, TAKI, Monopoly,* or football, we are facilitating the child's hidden "violent" traits to come to light:

> [In the] two worlds that blend in a relational field, giving life to many scenarios that differ each time..., [t]he patient's inhibited parts, the violent traits hidden inside him, are encouraged to come to light and to meet with the characters that the intuitive and narrative skills of the analyst can create.
>
> (Ferro & Nicoli, 2017, p. xiii)

Collovà, a colleague of Ferro's from Pavia, Italy, describes the required state of mind of the analytical therapist in the bi-personal field thus:

> ...[The] analyst, unlike the analysand, regresses only partially; this allows him [/her] to avoid being overwhelmed by the paralysing dynamics of the field, keeping a free ego that allows him/[her] to adjust the input voltage. In practice, the analyst retains a vision that is both internal...and external.
>
> (Collovà, 2017, p. 14)

Note that this vision, which is both internal and external, is reminiscent of Benjamin's concept of the "third in the one*"*, the primary object holding the newborn infant's needs, anxieties, and its whole being, in their mind. As illustrated in the game of *Talisman* with Noam, this attuned adjustment or calibration of the "input voltage" is vital for work with children in more disturbed states of mind, children like Noam, whose container is so limited and woefully inadequate that β elements are continually and violently evacuated and expelled. We use our therapeutic intuition to guide us as to when we should let the child be the all-powerful oligarch who owns all the pricy hotels on the board, as we play the part of the penniless pauper, and when we should assert our potency, act like a wily business entrepreneur, buy our own properties, and build our own hotels. Square by square, space by space, move by move, transformations in the game take place, both literally and metaphorically.

Ferro and Molinari (2018) liken the analyst's role to that of a filmmaker/editor. Many adults in less disturbed states of mind and some children can metabolise and narrate their experiences such that the therapist has the luxury of being part of the audience, as it were, watching the patient's "home movies" and co-constructing with them "a dream about a dream". In these cases, psychic space, thirdness, the one in the third, and triangular space are available in the psychotherapy room. Most children's ability to narrate the workings of the psyche as a coherent story or film is less well developed. These authors suggest that when the child plays in the analytic playroom, it is as if the therapist is *"*immersed in the moment in which things are created. It is as though by magic we are on the set, in the place where dreams [or nightmares] are formed" (Ferro and Molinari, 2018, p. 122). The quality of the dream/play the child presents they likened to the quality of the images in a spool of film and varies along a spectrum: from a collection of badly degraded images through raw unedited disparate images, to whole intact film segments that just need a quiet space in which to do a touch of editing and organising with another mind present. For children whose container is "extremely tiny – tenuous, fragmented [and] brittle", children whose alpha function is so limited that they cannot yet dream or play, "what is needed [in psychotherapy] is to construct together a place in the mind where dreams are given life" (Ferro and Molinari, 2018, pp. 122–123).

Our formulation now becomes slightly more elaborate, but can encompass this view of dreaming and playing as processes that fuel one another in a cyclic process and comprise the central tenet of contemporary psychoanalytic theory and practice "living and dreaming the experience together":

(transference ↔ countertransference ↔ reverie) + total situation ↔ dreaming ↔ narration, play, and playing = living and experiencing together with the other

As Ferro puts it, it is upon the therapist to use their therapeutic intuition and understanding of the "total situation" in the moment to create "characters" and to narrate/enact these characters' actions and words through the patient-therapist interaction or game, all in such a way that the "patient's inhibited parts", anguish and violent pain, can come to light and be transformed through the game.

I end this chapter with a vignette from a therapy with one such traumatised child, Paulina, whose container was so damaged that it felt as if all content was evacuated from her mind before she even entered the therapy room. Over a period of many months, Paulina frequently slept through the entirety of the sessions, an empty evacuating dissociated sleep. When she did use the toys and games in the therapy room, her play was more like Green's (2005) negative play (–P), which he likened to Bion's –K, (described in Chapter 7), what could also be called in the context of this discussion, negative dreaming. The images in this child's film were not only degraded: they were distorted and disconnected at best, and mostly totally burnt, bleached, and blanked out. The breakthrough in the therapy came from a most unexpected direction, not through play with dolls (though many times both she and I made huge efforts at make-believe play), not through the obvious more visceral games of *Monopoly*, War, *TAKI,* and football favoured by many of the children I work with, but through *Code Breaker* (*Mastermind*), a game usually reserved for my more cerebral patients who need a break from the heat of these competitive interactive games, but which this child "magically" turned into a persecutory instrument of treacherous cruelty.

VIGNETTE P   *Code Breaker* turned instrument of torment

Paulina, a ten-year-old child, whose family history was riddled with secrets, abuse, and abandonment, a pretty girl but dead inside, was unable to engage in any real play. She repeatedly drew stereotypical pictures of fairies and told endless stories about them, which had no plot, no beginning, middle, or end. She "played" with the small dolls and doll's house in the room, but had no idea what to do with them. She would repeatedly pair the dolls up obsessively on the carpet, only to pack them away again silently and mechanically a few minutes later. This went on for months on end. I felt as if all life was being sucked out of me and that I was at a therapeutic impasse. I tried engaging her in the play with dolls, elaborating on the stories about the fairies, but my play and hers remained lifeless.

After more than a year of such sessions, week after week, month after month, it was Paulina who found the way out. One day, she pulled out the game *Code Breaker* from the cupboard and demanded we play. An objective competitive game, par excellence, that involves guessing a code made up of four coloured pegs, which has been chosen by the other player and hidden from view. "Not a chance", I thought. "Paulina has almost no faculty for mentalisation, she hasn't a hope of understanding the game. This game will get us nowhere". I could not have been more mistaken. As Paulina became increasingly involved in the game, she began to use it to tyrannise and terrorise me, to reduce me to helplessness and hopelessness, and thereby was able to convey to me the violent anxiety and despair of her emotional and physical daily existence, something she had been totally unable to do verbally or via creative play and drawing.

Paulina insisted on rigidly remaining in total omnipotent control of the game, choosing the four-colour code herself, turn after turn, refusing to allow me to have a turn to choose a code myself for her to guess. Moreover, she found it unbearable if I succeeded in cracking her code. I felt trapped between two impossible options. I either had to erase my own mind and not think. Or if I allowed my mind to live and breathe, Paulina experienced this as a threat of annihilation (cf. Britton's theory of hypersubjectivity, Subchapter 7.3). It was as if she felt my mind would engulf hers or erase hers. When I did venture towards some spontaneous gesture, by daring to guess one of the pegs correctly, she returned fire by tightening her tyrannical hold on me and, unbeknownst to me, "replaced" one or more of the coloured pegs with a blank hole. At some point, I deciphered this code, where something had been replaced by nothing – a code that can be conceived of theoretically as a concretisation of –K or even a form of negative hallucination (Green, 1997, 1999, see Chapter 6). Again, Paulina could not bear the functioning of my mind. But equally, I knew she *needed* my mind to function, to contain the overwhelming anxiety and nameless dread (Bion, 1962) that had become part and parcel of our sessions. This meant using the pegs as characters in the game to communicate what had been contained, and what I felt Paulina could "hear" through the game without feeling persecuted or annihilated. I knew Paulina felt more in control in the rounds of the game, which involved me failing to decipher her code, so I deliberately placed my pegs incorrectly round after round. This was not so easy as my incorrect guesses were met with scorn and derision from Paulina, which, despite the fact that I had consciously chosen to lose the game, hit hard and resonated forcefully, at times intolerably, in my countertransference. After a few such rounds, the game began to feel stagnant, and I decided that it was time to introduce a new narrative derivative/character into the game who would discover Paulina's ruse. Paulina chose her code, and I responded as before, gradually honing in on the coloured pegs in her code. "Aha!" I said, "There's only one possibility – there is no peg there at all. Nothing. A no-thing peg!"

Paulina was enraged at my discovery and immediately upped her game, responding by creating a new more terrifying monster, infused with cruelty and anxiety. She began filling the blank holes with any foreign matter that came to hand: small animal models, plasticine, even dirty tissues. Sometimes I felt that she took sadistic pleasure in seeing me struggle, disoriented, and give up. This was indeed the magic, black magic perhaps, of which Ferro and Molinari (Bion, 1962) write, where the child's game becomes the film set itself. I found myself immersed in Paulina's traumatic persecutory horror-filled inner world, living/dreaming/suffering it together with her, a world she enacted and narrated through the characters of secret codes, coloured pegs, empty holes, and discarded pieces of old plasticine, all of which had "magically" morphed into instruments of persecutory disorientation and "gaslighting" in an ostensibly innocent game. It felt as if Paulina was draining the game of any childish playful innocence and contaminating it with indigestible life-threatening poisons. Eigen's concept of *toxic nourishment* came to mind (1999). I thought of Paulina's tragically traumatic family history and the toxic impingements in her life. I talked to her of my feelings of powerlessness, of confusion and disorientation, of fear and hopelessness in the face of the ever-changing, unpredictable reality: of the code, of the pegs and their bizarre replacements, all in the language of the game.

And gradually, Paulina began to talk of events at home, of the lack of food and hot meals, of the unfamiliar men her mother brought home, of her wish and plans to run away and live on her own.

Notes

1 The concepts of reverie, α- and β-elements will be discussed further in the next section in the context of Bionian dreaming and thinking.
2 For description of the board game *Talisman*, see https://en.wikipedia.org/wiki/Talisman_ (board_game) and https://boardgamegeek.com/boardgame/27627/talisman-revised-4th-edition.

Bibliography

Alvarez, A. (1983). Problems in the use of the counter-transference: Getting it across. *Journal of Child Psychotherapy, 9*(1), 7–23.
Alvarez, A. (1989). Development toward the latency period: Splitting and the need to forget in borderline children. *Journal of Child Psychotherapy, 15*(2), 71–83.

Alvarez, A. (1997). Projective identification as a communication its grammar in borderline psychotic children. *Psychoanalytic Dialogues, 7*(6), 753–768.

Alvarez, A. (1998). Failures to link: Attacks or defects?: Some questions concerning the thinkability of Oedipal and pre-Oedipal thoughts. *Journal of Child Psychotherapy, 24*(2), 213–231.

Alvarez, A. (2010). Levels of analytic work and levels of pathology: The work of calibration. *International Journal of Psychoanalysis, 91*(4), 859–878.

Alvarez, A. (2012). *The Thinking Heart: Three Levels of Psychoanalytic Therapy with Disturbed Children.* Routledge.

Atwood, G. E., & Stolorow, R. D. (2014). *Structures of Subjectivity: Explorations in Psychoanalytic Phenomenology and Contextualism* (2nd ed.). Routledge.

Baranger, M. (2012). The intrapsychic and the intersubjective in contemporary psychoanalysis. *International Forum of Psychoanalysis, 21*, 3–4, 130–135.

Baranger, M., & Baranger, W. (2008). The analytic situation as a dynamic field. *The International Journal of Psychoanalysis, 89*(4), 795–826.

Bellinson, J. (2000). Shut up and move: The uses of board games in child psychotherapy. *Journal of Infant, Child, and Adolescent Psychotherapy, 1*(2), 23–41.

Bellinson, J. (2002). *Children's Use of Board Games in Psychotherapy.* Jason Aronson.

Benjamin, J. (1988). *The Bonds of Love: Psychoanalysis, Feminism, and the Problem of Domination.* Pantheon.

Benjamin, J. (1990). An outline of intersubjectivity: The development of recognition. *Psychoanalytic Psychology, 7*(Suppl), 33–46.

Benjamin, J. (1995). *Like Subjects, Love Objects: Essays on Recognition and Sexual Difference.* Yale University Press.

Benjamin, J. (2007). *Intersubjectivity, Thirdness, and Mutual Recognition. A Talk Given at the Institute for Contemporary Psychoanalysis.* Los Angeles. https://terapia.co.uk/wp-content/uploads/2020/05/Reading-14-Jessica-Benjamin-Intersubjectivity.pdf

Bion, W. R. (1962). *Learning from Experience.* Tavistock.

Bion, W. R. (1967). *Second Thoughts: Selected Papers on Psychonalysis.* Heinemann.

Bion, W. R. (2019). *Four Discussions with WR Bion.* Harris Meltzer Trust.

Brady, M., Tyminski, R., & Carey, K. (2012). To know or not to know: An application of Bion's K and–K to child treatment. *Journal of Child Psychotherapy, 38*(3), 302–317.

Carroll, L. (1999). *The Annotated Alice: The Definitive Edition.* WW Norton & Company.

Caruth, E. G. (1988). How you play the game: On game as play and play as game in the psychoanalytic process. *Psychoanalytic Psychology, 5*(2), 179–192.

Civitarese, G. (2012). *The Violence of Emotions: Bion and Post-Bionian Psychoanalysis.* Routledge.

Civitarese, G. (2019). Bion's O and his pseudo-mystical path. *Psychoanalytic Dialogues, 29*(4), 388–403.

Civitarese, G., & Ferro, A. (2018). *The Analytic Field and Its Transformations.* Routledge.

Collovà, M. (2017). The setting as a locus of possible transformations. In A. Ferro (Ed.), *Contemporary Bionian Theory and Technique in Psychoanalysis* (pp. 1–43). Routledge.

Ferro, A. (1992). Two authors in search of characters: The relationship, the field, the story. *Rivista Di Psicoanalisi, 38*(1), 44–90.

Ferro, A. (2003). *The Bi-Personal Field: Experiences in Child Analysis.* Routledge.

Ferro, A. (2006). Clinical implications of Bion's thought. *The International Journal of Psychoanalysis, 87*(4), 989–1003.

Ferro, A. (Ed.). (2017). *Contemporary Bionian Theory and Technique in Psychoanalysis* (First edition). Routledge.

Ferro, A., & Molinari, E. (2018). The analyst as dreaming filmmaker. In C. Bonovitz & A. Harlem (Eds.), *Developmental Perspectives in Child Psychoanalysis and Psychotherapy* (pp. 119–140). Routledge.

Ferro, A., & Nicoli, L. (2017). *The New Analyst's Guide to the Galaxy: Questions about Contemporary Psychoanalysis*. Karnac Books.

Fonagy, P., & Target, M. (1998). Mentalization and the changing aims of child psychoanalysis. *Psychoanalytic Dialogues*, *8*(1), 87–114.

Ghent, E. (1990). Masochism, submission, surrender: Masochism as a perversion of surrender. *Contemporary Psychoanalysis*, *26*(1), 108–136.

Green, A. (1997). The intuition of the negative in playing and reality. *International Journal of Psycho-Analysis*, *78*, 1071–1084.

Green, A. (1999). *The Work of the Negative*. Free Assn Books.

Green, A. (2005). *Play and Reflection in Donald Winnicott's Writings*. Karnac Books.

Grotstein, J. S. (2008). The overarching role of unconscious phantasy. *Psychoanalytic Inquiry*, *28*(2), 190–205.

Grotstein, J. S. (2018a). *A Beam of Intense Darkness: Wilfred Bion's Legacy to Psychoanalysis*. Routledge.

Grotstein, J. S. (2018b). *But at the Same Time and on Another Level: Psychoanalytic Theory and Technique in the Kleinian/Bionian Mode*. Routledge.

Heimann, P. (1950). On counter-transference. *International Journal of Psycho-Analysis, 31*, 81–84.

Heimann, P. (1977). Further observations on the analyst's cognitive process. *Journal of American Psychoanalytic Association*, *25*, 313–333.

Heimann, P. (2005). Counter-transference. In P. Heimann & M. Tonnesmann (Eds.), *About Children and Children-No-Longer: Collected Papers 1942–80* (pp. 55–59). Routledge.

Herman, J. L. (2000). Treating the cheater: An ego and self psychological approach to working through of the cheating syndrome in the treatment of latency children. *Journal of Infant, Child, and Adolescent Psychotherapy*, *1*(2), 59–70.

Joseph, B. (1998). Thinking about a playroom. *Journal of Child Psychotherapy*, *24*(3), 359–366.

Klein, M. (Ed.). (1932). The technique of analysis in the latency period. In *The Psychoanalysis of Children* (pp. 94–121). Hogarth Press.

Klein, M. (Ed.). (1975). Personification in the play of children. In *Love, Guilt and Reparation and Other Works 1921–1945* (pp. 199–209). Hogarth Press.

Krimendahl, E. (2000). "Did you see that?": A relational perspective on children who cheat in analysis. *Journal of Infant, Child, and Adolescent Psychotherapy*, *1*(2), 43–58.

Meeks, J. E. (1970). Children who cheat at games. *Journal of the American Academy of Child Psychiatry*, *9*(1), 157–170.

Meeks, J. E. (2000). Reflections on children who cheat at games: A commentary. *Journal of Infant, Child, and Adolescent Psychotherapy*, *1*(2), 71–75.

Molinari, E. (2017a). *Field Theory in Child and Adolescent Psychoanalysis: Understanding and Reacting to Unexpected Developments*. Taylor & Francis.

Molinari, E. (2017b). Variations on a theme: Child and adolescent analysis. In A. Ferro (Ed.), *Contemporary Bionian Theory and Technique in Psychoanalysis* (pp. 176–216). Routledge.

Molinari, E. (2018). The art of fielding. *Romanian Journal of Psychoanalysis*, *11*(2), 87–96.

Ogden, T. H. (1994). The concept of interpretive action. *Psychoanalytic Quarterly*, *63*, 219–245.

Ogden, T. H. (2004a). On holding and containing, being and dreaming. *The International Journal of Psychoanalysis*, *85*(6), 1349–1364.

Ogden, T. H. (2004b). This art of psychoanalysis: Dreaming undreamt dreams and interrupted cries. *The International Journal of Psychoanalysis*, *85*(4), 857–877.

Ogden, T. H. (2019). Ontological psychoanalysis or "What do you want to be when you grow up?" *Psychoanalytic Quarterly*, *88*(4), 661–684.

Ogden, T. H. (2020). Toward a revised form of analytic thinking and practice: The evolution of analytic theory of mind. *Psychoanalytic Quarterly*, *89*(2), 219–243.

Oren, A. (2008). The use of board games in child psychotherapy. *Journal of Child Psychotherapy*, *34*(3), 364–383.

Poe, E. A. (1927). *The Works of Edgar Allan Poe, in One Volume: Complete Tales and Poems* (p. 8). WJ Black.

Racker, H. (1957). The meanings and uses of countertransference. *Psychoanalytic Quarterly*, *26*, 303–357.

Saar, N., Bar, M., & Gothelf, D. (2017). Understanding cheating in board games play therapy with children. *Sihot/Dialogue: Israel Journal of Psychotherapy*, *31*(3), 211–217.

Schneider, J. A. (2010). From Freud's dream-work to Bion's work of dreaming: The changing conception of dreaming in psychoanalytic theory. *The International Journal of Psychoanalysis*, *91*(3), 521–540.

Segal, H. (1957). Notes on symbol formation. *International Journal of Psycho-Analysis*, *38*, 391–397.

Segal, H. (1978). On symbolism. *The International Journal of Psychoanalysis*, *59*, 315–319.

Steiner, J. (2003). *Psychic Retreats: Pathological Organizations in Psychotic, Neurotic and Borderline Patients*. Routledge.

Stolorow, R. D., & Atwood, G. E. (1984). Psychoanalytic phenomenology: Toward a science of human experience. *Psychoanalytic Inquiry*, *4*(1), 87–105.

Winnicott, D. W. (1965). *The Maturational Processes and the Facilitating Environment: Studies in the Theory of Emotional Development*. Karnac.

Winnicott, D. W. (Ed.). (1971). The use of an object and relating through identifications. In *Playing and Reality* (pp. 101–111). Penguin Books.

Winnicott, D.W. (Ed.). (1977). Hate in the countertransference 1947. In *Through Paediatrics to Psycho-Analysis* (pp. 194–204). Karnac.

Chapter 9

Conclusion

This book has aimed to reveal the complexities and challenges of middle childhood, rediscovering what has been deemed latent and dormant, concealed beneath the surface of the proverbial industrious good citizen portrayed by Erikson (1950). My intent is to reconnect the disconnect between psychodynamic theory and the emotional turbulence (Bion, 1976) bubbling beneath the superficial banality, inflexibility, and defensiveness of the post-oedipal child's psyche, and from there, to accompany the school-aged child into the analytic playroom and explore the richness, variety, and therapeutic power of the game-play of middle childhood as a *bone fide* psychoanalytic language.

Sigmund Freud talked of post-oedipal children as losing their charm, as stupider than their younger siblings; Anna Freud emphasised the defences and the obsessional tendencies of this group; Klein bemoaned the restricted imagination and reserved attitudes of the post-oedipal pre-pubertal child; Winnicott asserted that children of this age should be left well alone, unless "very ill indeed". All used words such as dull, boring, limited, repressed, and obsessional to describe this critical stage of child development, long regarded in the field as years of supposed quiescence, a period of "latency". Klein and Winnicott shied away from treating this age group, citing the well-documented rigid defences and superego of the latency period, and the sexual impulses and conflicts that are presumed inaccessible in their underground hideout, banished until puberty. Generations of child psychotherapists after them have followed their lead. Still today, many practitioners, novices, and experienced clinicians regard children in the 8–13 age range as rather a chore to treat.

The historical critique of the child psychoanalytic literature (Chapter 2) revealed whole generations of school children seen in the analytic playrooms of yesteryear, but neither properly heard nor properly held in the collective mind of the field of child psychoanalysis. Until the turn of the century, most psychodynamic texts sketched out the stage of middle childhood only cursorily, painting these years in monochrome tones, compared to the florid vibrant colours used to describe the psyches of their older and younger, vociferous, somewhat exhibitionist, siblings.

DOI: 10.4324/9781003425229-12

The natural language of play of middle childhood suffered a similar fate and was excluded for decades from the classical analytic playroom. These forms of game-play and communication typical of the post-oedipal pre-pubertal years were all but dismissed until the turn of the last century, considered unsuitable for analytic work because of their structure and marked difference in dialect from the language of pretend play with dolls and small objects characteristic of early childhood.

Given the little attention paid in the field to middle childhood and game-play over almost a full century of child psychoanalysis and psychotherapy, it is small wonder that even today, engaging school-aged children psychotherapeutically in the traditional child analytic playroom is frequently still regarded as baffling and even boring. In this book, I have presented a reformulation of the technique and language of analytic psychotherapy to fit the enigmatic and often misunderstood psyche of middle childhood. I would add that, in the wake of the Covid-19 pandemic, such a reappraisal of child psychotherapy technique has become especially urgent given the recent sharp increase in the numbers of school-aged children found to be suffering from mental health problems across the globe, and the well-documented high levels of dropout from treatment seen in this age group.

9.1 The wave-particle child: A developmental reconceptualisation

The critique of the contemporary developmental texts on middle childhood (Chapter 3) pointed the way to a paradoxical "wave-particle" picture of the psyche of the school-age child: a psychic organisation which is constantly changing and evolving, and yet at the same time ordered and structured, simultaneously both "moving dynamic wave" and "stable particle". Some aspects of the child's psyche do seem to become quiescent in the post-oedipal years. Certain conflicts and impulses are pushed aside, to be classified and boxed away for later times, whilst other aspects of the psyche and the mind develop and change at an astounding rate. As Klein (1952) herself first suggested, the post-oedipal period should still be regarded as a period of flux, of work in progress, where the solution to the oedipal complex is not yet stable, and the child continues to oscillate between what Klein called the schizoid-paranoid position and the depressive position. Broadening this perspective, middle childhood can be characterised as a period of development where the impetus towards structure and stability is in constant tension with forces for emotional change and psychic restructuring. Despite the supposed equanimity of middle childhood, the potential for upset, anxiety, and even turmoil can clearly be seen to be ever present in children of this age. Paraphrasing slightly Wilson's (1989) words (quoted at the end of Chapter 3): "despite [the] virtue of composure and orderly growth [in middle childhood], [the child's psyche] nevertheless sits perilously at the mercy of numerous disruptive forces."

From the in-depth developmental discussion in Part I, it can be seen that the psyche of what I have called the "wave-particle" child is far from the rigid structure posited especially by Freud, Anna Freud, and the ego psychologists. Neurologically, hormonally, cognitively, emotionally, and socially, children between the ages of 6 and 12 are changing and developing rapidly and fundamentally, although these changes are less dramatic and tempestuous than in toddlerhood or in adolescence. There is a semblance of structure and order in their psyche to be respected and cultivated, as Alvarez (1989, 2012) wisely reminds us. The reconceptualisation of the developmental stage of middle childhood, in terms of duality and flux, stability, structure, *and* emotional turbulence, has deep repercussions for child psychotherapy in the primary school years. Children of this age are more vulnerable and have a more fragile psychic structure than was previously thought and many are in great need of professional help to negotiate their developmental path through these years. This picture of a constantly developing, still flexible, and malleable psyche implies that psychotherapeutic intervention is not only often critically important in middle childhood, but also has the potential to be highly effective.

9.1.1   *Beyond the triangular to the polygonal*

The primary task of middle childhood, since time immemorial, has been to go out into the world as an autonomous individual with agency and responsibility and to take a role in society, albeit still under the auspices of the parental home (unlike in adolescence). Superficially, this might appear to be a natural, straightforward developmental step. Parents, educators, and practitioners alike have barely paused to think about what this giant developmental leap actually entails for the child. Middle childhood is a period of negotiation through a multiplicity of relations: siblings, aunts, uncles, grandparents and cousins, peers, teachers, scout leaders, and sports coaches. Significant also are the parents' own internalised polygonal web of relations, and their external social and professional worlds, from which the child is excluded, but whose presence as significant other in the parents' world is strongly felt. I believe that the term triangularity does not do justice to these intra-psychic and inter-psychic complexities and have suggested the term *polygonality* as metaphor for the complexity of this wider interpersonal and intersubjective field. Internalising this polygonal inter-psychic and intra-psychic complexity presents a particularly challenging developmental task for the immature and as yet unstable psyche of the school-aged child. If the child is to successfully negotiate this process, infant omnipotence must gradually be replaced by a sense of agency and potency in the real world, and the nascent capacities for self-reflection, self-regulation, and mentalisation with which the child enters middle childhood must be honed and bolstered.

Middle childhood, then, can be reconceptualised as a period of constant psychic flux and change where the psyche is developing beyond the triangular into the polygonal space. In this context, I believe it is critical to revise psychoanalytic understanding of the resolution of the Oedipus conflict in broader non-gendered, non-patriarchal, non-sexist terms in line with contemporary thinkers such as Scarfone (2019), Fiorini (2016, 2019), and Balsam (2001, 2010). Building on these authors' work, I have argued here that the developing child should be seen as grappling with the "enigma of difference" (between the sexes and the generations), "alterity" (the other as outside of the self and the self as other to an-other) and the "fact of incompleteness" (relinquishing omnipotent beliefs and wishes of "having it all", beyond the narrow connotations of possessing both the female and male sex organs). These are complexities of "polygonal" internal and external object relations that reach well beyond the triangular so-called oedipal level, and the stresses and pitfalls for the child negotiating this multiplicity of relations are great. Working through these issues, accepting one's own alterity and incompleteness, is a prerequisite for the child's crystallising identity and for the differentiation and integration of the self. This could be said to be the work of a lifetime, and middle childhood is undoubtedly a critical stage in this lifelong developmental task.

A corollary to this polygonal view of psychic development in middle childhood is the understanding that matters of gender identity and sexuality are clearly not placed on the back burner during middle childhood, as classical psychodynamic theory has led us to believe. Questions of sexuality and gender identity are high on the public agenda today, and children are exploring these questions at an ever-younger age, both inside the psychotherapy room and outside. Approaching these matters within a polygonal nuanced flexible framework of definitions and identifications, as outlined in this book, is complex. However, such an approach enables the child in psychotherapy to explore for themselves more honestly and more deeply the many and varied aspects of gender identity and sexuality which have traditionally been regarded as belonging either to the masculine or the feminine, the male or the female, and the maternal or the paternal.

9.1.2   The language of play in middle childhood

Throughout these chapters, I have highlighted what is plain to see in any school playground, child's bedroom, or local park: the natural language of play and communication of this age group reflects the wave-particle nature of their psyche and the polygonal world of intra-psychic and interpersonal relations. The momentous shifts in all spheres of development propel the school-aged child towards rule-bound competitive games and organised group activities (Freud, 1963; Piaget, 1962; Plaut, 1979). They naturally shy away from the regressive pull of the toys and play materials of early childhood presented in the traditional child psychotherapy room. Instead, these older children tend instinctively towards the more sophisticated language of structured games, of hierarchy, compartmentalisation, and acquisitiveness that is the natural arena of play in middle childhood. This territory is occupied by games like football, French skipping, *Monopoly, Cheat, War*, and *Speed/Spit,* which superficially seem highly structured and restricted by rules and by predetermined contents and symbols. But beneath the surface of these games is a rich and varied world of imagination and playfulness, seething with emotion and conflict. These are games that have been designed and refined, usually unintentionally, by generations of creative children and adults to engage children's attention and enable them to practice their burgeoning physical, cognitive, and social abilities, whilst simultaneously releasing and working through emotional and physical energy and sexual and aggressive impulses, all within the metaphor of the game.

This is a language of play and intra-psychic and inter-psychic communication that has been overlooked and often rejected by the major schools of child analytic psychotherapy (Chapter 4), a fact which is all the more puzzling given that analytic thinkers from Melanie Klein and Anna Freud, through Winnicott, to Alvarez, Ferro and Paulina Kernberg today, have all stressed the utmost importance of meeting the child at their level and communicating in their language. Texts on psychoanalytic child psychotherapy emphasise the dual purpose of play in the analytic setting, both as a channel for communication with the unconscious and as enabling cognitive, emotional, social, and physical development. I have argued that game-play indeed serves both of these purposes (Chapter 5). It is the wave-particle child's natural language of intra-psychic and interpersonal communication, and its many forms (board games, ball games, sports, collections, and bartering) are today widely recognised as vital to all these aspects of the children's development. The squares, lines, boxes, rules, and regulations of these traditional children's games are the *lingua franca* of middle childhood. I have shown how, like dolls and toy cars for the younger child, the pawns, bats and balls, dices, and cards, even the rules and the gameboards themselves, serve as external phenomena (Winnicott, 1971) to be manipulated by the older child and infused with dream elements for playing in the transitional space. It is the "aliveness", the natural curiosity, and the spontaneity of the child's true self, which transform everyday board games, card games, and ball games into Winnicottian transitional spaces of creative play (Chapter 6). Moreover, this is only part of their therapeutic power: the storylines of these games of commerce, battlefields, superheroes, and sports can be seen to offer safe developmentally appropriate metaphors and "covers" for expressing and exploring even violent and visceral anxieties, impulses, and passions. Moreover, the inherent interactive nature of these games brings the patient-therapist transference–countertransference matrix to the fore and serves as an essential and powerful tool through which to enter and grapple with the emotional turbulence of the child's inner world.

9.2 Clinical theoretical formulation

There have been a few seminal papers published in the last two decades that have finally placed game-play centre-stage as the "therapy itself" in middle childhood (Beiser, 1979; Bellinson, 2000, 2002; Herman, 2000; Krimendahl, 2000; Meeks, 1970, 2000; Oren, 2008; Saar et al., 2017). I have built upon the ideas and insights of these papers to develop the detailed clinical theoretical formulation outlined in this book: specifically with regard to the triangular, and what I have termed the polygonal, space; the transference–countertransference matrix; the intersubjective; and 21st-century theories on Winnicottian and Bionian playing, thinking, and dreaming.

9.2.1 Expanding psychic space at the polygonal level

When viewed through the polygonal prism of psychic development, the psychotherapeutic paradigm based on the playroom of early childhood can be seen to be heavily weighted towards the domain of what has been traditionally regarded as the maternal. This paradigm of the mother-infant dyad, associated with boundlessness, receptivity, subjectivity, and being, has long been privileged in child psychoanalysis over the traditionally paternal, the domain of productivity, emancipation, cognition, and doing. I contend that the simple addition to the child psychotherapy room of the traditional structured games of middle childhood, symbolic of the "objective" and "exciting" outside world, bounded in time and place, a world of competition, action, and discovery, naturally redresses this long-standing imbalance. Furthermore, the multiplayer structure of many board games, such as *Frustration, Cluedo, Monopoly,* or *Talisman,* with their four-sided boards and choice of different pawns or cards, immediately lays down a polygonal field of play and projection of internal objects onto the playing board.

I have shown how, in these "polygonal" states of mind–in which a child strives towards individuation, autonomy, and symbolisation–board games, card games, and competitive ball games lay down, a priori, a degree of separation between the self and other(s) (Subchapter 7.1). In these more integrated states of mind, themes of self-confidence, impulse control, potency and agency, of difference and similarity, gender identity, and sexuality, can all be explored within the safety of the analytic playroom and through the medium of the interactive competitive game. Issues of cheating in the game-play are central to the therapeutic work: it is upon the therapist to decide when to impose limits and when to encourage flexibility and allow a modicum of mischief and playful dishonesty to enter the child's play (Subchapter 7.1). It is important to note that at the polygonal/triangular level of functioning, the therapeutic work takes place largely on the symbolic level, through the metaphor of the game, as opposed to "under cover" of the game. (This distinction is further elaborated below.) The quality of play and the tone and atmosphere of the transference–countertransference are key to differentiating these two modes of playing. When remaining largely within the metaphor of the game, the child maintains an intuitive acceptance of "plausible deniability"; they understand at a very basic level that "it is just a game", and there is far less urgency in their need to win, and less tyranny in their control over the game.

9.2.2 From the dyad to the triad

Most wave-particle children who are referred to psychotherapy are more "wave" than "particle"; their triangular psychic structure is still very much a work in progress, and polygonal issues remain out of their grasp. Here too, in these more disturbed states of mind, structured competitive games come into their own. These games have one foot in reality, the other in fantasy. The pawns, the board, the bats, balls, and goalposts are all tangible, and belong to the realm of the "other", the outside world, the parental organising and limiting function. But the play itself is also heavily coloured by the child's inner world, the game is a "moving target" and unpredictable, and the storyline is pure fantasy, available for the child to embellish and infuse with their own dream (and nightmare) elements (as Winnicott and Bion put it). I have argued that for the wave-particle child, the combination of a "playful" therapist and structured games can usefully and effectively function as a bridge between the wave and the particle, the subjective and the objective, and as a "user-friendly" tool for developing and strengthening the capacity for mentalisation in children on the cusp of triangulation and thirdness.

The vignettes and the clinical analysis of game-play in Subchapter 7.2 demonstrate that these games can forge the critical "missing link" (Britton, 1989) in the tragically flattened triangular space of children in more deeply disturbed states of mind. Such children are in dire need of psychotherapy in order to help them reorganise their inner private selves quietly, safely, at their own pace, but the challenges these fragile explosive and disorganised children present to child psychotherapists are formidable. Alvarez (1989) emphasises the borderline child's developmental need for distancing and splitting off of threatening material and traumatic events in order to allow thinking and psychic organisation and structuring to take place. I have shown how the traditional games of middle childhood inherently offer such structure, and the predetermined contents and rules serve as the safety gear these children need in order to approach their highly turbulent inner world, safely, carefully, and without injury. It is in this context that I refer to these games as serving as "a cover" rather than a metaphor, under whose guise the child can express their emotional turbulence and direct their vengeful rage and vindictive envy towards the therapist. The very framework of the game, the pawns, the squares, and the dice, protects the child from having to take ownership of these threatening and overwhelming emotions. The game acts as a conduit through which to express threatening and frightening anxieties and psychic pain. The therapist is often experienced by the child as a threat to their potency/omnipotence, and the game may feel like an existential fight for survival, and yet the pretend mode is nevertheless active. I have likened the therapeutic work with such hyper-subjective and hyper-objective (Britton, 2004) children to shifting the vertices of subjectivity and objectivity, inner and outer reality, the pretend world, and the real world, slowly and gradually, outwards and upwards, from a highly skewed paranoid-schizoid triangle, towards a more balanced and spacious, more equilateral, triangular transitional psychic space.

9.2.3 Containing, dreaming, and living the experience together in the analytic playing field

Many children referred to therapy are survivors of long-term abuse, deprivation, and chronic trauma – they have very little experience of benign containing objects who can contain and metabolise their inner terror and pain. They have learnt to communicate only obliquely. Not only are these children developmentally averse to verbal emotional communication, but bitter past life experience has also taught them that direct expression of their anxiety and inner hurt can be dangerous. Nevertheless, on some level, they have not given up hope.

Children in disturbed and disorganised states of mind need the therapist to contain and digest the anxiety, rage, inadequacy, and despair that continuously overwhelm their psyche. I have shown in the last chapter how interactive game-play with the child in the psychotherapy playroom can be seen as an example of the Kleinian total transference situation par excellence. The child enters the therapy room, chooses a game, and challenges the therapist to enter with them into the fray of their inner psyche, played out between the goalposts or across the wilds of the Monopoly board. The child's choice of game, the way they play, and moreover the way they cheat, their subjective perception of the therapist, whether as benign competitive opponent or as existential threat, all these are reflections and projections of the child's deepest anxieties and phantasies. The framing structure of the therapist-cum-game-play enables the metabolised products of the child's raw feelings and "unthought thoughts" to be translated into words and interventions-in-game that can be tolerated by the child and slowly internalised. Therapeutic responses and interventions take place through the medium of the game. We surrender rather than submit (Ghent, 1990) to the child's cheating and omnipotent control, and let the game take its course accordingly. Initially, the pawns are moved, the cards played, and the goalposts set, all according to the child's stipulations and strict orders. The therapist may at most reflect out loud on the child's existential need to win, the fear and the hurt of feeling impotent, stupid, and humiliated, but only in non-specific, third person, not even therapist-centred, interpretations. Through the introjection of the repeated experience of the therapist's reverie, the child's own capacity for reverie expands. Gradually, the therapeutic interventions can be taken one step further, and the therapist can add into the game-play elements of transmutative surprise or challenge, manipulating the external phenomena in the transitional space. These benign transmutative intra-psychic and inter-psychic experiences (a pawn taken by the therapist or a goal scored against the child, a surprise double six thrown by the child, or a round of *TAKI/UNO* won without cheating) are lived together by child and therapist in the game-play and the child's own container expands.

The journey through the history of child psychoanalysis and the reformulation of game-play in the context of child psychotherapy in middle childhood brought me to the final chapter (Chapter 8) to Ferro and Civitarese's bi-personal analytic field theory. Viewed through this conceptual lens, the child's play is seen as "narrating" the entire web of projective identifications active in their inner world and intersubjective environment, to be explored and metabolised in the polygonal multi-poled field of the game-play. Whether the child chooses to play Cheat or chess, toss a football in the air, paint our portrait, or organise a doll's tea party is of relatively little importance. The royalties in a pack of cards; the pawns on the chessboard; the characters in *Talisman*; and even the money and the properties themselves in a game of *Monopoly*; all come alive to narrate, metabolise, and transmute the story of the child's inner psyche. This "magic of anonymity" (Fonagy & Target, 1998) takes place naturally in the game-play.

At the more benign levels of triangular and polygonal states of mind (Subchapter 7.1), the therapist's role is more one of "editor", "translator", or "narrator" of the child's narrative. At the more disturbed and terrorised states of mind (Subchapters 7.2 and 7.3 and Chapter 8), the therapist and the child often find themselves as if trapped against their will in a horror movie, unable to move, unable to scream, unable to make sense of the carnage and the terror to which they are subjected; all in the guise of a children's "innocent" board game. The growth in "alive experiencing" (Winnicott, 1971) and spontaneity in the child comes only slowly, and the process is most often laden with anxiety, turmoil, and psychic pain, for child and for therapist alike. This is especially true in states of psychic deadness, where the pictographs of the child's psyche are often so faint, disjointed, incomplete, and bleached almost beyond recognition (Ferro & Molinari, 2018), that the therapist may spend months groping around in the dark, searching for a glimmer of insight and movement.

9.3   An afterthought

We have come a long way from the classical psychoanalytic concept of latency as a period of stasis and stagnation, and the concomitant long-standing blind opposition in the field to structured games in the analytic playroom. And yet, I cannot help but wonder if board games, card games, and ball games in psychoanalytic child psychotherapy are becoming more acceptable only because we are today in the throes of the modern electronic revolution. Once regarded as pastimes of the lazy, games like *Monopoly* and *UNO* have recently gained almost romantic status in the eyes of educators and parents, regarded as treasured relics of yesteryear, when compared to "mindless" computer games. The same disparaging epithets once used to describe card games and board games are applied today to almost any games involving modern technology. As we have seen, contemporary theory sees the psychoanalytic psychotherapist's role as facilitating the patient's capacity to play, dream, think, and communicate, a role that transcends the specifics of the child's chosen toy or game in any particular session. Perhaps, then, we should try and avoid this repetition compulsion and adopt a broader, more receptive approach to technique and to our tools of the trade in order to meet the child patient where they are, in the game they choose, be it the doll's house, a card game, or the latest mobile phone app. Take for example the following short excerpt from a therapy with a rather grumpy and uncooperative 13-year-old boy:

Maybe smartphones really are smart, even in therapy

A child takes out his mobile phone and starts playing what he calls "the surgeon's game". My heart sinks. "There he goes again, hiding behind his mobile phone", I think to myself. I wonder whether I should set any limits, and if so, what kind? Should I insist that this session we go "phone free", even though that is bound to put this already sullen 13-year-old in an even worse mood? As I am debating with myself, he pipes up and starts spontaneously telling me about the game: "Every time I manage to operate successfully and mend a broken bone I gain points, one for a finger, five for a hand, twenty for a hip, and so on!" I can't believe my ears: this is a young adolescent whose family history contained much illness and many hospitalisations, and whose father specifically had broken his bones repeatedly as a child. I have to admit to myself reluctantly that maybe mobile phones can also be a useful therapeutic tool. He goes on playing, I ask questions, and he involves me in his successes and failures. I say: "Breaking bones is really painful and scary. It must be an amazing feeling to be a surgeon and to be able to fix them just like that!" "Yeah, it's so cool!", he replies.

The 2020 global Covid-19 pandemic catapulted the psychoanalytic community into the 21st century, necessitating flexibility and change. Children's voices were once again muffled and stifled. Children were forgotten at home for months on end by governments all over the world, their emotional, social, and developmental needs neglected, even when simple solutions like structured outdoor classrooms and sports activities were relatively simple to organise and readily available. School-aged children are not "left well alone": they should not be intruded upon, and they need autonomy and independence, but they also need holding and structure. I embarked upon this project well before the pandemic had become a reality. But as the pandemic unfolded and I watched with dismay as government after government failed its country's children, especially those from deprived inner-city neighbourhoods with high unemployment and few open spaces, I felt an increasing sense of urgency in my writing.

Children know what they want. The sales of board games soared during the pandemic. Parents and children reported that playing these games was a welcome relief from the screens that had become their main connection with the outside world. Online gaming increased even more dramatically: up by at least 90%, many reports claim. Whilst some online articles report these figures with gloom and doom, many highlight the social and emotional benefits of gaming even amongst preadolescents, citing research showing that playing the popular online interactive video games of today often leads to an increase in the time children spend with friends and to improvement in conflict resolution skills, even to an improvement in measures of creativity and emotional well-being. Children today are communicating more and more via online games, instead of via game-play in the schoolyard, local playground, out in the streets, or in their homes. They do not chat on Zoom with their friends, any more than they chatted on the telephone or played with dolls or cars in the sandbox together before Covid-19. Structured games, online and offline, are their emotional and social lifeline.

9.4   Future directions

I have attempted in these chapters to flesh out the clinical theory and practice of game-play in the analytic playroom, to furnish child analytic therapists with a conceptual framework through which to understand the language that most children in middle childhood naturally use to communicate when they enter the child psychotherapy room. This has been a clinically focused conceptual exploration. Multiple questions remain to be investigated in future conceptual, clinical, and empirical research. Outcome data are needed from public child mental health clinics where structured games are included as a matter of course in the psychotherapy playroom. We also need to develop research tools that can trace the therapeutic game-play process qualitatively and quantitatively. Questions of game-play on smartphones and on computers online have barely been explored: where and how does this new technology enter the child psychoanalytic discourse?

Today, more than ever, school-aged children need to be seen and heard, spoken to and listened to, engaged with at eye level, in their own language of play and communication. The average 40% dropout rate in child psychotherapy is a wake-up call. With an estimated more than 20% of school children struggling with mental health issues in the wake of the pandemic, I believe it is essential that mental health clinics act urgently to explore novel therapeutic approaches in order to engage these children more effectively in psychotherapy and reduce the treatment dropout rate. In this context, my hope is that this book will contribute to rethinking the theory and technique of psychodynamic psychotherapy in middle childhood.

Bibliography

Alvarez, A. (1989). Development toward the latency period: Splitting and the need to forget in borderline children. *Journal of Child Psychotherapy*, *15*(2), 71–83.

Alvarez, A. (2012). *The Thinking Heart: Three Levels of Psychoanalytic Therapy with Disturbed Children*. Routledge.

Balsam, R. H. (2001). Integrating male and female elements in a woman's gender identity. *Journal of American Psychoanalytic Association*, *49*(4), 1335–1360.

Balsam, R. H. (2010). Where has oedipus gone? A turn of the century contemplation. *Psychoanalytic Inquiry*, *30*(6), 511–519.

Beiser, H. R. (1979). Formal games in diagnosis and therapy. *Journal of the American Academy of Child Psychiatry*, *18*(3), 480–491.

Bellinson, J. (2000). Shut up and move: The uses of board games in child psychotherapy. *Journal of Infant, Child, and Adolescent Psychotherapy*, *1*(2), 23–41.

Bellinson, J. (2002). *Children's Use of Board Games in Psychotherapy*. Jason Aronson.

Bion, W. R. (1976). Emotional turbulence. In F. Bion (Ed.), *Clinical Seminars and Other Works*, 295–305.

Britton, R. (2004). Subjectivity, objectivity, and triangular space. *The Psychoanalytic Quarterly*, *73*(1), 47–61.

Britton, R. (1989). The Missing Link: Parental Sexuality in the Oedipus Complex. In R. Britton, M. Feldman, & E. O'Shaughnessy (Eds.), *The Oedipus Complex Today Clinical Implications*. Karnac.

Erikson, E. H. (1950). *Childhood and Society* (2nd ed.). Norton (1963).

Ferro, A., & Molinari, E. (2018). The analyst as dreaming filmmaker. In C. Bonovitz & A. Harlem (Eds.), *Developmental Perspectives in Child Psychoanalysis and Psychotherapy* (pp. 119–140). Routledge.

Fiorini, L. G. (2016). Intersubjectivity, otherness, and thirdness: A necessary relationship. *International Journal of Psycho-Analysis, 97*(4), 1095–1104.

Fiorini, L. G. (2019). Deconstructing the feminine: Discourses, logics and power. Theoretico-clinical implications. *The International Journal of Psychoanalysis, 100*(3), 593–603.

Fonagy, P., & Target, M. (1998). Mentalization and the changing aims of child psychoanalysis. *Psychoanalytic Dialogues, 8*(1), 87–114.

Freud, A. (1963). The concept of developmental lines. *Psychoanal Study of the Child, 18,* 245–265.

Ghent, E. (1990). Masochism, submission, surrender: Masochism as a perversion of surrender. *Contemporary Psychoanalysis, 26*(1), 108–136.

Herman, J. L. (2000). Treating the cheater: An ego and self psychological approach to working through of the cheating syndrome in the treatment of latency children. *Journal of Infant, Child, and Adolescent Psychotherapy, 1*(2), 59–70.

Klein, M. (1952). Some theoretical conclusions regarding the emotional life of the infant. In Klein, Heimann, Isaacs and Riviere (Eds.), *Developments in Psycho-Analysis* (Vol. 3, pp. 198–236). Hogarth Press.

Krimendahl, E. (2000). "Did you see that?": A relational perspective on children who cheat in analysis. *Journal of Infant, Child, and Adolescent Psychotherapy, 1*(2), 43–58.

Meeks, J. E. (1970). Children who cheat at games. *Journal of the American Academy of Child Psychiatry, 9*(1), 157–170.

Meeks, J. E. (2000). Reflections on children who cheat at games: A commentary. *Journal of Infant, Child, and Adolescent Psychotherapy, 1*(2), 71–75.

Oren, A. (2008). The use of board games in child psychotherapy. *Journal of Child Psychotherapy, 34*(3), 364–383.

Piaget, J. (1962). *Play, Dreams and Imitation.* Norton.

Plaut, E. A. (1979). Definition of Play. *Psychoanalytic Study of the Child, 34,* 217–232.

Saar, N., Bar, M., & Gothelf, D. (2017). Understanding cheating in board games play therapy with children. *Sihot/Dialogue: Israel Journal of Psychotherapy, 31*(3), 211–217.

Scarfone, D. (2019). The feminine, the analyst and the child theorist. *International Journal of Psycho-Analysis, 100*(3), 567–575.

Wilson, P. (1989). Latency and certainty. *Journal of Child Psychotherapy, 15*(2), 59–69.

Winnicott, D. W. (1971). *Playing and Reality.* Penguin Books.

Winnicott, D. W. (1971). The use of an object and relating through identifications. In D.W. Winnicott, *Playing and Reality* (pp. 101–111). Penguin Books.

Index

100, 101, 106, 128, 135, 143–145, 149,
169, 175, 181–182, 199, 201, 208–210,
216, 217, 219, 222, 225–228, 233–235,
247, 249, 252

jacks/five stones *see* five-stones
Jemerin, J.M. 3, 34, 46, 61
Joseph, Betty 81, 83, 84, 122, 217, 223,
229
juvenile stage, in development 41, 44, 46

K and-K, Knowledge (psychic), Bion *see*
thinking, in Bionian and post-Bionian
theory; dreaming
Kazdin, A.E. 3
Keats, J. (negative capability) 140, 221
Kegerreis, S. 84
Kernberg, P.F. 9, 147, 249
Kessler, R.C. 2, 3, 58
Khan, M.R. 88–89
Klein, M., Kleinian approaches to child
psychoanalysis 1, 7–9, 35–36, 38, 39,
55, 77–85, 91, 99, 103, 104, 111–113,
116, 118–119, 138, 178, 186, 199, 217,
218, 221–222, 229, 230, 245–246, 252
Knight, R. 4, 6, 7, 38, 39, 41, 43, 44, 47–
49, 56, 57, 60, 61, 63
Kohlberg, L. 59, 60
Kohut, H. 61, 121, 164, 179
Krimendahl, E. 10, 99, 100, 105, 114, 172,
217, 249

Lacan, J. 179, 210
language: of achievement *see* negative
capability, and work of the negative;
of communication *see* game-play,
as language of intra-psychic and
inter-psychic communication
Lanyado, M. 8, 90
latency: classical psychoanalytic view 1,
3, 5–7, 10, 11, 23, 32–39, 41, 43, 49,
57–58, 62–63; contemporary critique of
38–49, 80, 82–83, 93, 98–99, 114, 128,
177, 211, 245–247, 253, 255; defences,
in classical psychoanalytic theory 1,
33–37, 50, 57, 84, 90–91, 96, 245;
etymological root of 7, 39; perceived
psychic stagnation in 1, 6, 7, 9, 11, 32,
33, 36, 39, 43, 68, 241, 253; quiescence
in 5, 6, 11, 32, 68, 246
learning *see* middle childhood, learning and
acquisition of knowledge in

Lenormand, M. 121–123, 126, 135, 136,
139, 141, 144–146, 149
lifeless play 137, 142, 188, 194, 201–203,
240
Locke, J. 42
Loewald, H.W. 62; *see also* oedipal
complex, classical theory and
contemporary reformulations
losing *see* winning and losing, especially
in game-play in child psychoanalytic
psychotherapy

Mahler, M. 96, 154, 179
masculine, the male and the paternal 64, 65,
69, 135, 155, 180, 198, 199, 248, 250
mastery *see* agency
masturbation 34, 35, 56, 119
maternal 64, 65, 118, 135, 155, 179–181,
198, 199, 248, 250
me, and not-me, in Milnerian and
Winnicottian thinking 85, 87, 125–127,
140, 148, 154, 194
Meeks, J.E. 9, 11, 99, 100, 114, 160, 168,
172, 173, 189, 217
Meersand, P. 6–8, 10, 47, 51, 54, 56, 57,
61–63, 66, 114, 117, 118, 124, 127, 136
Meitner, L. (Nuclear Physicist) 140, 150
mentalisation *see* game-play in child
psychoanalytic psychotherapy, and
mentalisation
messianic *see* Bion, W.R., Establishment,
and the Messianic/Mystic
metabolisation in contemporary PA theory;
in game-play 102, 104, 121, 221, 224,
233–238, 251, 252
metaphor, analytic work within the
metaphor of play and game 61, 67, 81,
95, 105, 120, 122, 123, 137, 139, 142,
143, 158, 169, 180, 184, 188, 195, 236,
238, 249–251
middle childhood: achievements,
developmental in 1, 4, 6, 39, 44, 55,
58, 61, 138; art, depiction of middle
childhood in 24, 26, 40; behaviour
problems in 2, 3, 35, 48, 61, 68, 88, 92,
95, 163, 171, 192, 203, 205, 221, 222,
236; body, and the bodily in 7, 24, 33,
38, 40, 44, 54–57, 60, 63, 64, 156, 162,
200; capacities and capabilities in 4, 6,
8, 24, 33, 41–45, 47, 49–51, 55–61, 67,
69, 77, 98, 114, 122, 126, 127, 140, 141,
157, 160–164, 166–169, 173, 174, 176,

transitional space *see* game-play in child psychoanalytic psychotherapy, and expanding the transitional space

transmutations in game *see* transformations in play, game and game-play

trauma, working with trauma and traumatised children 58, 86, 94, 97, 102, 103, 141–143, 146–148, 150, 163, 178, 191, 196, 216, 224, 226, 230, 232, 239, 241, 251

triadic relations, development towards; and in middle childhood 62, 63, 154, 159, 178, 179, 188, 191, 198, 250; *see also* triangular space

triangular space 58, 62, 63, 153–155, 169, 176, 178, 180–182, 185, 189, 191–197, 199–201, 203, 205, 207, 209, 247–251, 253; enigma of difference 63–65, 156, 248; incompleteness, fact of 63–65, 156, 248

Trowell, J. 65, 179

turmoil, emotional 48, 103, 216, 218, 245–247, 249, 251, 253

Tustin, F. 135, 147, 148

tyranny of child-patient in psychotherapy *see* game-play in child psychoanalytic psychotherapy, with "difficult to treat" children

uncanny, the 202, 208

uncertainty(ies) 140; in middle childhood, in play and game-play 50, 59, 140, 141, 176

unconscious, access to and expression of via play and game-play 8, 34, 38, 78–82, 84–86, 90, 92, 94, 100, 101, 111–115, 118–121, 127, 128, 143, 145, 147, 149, 197, 199, 229–233, 249

Unheimlich *see* uncanny, the

unintegration 139, 145, 150

unknown, and unpredictable in game-play *see* negative capability, and work of the negative

unpleasure 33, 77, 102

vignettes *see* game-play in child psychoanalytic psychotherapy, vignettes and clinical examples

violence of emotion, in post-Bionian theory: in child patients in psychotherapy 103, 170, 222, 226, 232, 238–240, 249

visceral emotions, in T-CT in game-play 114, 122, 155, 159, 197, 205, 217, 224, 230, 232, 239, 249

volleyball 156, 157, 166

Waddell, M. 47, 48, 50, 54, 57, 60, 61, 66, 67, 161

War, card game 96, 120, 137, 138, 149, 155, 176, 177, 183, 189, 206, 226, 236

wave-particle child *see* middle childhood, wave particle as metaphor for

wave–particle duality in physics, paradox 50

Winnicott, D.W.: and latency 1, 8, 9, 36–39, 58, 61, 77, 79, 85–89, 245, 249, 251, 253; and play and playing 1, 8–10, 79, 85–89, 100, 102, 106, 111, 112, 121–126, 128, 135–138, 143–149, 179, 182, 193, 194, 224–226, 232–234, 245, 249, 251, 253; sanity, as developmental achievement in latency, contrasted with madness 36–38, 207, 220; squiggle game 9, 36, 38, 87, 116, 124, 139; *see also* game-play in child psychoanalytic psychotherapy, and expanding the transitional space

Winnicottian *see* Winnicott, D.W., and play and playing

winning and losing, especially in game-play in child psychoanalytic psychotherapy 8, 10, 89, 98, 102, 115, 122, 137, 138, 146, 157, 159, 164, 167–172, 174–177, 182–184, 188–191, 195–198, 200, 205, 218, 220, 224–228, 236, 237, 240, 245, 250, 252

work of the negative *see* negative capability, and work of the negative

Youell, B. 47, 48, 54, 56, 59

For Product Safety Concerns and Information please contact our EU
representative GPSR@taylorandfrancis.com
Taylor & Francis Verlag GmbH, Kaufingerstraße 24, 80331 München, Germany

www.ingramcontent.com/pod-product-compliance
Lightning Source LLC
Chambersburg PA
CBHW050339270326
41926CB00016B/3518

* 9 7 8 1 0 3 2 5 4 5 0 6 6 *